TABLE OF CONTENTS

WESTERN HERITAGE: MAN'S ENCOUNTER WITH HIMSELF AND THE WORLD

A Journey for Meaning

Edited by

Francis R. Gendreau
Angelo Caranfa

Stonehill College

University Press of America,™ Inc.

Library of Congress Cataloging in Publication Data
Main entry under title:

Western heritage.

Includes index.
1. Man—Addresses, essays, lectures. I. Gendreau,
Francis R., 1943-   . II. Caranfa, Angelo.
BD450.W484   1984   128   84-17268
ISBN 0-8191-4251-4 (alk. paper)
ISBN 0-8191-4252-2 (pbk. : alk. paper)

Who am I, whence do I come that I am
                          as I am...?

                    Thomas Mann, <u>Meditations
                    of an Unpolitical Man</u>.

A wandering Aramean was my father; and
he went down into Egypt and sojourned
there. few in number; and there he became
a nation, great, mighty, and populous.

                         <u>Deuteronomy</u> 26:5.

ACKNOWLEDGEMENTS

Our theme, man's journey into Western Heritage, has taken us across three thousand and more years of history, from Genesis to the present. The road which we have travelled is not an original one. However, the selection and the placement of the stones side by side are totally our own design. In this process we have learned how little we do know, and how many more steps we must still take before we stand speechless, contemplating the fragility of Western Civilization and of man himself. But we have experienced, at least for a moment, the joy of a delectable pain in the waiting for the completion of this book. There were moments, we must say, when we thought that we would not be able to continue our travel. However, the encouragement and love given us by our families made it possible for us to persevere: we thank them with a silent tear and quiet smile.

A special acknowledgement must go the Academic Dean of Stonehill College, the Rev. Robert J. Kruse who approved the funding for this project. We are deeply indebted to Professor Raymond Pepin and his secretary, Peggy Karp, for their computer expertise and typing respectively, without which this journey of ours would have been more difficult to undertake. Also, a thank you goes to Mary Camara and June Buckley for being so patient and kind as they typed and xeroxed the manuscript. In the preparation of the manuscript a considerable burden was placed upon the library staff, and need we say that the response was always prompt and filled with kindness. Hence, thanks are in order to Carol Fraser, library director, and to Edward Hynes, Jean Pearce, Robert Bouchard-Hall, Madeline Foster, Joyce Vacchi, Christine Reynolds, and Cheryl Anderson: together they made the travelling less painful. Finally, our deep-felt gratitude is also due to Marie Malone and Professor Constance Schick of the Modern Language Department, who read and reread the manuscript, pointing out awkward sentence structure, typographical errors, and so forth. Their constructive criticisms had one aim; to make us clarify more and more our intentions, thereby leading us gently to write in a most simple, precise and clear form. In

the end, we alone are responsible for the errors and
unclarities that one may find in the book.

Francis R. Gendreau

Angelo Caranfa

COPYRIGHT ACKNOWLEDGMENTS

1

PREFACE

<u>Western Heritage</u>: <u>Man's</u> <u>Encounter</u> <u>with</u> <u>Himself</u> <u>and</u> <u>the</u> <u>World</u> is designed to make one aware of the value systems which animate Western Civilization. As the reader will discover, this introductory text is not a study in philosophy strictly speaking; rather, it considers the philosophical life from a broader perspective. It traces contemporary life back to the most fundamental and ultimate ground of our Western Heritage, that is, the Judaeo-Christian and Greco-Latin tradition. The thread of the narration is the conflict and continuity of human values, and its underlying theme is man's encounter with the voices of time. The focus here is on the enduring side of philosophical positions from the viewpoints of theologians, scientists, literati, social and political philosophers who have attempted to define human nature or man himself.

If this study, then, transmits any approaches, it is to recall contemporary man - a man in exile in an absurd and Godless universe - back to his cultural beginning: to make him relive his destiny in the first man's exodus from the Garden from which the search for meaning, the quest for knowledge, and the desire for eternal life have their origin. We hope that through this work the reader reexperiences those "moments of truth" which underscore the contention that Western Culture has for its ultimate foundation Biblical ideals subsequently redefined by various philosophical schools. The rising tide of existential humanism in the philosophies of Kierkegaard, Nietzsche and Sartre, the ascendancy of social and biological engineering in the thoughts of Skinner, Wilson and Lorenz, and the literary relativism of Beckett, Pinter and Ionesco all reflect not only a redefinition of certain Biblical truths, but also their transformation. Where, on the one hand, Biblical humanism grounds itself in the mystery of God's Creation, on the other hand, contemporary humanism has for its foundation man's human and social perfectibility. On philosophic grounds, today's humanism defines man as Creator of his

xvii

own values aspiring, as Sartre says, towards being God. That is why the same humanistic view explains man as a nothing, as a force of passions. For without a doubt, man is nothing if his passion is to be God.

Accordingly, this study is directed to the "beginnings" of historical movements without, at the same time, being just a collection of readings in the history of ideas. Thematically arranged, the readings should lead the reader back to the various historical starting points, allowing him to pause, now and then, on other paths, but always inviting him to move on in the direction of other disciplines - theology, philosophy, history, literature, psychology, sociology, mathematics, the natural and the biological sciences, the arts and languages. The readings speak within a universal framework even though they may be selected from a variety of methodologies. The philosopher, the theologian, the artist, the historian, the poet, the sociologist, the psychologist, the mathematician, the scientist, the linguist and the common man live in and see the same world and each in his own language tries to penetrate or uncover the ultimate structure of man's existence. In a way, they are all engaged in a discourse by which the definition of man obtains its clearest meaning.

Hence, the selection of the original readings is related to the need they are intended to serve: to illuminate the reader's life experiences within the historical process through the eyes of great minds, minds that have contributed to the building of our Western Heritage. In fact, we do hope that the readings whose concentration rests on three themes - <u>MAN IN A GOD-CENTERED WORLD</u>, <u>MAN IN A NATURE-CENTERED WORLD</u>, <u>MAN IN A HUMAN-CENTERED WORLD</u> - will ground the reader in the universal value-system of Western Civilization as she struggles now, as she did before, for her survival. Here lies the originality and the need for writing this book.

Francis R. Gendreau

Angelo Caranfa

Introduction

Three very distinctive philosophies of the human person have been chiseled out of western man's experience of himself and his place in the world:

1. The human person viewed as an individual made in the image of God and whose ultimate happiness rests in the attainment of union (reunion) with God;

2. The human person viewed as an individual ultimately created by God, but now governed by both natural laws and natural dispositions and, accordingly, whose ultimate happiness (perfectibility) depends to a great extent on his ability to control nature;

3. The human person viewed as an individual who lives in a godless universe and who is in part the product of blind evolutionary forces but who, nevertheless, is capable of bringing meaning into his life by actualizing his role as creator.

Clearly, the basis for distinguishing each of these philosophies of the human person consists of very distinctive views of the universe or world that man inhabits. Philosophers generally refer to their views of the universe as their _metaphysics_ or, at times, their _philosophy_ _of_ _nature_ (cosmology). Accordingly, the first view which clearly locates the human person in a God-centered universe is based on a _theistic_ metaphysics. The second view, however, which obviously locates the human person in a Nature-centered universe is based on a _naturalistic,_ _materialistic,_ or _mechanistic_ metaphysics that still retains a limited role for God. Finally, the third view has eclipsed God from the universe and so, in one sense, still retains a naturalistic and materialistic orientation, but very obviously points to man's supremacy over nature, - in fact, now performing "creator" functions. For want of a better label to identify this metaphysical view, the label <u>anthropocentric</u> metaphysics will serve our present purpose.

This collection of readings (many of which are classics) reveals both the identifying characteristics and the historical evolution of each of these philosophies of the human person and the metaphysical perspective upon which each is based.

All three philosophies have had supporters throughout the history of western philosophy. However, the careful observer of that history cannot fail to recognize that each philosophy of the human person has been particularly in the foreground during certain historical time-frames. Accordingly, the position that maintains that man lives in a God-centered universe was especially dominant during the ancient classical period and continued to be so until the 14th century A.D. The philosophy of the human person locating him in a nature-centered universe, however, was particularly prominent during the the 18th century with events and developments of the 14th to 17th centuries serving as the basis and background for such prominence. Finally, the philosophy of the human person that locates him in a godless universe and which envisions man as the new "creator" has very definitely become the most striking philosophy of our own time with the 19th century serving as the fertile ground in which such a viewpoint germinated.

Inasmuch as it is possible to identify each philosophy of the human person as particularly prominent during very definite time-frames, in addition to organizing the readings chronologically, we will also arrange them under the three aforementioned categories:

    I.   MAN IN A GOD-CENTERED WORLD;

    II. MAN IN A NATURE-CENTERED WORLD;

    III. MAN IN A HUMAN-CENTERED WORLD.

The reader is cautioned not to conclude that because the readings are arranged chronologically under these

three categories that there are no contemporary
thinkers, for example, who hold the view that man
inhabits a God-centered universe. This is clearly
false. The classification of the readings in the
manner heretofore described merely serves to focus the
attention of the reader to a particular philosophy and
yet, at the same time, to provide a sense of historical
continuity and development.

The remainder of this introduction attempts to
explain the characteristics of each philosophy so that
the reader may have a clearer sense of the whole before
he begins reading the thought of the selected
representatives of that philosophical position.

PART I.

MAN IN A GOD-CENTERED WORLD

The view of human nature that portrays man as created
in the image of, as bearing a likeness to, as having an
affinity with, or, more simply, as mirroring God has
manifested itself within three traditions of the
ancient and medieval periods of western philosophy:
the Biblical tradition as articulated in the Old and
New Testaments; the Greco-Roman tradition in the
writings of Plato (427-347 B.C.), Aristotle (384-322
B.C.), and the Roman stoic Marcus Aurelius (121-180
A.D.); and the Christian philosophical tradition of
Gregory of Nyssa (c. 330-c. 394), Thomas Aquinas
(1224-1274), and Catherine of Siena (1347-1380). Let
us proceed to an examination of the essential features
of each of these traditions.

A. <u>The</u> <u>Biblical</u> <u>Tradition</u>: <u>The</u> <u>Old</u> <u>and</u> <u>New</u> <u>Testament</u>
<u>Image</u> <u>of</u> <u>Man</u>. For Biblical man, the truth of being
human consists in the fundamental realization that man
is not God, but is a creature made in the image and
likeness of God, a God who created man for a specific
purpose. In the language of Proverbs 8: "Unto you, O
men I call, and my voice is to the sons of man;" and,
in St. Paul's Epistle to the Romans, Paul instructs the
Romans that "the Spirit himself and our spirit bear
united witness that we are children of God." However,

in addition to being God's witness, man is also
declared in Genesis to be the designated master of all
creation, from the fowl of the air to the fishes in the
depths of the sea to the animals on the earth.
Accordingly, the Bible reveals that man was created to
have knowledge of the Creator and to praise, glorify,
and love God and, by the beauty and majesty of
creation, to see himself as a "breath of life," as a
"living soul" in God's creative love.

   However, this "living soul" became stained as a
result of the sin of Adam and Eve. They ignored God's
command that they not eat of the tree of knowledge and
of life, and consequently were expelled from the Garden
of Eden.   Subsequently, Moses received the Law which
provided fallen man with guiding principles by which he
ought to conduct his life.   Finally, those of the
Christian religion believe that Jesus Christ is the
messiah prophesied by such Hebrew prophets as Isaiah
and Daniel. He is believed to be the new Adam who was
sent by His Father and who, together with the Holy
Spirit, is the way to salvation - the way back to God.
The New Testament authors repeatedly convey the basic
message that Jesus Christ had not come to abolish the
law and the prophesies but to fulfill them, and that by
His Incarnation, Death, and Resurrection, He had once
again restored man to spiritual health, to the image
and likeness of God, the Father.   The Christian
viewpoint that is very clearly found in the gospels and
taught by Paul in his letters to the Romans,
Corinthians and Ephesians was more fully interpreted
and articulated by Church Fathers, such as St. Gregory
of Nyssa, by theologian-philosophers, such as St.
Thomas Aquinas, as well as by religious mystics such as
St. Catherine of Siena.   Before we turn to these
thinkers, let us examine the essential features of the
Greco-Roman tradition in the thoughts of Plato,
Aristotle, and Marcus Aurelius, thoughts which exerted
a considerable influence on medieval theology and
philosophy.

B.   The Greco-Roman Tradition: Plato, Aristotle and
Marcus Aurelius. Despite very real differences between
them on certain philosophical issues, Plato, Aristotle,
and Marcus Aurelius, three of the foremost
representatives of the Greco-Roman tradition,
unequivocally speak of man as possessed of a "divine
element" which enables him to know and contemplate the

divine. The fact that they were so clear on this matter explains in part why both Plato and Aristotle influenced the early Church Fathers and the theologian-philosophers of the early and high Middle Ages.

Plato's view of man, briefly stated, is that each man is a soul imprisoned in a body. How and why the soul came to be a prisoner in a human body is never made clear by Plato. What is clear in his writings is that man's ultimate end is to free himself from his incarceration in the body so that he may come to possess truth (real being). In the <u>Phaedo</u>, one of Plato's more substantive dialogues, the soul is simply identified with mind (intelligence) which is in pursuit of truth. Plato maintains that the body (the senses) prevents one from attaining genuine or pure knowledge which, Plato emphatically insists, can only be attained by the mind (i.e., the soul) alone. And he attains to the purest knowledge of them [essences] who goes to each with the mind alone, not introducing or intruding in the act of thought sight or any other sense together with reason, but with the very light of the mind in her own clearness searches into the very truth of each; he who has got rid, as far as he can, of eyes and ears, and, so to speak, the whole body, these being in his opinion distracting elements which when they infect the soul hinder her from acquiring truth and knowledge.

In the <u>Phaedrus</u>, probably written later than the <u>Phaedo</u>, Plato's discussion of the nature of man and, more particularly, the nature of the soul, is much more detailed. Plato compares the soul to a pair of winged horses pulling a chariot guided by a charioteer. In the case of the gods, Plato tells us, the winged horses and the charioteers are all of noble descent. However, in the case of human beings, the charioteer drives one winged horse which is noble and of noble breed and a second winged horse which is ignoble and of ignoble descent. Plato observes that in the case of the human soul, then, the driving of the horses proves to be a difficult task for the charioteer.

Plato maintains that the soul in her totality "has the care of inanimate being everywhere.... When perfect and fully winged the soul soars upward and orders the whole world," whereas the imperfect soul,

xxiii

losing her wings, droops in her flight and eventually
settles on the earth and receives an earthly frame (a
body). It is precisely this composition of soul and
body which is called a living mortal creature. For an
immortal creature, however, Plato points out that "no
such union can be reasonably believed to be."

Despite the differences between mortal and immortal
creatures, Plato observes that "the wing is the
corporeal element which is most <u>akin to the divine</u>, and
which by nature tends to soar aloft and carry that
which gravitates downwards into the upper region, which
is the habitation of the gods." In other words, Plato
clearly maintains that there is a <u>likeness</u> that all
souls share whether they be the souls of immortal or
mortal creatures.

As for the meaning of the metaphor used by Plato in
the <u>Phaedrus</u>, the charioteer undoubtedly symbolizes the
rational element of the soul, while the winged horses
represent the emotional elements of the soul (the noble
horse symbolizing the spirited or courageous element of
the soul, while the ignoble horse signifying the
appetitive element of the soul). In short, then, Plato
speaks of the human soul as consisting of three parts
or three principles of action. Reason, the rational
part, distinguishes man from brutes in that it seeks
the truth or wisdom which is its proper good or end.
The Appetitive part of the soul, on the other hand,
seeks pleasure and earthly goods, while the Spirited
part is "a lover of honour and modesty and temperance
and the follower of true glory." As Plato points out,
the spiritual part needs "no touch of the whip but is
guided by word and admonition only." It is therefore
the natural ally of Reason.

Plato indicates that to the extent that Reason
beholds true being, the "wing on which the soul soars
is nourished." Hence, Plato insists that philosophy
(the love of wisdom) is important. It is that activity
which enables the human soul to be most <u>like</u> God (Zeus)
and the other gods. Philosophy is contrasted with
philosoma, the love of the body which love is
destructive of man's true nature, that is, a soul
consisting of a rational element and two affective
elements, one of which, the spirited element, lifts man
to his true destiny - the contemplation of truth (real
being).

xxiv

Aristotle, although a student of Plato, eventually came to have serious misgivings about the psychology, epistemology (theory of knowledge), and metaphysics of Plato. In particular, he rejected the dualism of soul and body in Plato's philosophy of man. Instead of viewing the soul as <u>that which lives</u> in a body, Aristotle speaks of the soul as <u>that by which a body lives</u>. Aristotle's view is rooted in his philosophy of nature wherein he speaks of the principles of mobile being as matter and form which coexist in a reciprocal way within every natural thing in a relationship of potency to act. Form (substantial form) is the principle by which a thing is the kind of thing it is. Matter (primary matter) is the principle of potentiality by which a thing (substance) can become a new thing possessing a new form. In man, as in all living things, the soul is the substantial form – a "ratio" or "formulable essence." As Aristotle observes: <<Since then the complex here is the living thing, the body cannot be the actuality of the soul; it is the soul which is the actuality of a certain kind of body....From all this it follows that the soul is in actuality a formulable essence of something that possesses potentiality of being besouled.>>

Aristotle distinguishes between different kinds of souls (that is to say, principles of life) inasmuch as there are different kinds of living things – namely, plants, animals and men. He maintains that the vegetative soul is the principle of life in plants by which they (plants) grow and reproduce. The sensitive soul is the principle of life in animals by which they (animals) grow, reproduce, sense, desire what they sense, and move. The rational soul is the principle of life in men by which they (men) participate in vegetative and animal existence and by which they are also capable of engaging in properly human activities, namely, knowing and willing. Possessed or "besouled" by the rational soul, man's end, Aristotle argues in the <u>Nicomachean Ethics</u>, consists in the actualization of those potentialities or powers of the soul that are properly and distinctively human powers. Consequently, Aristotle maintains that man perfects himself in the <u>contemplation of God</u>, which Aristotle identifies as pure form or self-thinking thought. Because <u>man has a divine element in him</u>, that is to say, the rational soul, it follows that man should become self-sufficient in thought as God is and not relish the practical life which can only serve to hinder him in his ultimate

xxv

pursuit. Aristotle does admit that man needs the
necessaries of life, but only to the extent that he is
freed to pursue those things which are in keeping with
his nature. <<For while a philosopher, as well as a
just man or one possessing any other virtue, needs the
necessaries of life, when they are sufficiently
equipped with things of that sort the just man needs
people towards whom and with whom he shall act
justly,.... but the philosopher, even when by himself,
can contemplate truth, and the better the wiser he is;
he can perhaps do so better if he has fellow workers,
but still he is the most self-sufficient.>>

   Aristotle observes that just as it would be absurd to
ascribe any practical virtues to God, so, by a process
of exclusion, Aristotle concludes that the social life
is inferior, "in a secondary degree," to the life of
contemplation which is the <u>God-like life in man</u>.

   Marcus Aurelius maintains that the soul of man is an
efflux from the deity.   So, even though we have bodies
like animals, we have reason or intelligence as the
gods do. Consequently, inasmuch as God is in man, we
must constantly attend to the divinity within us, for
it is only in this way that we can have any knowledge
of the nature of God.   The human soul is in a sense a
portion of the divinity, and the soul alone has
communication with the deity.   <<For with his
intellectual part alone God touches the intelligence
only which has flowed and been derived from himself
into these bodies.>>

   It is by living a divine life that man approaches to
a knowledge of the divinity.   It is by following the
divinity within, that man comes nearest to the deity,
the supreme good. In short, then, Marcus clearly places
himself within the Greek philosophical tradition with
his insistence that man bears a divine stamp, a kinship
with the Divine.

C.   <u>The Christian-Philosophical Tradition</u>.   God's
infinite love, now His Law, is the theme of Catherine
of Siena in the <u>Dialogue</u> which takes the form of an
exchange between God and herself.   She, like Old
Testament authors, summons man back to God. However,
unlike their claim that the "bridge" to God is by way

xxvi

of the Law, she sees man's return to God through the mediation of the soul in God's gift of faith. "It is in reason that the light of faith is held, and one cannot lose the one without losing the other. I made the soul after my own image and likeness, giving her memory, understanding and will." In other words, for Catherine, as for the early Church Fathers and the theologian-philosophers of the schools, man is open to the reality of Creation only if the soul's powers (that is to say, memory, understanding and will) are in a harmonious unity with God's will. True to the Christian thesis advanced by St. Paul that Christ's Incarnation, Death, and Resurrection have restored fallen man to the image and likeness of God, Catherine sees God's "breath" as received by, and mirrored in the soul which is moved by God's divine light or love which shines in man through Christ. "This is the enlightenment of the mind, which sees itself reflected in the warm-hearted love I have shown you in Christ crucified, as in a mirror." If, then, man lives a life according to the understanding that Christ is God's "breath" in him, he is in a position to go "upwards," to mount what Catherine calls the three stairs - the body, mind, and spirit - in short, to move from the lower to the higher bridge in an ascent that is a return to God, a rebirth, a recreation, and a regeneration. The Christian man, then, who lives by the Incarnation, Death, and Resurrection of Christ, not only lives by God's Law, but is also drawn to God with all the powers of the soul.

Whereas Catherine speaks of the soul and its powers as made in the image and likeness of God, Gregory of Nyssa, in his treatise <u>On the Making of Man</u>, observes that since the soul and mind is "in its likeness to the archetype," it follows that "likeness to God" and "rational nature" go hand in hand. As Gregory maintains: "But perfect bodily life is seen in the rational (I mean the human) nature, which both is nourished by and endowed with sense, and also partakes of reason and is ordered by mind." Accordingly, Gregory argues that since the most beautiful is Divinity itself to which all things move, it follows that the soul, being the "archetype" in man of "divine beauty," moves in the direction of God.

In the thirteenth century, Thomas Aquinas, theologian-philosopher and unquestionably the most important representative of the medieval-Scholastic tradition, summed up the Christian view of man in his On the Truth of the Catholic Faith (Summa Contra Gentiles): "From the fact that they acquire the divine goodness, creatures are made like unto God. Therefore, if all things tend to God as their last end, so as to acquire His goodness, it follows that the last end of things is to become like unto God." Consequently, if man is created in the image and likeness of God, and since God is Divine Reason, Divine Intellect, as well as the principle of motion and being, it follows that there is no other distinctive attributes of man than his intellect and will. However, for Thomas Aquinas, like Paul and Gregory had observed before him, and Catherine of Siena would echo after him, man is not only a rational being endowed with understanding and will, but he is also a man of faith requiring God's love and grace for the complete actualization of the self. Thus, man's destiny lies in the life, and in the truth of faith, a truth that is taught by the visible Church, otherwise man is doomed to remain a prisoner of his earthly existence. "So, you see," Catherine subsequently remarks, "the bridge has walls and a roof of mercy. And...the Holy Church is there to serve the bread of life and the blood, lest the journeying pilgrims, my creatures, grow weary and faint on the way."

This, then, is the Christian view of man: man is made in the likeness of God, and his ultimate purpose is to love God - a purpose that is fulfilled by those who live by the truth that Christ proclaimed; namely, that He came to perfect the Law of the Old Testament by His Incarnation, Death, and Resurrection. This perfected Law is implanted in man as the Spirit of Love. Obedient to the Trinitarian unity of Love (namely, God's Law which is the incarnate, crucified, and risen Christ who continues to live in man by his spirit of love), the Christian man experiences himself as born of God and as son of the Father in the glory of Christ, the Son, whose Spirit is constantly alive in the Church.

In conclusion, despite points of difference existing between the Biblical, Greco-Roman, and the Christian-Scholastic views of the nature of man, there emerges a unified image of man who is a being akin to, and whose end lies in union with God.

PART II.

MAN IN A NATURE-CENTERED WORLD

Both the Judaeo-Christian and Greco-Latin tradition, with their emphasis on right reason and contemplation, tell us that man can attain God's likeness in his use of memory, understanding and will.   Man perfects himself only in so far as he beholds the eternal, the immaterial and the unchanging Forms, Being or God Himself.

As contrasted with this image of man, the view of man as located in a Nature-centered world represents indeed a shift to earthly concerns.   In a Nature-centered world, man perfects himself in action, not contemplation, in the appetitive element of the soul, not the rational, in nature as driven by an internal principle, a principle which is revealed by the knowledge of the new sciences, mathematics and physics, not in nature as ordained to a higher end, <u>telos</u>. When this view reaches its mature consciousness in the Enlightenment philosophy of Rousseau, the question of the nature of man coincides with that of the natural sciences and the appearance of the social order as an artificial commonwealth.   Man becomes a <u>homologue</u> of nature, and nature is revealed "in the hearts of men" and in mathematical symbols.

In his dialogue with St. Augustine, Petrarch captures this shift in outlook; he penetrates the existential tension between the eclipse of the Judaeo-Christian and Greco-Latin tradition on the one hand, and the emergence of a new era with the emphasis on earthly love and fame, on the other hand. According to Petrarch, man's concern with "mortal rewards" invariably leads him to forget his eternal beginning: that he was created for the glory of God, thereby losing himself in the world of Humanity. Man will busy himself with concrete situations, forgetting ultimate concerns such as sin and guilt, birth and death. "Death may strike at any moment. Time is short; it is dangerous to make any postponements."

xxix

If Petrarch announces the coming of man in his desire
for worldly fame, Pico's originality is clear:
influenced by the rediscovery of the classical
heritage, he goes beyond the Christian-Scholastic
tradition, to the pagan and cabalistic philosophy of
Hermes Trismegistus. The Greco-Roman world saw the
universe as consisting of hierarchical layers, each
representing a different form of reality, extending
from the lowest to the highest in God. Within this
rational order each type of creature has its own place,
and human will could ascend as high as God, making of
man a participant in the divine essence. Of man, Pico
writes: "Thou, constrained by no limits, in accordance
with thine own free will,...shalt ordain for thyself
the limits of thy nature." Though this view is
suggestive of Sartre's philosophy which makes of man an
indeterminate being, Pico still operates within the
classical-scholastic heritage in praising man as a
"great miracle" worthy of admiration beyond all other
creatures.

Thus, within the Neoplatonic and cabalistic
three-fold division of the universe-intelligible,
rational and sensory, or intelligible, celestial and
material - man, according to Pico, belongs to all
three: he has a corruptible nature, a celestial and
invisible nature derived from the stars and under their
control, and a soul given to him by God and endowed
with divine knowledge. Hence, as a microcosm of
nature, man is to be understood in the light of
practical sciences such as magic and astrology. To
understand man requires a science of nature. "Then let
us fill our well-prepared and purified soul with the
light of natural philosophy, so that we may at last
perfect her in the knowledge of things divine."

Like Pico, Machiavelli shares the temper of his age:
he sees man capable of compassion, gratitude, piety,
love of humanity and of God. But self-love, or the
desire to glorify oneself abolishes all the natural
virtues - prudence, temperance, fortitude and justice -
by which man leads the moral life, bringing him closer
to the nature of a brute. Machiavelli sees human nature
as a struggle of ambition, avarice and weakness and
fear of death. "No animal can be found that has a
frailer life, and has for living a stronger desire,
more disordered fear or greater madness." It is
because of this struggle in the psyche of man that

man's existence is less desirous than that of a hog which accepts the limits of his nature; "because in this mud I live more happily; here without anxiety I bathe and roll myself."

This image of man as both frail, vulnerable, vain and presumptuous finds another expression in the thoughts of Montaigne. Indeed, the French luminary considered presumptuousness as the source of man's ills. He ridicules man for believing himself to be the master of the world: "who has sealed him this privilege?" And the answer is: no one. For ignorance, more than knowledge, is man's universal condition, and it is by vanity alone that he makes himself equal to God. In fact, man's knowledge cannot even penetrate the smallest part of the universe, nor will it ever understand the animal world, or ever comprehend man himself. For whatever the relation between animal and man, the animal world seems superior to that of man; man alone, among other animals, is naked, tied and bound; "man can neither walk, nor speak, nor eat, nor do anything but cry." So that man merely obeys the same law and the same fortune that other creatures do; and, if he remains within the bounds of the natural order, he will prosper; if, on the other hand, through freedom of imagination and arrogance, he tries to go outside nature, then sin, disease, confusion and despair result. "It is not in our power to acquire a fairer recommendation than to be favored by God and nature." For God and nature favor all things equally.

It seems no accident that the break with the classical-scholastic tradition, a break to which Petrarch alluded in his dialogue with Augustine, is carried on in the name of man over and against the Church, and in the name of feelings over and against reason. In the Reformation philosophy of Luther and Calvin the appeal to earthly experiences replaces the law of nature or reason, private experiences become the links to salvation, and creation is identified with God's unknowable will, as opposed to God's rationality in an ordered universe. In protest against the classical-scholastic view of man, and in the interest of the emerging new social and political order, Luther tells us that man is corrupt and that man's natural faculties are destitute of goodness and truth. But Calvin, unlike Luther, does admit that the Fall did not wipe out reason completely, but that she is weakened by the weight of the flesh; that however corrupt man is, there remains in him "some sparks" of understanding. To both Luther and Calvin, faith alone, not good works, is the only power by which man is restored to his original goodness prior to the Fall. "Ask reason herself," writes Luther, "whether she is not convinced and compelled to confess that she is foolish and rash in not allowing the judgement of God to be incomprehensible, when she admits that everything else divine is incomprehensible." Hence, salvation must precede right conduct, and right conduct does not come from the soul's upward movement into God through the sacramental system of the Church; instead, Christian man is already saved by faith alone in Christ's gospel. Thus, the primary and only means to understand man is through faith alone; classical-scholastic philosophy is no longer a reliable tool to such an end because the soul, God's divine archetype in man, has no power to open herself up to the mystery of God's love.

With Descartes, modern man is born. Modern in that man is understood from the light of mathematical sciences. Convinced that everything in nature is a product of mechanical contact between particles of material substances, Descartes, in his attempt at defining God, body and man, inquires first into the nature of substance. That substances exist, Descartes has little doubt; "That is why from the fact that we now have, e.g. the idea of an extended or corporeal substance, although we do not yet know certainly whether such really exists at all, we may yet conclude that it may exist; and if it does exist, any one portion of it which we can demarcate in our thought must be distinct from every other part of the same substance." A substance, then, has a principle attribute, and the attribute of a corporeal substance is extension, while that of the soul or mind is thought. And although body and soul are one in the nature of man, they still remain distinct one from the other. The proof that man is a composite of two really distinct substances rests on the notion that God exists. "And first of all, because I know that all things which I apprehend clearly and distinctly can be created by God as I apprehend them it suffices that I am able to apprehend one thing apart from another clearly and distinctly in order to be certain that one is different from the other, since they may be made to exist in separation at least by the omnipotence of God;...and, therefore just because I know certainly that I exist,...I rightly conclude that my essence consists solely in the fact that I am a thinking thing...I possess a distinctive idea of body, inasmuch as it is only an extended and unthinking thing...."

The self, then, is a substance whose essence is to think, and that this substance is "really distinct" from any physical body in that the latter "is only an extended and unthinking thing." And since thought is the essence of the mind, all faculties of thinking, from emotions to perceptions to imagination to understanding and volition are equally modes of thought. So that body and soul reciprocally effect each other; through the emotions or passions the body acts on the soul, while through the will the soul moves the body. This interaction takes place at the pineal gland which, in turn, opens up the brain, effecting the "animal spirits" which transmit the message through the various nerves, causing the muscles to move the body. "And I ought in no wise to doubt the truth of such matters, if, after having called up all my senses, my memory, and my understanding, to examine them, nothing is brought to evidence by any one of them which is repugnant to what is set forth by the others. For because God is in no wise a deceiver, it follows that I am not deceived in this."

Not surprisingly, we see in Pascal the skepticism of Montaigne and the influence of the Cartesian doubt. Like Montaigne, he places the wisdom of the heart above that of mathematics and physics, even though his starting point is his Cartesian view that man is obviously made to think. Nor does he fail to carry the Cartesian dualism which separates mind from body. "Man is to himself the most wonderful object in nature; for he cannot conceive what the body is, still less what the mind is, and least of all how a body should be united to a mind."

It is from this view-point that Pascal considers both human wisdom and scientific knowledge inadequate tools to an understanding of man. On the one hand, human wisdom cannot grasp man's place in this vast universe; on the other hand, scientific knowledge cannot penetrate the least particle of nature. This, then, is man's natural condition: "A nothing in comparison with the Infinite, an All in comparison with Nothing, a mean

between nothing and everything."   Yet, man burns with
desire to find a solid ground on which he can bridge
these two extremes.   That bridge is God.   "These
extremes meet and reunite by force of distance, and
find each other in God, and in God alone." To Pascal,
then, man is incomplete, he is restless and in despair
without God who touches the heart, not the intellect.
For the intellect to Pascal holds the same position in
the world of thought as the body holds in the economy
of nature.   Faith, therefore, does not complete or
perfect reason, but it is a living mystery beyond human
understanding: like Kierkegaard after him, Pascal
considers faith a passion of the heart, and through the
heart man comes to a knowledge of first principles.

    Under the influence of Locke's view that ideas, not
real things, are the object of knowledge, and in
continuity with Berkeley's notion that perception is
the criterion of reality, Hume views man as "a bundle
or collection of different perceptions, which succeed
each other with an inconceivable rapidity, and are in
perpetual flux and movements."   There is nothing that
remains essentially permanent or unchanged in man. The
human mind is a system of different perceptions linked
together by the relation of cause and effect,
influencing, modifying and even cancelling each other.
"But this is still more remarkable, when we add a
sympathy of parts to their _common end_, and suppose that
they bear to each other, the reciprocal relation of
cause and effect in all their actions and operations."

    In this respect, the Self is like a republic in which
the members are united by the reciprocal ties of
subordination; and, just as the republic may change its
members, its laws and constitution, so, too, the same
person may change his disposition and character without
losing his identity.   This is so because "Whatever
changes he endures, his several parts are still
connected by the relation of causation." This relation
of cause and effect among different perceptions is
shown to us by the memory which discovers personal
identity. Thus, the belief in the Self as simple and
identical substance from the principles of Resemblance,
Causation and Contiguity is not valid. Identity is not
a property of the outside world, the world of objects,
but is a product of the mind, and it depends on the
"relations of ideas" which produce Identity by means of
"an easy transition" they effect.

xxxiv

Pope seizes on the Newtonian view of the universe, on
the natural philosophy of Locke and Hume, and on the
deism of his day to give us an image of man based upon
"what we can reason" or know of man in nature. In
nature, Pope sees nothing but the unfolding of the
"ways of God to man;" he sees a chain "that draws all
to agree" that there is a design, a cause, a God, "The
great directing <u>MIND</u> of <u>ALL</u>," that maintains created
things in their proper course. And within this organic
whole, nature balances good with evil, so that what
look like natural catastrophes or moral imperfections
on the part of man are really parts of a larger and
perfect unity.

In a way, then, man is a blessed creature in that he
is as perfect as he ought to be, or perfect within his
own sphere; he is even ignorant of the "book of Fate."
And although man is blind to his "future bliss," God
has endowed him with hope as his blessing, a natural
disposition by which the "untutored mind" sees the
world as moved by "general laws," up to "the first
Almighty cause," regulating all things from matter and
motion, to animals and angels. To hope otherwise, to
go beyond the boundaries of his own sphere is to suffer
the delusion of pride. "Aspiring to be Gods, if Angels
fell,/ Aspiring to be Angels, Men rebel;/And who but
wishes to invert the laws/of <u>Order</u>, sins against the
Eternal Cause." For man's happiness is to submit to
the law of his own nature which is relative to the
perfect and harmonious whole. Resignation, rather than
the desire to attain the highest good, is man's
ultimate bliss. "Whatever is, is <u>RIGHT</u>;" for Nature
and man are intrinsically linked so as to reveal God's
Providence which "is kept in Nature, and is kept in
Man."

In continuity with Pope's naturalism, La Mettrie
defines man as "a complicated machine" difficult to
understand from the <u>a priori</u> method of the philosophers
who locate his essence in the "wings of the spirit" or
soul. It is rather the <u>a posteriori</u> procedure of the
physician-philosopher which alone can reveal the nature
of man. This method rests on the observation that "The
human body is a machine which winds its own springs.
It is the living image of perpetual movement.
Nourishment keeps up the movements which fever excites.
Without food, the soul pines away, goes mad, and dies
exhausted."

xxxv

The soul, then, is correlative to the body, and just as the body goes through various stages of development, so too the soul. Accordingly, to study the nature of the soul is to understand the organization of the body, most importantly that of the brain: the brain controls both the faculties of the soul, as well as other bodily functions. "For finally, even if man alone had received a share of natural law, would he be any less a machine for that?" Natural law, tells us La Mettrie, is a "principle of motion" or a material and sensible part of the brain, not a product of revealed truths or contemplation. Consequently, the soul is matter in motion. "Given the least principle of motion, animated bodies will have all that is necessary for moving, feeling, thinking, repeating, or in a word for conducting themselves in the physical realm, and in the moral realm which depends upon it." But both the nature of matter and motion is beyond the understanding of biological laws. "Let us then submit to an invincible ignorance on which our happiness depends." For if we listen to the "convinced materialist," the one who tells us that man is a machine or a mere animal following the natural law, then, we will even respect and love others from the moral principle: do unto others as you would have them do unto you. Convinced of this, La Mettrie boldly concludes that man is a machine "and that in the whole universe there is but a single substance differently modified."

PART III

MAN IN A HUMAN-CENTERED WORLD

We began this introduction with an account of man in a God-centered universe, selecting readings from the Bible, Plato, Aristotle, Marcus Aurelius, Gregory, Thomas Aquinas and Catherine of Siena. Man in a God-centered world denotes the idea that man is created in the image and likeness of God, capable of rational thought and willing the highest good, namely, God Himself. To the Christians, God's plan to man is revealed in the Incarnation, Death and Resurrection of Christ, the Son, in the Spirit breathed into the Church

in its Apostolic Tradition. This view is dethroned by
an image of man that emphasizes Nature, drawing from
Italian humanists, Reformers, and seventeenth and
eighteenth century philosophers. Natural man is
opposed to supernatural man, and nature (understood as
material reality) is opposed to transcendence. Whereas
man's nature in classical-scholastic thought is located
between that of animals and that of angels, natural man
finds his essence in the savage "whose untutored mind,"
says Pope, sees God in the "general laws" of Nature.
Moreover, Nature-centered world defines man as a
machine perfectible through the light of science and
reason in the construct of a rational social order.

   Man in a Human-centered world transforms these two
images by inverting the relationship God-man to
Man-god. In this world man believes that "the
unexamined life" is the only life worth living, and
that the mystery of existence is merely idle
speculation: life begins and ends in society. To be
human means to live in the cave, in the underground; it
means to experience oneself as an insect, a spider and
a rat; it means to be mad, spiteful and forceful. In
short, it means to divorce oneself from family ties,
history and God: it means the loss of belief in the
value system of Western Heritage and, at the same time,
the affirmation that through psychological, social and
biological engineering man can in fact perfect his
world by the total elimination of good and evil. The
good life will have an experimental justification, not
a rational and spiritual one.

   It is Feuerbach who paves the way for man's secular
concerns: what Feuerbach does is to humanize God by
inverting Him. In this inversion, man's knowledge of
God is man's knowledge of himself in his essential
nature, that is, the life which man lives in his
relation to his species. Hence, where there is this
consciousness, there is a capacity of science; science
is knowledge of species. "But only a being to whom his
own species, his own nature, is an object of thought,
can make the essential nature of other things or beings
an object of thought." What defines man, then, is his
relation to himself, and others are the means by which
he objectifies his own essence in absolute terms. The
"Absolute" is man's essence; "The power of the object
over him is therefore the power of his own nature."

Unlike the animal which cannot think of his own species, man is himself at once I and Thou; his species, not merely his individuality, is an object of thought.   To understand the nature of man is to understand that he can transcend his limited nature and thereby perfect himself in the consciousness of the infinite where "the conscious subject has for his object the infinity of his own nature." In this way, every individual is nothing but his own God, the highest conscious being in himself.   And the goal of a self-conscious individual is to will, to love and to reason. "To will, to love, to think, are the highest powers, are the absolute nature of man as man, and the basis of his existence."

It remains for Darwin to play the role of Descartes for the biological sciences, to link the animal kingdom around a central idea that the principle of evolution merely reveals the biological adaptation of the species to the environment. And whereas Montaigne and La Mettrie had alluded to a similar conclusion, Darwin goes further in that he sees nothing at all in man which cannot be traced back to the law of modification by natural selection and the rule of the survival of the fittest. "On the contrary, at every stage in the process of modification, all the individuals which were in any way better fitted for their condition of life, though in different degrees, would have survived in greater numbers than the less well-fitted." Thus, man slowly but surely modifies his animal stock, and unconsciously elevates himself from his animal existence to a social and a religious being.

Accordingly, Darwin argues that man's mental powers, his sense of morality and a belief in God are subject to the same law of natural selection. What animals know is what they learn from instincts; what man knows comes from his emotion of sympathy which makes him unite with others and take pleasure in the company of others.   Ultimately, belief in God, a belief which seems to arise from a considerable advance in the faculties of reason, imagination, curiosity, wonder and cultural progress, distinguishes man from his animal ancestry. "The idea of a universal and beneficent Creator does not seem to arise in the mind of man, until he has been elevated by long-continued culture." It is clear, concludes Darwin, that although evolution points to man as the fittest to survive, that he has

descended from animal form and that he has made for
himself an advanced culture, there still remains in him
the stamp of his "lowly origin."

   To say with Darwin that there is evolution is to say
that there is a development in nature and in the animal
kingdom. This Nietzsche rejects. Instead, he insists
that what seems to be an order in the universe, in
culture and in man is merely a blind path, a chaos
where everything eternally recurs in the same
succession and sequence. To say that everything
returns also implies an order. But the order to which
Nietzsche alludes is the one in which there is no God.
Hence, evolution is not progress but illusion, life is
not happiness but a disease, beauty is not harmony but
disorder, goodness is not the way to God but away from
Him, man is not rational but mad, with no final resting
place open to him: he is homeless, and the man who is
strong enough to accept the meaninglessness of life is
master indeed of this universe.   "What did we do when
we unchained this earth from its sun? Whither is it
moving now? Whither are we moving now? Away from all
suns? Are we not plunging continually? Backward,
sideward, forward, in all directions? Is there any up
or down left?" No, there is no heaven or earth: man
journeys in an "infinite nothingness;" not because
Christ has arisen, but because "we" have killed God,
the God of all religions; the churches themselves have
become "the sepulchers of God."

   With the death of God Nietzsche draws upon the
"Superman" to replace Him.   "Man is something that is
to be surpassed. What have ye done to surpass man?"
To surpass man, teaches Zarathustra, is to return him
to the earth, to make him not believe those who speak
of superearthly hopes: "Once blasphemy against God was
the greatest blasphemy; but God died, and therewith
also those blasphemers." This means that man must
abandon the notions of the soul, happiness, reason,
virtue, justice, piety, sin, sacrifice and love,
concepts that have been associated with
classical-scholastic tradition, and instead must walk
the rope set over an abyss, a rope which stretches
between two points, the animal and that of Superman.
"What is great in man is that he is a bridge and not a
goal: what is lovable in man is that he is an
over-going and a down-going;" for man is going over
across the rope towards the Superman and, at the same

time, he is going down the rope to sacrifice himself in order to make possible the world of the Superman. "I love him whose soul is deep even in the wounding, and may succumb through a small matter: thus goeth he willingly over the bridge."

Having spoken these words to the people assembled in the market-place, Zarathustra then remains silent, for he knows that he is not understood. After a short pause. he went on to speak of "the last man" and of "the higher man." The truth of the last man is that his species is like that of the ground-flea whose life-existence does not go beyond the pleasures of the moment. The last man is in fact every man, and every man is equal to one another in that all want material goods: this last man is the market-place man, the mob man, the mass man, the segmented man, the slave man who wants to both rule and obey, but finds them too burdensome; "Give us the last man! make us into these last men!" shout the people at Zarathustra. The last man marks the end of a degenerate Western culture and, at the same time, it is the origin from which "the higher man" will emerge and rule over the future. "Now only cometh the great noontide, now only doth the higher man become-master!" This higher man is like a creator god, creating order out of the dust into which civilization has returned after centuries dominated by the kingdom of God and the morality of mediocrity and utility. "Before God! - Now however this God hath died! Ye higher men, this God was your greatest danger."

In continuity with Darwin's idea that man is an organism obeying natural laws, Mead understands man as a process, a relation. To Mead the self has meaning only in so far as there is a group; it is out of the interaction which the individual has with the group that the self emerges with further mental differentiation, to finally grasp the meaning of his actions as they affect others. "When we reach a self we reach a certain sort of conduct, a certain type of social process which involves the interaction of different individuals and yet implies individuals engaged in some sort of co-operative activity. In that process a self, as such, can arise."

For the self to arise there must be reflective activities, that is, activities by which the "I"

internalizes gestures, roles and conduct of the
"generalized other" or group. This internalized other
forms the "me" of the self. Hence, it is from the
inner dialogue which the "I" has with the "me" that the
self learns to think, judge and become a responsible
individual; he completes himself only in so far as he
takes on the attitudes of others and acts toward
himself as others act. Reflexivity, then, allows the
individual to separate himself from the "generalized
other" and to converse with himself, although this
conversation is conducted equally with society at
large. "The essence of the self, as we have said, is
cognitive: it lies in the internalized conversation of
gestures which constitutes thinking, or in terms of
which thought or reflection proceeds. And hence the
origin and foundation of the self, like of those of
thinking, are social."

    Essentially. the self is a social process, a process
with two distinguishable phases, the "I" and the "me."
The self develops as he alters his response to the "me"
both individually and collectively. The attitudes
which he takes toward others are present in his own
experience, but his response to them contains a new
element, the cognitive factor. It is through this
process that the self becomes a free individual; he
becomes a self-conscious being, aware of himself and
the environment.

    Like Mead, and in the naturalism advanced by Hume, La
Mettrie and Darwin, Dewey conceives of man as an
organism sharing the same organic processes with other
lower animals. And whereas Dewey criticizes Hume for
identifying customs or habits with human nature, he
also abandons the Helvetian notion that man is
malleable in that he is a bundle of instincts. These
two views, insists Dewey, are inadequate; where the
former places man's perfectibility in the environment,
the latter places it in man: to change customs
involves changing human nature. Dewey also sees that
the combination of the two presents a problem in that
it might be easy to exchange the influence of one for
that of the other, if not totally identify the one with
the other. Hence, to Dewey human nature is the
conflict between "impulses" or "native activity" on the
one hand, and "acquired habits" on the other hand.
That is to say, "social conditions," rather than "an
old and unchanged Adam" affect the habits of the

individual and, at the same time, "impulses" affect the environment. This being the case, "Habits once formed perpetuate themselves by acting unremittingly upon the native stock of activities. They stimulate, inhibit, intensify, weaken, select, concentrate and organize the latter into their own likeness. They create out of the formless void of impulses a world made in their own image."

Accordingly, man is a creature of acquired habits, not of reason or instincts. Some activities proceed from the "impulses" of the individual which, in turn, set up reactions in the environment where others approve, disapprove, protest, encourage, share, react, or even leave the individual alone in his response. Conduct, then, is always shared; it is not the moral imperative "ought" that says that conduct should be social; instead, what is social is either good or bad. Slavery and wars, for example, like pity and sympathy, are not physiological and psychological necessities, even though they are woven out of man's needs and desires, as much as they are social phenomena "in their mutual inhibitions and reinforcements." In this way "impulses" are plastic in terms of the ways in which they may be channelled: their direction depends upon reinforcements and inhibitions supplied by the social environment. Hence, the same impulses may give rise to different modes of behaviors under different social conditions. Social conditions can be changed to facilitate a desirous behavior. "But the remedy lies in the development of a new morale which can be attained only as released impulses are intelligently employed to form harmonious habits adapted to one another in a new situation." Intelligence or thought is called upon to direct "impulses" toward a reorganization of old habits, or to fashion new ones. Here is where education comes in: to direct the growth process of the individual intelligently and to harmonize such a growth with the goals of society.

Cassirer uses the theoretical foundation of the biologist, von Uexkull, to ask the question: "Is it possible to make use of the scheme proposed by Uexkull for a description and characterization of the human world?" According to that scheme, reality is not a unique and homogeneous thing; it is diversified, having as many different patterns as there are different organisms. Unlike Darwin who held that the history of living things is an evolution from the lowest form to the highest in man, von Uexkull believes that every organism has its own world because it has its own experience. The clue to understanding animal life, von Uexkull maintains, is that all organisms have structures by which they adapt or fit into the environment, that is, they all have a receptor system and an effector system. These two structures together constitute what Uexkull calls, the <u>functional circle</u> of the animal.

Obviously, insists Cassirer, the human world forms no exception to the biological world. Yet, the functional circle of man is not only quantitatively larger, but it has undergone a qualitative change; in the human world there exists a third structure, a <u>symbolic system</u>, which completes the circle. Man, therefore, is not only a stimulus-response animal, but he is linked to the world by symbols; and, instead of dealing with things themselves, man in a sense is constantly conversing with himself; he finds himself in the midst of a fairy tale universe veiled with or enveloped by myths, language, art, religion, science and history itself.

Cassirer's inquiry into the nature of man takes him back to Plato by way of Comte's positivism and through Dewey's criticism of James' psychology. The philosophical analysis of man as a symbolic animal cannot do more than point out that the various methods used to define man are not exhaustive: what is needed instead is a philosophy of <u>symbolic forms</u>. This new method, insists Cassirer, does not reject the metaphysical, the scientific, the biological and the psychological studies of man, but complements them by transferring them to a new center of analysis called <u>functional analysis</u>. Within this center, man is defined as a functional being, that is, a system of human activities with a common origin. "Language, myths, religion, art, science, history are the constituents, the various sectors of the circle." Furthermore, the philosophy of symbolic forms shows that human activities are a polarity of two opposing tendencies, one which seeks to preserve old forms, while the other tends to destroy them in order to create new ones. In the course of time what varies is the proportion of the opposing factors with one factor emerging at one time, the other emerging at another time. This, according to Cassirer, is the creative process which determines the character of the single forms and gives to each of them its particular physiognomy. Thus, language, myths, religion, art, science and history express human consciousness and the power of man to create for himself an "ideal" world. "Human culture taken as a whole may be described as the process of man's progressive self-liberation."

Along with Freud, Jung realizes that man's psychic experiences which have become conscious can be repressed into the unconscious. Like Freud, Jung's analytical psychology takes into account the existence of the unconscious. Unlike Freud, who felt that man's forgotten content constitutes the individual's life experience, Jung maintains that there exists a deeper layer called collective unconscious which is identical in all men since it is universal in scope. And whereas the _personal unconscious_ consists of the individual's constellation of emotions and ideas called complexes, the collective unconscious consists of inherited possibilities of ideas known as _archetypes_. "The archetype is essentially an unconscious content that is altered by becoming conscious and by being perceived, and it takes its colour from the individual consciousness in which it happens to appear."

The notion of _archetype_, Jung explains, can be traced back to Philo Judaeus, Irenaeus and even Plato; it denotes "primordial types" from which copies are made, or "universal images" that have existed ever since the beginning of civilization. For example, primitive tribal lore, fairytales, myths and dreams reveal archetypal experiences; but where tribal lore and myths express the universal or collective unconscious of the individual, dreams manifest the opposite phenomenon. Irrespective of their revelation, however, archetypal experiences in a sense point to man's unconscious drama which becomes conscious by means of projection. Projection transforms the objective world into the replica of the individual's subjective psyche. "Primitive man impresses us so strongly with his subjectivity that we should really have guessed long ago that myths refer to something psychic. His knowledge of nature is essentially the language and outer dress of an unconscious psychic process....He simply didn't know that the psyche contains all the images that have ever given rise to myths, and that our unconscious is an acting and suffering subject with an

xliv

inner drama which primitive man rediscovers, by means of analogy, in the processes of nature both great and small."

Consciousness, that is, the process by which the individual becomes a separate and indivisible whole, is the relation between unconscious experiences and the ego. According to Jung, no unconscious material can become conscious without an ego to which it refers. "Consciousness needs a centre, an ego to which something is conscious." Unlike Freud and Janet, Jung insists that his treatment of neurosis and psychosis points to an ego, a center that crystallizes itself around accumulated emotions, feelings, thoughts and memories which have always existed potentially. or _in potentia_, and which express the affect state of the individual's unconscious. For example, where on the one hand the affect state of a psychotic may reveal an ego that is displaced by the unconscious, on the other hand, in a normal person the unconscious collaborates with the conscious without any disturbance, so that the ego becomes aware of its own unconscious layers. "The collaboration of the unconscious is intelligent and purposive, and even when it acts in opposition to consciousness its expression is still compensatory in an intelligent way, as if it were trying to restore the lost balance." The ego, however, can fail to achieve "individuation" either by refusing to acknowledge those emotions and attitudes that are painful to admit (Jung calls this the shadow), or by failing to assimilate into consciousness the dual aspect of the unconscious, namely, the feminine and the masculine personality. According to Jung, man has a feminine side of him and woman has a masculine side of her respectively known as _anima_ and _animus_ and which bring into consciousness a hidden psychic life: they represent man's ancestry in feelings, thoughts and life itself. "No wonder their nature is strange, so strange that their irruption into consciousness amounts to a psychosis." This means that the individual develops by conflict and collaboration: the ego emerges with a new consciousness as it struggles to assimilate its personal unconscious (shadow) with the two incongruous halves of the collective unconscious (_anima_ and _animus_).

Against Jung's psychology which admits that the individual's behaviours cannot be predicted from the study of the unconscious, and that it is difficult to decide whether a manifestation of the unconscious can be interpreted as an effect or an aim, Skinner, on the other hand, while agreeing with Freud against Jung in saying that human actions are lawful, disagrees with Freud's theory of the id, ego and super-ego. "We may quarrel with any analysis which appeals to a self or personality as an inner determiner of action, but the facts which have been represented with such devices cannot be ignored." Yet, Skinner in a way ignores Freud's postulate by saying that it is not scientific, that is, it cannot be observed from the inductive method of the scientist and, therefore, it cannot adequately explain human behaviours. As with Freud, however, Skinner gives a pure naturalistic interpretation of human behaviours.

In dealing with human behaviours, insists Skinner, one needs to measure only the cause-effect relationship without any reference to the structures of the unconscious. In short, one has to explain the "unified system of response" and the various relationships which exist among them. From this, Skinner admits, like Mead and Dewey, that "responses" are organized around certain given "stimuli" and that present with the stimulus-response there is "reinforcement." The fact that the behaviours of one may be different in different circumstances is evidence for the postulate that external variables, of which "responses" are a function, determine behaviours. For example, a motion to adjourn a meeting which has run through the lunch hour may reveal "the hungry man's speaking." Thus, one's behaviour may be different before and after a healthy meal. Consequently, if the outside environment is not consistent with producing a certain kind of response, the behaviour is performed with less frequency. So that one should not be surprised, for example, if the pious churchgoer on Sunday becomes an aggressive, unscrupulous businessman on Monday. For he possesses two response systems appropriate to different sets of circumstances, and his inconsistency is no greater than that of the environment which conditions him to go to church on Sunday and to work on Monday. Conflict may arise when the same individual may be asked in church to examine his business actions, while on Monday he may be engaged in some sort of transactions with the church. Resolution revolves around the extent to which a response works either to the advantage or disadvantage of the community. "These two sets of variables account, not only for the membership of each group of responses, but for the relation between them which we describe when we say that one personality is engaged in controlling the other. Other kinds of relations between personalities are evident in the processes of making a decision, solving a problem, or creating a work of art."

Hence, if indeed behaviours consist of such responses, then a scientific analysis of human behaviours "dispossesses autonomous man" and turns the control over to the environment. Does not this make of man a victim to others, asks Skinner? Certainly men have been victims, as they have been victimizers, but where it is true that man may be controlled by the environment, "it is an environment which is almost wholly of his own making." In fact, continues Skinner, the physical and social worlds are largely man-made and culture is a witness to the exercise in self-control. As the individual controls himself by manipulating the outside world, "so the human species has constructed an environment in which its members behave in a highly effective way." Obviously, there have been mistakes made and they will continue to be made, with no assurance that the environment man has made for himself will continue to provide gains which outstrip the losses; but man, for better or for worse, is what he has made of himself. Therefore, there is nothing inconsistent with the fact that in engineering and controlling the environment, one man is the controller, the other the controlled. In the final analysis, man will continue to have power over the environment to no limits, but the "human species," concludes Skinner, "will never reach a final state of perfection before it is exterminated."

But for Sartre, as for Nietzsche before him, and against Skinner's explanation of human nature in terms of conditioning behaviors, "human life begins on the far side of despair." Despair is a precondition to life, and life begins only after man has experienced the anxiety that accompanies man's awareness of a meaningless, purposeless and distant universe. God, Nature, society, personal and interpersonal relationships, says Sartre, are merely illusory devices by which man protects himself from seeing that he is totally alone, a stranger to himself and in exile in this rotten and absurd world. "Outside nature," says Orestes in the play _The Flies_, "against nature, without

excuse, beyond remedy, except what remedy I find within
myself." The world, and with it man himself, has no
longer a center; everything is disconnected from
everything else and man, instead of touching the other,
merely glides by the other, sharing only nausea and
anguish. "Farewell, my people," says again Orestes,
"try to reshape your lives. All here is new, all must
begin anew."

With this view Sartre annihilates not only the
Judaeo-Christian and Greco-Roman world view, but also
the naturalism, the materialism, the rationalism, the
historicism and the behaviouralism of subsequent
theories on man and his world: they all crumble under
this barren, futile, dark and ugly existence where man
is called to begin anew, to start from nothingness.
And, according to Sartre, to begin anew means that the
only life that exists is the reshaped one, the
life that the individual lives in the world which he
himself has made, and for which he, as creator, is
ultimately responsible. "I _am_ my freedom," says
Orestes to Zeus, "no sooner had you created me than I
ceased to be yours." And to say that man is his
freedom is to reject the various polarities of reality
in the notions such as objective-subjective,
being-becoming, essence-accident, ideal-real,
soul-body, thought-action, cause-effect, God-man
and to affirm instead that existence precedes essence.
This means that man is not a product of God's love nor
of revelatory truths in the Incarnation, Death and
Resurrection of Christ nor of contemplation nor of
evolution nor of psychology nor of culture, but that he
_is_, and that only afterwards he defines _what_ he is:
"Man is nothing else but what he makes of himself."
Such is the first principle of existentialism,
otherwise known as subjectivity.

But what man _is_ is his own _choices_, and through them
he _makes_ himself _what_ he is, namely, a free and
responsible being. This does not mean that man becomes
responsible for his own individuality alone, but that
in choosing himself he chooses humanity. Thus, there
can be no objective commands or external rules by which
man legitimizes his actions; man alone creates his own
values with no outside world, and for that matter no
inner world, prescribing to him what he "ought" to do
and be. Here lies man's existential dizziness and the
awesome burden of responsibility. Where, on the one

hand, man is condemned to freedom, on the other hand, existence requires constant choices, renewed awareness that there is nothing beyond anguish and despair. "In this sense we may say that there is a universality of man; but it is not given, it is perpetually being made. I build the universal in choosing myself; I build it in understanding the configuration of every other man, whatever age he might have lived in." Freedom requires both total involvement or engagement and unfulfilled possibilities, for whatever state man is in, there is always the possibility for renewed choices, for making himself the creator of the world in which he simply exists. "But I shall not return under your law," says Orestes to Zeus, "I am doomed to have no other law but mine....For I, Zeus, am a man, and every man must find out his own way."

Accordingly, there is no particular way, no right way by which man lives his freedom; all that he can do is condemn the pretentions that he is free, the hypocrisy that he lives an authentic life, the fear of engagement, the illusion of customs. The only road that exists for him and from which there is no exit is that of exile; to shrink from this path is to avoid the responsibility of freedom and, therefore, the possibility of creating for himself his own values. "At heart, what existentialism shows is the connection between the absolute character of free involvement, by virtue of which every man realizes himself in realizing a type of mankind,...and the relativeness of the cultural ensemble which may result from such a choice; it must be stressed that the relativity of Cartesianism and the absolute character of Cartesian involvement go together."

Disagreeing with Skinner, Dewey and Mead who say that human behaviours are functions of the environment, Professor Wilson, who bases his theory of human nature on Darwin's propositions of natural selection, genetic inheritance, environmental necessity and the struggle for existence, believes that to understand man is to use the empirical method of biology. Biological research alone can increase man's understanding of himself and society. To the extent that this is true, Wilson soon adds that it presents man with two spiritual dilemmas: one, that man has no purpose beyond his genetic history; two, that human values are innate, not environmental. This granted, biological knowledge becomes indispensible to the solution of these problems. Thus, Wilson studies man from the presupposition that he is a biological organism with a system of censors and motivators which guides him beyond his immediate environment and toward that which his genetic code automatically steers him. "I believe that the human mind is constructed in a way that locks it inside this fundamental constraint and forces it to make choices with a purely biological instrument. If the brain evolved by natural selection, even the capacities to select particular esthetic judgments and religious beliefs must have arisen from the same mechanistic process."

Thus, in the ultimate formulation of the question, what is man, and in his explanation of human nature, Wilson's biological approach is no less important than that of Descartes, Hume and La Mettrie. While retaining and developing their theories that man is a thinking thing controlled by the motor activities of the body, that man is a bundle of perceptions, and that man is a machine with the brain as his main spring, Wilson lays the ground work for a "sociobiology" of man. He demonstrated experimentally that everything, from man's mental apparatus to his social institutions, is a device by which man survives and reproduces the genes and the group of people most fitted to survive. Consequently, man is seen as having no higher purpose than self-glory. Marxism, like other secular religions, says Wilson, offers little more than the promises of material welfare and an escape from the consequences of human nature; it is also motivated by self-aggrandizement.

The important point of Wilson's biological study is that it considers man in the like of any other organism, possessing a system of instinctual censors and motivators which enable him to direct his course towards his communal nature. At this point the second dilemma emerges: "Which of the censors and motivators should be obeyed and which ones might be better curtailed or sublimated?" Man alone, answers Wilson, must decide this question; he alone has to choose among the alternative censors and motivators which he has inherited. This means that at some point in time, if not now, man must shift his course from an automatic control to a "precise steering" based on biological, not philosophical nor theological nor psychological nor sociological knowledge. "The only way forward is to study human nature as part of the natural sciences, in an attempt to integrate the natural sciences with the social sciences and humanities." Wilson cannot conceive of a better method than the one which produces hard-won empirical analysis of man derived from the laws of biology. He even tells us not to fear this new approach. Instead, he goes on to say, social scientists should absorb the relevant results of biological studies and should even beg the biologists to continue their investigation of biological man to a point when it might become possible for the social scientists to imitate the most perfect nuclear family in the like of that found in the white-handed gibbon. In short, what the biological method explains is the hope in human and social perfectibility. "Human genetics is now growing quickly along with all other branches of sciences. In time, much knowledge concerning the genetic foundation of social behavior will accumulate. and techniques may become available for altering gene complexes by molecular engineering and rapid selection through cloning. At the very least. slow evolutionary change will be feasible through conventional eugenics. The human species can change its own nature." What man will choose. no one can say. But what Wilson hopes to achieve with his new materialism is to reintroduce into our culture that philosophical "sense of wonder" which speaks more of the things we do not know than those we do know.

PART IV.

CONCLUSION

Thus, the question of the nature of man remains and the search for a clear and adequate understanding of its meaning goes on. Nothing, we think, can be more truthful than "the truth" that man is a widening path that has been paved with stones of the Judaeo-Christian and Greco-Roman tradition, naturalism, rationalism, empiricism, behavioralism, nihilism and existentialism all mixed together, yet existing separate from each other. while building on each other, to constitute Western Heritage. For the reader the net effect should be a feeling of journeying, of searching, of wondering, of begging, of engagement and of conversing with the

li

Road which is his cultural ancestry. The reader is invited to be a witness, as well as a humble participant, and to intervene reverently as a philosopher-child in both asking the question about man and in respecting the world which he has inherited and tries to understand. This does not simply mean that he be honest, authentic and sincere in his travels for "the truth" about man and his universe, but that he must realize the falsehood of such a truth if he encounters it; that is, he must understand that no one is privileged to possess ultimate truth. but that he must, like a child, constantly wonder about the nature of "truth itself." He must see that every stop in his journey is indeed a communion with the past, an engagement in the delicate construction of an ever-present now, and a waiting for the last steps to be taken, but never to expect to take them; for to expect a final truth about human nature is to deny that man is a journeyer, an itinerant, a beggar always ready for the call. next, please! This has been the purpose of this book: not to give the answer to the question, but to call the reader to begin his pilgrimage on the way to self-liberation.

Although we have explained the various readings under MAN IN A GOD-CENTERED WORLD, MAN IN A NATURE-CENTERED WORLD and MAN IN A HUMAN-CENTERED WORLD as if they are in conflict for "the truth" about human nature, they should not be seen necessarily as antithetical to each other, rather as images emanating from, and returning to the mirror which is Western Civilization. And where the reader is free to choose one image over another. our emphasis here is on the "whole truth" of human nature as that truth comes down to us through the original writings of great minds, minds that have contributed to the building of the Road. Hence, the reader is called to see that every image hides the total truth. while, at the same time, it reveals a particular truth about man and his world. Furthermore, the reader is called to understand that where there might be other images of man, our three-fold division serves merely the purpose of organizing the many selections around a center so as to make the traveling less weary. As for the selections themselves, we have tried to make them short and representative of the times they speak.

lii

Thus, the reader sees in time the accumulated seconds
of yesterdays, the minutes of todays and the hours of
tomorrows as they take on increasing importance for the
reader himself. And, as he walks back in time from the
land of Wilson which places man in the innate mechanism
of censors and motivators, to the Biblical soil which
roots man in the image and likeness of God, through
Cassirer's path of man as a symbolic animal, he notices
Descartes' man as a thinking thing.   Then, on his way
to Darwin's natural path. he encounters Rousseau's
savage man and La Mettrie's man as a machine. Slowly,
and as he turns himself in the direction of Hume, he
sees Mead, Dewey and Skinner standing there claiming,
each in his own way, that man is conditioned by the
very Road he is on. But now, as he keeps on walking in
a crowded path he, nevertheless, still finds himself
journeying alone in anguish, estranged from everything
around him in a meaningless universe of Sartre,
Nietzsche and Pascal, despairing, like a mad man, that
the Road leads nowhere.   Yet, as he trembles for a
deeper communion with himself and the world around him.
he sees a sign that leads him to the dream world of
Jung's personal and collective unconscious.   There,
still in a dream and as he prepares himself to take the
next distance, he may recall the divine archetype in
the by-ways of Aquinas, Gregory, Marcus Aurelius,
Aristotle and Plato. And, if he dreams long enough, he
may even find himself being urged by Catherine to carry
on, to ascend the eternal Way in obedience to Christ's
love. Rested and refreshed in his pilgrimage by the
sacraments of the Church, he is now prepared to enter
St. Paul's land of a new life in the Incarnation, Death
and Resurrection of Christ in the Spirit of God, but
only after he is justified by faith alone in the
resurfaced road of Luther and Calvin. However distant
the journey might have been, with all its side paths,
turns and steeper passes, he may still hear Petrarch's
echoing words not to lose himself in the corrupt
landscape of Machiavelli and Montaigne, or in the hymn
of praise by Pico, Pope and Feuerbach, but to go
forward, to take the last steps into the desert of the
Old Testament from which his dust-like existence had
its mysterious birth.   In the words of Ecclesiasticus:
"He himself made man in the beginning and then left him
free to make his own decision."   For this, man must be
thankful. His task now is not to stop, but to move on,
perhaps solitary and tired, weaker and weaker, in his
pilgrimage to seek what is both good and evil.
beautiful and ugly, sacred and profane in the Road. The
pain to find and to build he must conceal; the truth to

pass on to others he must speak silently. But he can
speak the truth only if he has measured and kissed the
stones on which he stands.

   This does not mean to accept the Road as defined by
the various images on human nature that we have
presented here, but instead to examine and criticize
with a logical mind the very assumptions on which these
images of man rest. It means not to affirm or deny the
question of human nature either by ignorance or
presumptuousness with a simple response, but to
question the question with a still better understanding
derived from the response the reader gives to a
particular image.   In short, we call the reader to
engage himself in a dialectic or philosophical analysis
of the original question in order to discover that
there are more questions to ask. For example, to raise
the question of human nature is also to ask what does
man seek. This implies that man is free or not free to
choose what he seeks.   In turn, this leads to the
question of man's relation with other men and,
therefore, it raises the question of the nature of
society. Ultimately, the question resolves itself into
a question of the nature of the universe and of man's
religious beliefs.   Is the universe made out of
nothing? Or is there a spiritual power responsible for
created things?   Or is the universe made out of
material particles in the like of quarks and electrons?
From these questions we hope that the reader, although
he finds himself engaged in a philosophical discourse.
is led to converse with other disciplines so that the
question reaches its most translucent center. The end
result is for the reader to construct for himself in a
most critical and synthetic way a clear and firm ground
on which to stand as he continues to endure the road
until the end.

   In these readings the end of man, or his freedom, can
be easily seen. Wilson, Darwin and La Mettrie, each in
his own way, tells us that man is biologically
determinate, whereas Skinner, Dewey, Mead and even Hume
claim that man is not free. but conditioned by past and
present social conditions. And where Luther and Calvin
see man as determinate by his original sin, Catherine.
Aquinas and Gregory, on the other hand, maintain that
man through his natural faculties can attain for
himself both his natural and supernatural happiness.
Machiavelli and Nietzsche point to man's psychological

urges as determinants of his choices. Sartre instead tells us that man is free to choose his own values. Pope limits freedom within the laws of nature, whereas Pico, in the tradition of Plato, Aristotle, Marcus Aurelius and the Scholastics, believes that man can achieve self-realization only in the exercise of reason and will. Jung, Cassirer and Feuerbach give us a cultural and psychological definition of freedom: man, they tell us, can transcend his own limitations and choose the ideal good for himself. So that the reader may ask which of these views is "the right" one. But he should not be surprised if he is asked to search further into the notions of eternal and divine laws, natural and positive laws, necessity, causation, free will. and so on. This is not to confuse him, but to make him see that there are other variables that must be clarified in order to arrive at a more precise notion of freedom. At the same time, however, the reader should realize that all philosophers speak with a unified voice about freedom; they all speak from the ground of human nature. and they all tell us that man seeks perfection, actualization, self-realization or self-liberation. Now, whether perfection is achieved from within a God-centered world, a Nature-centered universe or a Human-centered world or outside these centers, the reader is cautioned not to conclude that today's man is closer to perfection than he was when he first emerged from the dust of the earth. The question, what is man, is as valid today as it was when it was first raised by the Psalmists who said: "Tell me, Yahweh, when my end will be, how many days are allowed me, show me how frail I am."

Francis R. Gendreau

Angelo Caranfa

PART I.

MAN IN A GOD-CENTERED WORLD

THE BIBLE: THE HEBREW AND CHRISTIAN SCRIPTURES

Although the Bible, strictly speaking, refers to the Old and New Testaments, nevertheless, it is a collection of many books united under one theme: man's encounter with the God of Creation, Revelation, and Redemption. Despite the diversity of stories, prophesies, lamentations, and songs that it contains, and despite the many problems of determining authorship as well as the time when various segments were written, the Bible does provide a single view of man or human nature: he is created in the image and likeness of the God Who revealed Himself to Abraham, Isaac and Jacob, and Who subsequently revealed Himself in the Incarnation, Death, and Resurrection of Jesus Christ.

As a book containing an account of God's creation of the world and man's encounter with God, other men, and the world, the Bible remains one of the ultimate sources of Western heritage. Yet, the Bible is not an historical document, that is to say, it was not written to provide an historical account. By its many parables and stories, the Bible focuses on the theme of salvation history: the intervention of God on behalf of a powerless and servile Israel. It is through Israel that God reveals his purpose to man and the created order. Through Israel, it seems as if civilization passes from a dark beginning to a morning of a new day; with the birth of Israel, Western man is introduced to the light of the world where everything finds its goodness in God's creative words: "And God said ..."

The readings that follow, taken from Genesis, Psalms, and Ecclesiasticus, provide us with an insight into the Old Testament image of man. The selections from the New Testament are taken from St. Paul's letters (epistles) to the Romans, Corinthians and Ephesians. The reader must keep in mind that there is one single image of man connecting the two Testaments. Nevertheless, the Old Testament emphasizes man's responsibility to God's Law, whereas the New Testament places emphasis on faith and love, as well as on truth, understanding, and obedience to God's Law, as the keys to salvation.

GENESIS 2:5-9; 15-25:

"And man became a living being."

At the time when Yahweh God made earth and heaven there was as yet no wild bush on the earth nor had any wild plant yet sprung up, for Yahweh God had not sent rain on the earth. nor was there any man to till the soil. However, a flood was rising from the earth and watering all the surface of the soil. Yahweh God fashioned man of dust from the soil. Then he breathed into his nostrils a breath of life, and thus man became a living being.

Yahweh God planted a garden in Eden which is in the east. and there he put the man he had fashioned. Yahweh God caused to spring up from the soil every kind of tree. enticing to look at and good to eat, with the tree of life and the tree of the knowledge of good and evil in the middle of the garden. . . .Yahweh God took the man and settled him in the garden of Eden to cultivate and take care of it. Then Yahweh God gave man this admonition. 'You may eat indeed of all the trees in the garden. Nevertheless of the tree of the knowledge of good and evil you are not to eat, for on the day you eat of it you shall most surely die.'

Yahweh God said, 'It is not good that the man should be alone. I will make him a helpmate.' So from the soil Yahweh God fashioned all the wild beasts and all the birds of the heaven.   These he brought to the man to see what he would call them; each one was to bear the name the man would give it. The man gave names to all the cattle, all the birds of heaven and all the wild beasts.   But no helpmate suitable for man was found for him. So Yahweh God made the man fall into a deep sleep. And while he slept, he took one of his ribs and enclosed it in flesh. Yahweh God built the rib he had taken from the man into a woman, and brought her to the man. The man exclaimed:

'This at least is bone from my bones,
    and flesh from my flesh!
    This is to be called woman,
    for this was taken from man.'

   This is why man leaves his father and mother and
joins himself to his wife, and they become one body.

   Now both of them were naked, the man and his wife,
but they felt no shame in front of each other.

ECCLESIASTICUS   15:14-19:

                    God made man free.

He himself made man in the beginning,
      and then left him free to make his
      own decisions.

If you wish, you can keep the commandments,
      to behave faithfully is within your power.

He has set fire and water before you;
      put out your hand to whichever you prefer.

Man has life and death before him;
      whichever a man likes better will be given
      him.

For vast is the wisdom of the Lord;
      he is almighty and all seeing.

His eyes are on those who fear him,
      he notes every action of man.

ECCLESIASTICUS 16:26-31; 17:1-14:

              God made man in his own image.

   When God created his works in the beginning,
he allotted them their portions as soon as they were
made.
      He determined his works for all time,

from their beginnings to their distant future.
      They know neither hunger nor weariness,
and they never desert their duties.
      None has ever jostled its neighbour,
they will never disobey his word.
      And afterwards the Lord looked at the earth,
and filled it with his good things.
      He covered its surface with every kind of animal,
and to it they will return.
      The Lord fashioned man from the earth,
to consign him back to it.
      He gave them so many days' determined time,
he gave them authority over everything on earth.
      He clothed them with strength like his own,
and made them in his own image.
      He filled all living things with dread of man,
making him master over beasts and birds.
      He shaped for them a mouth and tongue, eyes and
ears,
and gave them a heart to think with.
      He filled them with knowledge and understanding,
and revealed to them good and evil.
      He put his own light in their hearts
to show them the magnificence of his works.
      They will praise his holy name,
as they tell of his magnificent works.
      He set knowledge before them,
he endowed them with the law of life.
      He established an eternal covenant with them,
and revealed his judgements to them.
      Their eyes saw his glorious majesty,
and their ears heard the glory of his voice.
      He said to them, 'Beware of all wrong-doing';
he gave each a commandment concerning his neighbor.

PSALM 8:4-9:

      Man crowned with glory and splendour.

. . . ah, what is man that you should spare a thought
for him,   the son of man that you should care for him?

Yet you made him little less than a god,
you have crowned him with glory and splendour,
made him Lord over the works of your hands,

6

set all things under his feet,

sheep and oxen, all these,
yes wild animals too,
birds in the air, fish in the sea
travelling the paths of the ocean.

Yahweh, our Lord,
how great your name throughout the earth!

PSALM 39:4-13:

Man's hope is in God.

'Tell me, Yahweh, when my end will be,
how many days are allowed me,
show me how frail I am.

"Look, you have given me an inch or two of life,
my life-span is nothing to you;
each man that stands on earth is only a puff of wind,
every man that walks, only a shadow,
and the wealth he amasses is only a puff of wind -
he does not know who will take it next.

So tell me, Lord, what can I expect?
My hope is in you.
Free me from all my sins,
do not make me the butt of idiots.
I am dumb, I speak no more,
since you yourself have been at work.

Lay your scourge aside,
I am worn out with the blows you deal me.
You punish man with the penalties of sin,
like a moth you eat away all that gives him pleasure -
man is indeed only a puff of wind!

Yahweh, hear my prayer,
listen to my cry for help,
do not stay deaf to my crying.
I am your guest, and only for a time,
a nomad like all my ancestors.
Look away, let me draw breath,
before I go away and am no more!

LETTER OF PAUL TO THE ROMANS 7:9-25; 8:3-8; 8:9-11; 8:14-17:

Everyone moved by the Spirit is a son of God.

Once, when there was no Law, I was alive; but when the commandment came, sin came to life and I died: the commandment was meant to lead me to life but it turned out to mean death for me, because sin took advantage of the commandment to mislead me, and so sin, through that commandment, killed me.

The Law is sacred, and what it commands is sacred, just and good. Does that mean that something good killed me? Of course not. But sin, to show itself in its true colours, used that good thing to kill me; and thus sin, thanks to the commandment, was able to exercise all its sinful power.

The Law, of course, as we all know, is spiritual; but I am unspiritual; I have been sold as a slave to sin. I cannot understand my own behavior. I fail to carry out the things I want to do, and I find myself doing the very things I hate. When I act against my own will, that means I have a self that acknowledges that the Law is good, and so the thing behaving in that way is not my self but sin living in me. The fact is, I know of nothing good living in me--living, that is, in my unspiritual self--for though the will to do what is good is in me, the performance is not, with the result that instead of doing the good things I want to do, I carry out the sinful things I do not want. When I act against my will. then, it is not my true self doing it, but sin which lives in me.

In fact, this seems to be the rule, that every single time I want to do good it is something evil that comes to hand. In my inmost self I dearly love God's Law, but I can see that my body follows a different law that battles against the law which my reason dictates. This is what makes me a prisoner of that law of sin which lives inside my body.

What a wretched man I am! Who will rescue me from
this body doomed to death? Thanks be to God through
Jesus Christ our Lord!

In short, it is I who with my reason serve the Law of
God, and no less I who serve in my unspiritual self the
law of sin....

...God dealt with sin by sending his own Son in a
body as physical as any sinful body, and in that body
God condemned sin. He did this in order that the Law's
just demands might be satisfied in us, who behave not
as our unspiritual nature but as the spirit dictates

The unspiritual are interested only in what is
unspiritual, but the spiritual are interested in
spiritual things. It is death to limit oneself to what
is unspiritual; life and peace can only come with
concern for the spiritual. That is because to limit
oneself to what is unspiritual is to be at enmity with
God: such a limitation never could and never does
submit to God's law...

...In fact, unless you possessed the Spirit of Christ
you would not belong to him. Though your body may be
dead it is because of sin, but if Christ is in you then
your spirit is life itself because you have been
justified; and if the Spirit of him who raised Jesus
from the dead is living in you, then he who raised
Jesus from the dead will give life to your own mortal
bodies through his Spirit living in you....

...Everyone moved by the Spirit is a son of God. The
spirit you received is not the spirit of slaves
bringing fear into your lives again; it is the spirit
of sons, and it makes us cry out, 'Abba, Father!' The
Spirit himself and our spirit bear united witness that
we are children of God. And if we are children we are
heirs as well: heirs of God and coheirs with Christ,
sharing his sufferings so as to share his glory....

FIRST LETTER OF PAUL TO THE CORINTHIANS; 2:7-16:

The insignificance of human wisdom.

...The hidden wisdom of God which we teach in our mysteries is the wisdom that God predestined to be for our glory before the ages began. It is a wisdom that none of the masters of this age have ever known, or they would not have crucified the Lord of Glory; we teach what scripture calls: the things that no eye has seen and no ear has heard, things beyond the mind of man, all that God has prepared for those who love him.

These are the very things that God has revealed to us through the Spirit, for the Spirit reaches the depths of everything, even the depths of God. After all, the depths of a man can only be known by his own spirit, not by any other man, and in the same way the depths of God can only be known by the Spirit of God. Now instead of the spirit of the world, we have received the Spirit that comes from God, to teach us to understand the gifts that he has given us. Therefore we teach, not in the way in which philosophy is taught, but in the way that the Spirit teaches us: we teach spiritual things spiritually. An unspiritual person is one who does not accept anything of the Spirit of God: he sees it all as nonsense; it is beyond his understanding because it can only be understood by means of the Spirit. A spiritual man, on the other hand, is able to judge the value of everything, and his own value is not to be judged by other men. As scripture says: Who can know the mind of the Lord, so who can teach him? But we are those who have the mind of Christ.

FIRST LETTER OF PAUL TO THE CORINTHIANS, 15:12-56:

Man is born again through the Resurrection of the new Adam

...Now if Christ raised from the dead is what has been preached, how can some of you be saying that there is no resurrection of the dead? If there is no resurrection of the dead, Christ himself cannot have been raised, and if Christ has not been raised then our

preaching is useless and your believing it is useless;
indeed, we are shown up as witnesses who have committed
perjury before God, because we swore in evidence before
God that he had raised Christ to life. For if the dead
are not raised, Christ has not been raised, and if
Christ has not been raised, you are still in your sins.
And what is more serious, all who have died in Christ
have perished. If our hope in Christ has been for this
life only, we are the most unfortunate of all people.

   But Christ has in fact been raised from the dead, the
first-fruits of all who have fallen asleep. Death came
through one man and in the same way the resurrection of
the dead has come through one man. Just as all men die
in Adam, so all men will be brought to life in Christ;
but all of them in their proper order: Christ as the
first-fruits and then, after the coming of Christ,
those who belong to him.   After that will come the
end, when he hands over the kingdom to God the Father,
having done away with every sovereignty, authority and
power. For he must be king until he <u>has put all his
enemies under his feet</u> and the last of the enemies to
be destroyed is death, for everything is to be <u>put
under his feet</u>.--Though when it is said that everything
is subjected, this clearly cannot include the One who
subjected everything to him.   And when everything is
subjected to him, then the Son himself will be subject
in his turn to the One who subjected all things to him,
so that God may be all in all.

   If this were not true, what do people hope to gain by
being baptised for the dead?   If the dead are not ever
going to be raised, why be baptised on their behalf?
What about ourselves?   Why are we living under a
constant threat? I face death every day, brothers, and
I can swear it by the pride that I take in you in
Christ Jesus our Lord.   If my motives were only human
ones, what good would it do me to fight the wild
animals at Ephesus? You say: <u>let us eat and drink
today; tomorrow we shall be dead</u>. You must stop being
led astray: 'Bad friends ruin the noblest people'.
Come to your senses, behave properly, and leave sin
alone; there are some of you who seem not to know God
at all; you should be ashamed.

   Someone may ask, 'How are dead people raised, and
what sort of body do they have when they come back?'

They are stupid questions. Whatever you sow in the ground has to die before it is given new life and the thing that you sow is not what is going to come; you sow a bare grain, say of wheat or something like that, and then God gives it the sort of body that he has chosen: each sort of seed gets its own sort of body.

Everything that is flesh is not the same flesh: there is human flesh, animals' flesh, the flesh of birds and the flesh of fish. Then there are heavenly bodies and there are earthly bodies; but the heavenly bodies have a beauty of their own and the earthly bodies a different one. The sun has its brightness, the moon a different brightness, and the stars a different brightness, and the stars differ from each other in brightness. It is the same with the resurrection of the dead: the thing that is sown is perishable but what is raised is imperishable; the thing that is sown is contemptible but what is raised is glorious; the thing that is sown is weak but what is raised is powerful; when it is sown it embodies the soul, when it is raised it embodies the spirit.

If the soul has its own embodiment, so does the spirit have its own embodiment. The first _man_, Adam, as scripture says, <u>became a living soul</u>; but the last Adam has become a life-giving spirit. That is, first the one with the soul, not the spirit, and after that, the one with the spirit. The first man, being from the earth, is earthly by nature; the second man is from heaven. As this earthly man was, so are we on earth; and as the heavenly man is, so are we in heaven. And we, who have been modelled on the earthly man, will be modelled on the heavenly man.

Or else, brothers, put it this way: flesh and blood cannot inherit the kingdom of God: and the perishable cannot inherit what lasts for ever. I will tell you something that has been secret: that we are not all going to die, but we shall all be changed. This will be instantaneous, in the twinkling of an eye, when the last trumpet sounds. It will sound, and the dead will be raised, imperishable, and we shall be changed as well. because our present perishable nature must put on imperishability and this mortal nature must put on immortality.

12

When this perishable nature has put on imperishability, and when this mortal nature has put on immortality, then the words of scripture will come true: _Death is swallowed up in victory_. _Death, where is your victory_? _Death- where is your sting_? Now the sting of death is sin, and sin gets its power from the Law....

LETTER OF PAUL TO THE EPHESIANS, 4:4-24:

Man is called to a new life.

...There is one Body, one Spirit, just as you were all called into one and the same hope when you were called. There is one Lord, one faith, one baptism, and one God who is Father of all, over all. through all and within all.

Each one of us, however, has been given his own share of grace, given as Christ allotted it. It was said that he would:

When he ascended to the height, he captured

prisoners, he gave gifts to men.

When it says, 'he ascended', what can it mean if not that he descended right down to the lower regions of the earth? The one who rose higher than all the heavens to fill all things is none other than the one who descended. And to some, his gift was that they should be apostles; to some, prophets, to some, evangelists; to some pastors and teachers; so that the saints together make a unity in the work of service, building up the body of Christ. In this way we are all to come to unity in our faith and in our knowledge of the Son of God, until we become the perfect Man, fully mature with the fulness of Christ himself.

Then we shall not be children any longer, or tossed one way and another and carried along by every wind of doctrine, at the mercy of all the tricks men play and

their cleverness in practising deceit. If we live by
the truth and in love, we shall grow in all ways into
Christ, who is the head by whom the whole body is
fitted and joined together, every joint adding its own
strength, for each separate part to work according to
its function. So the body grows until it has built
itself up, in love.

   In particular, I want to urge you in the name of the
Lord, not to go on living the aimless kind of life that
pagans live. Intellectually they are in the dark, and
they are estranged from the life of God, without
knowledge because they have shut their hearts to it.
Their sense of right and wrong once dulled, they have
abandoned themselves to sexuality and eagerly pursue a
career of indecency of every kind. Now that is hardly
the way you have learnt from Christ, unless you failed
to hear him properly when you were taught what the
truth is in Jesus.   You   must give up your old way of
life; you must put aside your old self, which gets
corrupted by following illusory desires.   Your mind
must be renewed by a spiritual revolution so that you
can put on the new self that has been created in God's
way, in the goodness and holiness of the truth....

PLATO

Plato (427-347 B.C.), the son of a wealthy and noble family, abandoned very early in his life a career in politics and instead turned to philosophy. After the death of Socrates, his mentor. and a few years of travel, Plato founded a school known as the Academy on the outskirts of Athens.   In addition to his teaching duties, he authored a significant number of dialogues which utilize Socrates as the principal speaker through whom Plato presents a view of reality, man, the purpose of human existence, etc. His philosophical speculation continues to have an enormous impact on philosophy to the present day.   In fact, the British-American philosopher.   Alfred   North   Whitehead (1861-1947), observed that the history of philosophy is but a series of footnotes to Plato.

In the selections that follow, Plato provides us with an insight into his philosophy of human nature and the purpose of human existence.   In the first selection, taken from the Phaedo, Socrates and his associates are discussing how a philosopher faces death. Socrates observes that the philosopher has no reason to fear death for he has been pursuing death and dying all his life. Socrates explains the meaning of this curious position by way of a discussion of the nature of death and the nature of the philosophical life which, for Plato, it becomes apparent to the reader, is the ideal human life.

In the Phaedrus, Plato offers an ingenious analogy of man's nature. and, more specifically. a view of the soul. He compares the soul to a charioteer driving a chariot led by two horses (one noble and the other ignoble). For Plato, the image signifies the soul's three parts: Reason, Spirit, and Appetite and the internal dynamics between these three faculties.

Both readings make it abundantly clear that Plato's view of man is dualistic (Man is a soul imprisoned in a

body) and that the underpinning of this view of man
lies in the conviction that there are two orders of
reality: a material world and world of Ideas or
Ideals. The soul of man is, properly speaking, an
inhabitant of the latter world but it must first be
released from the chains that confine it to the
material world.

PHAEDO:

The philosopher practises dying.

...And now, O my judges, I desire to prove to you
that the real philosopher has reason to be of good
cheer when he is about to die, and that after death he
may hope to obtain the greatest good in the other
world. And how this may be, Simmias and Cebes, I will
endeavour to explain. For I deem that the true votary
of philosophy is likely to be misunderstood by other
men; they do not perceive that he is always pursuing
death and dying; and if this be so, and he has had the
desire of death all his life long, why when his time
comes should he repine at that which he has been always
pursuing and desiring?

Simmias said laughingly: Though not in a laughing
humour, you have made me laugh, Socrates; for I cannot
help thinking that the many when they hear your words
will say how truly you have described philosophers, and
our people at home will likewise say that the life
which philosophers desire is in reality death. and that
they have found them out to be deserving of the death
which they desire.

And they are right, Simmias, in thinking so, with the
exception of the words "they have found them out"; for
they have not found out either what is the nature of
that death which the true philosopher deserves, or how
he deserves or desires death. But enough of them:--let
us discuss the matter
among ourselves. Do we believe that there is such a
thing as death?

To be sure, replied Simmias.

Is it not the separation of soul and body? And to be dead is the completion of this; when the soul exists in herself. and is released from the body and the body is released from the soul, what is this but death?

Just so, he replied.

There is another question, which will probably throw light on our present enquiry if you and I can agree about it:--Ought the philosopher to care about the pleasures--if they are to be called pleasures--of eating and drinking?

Certainly not, answered Simmias.

And what about the pleasures of love--should he care for them?

By no means.

And will he think much of the other ways of indulging the body, for example, the acquisition of costly raiment, or sandals, or other adornments of the body? Instead of caring about them, does he not rather despise anything more than nature needs? What do you say?

I should say that the true philosopher would despise them.

Would you not say that he is entirely concerned with the soul and not with the body? He would like, as far as he can, to get away from the body and to turn to the soul.

Quite true.

In matters of this sort philosophers, above all other men, may be observed in every sort of way to dissever the soul from the communion of the body.

Very true.

Whereas, Simmias, the rest of the world are of opinion that to him who has no sense of pleasure and no part in bodily pleasure, life is not worth having; and that he who is indifferent about them is as good as dead.

That is also true.

What again shall we say of the actual acquirement of knowledge?--is the body, if invited to share in the enquiry, a hinderer or a helper? I mean to say, have sight and hearing any truth in them? Are they not, as the poets are always telling us, inaccurate witnesses? And yet, if even they are inaccurate and indistinct, what is to be said of the other senses?--for you will allow that they are the best of them?

Certainly. he replied.

Then when does the soul attain truth?--for in attempting to consider anything in company with the body she is obviously deceived.

True.

Then must not true existence be revealed to her in thought, if at all?

Yes.

And thought is best when the mind is gathered into herself and none of these things trouble her--neither sounds nor sights nor pain nor any pleasure,--when she takes leave of the body, and has as little as possible

to do with it, when she has no bodily sense or desire.
but is aspiring after true being?

   Certainly.

   And in this the philosopher dishonours the body; his
soul runs away from his body and desires to be alone
and by herself?

   That is true.

   Well. but there is another thing, Simmias: Is there
or is there not an absolute justice?

   Assuredly there is.

   And an absolute beauty and absolute good?

   Of course.

   But did you ever behold any of them with your eyes?

   Certainly not.

   Or did you ever reach them with any other bodily
sense?--and I speak not of these alone, but of absolute
greatness, and health, and strength. and of the essence
or true nature of everything.   Has the reality of them
ever been perceived by you through the bodily organs?
or rather. is not the nearest approach to the knowledge
of the several natures made by him who so orders his
intellectual vision as   to   have   the most exact
conception of the essence of each thing which he
considers?

   Certainly.

And he attains to the purest knowledge of them who
goes to each with the mind alone. not introducing or
intruding in the act of thought sight or any other
sense together with reason, but with the very light of
the mind in her own clearness searches into the very
truth of each; he who has got rid, as far as he can, of
eyes and ears and, so to speak, of the whole body,
these being in his opinion distracting elements which
when they infect the soul hinder her from acquiring
truth and knowledge--who, if not he, is likely to
attain to the knowledge of true being?

What you say has a wonderful truth in it. Socrates,
replied Simmias.

And when real philosophers consider all these things,
will they not be led to make a reflection which they
will express in words something like the following?
"Have we not found," they will say, "a path of thought
which seems to bring us and our argument to the
conclusion, that while we are in the body. and while
the soul is infected with the evils of the body, our
desire will not be satisfied? and our desire is of the
truth. For the body is a source of endless trouble to
us by reason of the mere requirement of food; and is
liable also to diseases which overtake and impede us in
the search after true being: it fills us full of
loves, and lusts, and fears, and fancies of all kinds,
and endless foolery. and in fact, as men say, takes
away from us the power of thinking at all. Whence come
wars, and fightings, and factions? whence but from the
body and the lusts of the body? Wars are occasioned by
the love of money, and money has to be acquired for the
sake and in the service of the body; and by reason of
all these impediments we have no time to give to
philosophy; and, last and worst of all, even if we are
at leisure and betake ourselves to some speculation.
the body is always breaking in upon us, causing turmoil
and confusion in our enquiries, and so amazing us that
we are prevented from seeing the truth. It has been
proved to us by experience that if we would have pure
knowledge of anything we must be quit of the body--the
soul in herself must behold things in themselves: and
then we shall attain the wisdom which we desire, and of
which we say that we are lovers; not while we live, but
after death; for if while in company with the body, the
soul cannot have pure knowledge, one of two things
follows--either knowledge is not to be attained at all,

or, if at all, after death. For then, and not till then, the soul will be parted from the body and exist in herself alone. In this present life, I reckon that we make the nearest approach to knowledge when we have the least possible intercourse or communion with the body, and are not surfeited with the bodily nature, but keep ourselves pure until the hour when God himself is pleased to release us.   And thus having got rid of the foolishness of the body we shall be pure and hold converse with the pure, and know of ourselves the clear light everywhere. which is no other than the light of truth." For the impure are not permitted to approach the pure. These are the sort of words, Simmias, which the true lovers of knowledge cannot help saying to one another, and thinking. You would agree; would you not?

Undoubtedly. Socrates.

But, O my friend, if this be true, there is great reason to hope that, going whither I go, when I have come to the end of my journey, I shall attain that which has been the pursuit of my life. And therefore I go on my way rejoicing, and not I only, but every other man who believes that his mind has been made ready and that he is in a manner purified.

Certainly. replied Simmias.

And what is purification but the separation of the soul from the body, as I was saying before; the habit of the soul gathering and collecting herself into herself from all sides out of the body; the dwelling in her own place alone. as in another life, so also in this, as far as she can;--the release of the soul from the chains of the body?

Very true, he said.

And this separation and release of the soul from the body is termed death?

To be sure, he said.

And the true philosophers, and they only. are ever
seeking to release the soul. Is not the separation and
release of the soul from the body their especial study?

That is true.

And, as I was saying at first, there would be a
ridiculous contradiction in men studying to live as
nearly as they can in a state of death, and yet
repining when it comes upon them.

Clearly.

And the true philosophers, Simmias, are always
occupied in the practice of dying, wherefore also to
them least of all men is death terrible. Look at the
matter thus:--if they have been in every way the
enemies of the body, and are wanting to be alone with
the soul, when this desire of theirs is granted, how
inconsistent would they be if they trembled and
repined, instead of rejoicing at their departure to the
place where, when they arrive, they hope to gain that
which in life they desired--and this was wisdom--and at
the same time to be rid of the company of their enemy.
Many a man has been willing to go to the world below
animated by the hope of seeing there an earthly love,
or wife, or son, and conversing with them. And will he
who is a true lover of wisdom, and is strongly
persuaded in like manner that only in the world below
he can worthily enjoy her, still repine at death? Will
he not depart with joy? Surely he will. O my friend,
if he be a true philosopher. For he will have a firm
conviction that there, and there only, he can find
wisdom in her purity. And if this be true, he would be
very absurd, as I was saying, if he were afraid of
death.

He would indeed, replied Simmias.

And when you see a man who is repining at the
approach of death. is not his reluctance a sufficient
proof that he is not a lover of wisdom, but a lover of
the body, and probably at the same time a lover of
either money or power, or both?

22

Quite so, he replied....

PHAEDRUS:

The nature of the human soul:

Reason, Spirit, and Appetite.

...The soul through all her being is immortal, for
that which is ever in motion is immortal; but that
which moves another and is moved by another, in ceasing
to move ceases also to live. Only the self-moving,
never leaving self, never ceases to move, and is the
fountain and beginning of motion to all that moves
besides. Now, the beginning is unbegotten, for that
which is begotten has a beginning; but the beginning is
begotten of nothing, for if it were begotten of
something, then the begotten would not come from a
beginning. But if unbegotten, it must also be
indestructible; for if beginning were destroyed, there
could be no beginning out of anything, nor anything out
of a beginning; and all things must have a beginning.
And therefore the self-moving is the beginning of
motion; and this can neither be destroyed nor begotten,
else the whole heavens and all creation could collapse
and stand still, and never again have motion or birth.
But if the self-moving is proved to be immortal, he who
affirms that self-motion is the very idea and essence
of the soul will not be put to confusion. For the body
which is moved from without is soulless; but that which
is moved from within has a soul, for such is the nature
of the soul. But if this be true, must not the soul be
the self-moving, and therefore of necessity unbegotten
and immortal? Enough of the soul's immortality.

Of the nature of the soul, though her true form be
ever a theme of large and more than mortal discourse,
let me speak briefly, and in a figure. And let the
figure be composite-a pair of winged horses and a
charioteer. Now the winged horses and the charioteers
of the gods are all of them noble and of noble descent,
but those of other races are mixed; the human
charioteer drives his in a pair; and one of them is
noble and of noble breed, and the other is ignoble and

of ignoble breed; and the driving of them of necessity gives a great deal of trouble to him. I will endeavour to explain to you in what way the mortal differs from the immortal creature. The soul in her totality has the care of inanimate being everywhere, and traverses the whole heaven in divers forms appearing:-when perfect and fully winged she soars upward, and orders the whole world; whereas the imperfect soul, losing her wings and drooping in her flight at last settles on the solid ground--there. finding a home, she receives an earthly frame which appears to be self-moved, but is really moved by her power; and this composition of soul and body is called a living and mortal creature. For immortal no such union can be reasonably believed to be; although fancy. not having seen nor surely known the nature of God, may imagine an immortal creature having both a body and also a soul which are united throughout all time. Let that, however, be as God wills, and be spoken of acceptably to him. And now let us ask the reason why the soul loses her wings!

The wing is the corporeal element which is most akin to the divine, and which by nature tends to soar aloft and carry that which gravitates downwards into the upper region, which is the habitation of the gods. The divine is beauty, wisdom, goodness, and the like; and by these the wing of the soul is nourished, and grows apace; but when fed upon evil and foulness and the opposite of good, wastes and falls away. Zeus, the mighty lord, holding the reins of a winged chariot. leads the way in heaven, ordering all and taking care of all; and there follows him the array of gods and demigods, marshalled in eleven bands; Hestia alone abides at home in the house of heaven; of the rest they who are reckoned among the princely twelve march in their appointed order. They see many blessed sights in the inner heaven, and there are many ways to and fro. along which the blessed gods are passing, every one doing his own work; he may follow who will and can, for jealousy has no place in the celestial choir. But when they go to banquet and festival, then they move up the steep to the top of the vault of heaven. The chariots of the gods in even poise. obeying the rein, glide rapidly; but the others labour, for the vicious steed goes heavily, weighing down the charioteer to the earth when his steed has not been thoroughly trained:--and this is the hour of agony and extremist conflict for the soul. For the immortals, when they are at the end of their course, go forth and stand upon the outside of heaven, and the revolution of the spheres carries them round, and they behold the things beyond. But of the heaven which is above the heavens, what earthly poet ever did or ever will sing worthily? It is such as I will describe; for I must dare to speak the truth. when truth is my theme. There abides the very being with which true knowledge is concerned; the colourless, formless, intangible essence, visible only to mind, the pilot of the soul. The divine intelligence, being nurtured upon mind and pure knowledge, and the intelligence of every soul which is capable of receiving the food proper to it, rejoices at beholding reality, and once more gazing upon truth. is replenished and made glad, until the revolution of the worlds brings her round again to the same place. In the revolution she beholds justice, and temperance, and knowledge absolute, not in the form of generation or of relation, which men call existence, but knowledge absolute in existence absolute; and beholding the other true existences in like manner. and feasting upon them. she passes down into the interior of the heavens and returns home; and there the charioteer putting up his horses at the stall, gives them ambrosia to eat and nectar to drink.

Such is the life of the gods; but of other souls, that which follows God best and is likest to him lifts the head of the charioteer into the outer world, and is carried round in the revolution, troubled indeed by the steeds, and with difficulty beholding true being; while another only rises and falls, and sees, and again fails to see by reason of the unruliness of the steeds. The rest of the souls are also longing after the upper world and they all follow, but not being strong enough they are carried round below the surface, plunging, treading on one another. each striving to be first; and there is confusion and perspiration and the extremity of effort; and many of them are lamed or have their wings broken through the ill-driving of the charioteers; and all of them after a fruitless toil, not having attained to the mysteries of true being, go away. and feed upon opinion. The reason why the souls exhibit this exceeding eagerness to behold the plain of truth is that pasturage is found there. which is suited to the highest part of the soul; and the wing on which the soul soars is nourished with this. And there is a law of Destiny, that the soul which attains any vision of truth in company with a god is preserved from harm until the next period, and if attaining always is

always unharmed. But when she is unable to follow, and
fails to behold the truth, and through some ill-hap
sinks beneath the double load of forgetfulness and
vice, and her wings fall from her and she drops to the
ground, then the law ordains that this soul shall at
her first birth pass, not into any other animal, but
only into man; and the soul which has seen most of
truth shall come to the birth as a philosopher, or
artist, or some musical and loving nature; that which
has seen truth in the second degree shall be some
righteous king or warrior chief; the soul which is of
the third class shall be a politician, or economist, or
trader; the fourth shall be a lover of gymnastic toils,
or a physician; the fifth shall lead the life of a
prophet or hierophant; to the sixth the character of a
poet or some other imitative artist will be assigned;
to the seventh the life of an artisan or husbandman; to
the eighth that of a sophist or demagogue; to the ninth
that of a tyrant;--all these are states of probation,
in which he who does righteously improves, and he who
does unrighteously, deteriorates his lot.

Ten thousand years must elapse before the soul of
each one can return to the place from whence she came,
for she cannot grow her wings in less; only the soul of
a philosopher, guileless and true, or the soul of a
lover, who is not devoid of philosophy, may acquire
wings in the third of the recurring periods of a
thousand years; he is distinguished from the ordinary
good man who gains wings in three thousand years:--and
they who choose this life three times in succession
have wings given them, and go away at the end of three
thousand years. But the others receive judgment when
they have completed their first life, and after the
judgment they go, some of them to the houses of
correction which are under the earth, and are punished;
others to some place in heaven whither they are lightly
borne by justice, and there they live in a manner
worthy of the life which they led here when in the form
of men. And at the end of the first thousand years the
good souls and also the evil souls both come to draw
lots and choose their second life, and they may take
any which they please. The soul of a man may pass into
the life of a beast, or from the beast return again
into the man. But the soul which has never seen the
truth will not pass into the human form. For a man
must have intelligence of universals, and be able to
proceed from the many particulars of sense to one
conception of reason;--this is the recollection of

those things which our soul once saw while following
God--when regardless of that which we now call being
she raised her head up towards the true being. And
therefore the mind of the philosopher alone has wings;
and this is just. for he is always, according to the
measure of his abilities, clinging in recollection to
those things in which God abides, and in beholding
which He is what He is. And he who employs aright
these memories is ever being initiated into perfect
mysteries and alone becomes truly perfect. But, as he
forgets earthly interests and is rapt in the divine,
the vulgar deem him mad, and rebuke him; they do not
see that he is inspired...

...For. as has been already said, every soul of man has
in the way of nature beheld true being; this was the
condition of her passing into the form of man. But all
souls do not easily recall the things of the other
world; they may have seen them for a short time only.
or they may have been unfortunate in their earthly lot,
and, having had their hearts turned into
unrighteousness through some corrupting influence, they
may have lost the memory of the holy things which once
they saw. Few only retain an adequate remembrance of
them; and they, when they behold here any image of that
other world, are rapt in amazement; but they are
ignorant of what this rapture means. because they do
not clearly perceive. For there is no light of justice
or temperance or any of the higher ideas which are
precious to souls in the earthly copies of them: they
are seen through a glass dimly; and there are few who,
going to the images, behold in them the realities, and
these only with difficulty. There was a time when with
the rest of the happy band they saw beauty shining in
brightness,--we philosophers following in the train of
Zeus, others in company with other gods; and then we
beheld the beatific vision and were initiated into a
mystery which may be truly called most blessed,
celebrated by us in our state of innocence, before we
had any experience of evils to come. when we were
admitted to the sight of apparitions innocent and
simple and calm and happy, which we beheld shining in
pure light, pure ourselves and not yet enshrined in
that living tomb which we carry about, now that we are
imprisoned in the body, like an oyster in his shell...

As I said at the beginning of this tale, I divided
each soul into three-- two horses and a charioteer; and

one of the horses was good and the other bad: the
division may remain, but I have not yet explained in
what the goodness or badness of either consists, and to
that I will proceed.   The right-hand horse is upright
and cleanly made; he has a lofty neck and an aquiline
nose; his colour is white, and his eyes dark; he is a
lover of honour and modesty and temperance, and the
follower of true glory; he needs no touch of the whip,
but is guided by word and admonition only. The other
is a crooked lumbering animal, put together anyhow; he
has a short thick neck; he is flat-faced and of a dark
colour, with grey eyes and blood-red complexion; the
mate of insolence and pride, shag-eared and deaf,
hardly yielding to whip and spur.   Now when the
charioteer beholds the vision of love, and has his
whole soul warmed through sense, and is full of the
prickings and ticklings of desire, the obedient steed,
then as always under the government of shame, refrains
from leaping on the beloved; but the other, heedless of
the pricks and of the blows of the whip, plunges and
runs away, giving all manner of trouble to his
companion and the charioteer, whom he forces to
approach the beloved and to remember the joys of love.
They at first indignantly oppose him and will not be
urged on to do terrible and unlawful deeds; but at
last, when he persists in plaguing them, they yield and
agree to do as he bids them.

And now they are at the spot and behold the flashing
beauty of the beloved; which when the charioteer sees,
his memory is carried to the true beauty, whom he
beholds in company with Modesty like an image placed
upon a holy pedestal. He sees her, but he is afraid
and falls backwards in adoration, and by his fall is
compelled to pull back the reins with such violence as
to bring both the steeds on their haunches, the one
willing and unresisting, the unruly one very unwilling;
and when they have gone back a little, the one is
overcome with shame and wonder, and his whole soul is
bathed in perspiration; the other, when the pain is
over which the bridle and the fall had given him,
having with difficulty taken breath, is full of wrath
and reproaches, which he heaps upon the charioteer and
his fellow-steed, for want of courage and manhood,
declaring that they have been false to their agreement
and guilty of desertion. Again they refuse, and again
he urges them on, and will scarce yield to their prayer
that he would wait until another time.   When the
appointed hour comes, they make as if they had

forgotten, and he reminds them, fighting and neighing and dragging them on, until at length he, on the same thoughts intent, forces them to draw near again. And when they are near he stoops his head and puts up his tail, and takes the bit in his teeth and pulls shamelessly. Then the charioteer is worse off than ever; he falls back like a racer at the barrier, and with a still more violent wrench drags the bit out of the teeth of the wild steed and covers his abusive tongue and jaws with blood, and forces his legs and haunches to the ground and punishes him sorely. And when this has happened several times and the villain has ceased from his wanton way, he is tamed and humbled, and follows the will of the charioteer, and when he sees the beautiful one he is ready to die of fear. And from that time forward the soul of the lover follows the beloved in modesty and holy fear.

And so the beloved who, like a god, has received every true and loyal service from his lover. not in pretence but in reality, being also himself of a nature friendly to his admirer, if in former days he has blushed to own his passion and turned away his lover, because his youthful companions or others slanderously told him that he would be disgraced. now as years advance, at the appointed age and time, is led to receive him into communion. For fate which has ordained that there shall be no friendship among the evil has also ordained that there shall ever be friendship among the good. And the beloved when he has received him into communion and intimacy, is quite amazed at the good-will of the lover; he recognises that the inspired friend is worth all other friends or kinsmen; they have nothing of friendship in them worthy to be compared with his. And when his feeling continues and he is nearer to him and embraces him. in gymnastic exercises and at other times of meeting, then the fountain of that stream, which Zeus when he was in love with Ganymede named Desire. overflows upon the lover, and some enters into his soul, and some when he is filled flows out again; and as a breeze or an echo rebounds from the smooth rocks and returns whence it came, so does the stream of beauty, passing through the eyes which are the windows of the soul, come back to the beautiful one; there arriving and quickening the passages of the wings, watering them and inclining them to grow, and filling the soul of the beloved also with love. And thus he loves, but he knows not what; he does not understand and cannot explain his own state;

he appears to have caught the infection of blindness
from another; the lover is his mirror in whom he is
beholding himself, but he is not aware of this. When
he is with the lover. both cease from their pain, but
when he is away then he longs as he is longed for. and
has love's image, love for love (Anteros) lodging in
his breast. which he calls and believes to be not love
but friendship only, and his desire is as the desire of
the other. but weaker; he wants to see him. touch him.
kiss, embrace him, and probably not long afterwards his
desire is accomplished. When they meet. the wanton
steed of the lover has a word to say to the charioteer;
he would like to have a little pleasure in return for
many pains, but the wanton steed of the beloved says
not a word, for he is bursting with passion which he
understands not;--he throws his arms round the lover
and embraces him as his dearest friend; and, when they
are side by side, he is not in a state in which he can
refuse the lover anything, if he ask him; although his
fellow-steed and the charioteer oppose him with the
arguments of shame and reason.

After this their happiness depends upon their
self-control; if the better elements of the mind which
lead to order and philosophy prevail. then they pass
their life here in happiness and harmony--masters of
themselves and orderly--enslaving the vicious and
emancipating the virtuous elements of the soul; and
when the end comes, they are light and winged for
flight, having conquered in one of the three heavenly
or truly Olympian victories; nor can human discipline
or divine inspiration confer any greater blessing on
man than this. If, on the other hand, they leave
philosophy and lead the lower life of ambition, then
probably, after wine or in some other careless hour.
the two wanton animals take the two souls when off
their guard and bring them together, and they
accomplish that desire of their hearts which to the
many is bliss; and this having once enjoyed they
continue to enjoy, yet rarely because they have not the
approval of the whole soul. They too are dear. but not
so dear to one another as the others, either at the
time of their love or afterwards. They consider that
they have given and taken from each other the most
sacred pledges, and they may not break them and fall
into enmity. At last they pass out of the body,
unwinged, but eager to soar. and thus obtain no mean
reward of love and madness. For those who have once
begun the heavenward pilgrimage may not go down again

to darkness and the journey beneath the earth. but they
live in light always; happy companions in their
pilgrimage, and when the time comes at which they
receive their wings they have the same plumage because
of their love...

5

ARISTOTLE

Aristotle (384-322 B.C.) was born in the Ionian city of Stagira in Chalcidice. At the age of seventeen he was sent to Athens where he entered Plato's Academy and remained there until Plato's death. twenty years later. After Plato's death. his nephew and heir, Speusippus, succeeded as head of the Academy. This development led Aristotle to leave the Academy and proceed first to Assos and then to the island of Lesbos. In 342. he accepted an invitation to serve as tutor to the son of Philip II of Macedon - the future Alexander the Great. Three years later he returned to his native Stagira and remained there until 335, at which time. he moved back to Athens to open his own school called the Lyceum. When Alexander the Great died in 323, the school was in danger of attack from the anti-Macedonian party in Athens and so. Aristotle fled to Chalcis where he died the following year.

The major works of Aristotle are principally scientific and philosophical in character. More specifically. he wrote treatises on logic, physics, psychology, natural history. and philosophy. that is to say, in metaphysics. ethics, politics, rhetoric and the art of poetry.

The first selection is taken from Book II, chapters 2 and 3 of the very important psychological work <u>On the Soul</u>. It becomes apparent to the careful reader that Aristotle's philosophy of man is not dualistic. Contrary to Plato. the soul is not a thing. It is a "ratio" or "formulable essence". It is the actuality of a certain kind of body that possesses the potentiality of being besouled. In short. the soul is not <u>that which lives</u>, but rather <u>that by which a body lives</u>. Aristotle also distinguishes between three different kinds of living things, namely, plants, animals. and men, and so. he speaks of three different kinds of soul.

In the second selection which is taken from the
Nicomachean Ethics, one can see the continuing
influence of Plato on Aristotle. Aristotle proposes
the view that happiness is activity in accordance with
virtue and that therefore it should be in accordance
with the highest virtue. He proceeds to point out that
"this will be that of the best thing in us." So, he
argues that contemplation is that activity.

ON THE SOUL:

The rational soul as formal cause of human life.

We resume our inquiry from a fresh starting-point by
calling attention to the fact that what has soul in it
differs from what has not in that the former displays
life. Now this word has more than one sense. and
provided any one alone of these is found in a thing we
say that thing is living. Living, that is, may mean
thinking or perception or local movement and rest, or
movement in the sense of nutrition, decay and growth.
Hence we think of plants also as living, for they are
observed to possess in themselves an originative power
through which they increase or decrease in all spatial
directions; they grow up and down, and everything that
grows increases its bulk alike in both directions or
indeed in all. and continues to live so long as it can
absorb nutriment.

This power of self-nutrition can be isolated from the
other powers mentioned, but not they from it--in mortal
beings at least. The fact is obvious in plants; for it
is the only psychic power they possess.

This is the originative power the possession of which
leads us to speak of things as living at all. but it is
the possession of sensation that leads us for the first
time to speak of living things as animals; for even
those beings which possess no power of local movement
but do possess the power of sensation we call animals
and not merely living things.

34

The primary form of sense is touch, which belongs to all animals. Just as the power of self-nutrition can be isolated from touch and sensation generally, so touch can be isolated from all other forms of sense. (By the power of self-nutrition we mean that departmental power of the soul which is common to plants and animals: all animals whatsoever are observed to have the sense of touch.) What the explanation of these two facts is, we must discuss later. At present we must confine ourselves to saying that soul is the source of these phenomena and is characterized by them. viz. by the powers of self-nutrition, sensation, thinking, and motivity.

Is each of these a soul or a part of a soul? And if a part. a part in what sense? A part merely distinguishable by definition or a part distinct in local situation as well? In the case of certain of these powers, the answers to these questions are easy, in the case of others we are puzzled what to say. Just as in the case of plants which when divided are observed to continue to live though removed to a distance from one another (thus showing that in _their_ case the soul of each individual plant before division was actually one. potentially many), so we notice a similar result in other varieties of soul, i.e. in insects which have been cut in two; each of the segments possesses both sensation and local movement; and if sensation, necessarily also imagination and appetition; for. where there is sensation, there is also pleasure and pain, and, where these. necessarily also desire.

We have no evidence as yet about mind or the power to think; it seems to be a widely different kind of soul, differing as what is eternal from what is perishable; it alone is capable of existence in isolation from all other psychic powers. All the other parts of soul. it is evident from what we have said, are. in spite of certain statements to the contrary, incapable of separate existence though, of course. distinguishable by definition. If opining is distinct from perceiving, to be capable of opining and to be capable of perceiving must be distinct. and so with all the other forms of living above enumerated. Further. some animals possess all these parts of soul, some certain of them only. others one only (this is what enables us to classify animals); the cause must be considered

later. A similar arrangement is found also within the
field of the senses; some classes of animals have all
the senses, some only certain of them, others only one,
the most indispensable, touch.

   Since the expression 'that whereby we live and
perceive' has two meanings, just like the expression
'that whereby we know'--that may mean either (a)
knowledge or (b) the soul, for we can speak of knowing
<u>by</u> or <u>with</u> either. and similarly that whereby we are in
health may be either (a) health or (b) the body or some
part of the body; and since of the two terms thus
contrasted knowledge or health is the name of a form,
essence, or ratio, or if we so express it an actuality
of a recipient matter--knowledge of what is capable of
knowing, health of what is capable of being made
healthy (for the operation of that which is capable of
originating change terminates and has its seat in what
is changed or altered); further, since it is the soul
by or with which primarily we live, perceive, and
think:--it follows that the soul must be a ratio or
formulable essence, not a matter or subject. For, as
we said, the word substance has three meanings--form.
matter. and the complex of both--and of these three
what is called matter is potentiality, what is called
form actuality. Since then the complex here is the
living thing, the body cannot be the actuality of the
soul; it is the soul which is the actuality of a
certain kind of body. Hence the rightness of the view
that the soul cannot be without a body, while it cannot
<u>be</u> a body; it is not a body but something relative to a
body.   That is why it is <u>in</u> a body, and a body of a
definite kind.   It was a mistake, therefore. to do
as former thinkers did, merely to fit it into a body
without adding a definite specification of the kind or
character of that body.   Reflection confirms the
observed fact; the actuality of any given thing can
only be realized in what is already potentially that
thing, i.e. in a matter of its own appropriate to it.
From all this it follows that soul is an actuality or
formulable essence of something that possesses a
potentiality of being besouled.

   Of the psychic powers above enumerated some kinds of
living things, as we have said, possess all, some less
than all. others one only. Those we have mentioned are
the nutritive, the appetitive, the sensory, the
locomotive, and the power of thinking. Plants have

none but the first, the nutritive, while another order of living things has this _plus_ the sensory. If any order of living things has the sensory, it must also have the appetitive; for appetite is the genus of which desire. passion, and wish are the species; now all animals have one sense at least. viz. touch, and whatever has a sense has the capacity for pleasure and pain and therefore has pleasant and painful objects present to it, and wherever these are present. there is desire. for desire is just appetition of what is pleasant. Further. all animals have the sense for food (for touch is the sense for food); the food of all living things consists of what is dry, moist, hot, cold, and these are the qualities apprehended by touch; all other sensible qualities are apprehended by touch only indirectly. Sounds, colours, and odours contribute nothing to nutriment; flavours fall within the field of tangible qualities. Hunger and thirst are forms of desire. hunger a desire for what is dry and hot, thirst a desire for what is cold and moist; flavour is a sort of seasoning added to both. We must later clear up these points, but at present it may be enough to say that all animals that possess the sense of touch have also appetition. The case of imagination is obscure; we must examine it later. Certain kinds of animals possess in addition the power of locomotion, and still another order of animate beings, i.e. man and possibly another order like man or superior to him. the power of thinking, i.e. mind. It is now evident that a single definition can be given of soul only in the same sense as one can be given of figure. For. as in that case there is no figure distinguishable and apart from triangle, etc., so here there is no soul apart from the forms of soul just enumerated. It is true that a highly general definition can be given for figure which will fit all figures without expressing the peculiar nature of any figure. So here in the case of soul and its specific forms. Hence it is absurd in this and similar cases to demand an absolutely general definition. which will fail to express the peculiar nature of anything that is, or again, omitting this, to look for separate definitions corresponding to each _infima species_. The case of figure and soul are exactly parallel; for the particulars subsumed under the common name in both cases--figures and living beings--constitute a series, each successive term of which potentially contains its predecessor. e.g. the square the triangle, the sensory power the self-nutritive. Hence we must ask in the case of each order of living things, What is its soul,

i.e. What is the soul of plant, animal. man? Why the
terms are related in this serial way must form the
subject of later examination.   But the facts are that
the power of perception is never found apart from the
power of self-nutrition, while--in plants--the latter
is found isolated from the former. Again, no sense is
found apart from that of touch, while touch _is_ found by
itself; many animals have neither sight, hearing, nor
smell. Again, among living things that possess sense
some have the power of locomotion, some not. Lastly.
certain living beings--a small minority--possess
calculation and thought, for (among mortal beings)
those which possess calculation have all the other
powers above mentioned, while the converse does not
hold--indeed some live by imagination alone, while
others have not even imagination.   The mind that knows
with immediate intuition presents a different problem.

It is evident that the way to give the most adequate
definition of soul is to seek in the case of each of
its forms for the most appropriate definition...

NICOMACHEAN ETHICS:

Man most like God in contemplative activity.

...The happy life is thought to be virtuous; now a
virtuous life requires exertion, and does not consist
in amusement.   And we say that serious things are
better than laughable things and those connected with
amusement, and that the activity of the better of any
two things--whether it be two elements of our being or
two men--is the more serious; but the activity of the
better is _ipso facto_ superior and more of the nature of
happiness. And any chance person--even a slave--can
enjoy the bodily pleasures no less than the best man;
but no one assigns a slave a share in happiness--unless
he assigns to him also a share in human life. For
happiness does not lie in such occupations, but, as we
have said before, in virtuous activities.

7

If happiness is activity in accordance with virtue,
it is reasonable that it should be in accordance with
the highest virtue; and this will be that of the best
thing in us.   Whether it be reason or something else
that is this element which is thought to be our natural
ruler and guide and to take thought of things noble and
divine. whether it be itself also divine or only the
most divine element in us, the activity of this in
accordance with its proper virtue will be perfect
happiness. That this activity is contemplative we have
already said.

Now this would seem to be in agreement both with what
we said before and with the truth. For, firstly, this
activity is the best (since not only is reason the best
thing in us, but the objects of reason are the best of
knowable objects); and secondly, it is the most
continuous, since we can contemplate truth more
continuously than we can do anything.   And we think
happiness has pleasure mingled with it. but the
activity of philosophic wisdom is admittedly the
pleasantest of virtuous activities; at all events the
pursuit of it is thought to offer pleasures marvellous
for their purity and their enduringness, and it is to
be expected that those who know will pass their time
more pleasantly than those who inquire.   And the
self-sufficiency that is spoken of must belong most to
the contemplative activity.   For while a philosopher.
as well as a just man or one possessing any other
virtue, needs the necessaries of life, when they are
sufficiently equipped with things of that sort the just
man needs people towards whom and with whom he shall
act justly. and the temperate man, the brave man, and
each of the others is in the same case. but the
philosopher. even when by himself, can contemplate
truth. and the better the wiser he is; he can perhaps
do so better if he has fellow workers, but still he is
the most self-sufficient.   And this activity alone
would seem to be loved for its own sake; for nothing
arises from it apart from the contemplating, while from
practical activities we gain more or less apart from
the action.   And happiness is thought to depend on
leisure; for we are busy that we may have leisure, and
make war that we may live in peace. Now the activity
of the practical virtues is exhibited in political or
military affairs, but the actions concerned with these
seem to be unleisurely. Warlike actions are completely
so (for no one chooses to be at war, or provokes war.
for the sake of being at war; any one would seem

absolutely murderous if he were to make enemies of his
friends in order to bring about battle and slaughter);
but the action of the statesman is also unleisurely,
and--apart from the political action itself--aims at
despotic power and honours, or at all events happiness,
for him and his fellow citizens--a happiness different
from political action, and evidently sought as being
different. So if among virtuous actions political and
military actions are distinguished by nobility and
greatness, and these are unleisurely and aim at an end
and are not desirable for their own sake, but the
activity of reason, which is contemplative, seems both
to be superior in serious worth and to aim at no end
beyond itself, and to have its pleasure proper to
itself (and this augments the activity), and the
self-sufficiency, leisureliness, unweariedness (so far
as this is possible for man), and all the other
attributes ascribed to the supremely happy man are
evidently those connected with this activity, it
follows that this will be the complete happiness of
man, if it be allowed a complete term of life (for none
of the attributes of happiness is <u>in</u>complete).

But such a life would be too high for man; for it is
not in so far as he is man that he will live so, but in
so far as something divine is present in him; and by so
much as this is superior to our composite nature is its
activity superior to that which is the exercise of the
other kind of virtue.   If reason is divine, then, in
comparison with man, the life according to it is divine
in comparison with human life.   But we must not
follow those who advise us, being men, to think of
human things, and, being mortal, of mortal things, but
must, so far as we can, make ourselves immortal, and
strain every nerve to live in accordance with the best
thing in us; for even if it be small in bulk, much more
does it in power and worth surpass everything. This
would seem, too, to be each man himself, since it is
the authoritative and better part of him. It would be
strange, then, if he were to choose not the life of his
self but that of something else.   And what we said
before will apply now; that which is proper to each
thing is by nature best and most pleasant for each
thing; for man, therefore, the life according to reason
is best and pleasantest, since reason more than
anything else <u>is</u> man.   This life therefore is also the
happiest.

But in a secondary degree the life in accordance with
the other kind of virtue is happy; for the activities
in accordance with this befit our human estate. Just
and brave acts, and other virtuous acts, we do in
relation to each other. observing our respective duties
with regard to contracts and services and all manner of
actions and with regard to passions; and all of these
seem to be typically human.   Some of them seem even to
arise from the body, and virtue of character to be in
many ways bound up with the passions.   Practical
wisdom, too, is linked to virtue of character, and this
to practical wisdom, since the principles of practical
wisdom are in accordance with the moral virtues and
rightness in morals is in accordance with practical
wisdom. Being connected with the passions also, the
moral virtues must belong to our composite nature; and
the virtues of our composite nature are human; so,
therefore. are the life and the happiness which
correspond to these. The excellence of the reason is a
thing apart; we must be content to say this much about
it, for to describe it precisely is a task greater than
our purpose requires. It would seem, however, also to
need external equipment but little, or less than moral
virtue does. Grant that both need the necessaries, and
do so equally, even if the statesman's work is the more
concerned with the body and things of that sort; for
there will be little difference there; but in what they
need for the exercise of their activities there will be
much difference. The liberal man will need money for
the doing of his liberal deeds, and the just man too
will need it for the returning of services (for wishes
are hard to discern, and even people who are not just
pretend to wish to act justly); and the brave man will
need power if he is to accomplish any of the acts that
correspond to his virtue, and the temperate man will
need opportunity; for how else is either he or any of
the others to be recognized?   It is debated, too,
whether the will or the deed is more essential to
virtue, which is assumed to involve both; it is surely
clear that its perfection involves both; but for deeds
many things are needed, and more, the greater and
nobler the deeds are. But the man who is contemplating
the truth needs no such thing, at least with a view to
the exercise of his activity; indeed they are. one may
say, even hindrances, at all events to his
contemplation; but in so far as he is a man and lives
with a number of people, he chooses to do virtuous

acts; he will therefore need such aids to living a human life.

But that perfect happiness is a contemplative activity will appear from the following consideration as well. We assume the gods to be above all other beings blessed and happy; but what sort of actions must we assign to them? Acts of justice? Will not the gods seem absurd if they make contracts and return deposits, and so on? Acts of a brave man, then, confronting dangers and running risks because it is noble to do so? Or liberal acts? To whom will they give? It will be strange if they are really to have money or anything of the kind. And what would their temperate acts be? Is not such praise tasteless, since they have no bad appetites? If we were to run through them all, the circumstances of action would be found trivial and unworthy of gods. Still, every one supposes that they <u>live</u> and therefore that they are active; we cannot suppose them to sleep like Endymion. Now if you take away from a living being action, and still more production, what is left but contemplation? Therefore the activity of God, which surpasses all others in blessedness, must be contemplative; and of human activities, therefore, that which is most akin to this must be most of the nature of happiness.

This is indicated, too, by the fact that the other animals have no share in happiness, being completely deprived of such activity. For while the whole life of the gods is blessed, and that of men too in so far as some likeness of such activity belongs to them, none of the other animals is happy, since they in no way share in contemplation. Happiness extends, then, just so far as contemplation does, and those to whom contemplation more fully belongs are more truly happy, not as a mere concomitant but in virtue of the contemplation; for this is in itself precious. Happiness, therefore, must be some form of contemplation.

But, being a man, one will also need external prosperity; for our nature is not self-sufficient for the purpose of contemplation, but our body also must be healthy and must have food and other attention. Still, we must not think that the man who is to be happy will need many things or great things, merely because he cannot be supremely happy without external goods; for

self-sufficiency and action do not involve excess, and
we can do noble acts without ruling earth and sea; for
even with moderate advantages one can act virtuously
(this is manifest enough; for private persons are
thought to do worthy acts no less than despots--indeed
even more); and it is enough that we should have so
much as that; for the life of the man who is active in
accordance with virtue will be happy.   Solon, too,
was perhaps sketching well the happy man when he
described him as moderately furnished with externals
but as having done (as Solon thought) the noblest acts,
and lived temperately; for one can with but moderate
possessions do what one ought.   Anaxagoras also seems
to have supposed the happy man not to be rich nor a
despot, when he said that he would not be surprised if
the happy man were to seem to most people a strange
person; for they judge by externals, since these are
all they perceive.   The opinions of the wise seem,
then, to harmonize with our arguments. But while even
such things carry some conviction, the truth in
practical matters is discerned from the facts of life;
for these are the decisive factor. We must therefore
survey what we have already said, bringing it to the
test of the facts of life, and if it harmonizes with
the facts we must accept it, but if it clashes with
them we must suppose it to be mere theory. Now he who
exercises his reason and cultivates it seems to be both
in the best state of mind and most dear to the gods.
For if the gods have any care for human affairs, as
they are thought to have, it would be reasonable both
that they should delight in that which was best and
most akin to them (i.e. reason) and that they should
reward those who love and honour this most, as caring
for the things that are dear to them and acting both
rightly and nobly.   And that all these attributes
belong most of all to the philosopher is manifest. He,
therefore, is the dearest to the gods. And he who is
that will presumably be also the happiest; so that in
this way too the philosopher will more than any other
be happy...

6

MARCUS AURELIUS

Marcus Aurelius Antoninus (121-180 A.D.), emperor of Rome and Stoic philosopher, was born of patrician stock in Rome as Marcus Annius Verus, and, after the early death of his parents, was brought up by his grandfather. He was introduced to the Stoic philosophy at the age of eleven and finding that his inclination was chiefly toward Stoicism, he attached himself to this--the strictest of the philosophical schools--even adopting the philosopher's simple dress and their mode of life. His industriousness and affectionate nature so impressed the emperor Hadrian that he advised Aurelius Antoninus, an uncle of Marcus, whom he had nominated as his successor, to adopt the boy and make him his heir. After his adoption, he assumed the name Marcus Aurelius Antoninus and proceeded to occupy himself with learning the art of government so that he would be ready to assume the responsibility of emperor of Rome, which fell on his shoulders in the year 161. However. he generously appointed Lucius Verus, the other adopted son of Antoninus, to share the throne as coemperor. Despite his gentleness and love of peace, his reign was marked by long and bloody wars against barbarian hordes, troubles of state, and domestic unhappiness. He died in 180 A.D. worn out by toil and anxiety while fighting against the barbarians on the Danube.

The _Meditations_ is the only extant work of Marcus Aurelius. Written in Greek during his lonely vigils in the Danubian marshes, its twelve books contain reflections on moral and religious topics which are set down often in a very unconnected fashion. The treatise expresses a Stoic philosophy, but one that clearly had been Romanized, for it does not adopt many of the physical and metaphysical views of the early Greek Stoic philosophers. The dominant issue taken up in the book is that of how life is to be lived well. For Marcus Aurelius, this issue was intimately connected with God and religion. As he observes in the selection that follows, God "with his intellectual part alone touches the intelligence only which has flowed and been

derived from himself into these bodies." Aurelius goes
on to say that if an individual also uses his
intelligence alone, which is an individual's
distinctive feature, he will rid himself of much
trouble.

MEDITATIONS:

Nothing is a man's own; all comes from the deity.

2. God sees the minds (ruling principles) of all men
bared of the material vesture and rind and impurities.
For with his intellectual part alone he touches the
intelligence only which has flowed and been derived
from himself into these bodies.   And if thou also
usest thyself to do this, thou wilt rid thyself of thy
much trouble. For he who regards not the poor flesh
which envelops him, surely will not trouble himself by
looking after raiment and dwelling and fame and such
like externals and show.

3. The things are three of which thou art composed, a
little body, a little breath (life), intelligence. Of
these the first two are thine, so far as it is thy duty
to take care of them; but the third alone is properly
thine. Therefore if thou shalt separate from thyself,
that is, from thy understanding, whatever others do or
say, and whatever thou hast done or said thyself, and
whatever future things trouble thee because they may
happen, and whatever in the body which envelops thee or
in the breath (life), which is by nature associated
with the body, is attached to thee independent of thy
will, and whatever the external circumfluent vortex
whirls round, so that the intellectual power exempt
from the things of fate can live pure and free by
itself, doing what is just and accepting what happens
and saying the truth: if thou wilt separate, I say,
from this ruling faculty the things which are attached
to it by the impressions of sense, and the things of
time to come and of time that is past, and wilt make
thyself like Empedocles' sphere,

All round, and in its joyous rest reposing;

and if thou shalt strive to live only what is really
thy life, that is, the present--then thou wilt be able

46

to pass that portion of life which remains for thee up
to the time of thy death, free from perturbations,
nobly, and obedient to thy own daemon (to the god that
is within thee).

4. I have often wondered how it is that every man
loves himself more than all the rest of men, but yet
sets less value on his own opinion of himself than on
the opinion of others. If then a god or a wise
teacher should present himself to a man and bid him to
think of nothing and to design nothing which he would
not express as soon as he conceived it, he could not
endure it even for a single day. So much more respect
have we to what our neighbours shall think of us than
to what we shall think of ourselves.

5. How can it be that the gods after having arranged
all things well and benevolently for mankind, have
overlooked this alone, that some men and very good men,
and men who, as we may say, have had most communion
with the divinity, and through pious acts and religious
observances have been most intimate with the divinity,
when they have once died should never exist again, but
should be completely extinguished?

But if this is so, be assured that if it ought to
have been otherwise, the gods would have done it. For
if it were just, it would also be possible; and if it
were according to nature, nature would have had it so.
But because it is not so, if in fact it is not so, be
thou convinced that it ought not to have been so:
--for thou seest even of thyself that in this inquiry
thou art disputing with the deity; and we should not
thus dispute with the gods, unless they were most
excellent and most just; --but if this is so, they
would not have allowed anything in the ordering of the
universe to be neglected unjustly and irrationally.

6. Practise thyself even in the things which thou
despairest of accomplishing. For even the left hand,
which is ineffectual for all other things for want of
practice, holds the bridle more vigorously than the
right hand; for it has been practised in this.

7. Consider in what condition both in body and soul a
man should be when he is overtaken by death; and
consider the shortness of life. the boundless abyss of
time past and future, the feebleness of all matter.

8. Contemplate the formative principles (forms) of
things bare of their coverings; the purposes of
actions; consider what pain is, what pleasure is, and
death, and fame; who is to himself the cause of his
uneasiness; how no man is hindered by another; that
everything is opinion.

9. In the application of thy principles thou must be
like the pancratiast. not like the gladiator; for the
gladiator lets fall the sword which he uses and is
killed; but the other always has his hand, and needs to
do nothing else than use it.

10. See what things are in themselves, dividing them
into matter, form and purpose.

11. What a power man has to do nothing except what God
will approve, and to accept all that God may give him.

12. With respect to that which happens conformably to
nature, we ought to blame neither gods, for they do
nothing wrong either voluntarily or involuntarily, nor
men, for they do nothing wrong except involuntarily.
Consequently we should blame nobody.

13. How ridiculous and what a stranger he is who is
surprised at anything which happens in life.

14. Either there is a fatal necessity and invincible
order. or a kind Providence, or a confusion without a
purpose and without a director.   If then there is an
invincible necessity, why dost thou resist? But if
there is a Providence which allows itself to be
propitiated, make thyself worthy of the help of the
divinity. But if there is a confusion without a
governor, be content that in such a tempest thou hast
in thyself a certain ruling intelligence. And even if
the tempest carry thee away, let it carry away the poor

flesh, the poor breath, everything else; for the intelligence at least it will not carry away.

15. Does the light of the lamp shine without losing its splendour until it is extinguished; and shall the truth which is in thee and justice and temperance be extinguished before thy death?

16. When a man has presented the appearance of having done wrong, say, How then do I know if this is a wrongful act? And even if he has done wrong, how do I know that he has not condemned himself? and so this is like tearing his own face. Consider that he, who would not have the bad man do wrong, is like the man who would not have the fig-tree to bear juice in the figs and infants to cry and the horse to neigh, and whatever else must of necessity be. For what must a man do who has such a character? If then thou art irritable, cure this man's disposition.

17. If it is not right, do not do it: if it is not true, do not say it. For let thy efforts be--.

18. In everything always observe what the thing is which produces for thee an appearance, and resolve it by dividing it into the formal, the material, the purpose, and the time within which it must end.

19. Perceive at last that thou hast in thee something better and more divine than the things which cause the various affects, and as it were pull thee by the strings. What is there now in my mind? Is it fear, or suspicion, or desire. or anything of the kind?

20. First, do nothing inconsiderately, nor without a purpose. Second, make thy acts refer to nothing else than to a social end.

21. Consider that before long thou wilt be nobody and nowhere. nor will any of the things exist which thou now seest. nor any of those who are now living. For all things are formed by nature to change and be turned and to perish in order that other things in continuous succession may exist.

22. Consider that everything is opinion, and opinion is in thy power. Take away then, when thou choosest. thy opinion, and like a mariner, who has doubled the promontory, thou wilt find calm, everything stable, and a waveless bay.

23. Any one activity whatever it may be, when it has ceased at its proper time suffers no evil because it has ceased; nor he who has done this act, does he suffer any evil for this reason that the act has ceased. In like manner then the whole which consists of all the acts, which is our life, if it cease at its proper time. suffers no evil for this reason that it has ceased; nor he who has terminated this series at the proper time, has he been ill dealt with. But the proper time and the limit nature fixes, sometimes as in old age the peculiar nature of man, but always the universal nature, by the change of whose parts the whole universe continues ever young and perfect. And everything which is useful to the universal is always good and in season. Therefore the termination of life for every man is no evil, because neither is it shameful, since it is both independent of the will and not opposed to the general interest, but it is good, since it is seasonable and profitable to and congruent with the universal. For thus too he is moved by the deity who is moved in the same manner with the deity and moved towards the same things in his mind.

24. These three principles thou must have in readiness. In the things which thou doest do nothing either inconsiderately or otherwise than as justice herself would act; but with respect to what may happen to thee from without, consider that it happens either by chance or according to Providence, and thou must neither blame chance nor accuse Providence. Second, consider what every being is from the seed to the time of its receiving a soul, and from the reception of a soul to the giving back of the same, and of what things every being is compounded and into what things it is resolved. Third, if thou shouldst suddenly be raised up above the earth, and shouldst look down on human things, and observe the variety of them how great it is, and at the same time also shouldst see at a glance how great is the number of beings who dwell all around in the air and the aether, consider that as often as thou shouldst be raised up, thou wouldst see the same things, sameness of form and shortness of duration. Are these things to be proud of?

25. Cast away opinion: thou art saved. Who then hinders thee from casting it away?

26. When thou art troubled about anything, thou hast forgotten this, that all things happen according to the universal nature; and forgotten this, that a man's wrongful act is nothing to thee; and further thou hast forgotten this, that everything which happens, always happened so and will happen so, and now happens so everywhere; forgotten this too, how close is the kinship between a man and the whole human race, for it is a community, not of a little blood or seed, but of intelligence. And thou has forgotten this too, that every man's intelligence is a god, and is an efflux of the deity; and forgotten this, that nothing is a man's own, but that his child and his body and his very soul came from the deity; forgotten this, that everything is opinion; and lastly thou hast forgotten that every man lives the present time only, and loses only this.

27. Constantly bring to thy recollection those who have complained greatly about anything, those who have been most conspicuous by the greatest fame or misfortunes or enmities or fortunes of any kind: then think where are they all now? Smoke and ash and a tale, or not even a tale. And let there be present to thy mind also everything of this sort, how Fabius Catullinus lived in the country, and Lucius Lupus in his gardens, and Stertinius at Baiae, and Tiberius at Capreae and Velius Rufus (or Rufus at Velia); and in fine think of the eager pursuit of anything conjoined with pride; and how worthless everything is after which men violently strain; and how much more philosophical it is for a man in the opportunities presented to him to show himself just, temperate, obedient to the gods, and to do this with all simplicity: for the pride which is proud of its want of pride is the most intolerable of all.

28. To those who ask, Where has thou seen the gods or how dost thou comprehend that they exist and so worshipest them, I answer, in the first place, they may be seen even with the eyes; in the second place neither have I seen even my own soul and yet I honour it. Thus then with respect to the gods, from what I constantly experience of their power, from this I comprehend that they exist and I venerate them.

29. The safety of life is this, to examine everything
all through, what it is itself, what is its material,
what the formal part; with all thy soul to do justice
and to say the truth.   What remains except to enjoy
life by joining one good thing to another so as not to
leave even the smallest intervals between?

30. There is one light of the sun, though it is
interrupted by walls, mountains, and other things
infinite. There is one common substance, though it is
distributed among countless bodies which have their
several qualities.   There is one soul, though it is
distributed among infinite natures and individual
circumscriptions (or individuals).   There is one
intelligent soul, though it seems to be divided. Now
in the things which have been mentioned all the other
parts, such as those which are air and matter, are
without sensation and have no fellowship: and yet even
these parts the intelligent principle holds together
and the gravitation towards the same.   But intellect
in a peculiar manner tends to that which is of the same
kin, and combines with it, and the feeling for
communion is not interrupted.

31. What dost thou wish? To continue to exist? Well,
dost thou wish to have sensation? Movement? Growth?
And then again to cease to grow?   To use thy speech?
To think?   What is there of all these things which
seems to thee worth desiring? But if it is easy to set
little value on all these things, turn to that which
remains, which is to follow reason and God. But it is
inconsistent with honouring reason and God to be
troubled because by death a man will be deprived of the
other things.

32. How small a part of the boundless and unfathomable
time is assigned to every man?   For it is very soon
swallowed up in the eternal.   And how small a part of
the whole substance?   And how small a part of the
universal soul? And on what a small clod of the whole
earth thou creepest?   Reflecting on all this consider
nothing to be great, except to act as thy nature leads
thee, and to endure that which the common nature
brings.

33. How does the ruling faculty make use of itself?
For all lies in this.   But everything else, whether it
is in the power of thy will or not, is only lifeless
ashes and smoke.

34. This reflection is most adapted to move us to
contempt of death, that even those who think pleasure
to be a good and pain an evil still have despised it.

35. The man to whom that only is good which comes in
due season, and to whom it is the same thing whether he
has done more or fewer acts conformable to right
reason, and to whom it makes no difference whether he
contemplates the world for a longer or a shorter
time--for this man neither is death a terrible thing.

36. Man, thou hast been a citizen in this great state
(the world):   what difference does it make to thee
whether for five years (or three)?   For that which is
conformable to the laws is just for all. Where is the
hardship then, if no tyrant nor yet an unjust judge
sends thee away from the state, but nature who brought
thee into it?   The same as if a praetor who has
employed an actor dismisses him from the stage.--"But I
have not finished the five acts, but only three of
them."--Thou sayest well, but in life the three acts
are the whole drama; for what shall be a complete drama
is determined by him who was once the cause of its
composition, and now of its dissolution: but thou art
the cause of neither.   Depart then satisfied, for he
also who releases thee is satisfied.

GREGORY OF NYSSA

Gregory of Nyssa (c. 330 - c. 394) was born into a wealthy Christian family in Cappadocia, a Roman province located in the mid-eastern part of Asia Minor. He rejected the invitation of his brother, Basil the Great, to join his monastic community and instead married and became a teacher of rhetoric. In 372, he was appointed bishop of Nyssa by Basil, bishop of Caesarea, but was deposed in 374 by a local synod dominated by the Emperor Valens and the Arian party. Gregory was restored to his see in 377 and subsequently began to move closer to his brother's monastic and theological ideals. From 379 to 394, he engaged more and more in writing and in the vigorous administration of his diocese. He was also actively involved in various synods at which he ardently defended the orthodox Trinitarian doctrine of the Council of Nicaea against the Arians. Among his most profound works are his <u>Commentary on the Song of Songs</u> and the <u>Life of Moses</u>.

In the selection that follows, taken from <u>On the Making of Man</u>, Gregory's philosophy of human nature surfaces. Man is spoken of as an image of God, the archetype, in that man has a rational nature, which both is nourished and endowed with sense, and also partakes of reason and is ordered by mind. Human nature, then, is the mean between the Divine and incorporeal nature, on the one hand, and the irrational life of brutes, on the other. To the extent that the life of man is governed by reason, it is drawn to divine excellence (beauty and goodness); however, to the extent that human life is governed by the irrational elements of its nature, it is drawn to evil. The true perfection of human nature, therefore, lies in the faith that Christ, the Son of God, became flesh, died, and resurrected, thereby restoring man to the likeness of Divine "archetypal" beauty and goodness.

ON THE MAKING OF MAN:

Man as likeness of divine archetype.

...Let us...consider...why the growth of things that
spring from the earth takes precedence, and the
irrational animals come next, and then, after the
making of these, comes man: for it may be that we
learn from these facts not only the obvious thought,
that grass appeared to the Creator useful for the sake
of the animals, while the animals were made because of
man, and that for this reason, before the animals there
was made their food, and before man that which was to
minister to human life.

But it seems to me that by these facts Moses reveals
a hidden doctrine, and secretly delivers that wisdom
concerning the soul, of which the learning that is
without had indeed some imagination, but no clear
comprehension. His discourse then hereby teaches us
that the power of life and soul may be considered in
three divisions. For one is only a power of growth and
nutrition supplying what is suitable for the support of
the bodies that are nourished, which is called the
vegetative soul, and is to be seen in plants; for we
may perceive in growing plants a certain vital power
destitute of sense; and there is another form of life
besides this, which, while it includes the form above
mentioned, is also possessed in addition of the power
of management according to sense; and this is to be
found in the nature of the irrational animals: for
they are not only the subjects of nourishment and
growth, but also have the activity of sense and
perception. But perfect bodily life is seen in the
rational (I mean the human) nature, which both is
nourished and endowed with sense, and also partakes of
reason and is ordered by mind.

We might make a division of our subject in some such
way as this. Of things existing, part are
intellectual, part corporeal. Let us leave alone for
the present the division of the intellectual according
to its properties, for our argument is not concerned
with these. Of the corporeal, part is entirely devoid
of life, and part shares in vital energy. Of a living
body, again, part has sense conjoined with life, and

part is without sense: lastly, that which has sense is again divided into rational and irrational. For this reason the lawgiver says that after inanimate matter (as a sort of foundation for the form of animate things), this vegetative life was made, and had earlier existence in the growth of plants: then he proceeds to introduce the genesis of those creatures which are regulated by sense: and since, following the same order, of those things which have obtained life in the flesh, those which have sense can exist by themselves even apart from the intellectual nature, while the rational principle could not be embodied save as blended with the sensitive,--for this reason man was made last after the animals, as nature advanced in an orderly course to perfection. For this rational animal, man, is blended of every form of soul; he is nourished by the vegetative kind of soul, and to the faculty of growth was added that of sense, which stands midway, if we regard its peculiar nature, between the intellectual and the more material essence, being as much coarser than the one as it is more refined than the other: then takes place a certain alliance and commixture of the intellectual essence with the subtle and enlightened element of the sensitive nature: so that man consists of these three: as we are taught the like thing by the apostle in what he says to the Ephesians, praying for them that the complete grace of their "body and soul and spirit" may be preserved at the coming of the Lord; using the word "body" for the nutritive part, and denoting the sensitive by the word "soul," and the intellectual by "spirit." Likewise too the Lord instructs the scribe in the Gospel that he should set before every commandment that love to God which is exercised with all the heart and soul and mind: for here also it seems to me that the phrase indicates the same difference, naming the more corporeal existence "heart," the intermediate "soul," and the higher nature, the intellectual and mental faculty, "mind."

Hence also the apostle recognizes three divisions of dispositions, calling one "carnal," which is busied with the belly and the pleasures connected with it, another "natural," which holds a middle position with regard to virtue and vice, rising above the one, but without pure participation in the other; and another "spiritual," which perceives the perfection of godly life: wherefore he says to the Corinthians, reproaching their indulgence in pleasure and passion,

"Ye are carnal," and incapable of receiving the more
perfect doctrine; while elsewhere, making a comparison
of the middle kind with the perfect, he says, "but the
natural man receiveth not the things of the Spirit:
for they are foolishness unto him: but he that is
spiritual judgeth all things, yet he himself is judged
of no man." As, then, the natural man is higher than
the carnal, by the same measure also the spiritual man
rises above the natural.

   If, therefore, Scripture tells us that man was made
last, after every animate thing, the lawgiver is doing
nothing else than declaring to us the doctrine of the
soul, considering that what is perfect comes last,
according to a certain necessary sequence in the order
of things: for in the rational are included the others
also, while in the sensitive there also surely exists
the vegetative form, and that again is conceived only
in connection with what is material: thus we may
suppose that nature makes an ascent as it were by
steps--I mean the various properties of life--from the
lower to the perfect form....

...And here, I think there is a view of the matter more
close to nature, by which we may learn something of the
more refined doctrines.   For   since the most beautiful
and supreme good of all is the Divinity Itself, to
which incline all things that have a tendency towards
what is beautiful and good, we therefore say that the
mind, as being in the image of the most beautiful,
itself also remains in beauty and goodness so long as
it partakes as far as is possible in its likeness to
the archetype; but if it were at all to depart from
this it is deprived of that beauty in which it was.
And as we said that the mind was adorned by the
likeness of the archetypal beauty, being formed as
though it were a mirror to receive the figure of that
which it expresses, we consider that the nature which
is governed by it is attached to the mind in the same
relation, and that it too is adorned by the beauty that
the mind gives, being, so to say, a mirror of the
mirror; and that by it is swayed and sustained the
material element of that existence in which the nature
is contemplated.

   Thus so long as one keeps in touch with the other,
the communication of the true beauty extends

proportionally through the whole series, beautifying by the superior nature that which comes next to it; but when there is any interruption of this beneficent connection, or when, on the contrary, the superior comes to follow the inferior, then is displayed the misshapen character of matter, when it is isolated from nature (for in itself matter is a thing without form or structure), and by its shapelessness is also destroyed that beauty of nature with which it is adorned through the mind; and so the transmission of the ugliness of matter reaches through the nature to the mind itself, so that the image of God is no longer seen in the figure expressed by that which was moulded according to it; for the mind, setting the idea of good like a mirror behind the back, turns off the incident rays of the effulgence of the good, and it receives into itself the impress of the shapelessness of matter....

We must, then, examine the words carefully: for we find, if we do so, that that which was made "in the image" is one thing, and that which is now manifested in wretchedness is another. "God created man," it says; "in the image of God created He him." There is an end of the creation of that which was made "in the image": then it makes a resumption of the account of creation, and says, "male and female created He them." I presume that every one knows that this is a departure from the Prototype: for "in Christ Jesus," as the apostle says, "there is neither male nor female." Yet the phrase declares that man is thus divided.

Thus the creation of our nature is in a sense twofold: one made like to God, one divided according to this distinction: for something like this the passage darkly conveys by its arrangement, where it first says, "God created man, in the image of God created He him," and then, adding to what has been said, "male and female created He them,"--a thing which is alien from our conceptions of God.

I think that by these words Holy Scripture conveys to us a great and lofty doctrine; and the doctrine is this. While two natures--the Divine and incorporeal nature, and the irrational life of brutes--are separated from each other as extremes, human nature is the mean between them: for in the compound nature of man we may behold a part of each of the natures I have mentioned,--of the Divine, the rational and intelligent element, which does not admit the distinction of male and female; of the irrational, our bodily form and structure, divided into male and female: for each of these elements is certainly to be found in all that partakes of human life. That the intellectual element, however, precedes the other, we learn as from one who gives in order an account of the making of man; and we learn also that his community and kindred with the irrational is for man a provision for reproduction. For he says first that "God created man in the image of God" (showing by these words, as the Apostle says, that in such a being there is no male or female): then he adds the peculiar attributes of human nature, "male and female created He them."

What, then do we learn from this? Let no one, I pray, be indignant if I bring from far an argument to bear upon the present subject. God is in His own nature all that which our mind can conceive of good;--rather, transcending all good that we can conceive or comprehend. He creates man for no other reason than that He is good; and being such, and having this as His reason for entering upon the creation of our nature, He would not exhibit the power of His goodness in an imperfect form, giving our nature some one of the things at His disposal, and grudging it a share in another: but the perfect form of goodness is here to be seen by His both bringing man into being from nothing, and fully supplying him with all good gifts: but since the list of individual good gifts is a long one, it is out of the question to apprehend it numerically. The language of Scripture therefore expresses it concisely by a comprehensive phrase, in saying that man was made "in the image of God": for this is the same as to say that He made human nature participant in all good; for if the Deity is the fulness of good, and this is His image, then the image finds its resemblance to the Archetype in being filled with all good.

Thus there is in us the principle of all excellence, all virtue and wisdom, and every higher thing that we conceive: but pre-eminent among all is the fact that we are free from necessity, and not in bondage to any natural power, but have decision in our own power as we please; for virtue is a voluntary thing, subject to no dominion: that which is the result of compulsion and force cannot be virtue.

Now as the image bears in all points the semblance of
the archetypal excellence, if it had not a difference
in some respect, being absolutely without divergence it
would no longer be a likeness, but will in that case
manifestly be absolutely identical with the Prototype.
What difference then do we discern between the Divine
and that which has been made like to the Divine? We
find it in the fact that the former is uncreated, while
the latter has its being from creation: and this
distinction of property brings with it a train of other
properties; for it is very certainly acknowledged that
the uncreated nature is also immutable, and always
remains the same, while the created nature cannot exist
without change; for its very passage from nonexistence
to existence is a certain motion and change of the
non-existent transmuted by the Divine purpose into
being....

...I may be allowed to describe the human image by
comparison with some wonderful piece of modelling.
For, as one may see in models those carved shapes which
the artificers of such things contrive for the wonder
of beholders, tracing out upon a single head two forms
of faces; so man seems to me to bear a double likeness
to opposite things--being moulded in the Divine element
of his mind to the Divine beauty, but bearing, in the
passionate impulses that arise in him, a likeness to
the brute nature; while often even his reason is
rendered brutish, and obscures the better element by
the worse through its inclination and disposition
towards what is irrational; for whenever a man drags
down his mental energy to these affections, and forces
his reason to become the servant of his passions, there
takes place a sort of conversion of the good stamp in
him into the irrational image, his whole nature being
traced anew after that design, as his reason, so to
say, cultivates the beginnings of his passions, and
gradually multiplies them; for once it lends its
co-operation to passion, it produces a plenteous and
abundant crop of evils....

THOMAS AQUINAS

Thomas Aquinas, theologian and philosopher declared to be the Doctor of the Catholic Church by Leo XIII in 1879, was born in Roccasecca, Italy, near Aquino, in 1224. After receiving an elementary education from Benedictine monks at Monte Casino, he attended the University of Naples where he became a master of arts. He entered the Dominican Order in 1244 and for the next 12 years pursued studies in both philosophy and theology, first at Paris, then at Cologne under the tutelage of Albert the Great, and then once again in Paris where in 1256 he was awarded the magistrate (doctorate) in theology. After being licensed to teach theology, he did so teach first at Paris until 1259 and then as a lecturer over a ten year period at various Dominican monasteries in the vicinity of Rome. In 1268 he returned to the University of Paris to teach theology, during which time he completed many of his writings. However, in 1272, he was called back to Italy to teach at the University of Naples. Early in 1274, on his way to Lyons, France, for the purpose of attending a church council, he died at Fossanova, Italy.

Thomas Aquinas did most of his writing from 1252-1273 while he was an active teacher. His writings consist of several large theological treatises (the most famous of which are his _Summa Theologiae_ and _Summa Contra Gentiles_ or _On the Truth of the Catholic Faith_, twelve commentaries on various treatises of Aristotle, commentaries on several books of the Bible, recorded disputations on theological and philosophical problems, and a large number of sermons, letters, and short treatises on philosophical and religious subjects.

His view of man owes much to Aristotle's _On the Soul_, to the Christian Platonism of St. Augustine, and to the Bible. The selection that follows is taken from the _Summa Contra Gentiles_, a work that was written as a manual of Christian doctrine intended for the use of Christian missionaries in Spain who were confronting the high intellectual culture of the Moslem world. In

the text provided, Thomas argues: 1. how God is the
end of all things; 2.   that all things tend to be like
unto God; 3.   how things imitate the divine goodness;
4.   that to know God is the end of every intellectual
substance; 5. that happiness does not consist in an
act of the will; 6.   that ultimate happiness consists
in contemplating God; and 7.   that man needs divine
help to attain that ultimate happiness.

ON THE TRUTH OF THE CATHOLIC FAITH:

Human happiness consists in comptemplating God.

Chapter XVIII: How God Is The End Of Things

It remains to ask how God is the end of all things.
This will be made clear from what has been said.

For He is the end of all things, yet so as to precede
all in being.   Now there is an end which, though it
hold the first place in causing in so far as it is in
the intention, is nevertheless last in execution. This
applies to any end which the agent establishes by his
action. Thus the physician by his action establishes
health in the sick man, which is nevertheless his end.
There is also an end which, just as it precedes in
causing, so also does it precede in being. Thus, that
which one intends to acquire by one's motion or action
is said to be one's end.   For instance, fire seeks to
reach a higher place by its movement, and the king
seeks to take a city by fighting. Accordingly, God is
the end of things as something to be obtained by each
thing in its own way.

Again. God is at once the last end of things and the
first agent, as we have shown. Now the end effected by
the agent's action cannot be the first agent, but
rather is it the agent's effect.   God, therefore,
cannot be the end of things as though He were something
effected, but only as something already existing and to
be acquired.

Further. If a thing act for the sake of something
already in existence, and if by its action some result
ensue, then something through the agent's action must
accrue to the thing for the sake of which it acts; and
thus soldiers fight for the cause of their captain, to
whom victory accrues, which the soldiers bring about by
their actions. Now nothing can accrue to God from the
action of anything whatever, since His goodness is
perfect in every way, as we proved in the First Book.
It follows, then, that God is the end of things, not as
something made or effected by them, nor as though He
obtained something from things, but in this way alone,
that He is obtained by them.

   Moreover. The effect must tend to the end in the
same way as the agent acts for the end. Now God, who
is the first agent of all things, does not act as
though He gained something by His action, but as
bestowing something thereby; since He is not in
potentiality so that He can acquire something, but
solely in perfect actuality, whereby He is able to
bestow. Things therefore are not ordered to God as to
an end to which something will be added; they are
ordered to Him to obtain God Himself from Him according
to their measure, since He is their end.

CHAPTER XIX: That All Things Tend To Be Like Unto God

From the fact that they acquire the divine goodness,
creatures are made like unto God.   Therefore, if all
things tend to God as their last end, so as to acquire
His goodness, it follows that the last end of things is
to become like unto God....

Further. All creatures are images of the first agent,
namely God, since <u>the agent produces its like</u>. Now the
perfection of an image consists in representing the
original by a likeness to it, for this is why an image
is made. Therefore all things exist for the purpose of
acquiring a likeness to God, as for their last end....

CHAPTER XX: How Things Imitate The Divine Goodness

From what has been said it is clear that the last end of all things is to become like God. Now, that which has properly the nature of an end is the good. Therefore, properly speaking, things tend to become like to God inasmuch as He is good.

Now, creatures do not acquire goodness in the way in which it is in God, even though each thing imitates the divine goodness according to its own manner. For the divine goodness is simple, being, as it were, all in one. For the divine being contains the whole fullness of perfection, as we proved in the First Book. Therefore, since a thing is good so far as it is perfect, God's being is His perfect goodness; for in God, to be, to live, to be wise, to be happy, and whatever else is seen to pertain to perfection and goodness, are one and the same in God, as though the sum total of His goodness were God's very being. Again, the divine being is the substance of the existing God. But this cannot be so in other things. For it was proved in the Second Book that no created substance is its own being. Therefore, if a thing is good so far as it is, and if no creature is its own being, none is its own goodness, but each one is good by participating in goodness, even as by participating in being it is a being.

Also. All creatures are not placed on the same level of goodness. For in some the substance is both form and actuality: such, namely, as are competent, by the mere fact that they exist, to be actually and to be good. But in others, the substance is composed of matter and form, and such are competent to be actually and to be good, though it is by some part of their being, namely, their form. Accordingly, God's substance is His goodness, whereas a simple substance participates in goodness by the very fact that it exists, and a composite substance participates in goodness by some part of itself....

CHAPTER XXV: That To Know God Is The End of Every
                 Intellectual Substance

Now, seeing that all creatures, even those that are devoid of reason, are directed to God as their last end, and that all reach this end in so far as they have some share of a likeness to Him, the intellectual creature attains to Him in a special way, namely, through its proper operation, by understanding Him. Consequently this must be the end of the intellectual creature, namely, to understand God.

For, as we have shown above, God is the end of each thing, and hence, as far as it is possible to it, each thing intends to be united to God as its last end. Now a thing is more closely united to God by reaching in a way to the very substance of God; which happens when it knows something of the divine substance, rather than when it reaches to a divine likeness. Therefore the intellectual substance tends to the knowledge of God as its last end.

Again. The operation proper to a thing is its end, for it is its second perfection; so that when a thing is well conditioned for its proper operation it is said to be fit and good. Now understanding is the proper operation of the intellectual substance, and consequently is its end. Therefore, whatever is most perfect in this operation is its last end; and especially in those operations which are not directed to some product, such as understanding and sensation. And since operations of this kind take their species from their objects, by which also they are known, it follows that the more perfect the object of any such operation, the more perfect is the operation. Consequently to understand the most perfect intelligible, namely God, is the most perfect in the genus of the operation which consists in understanding. Therefore to know God by an act of understanding is the last end of every intellectual substance....

Furthermore. In all mutually ordered agents and movers, the end of the first agent and mover must be the end of all, even as the end of the commander-in-chief is the end of all who are soldiering under him. Now of all the parts of man, the intellect is the highest mover, for it moves the appetite, by proposing its object to it; and the intellective appetite, or will, moves the sensitive appetites, namely the irascible and concupiscible. Hence it is that we do not obey the concupiscence, unless the will command; while the sensitive appetite, when the will has given its consent, moves the body. Therefore the end of the intellect is the end of all human actions. <u>Now the intellect's end and good are the true</u>, and its last end is the first truth. Therefore the last end of the whole man, and of all his deeds and desires, is to know the first truth, namely, God.

Moreover. Man has a natural desire to know the causes of whatever he sees; and so through wondering at what they saw, and not knowing its cause, men first began to philosophize, and when they had discovered the cause they were at rest. Nor do they cease inquiring until they come to the first cause; and <u>then do we deem ourselves to know perfectly when we know the first cause</u>. Therefore man naturally desires, as his last end, to know the first cause. But God is the first cause of all things. Therefore man's last end is to know God.

Besides. Man naturally desires to know the cause of any known effect. But the human intellect knows universal being. Therefore it naturally desires to know its cause, which is God alone, as we proved in the Second Book. Now one has not attained to one's last end until the natural desire is at rest. Therefore the knowledge of any intelligible object is not enough for man's happiness, which is his last end, unless he know God also, which knowledge terminates his natural desire as his last end. Therefore this very knowledge of God is man's last end.

Further. A body that tends by its natural appetite to its place is moved all the more vehemently and rapidly the nearer it approaches its end. Hence Aristotle proves that a natural straight movement cannot be towards an indefinite point, because it would not be more moved afterwards than before. Hence that which tends more vehemently to a thing afterwards than before is not moved towards an indefinite point but towards something fixed. Now this we find in the desire of knowledge, for the more one knows, the greater one's desire to know. Consequently, man's natural desire in knowledge tends to a definite end. This can be none other than the highest thing knowable, which is God. Therefore the knowledge of God is man's last end.

Now the last end of man and of any intelligent substance is called <u>happiness</u> or <u>beatitude</u>, for it is this that every intellectual substance desires as its last end, and for its own sake alone. Therefore the last beatitude or happiness of any intellectual substance is to know God....

CHAPTER XXVI: Does Happiness Consist In An Act Of The Will?

Since the intellectual substance attains to God by its operation, not only by an act of understanding but also by an act of the will, through desiring and loving Him, and through delighting in Him, someone might think that man's last end and ultimate happiness consists, not in knowing God, but in loving Him, or in some other act of the will towards Him; especially since the object of the will is the good, which has the nature of an end, whereas the true, which is the object of the intellect, has not the nature of an end except in so far as it also is a good. Therefore, seemingly, man does not attain to his last end by an act of his intellect, but rather by an act of his will....

But this can be clearly shown to be impossible.

For since happiness is the proper good of the intellectual nature, it must needs become the intellectual nature according to that which is proper thereto. Now appetite is not proper to the intellectual nature, but is in all things, although it is found diversely in diverse things. This diversity, however, arises from the fact that things are diversely related to knowledge. For things wholly devoid of knowledge have only a natural appetite; those that have a sensitive knowledge have also a sensitive appetite, under which the irascible and concupiscible appetites are comprised; and those which have intellectual knowledge have also an appetite proportionate to that knowledge, namely, the will. The will, therefore, in so far as it is an appetite, is not proper to the intellectual nature, but only in so far as it is dependent on the intellect. On the other hand, the intellect is in itself proper to the intellectual nature. Therefore, beatitude or happiness consists principally and essentially in an act of the intellect, rather than in an act of the will....

CHAPTER XXXVII: That Man's Ultimate Happiness
Consists in Contemplating God

...It is not possible that man's ultimate happiness
consist in comtemplation based on the understanding of
first principles; for this is most imperfect, as being
most universal, containing potentially the knowledge of
things. Moreover, it is the beginning and not the end
of human inquiry, and comes to us from nature, and not
through the pursuit of the truth. Nor does it consist
in contemplation based on the sciences that have the
lowest things for their object, since happiness must
consist in an operation of the intellect in relation to
the most noble intelligible objects.   It follows then
that man's ultimate happiness consists in wisdom, based
on the consideration of divine things....

CHAPTER CXLVII: That Man Needs Divine Help To Attain
                   Happiness: Happiness achieved only
                   with divine help.

...No instrument can achieve its ultimate perfection by
the power of its own form, but only by the power of the
principal agent, although by its own power it can
provide a   certain   disposition   to   the ultimate
perfection. Indeed, the cutting of the lumber results
from the saw according to the essential character of
its own form, but the form of the bench comes from the
skilled mind which uses the tool.   Likewise, the
breaking down and consumption of food in the animal
body is due to the heat of fire, but the generation of
flesh, and controlled growth and similar actions, stem
from the vegetative soul which uses the heat of fire as
an instrument.   Now, all intellects and wills are
subordinated as instruments under a principal agent to
God, Who is the first intellect and will. So, their
operations must have no efficacy in regard to the
ultimate perfection which is the attainment of final
happiness, except through the divine power. Therefore,
a rational nature needs divine help to obtain the
ultimate end.

Furthermore, there are many impediments presented to
man in the attaining of his end. For he is hindered by
the weakness of his reason, which is easily drawn into
error by which he is cut off from the right way of

reaching his end. He is also hindered by the passions
of his sensory nature, and by the feelings whereby he
is attracted to sensible and lower things; and the more
he attaches himself to these, the farther he is removed
from his ultimate end, for these things are below man,
whereas man's end is above him. He is further hindered
by frequent bodily illness from the carrying out of his
virtuous activities   whereby   he   may   tend   toward
happiness.   Therefore,   man   needs   divine help, but he
may fall completely short   of   the   ultimate   end as a
result of these obstacles.

   Hence, it is said, in John (6:44): "No man can come
to Me, except the Father, Who hath sent Me, draw him,"
and again: "As the branch cannot bear fruit of itself,
unless it abide in the vine, so neither can you, unless
you abide in Me" (John 15:4)....

CATHERINE OF SIENA

Catherine of Siena (1347-1380) was born in a district of Siena called Fontenbrada. Her proximity to the cloister of San Domenico made it easy for Catherine to be influenced by the Dominicans. In fact, at the age of twenty-one, she entered an order of Saint Dominic known as the Mantellate, devoted to service to the poor and the sick. In addition to serving the needs of the sick, especially while the plague was sweeping through Siena, Catherine also became involved in the politics of the day, when, in 1375, she persuaded the cities of Pisa and Lucca not to join the anti-papal league. The following year, the city of Florence called on Catherine to mediate between the papacy of Gregory XI and the various city-states which had been placed under papal authority. But she soon found herself being distrusted by the Signoria who, in turn, sent their own delegates to negotiate at Avignon. Consequently, she turned her attention to the concerns of clergy reform and the return of the papacy to Rome. She returned to Siena in 1377 where she founded a monastery, and in the same year wrote <u>The Dialogue</u>. She died in the year 1380 after a severe illness.

In <u>The Dialogue</u>, Catherine captures the Christian image of man, complementing in beautiful prose the views of Gregory of Nyssa and Thomas Aquinas. Man is portrayed as a "mirror" of God in Christ whose way to holiness comes through memory, understanding, and will, on the natural level, but in faith and in love of the Spirit of God, on the spiritual level. The bridge to these two lives is the Church and her Trinitarian revelation of God, the Father, God, the Son, and God, the Holy Spirit.

THE DIALOGUE:

     Christ and the Church as man's bridge to God.

     I want you to understand this, my daughter: I
created humankind anew in the blood of my only-begotten
Son and reestablished them in grace, but they have so
scorned the graces I gave them and still give them!
They go from bad to worse, from sin to sin, constantly
repaying me with insults.   And they not only fail to
recognize my graces for what they are, but sometimes
even think I am abusing them -- I who want nothing but
their sanctification! I tell you it will go harder for
them in view of the grace they have received, and they
will be deserving of greater punishment. They will be
more severely punished now that they have been redeemed
by my Son's blood than they would have been before that
redemption, before the scar of Adam's sin was removed.

     It is only reasonable that those who receive more
should give more in return, and the greater the gift,
the greater the bond of indebtedness. How greatly were
they indebted to me, then, since I had given them their
very existence, creating them in my image and likeness!
They owed me glory, but they stole it from me and took
it to themselves instead.   They violated the obedience
I had laid on them and so became my enemies. But with
humility I destroyed their pride: I stooped to take on
their humanity, rescued them from their slavery to the
devil, and made them free.   And more than this -- can
you see? -- through this union of the divine nature
with the human, God was made human and humanity was
made God.

     What indebtedness -- to have received the treasure of
the blood by which they are created anew in grace! So
you see how much more they owe me after their
redemption than before. For now they are bound by the
example of the incarnate Word, my only-begotten Son, to
give me glory and praise. And then they will pay their
debt of love for me and for their neighbors, as well as
true and solid virtue as I described for you earlier.

     Because they owe me so much love, if they refuse it
their sin is all the greater, and my divine justice

punishes them so much more severely in eternal damnation. False Christians fare much worse there than do pagans. The fire of divine justice torments them the more, burning without consuming; and in their torment they feel themselves being eaten by the worm of conscience, which eats away without eating up -- for the damned for all their torment cannot cease to exist. Indeed, they beg for death but cannot have it: They cannot cease to exist. By their sin they can lose the life of grace, but not their very being.

So sin is punished far more severely after people have been redeemed by the blood than before. For they have received more, but they seem to ignore it and to take no notice of their evil deeds. Though I once reconciled them to myself through the blood of my Son, they have become my enemies.

But I have one remedy to calm my wrath: my servents who care enough to press me with their tears and bind me with the chain of their desire. You see, you have bound me with that chain -- and I myself gave you that chain because I wanted to be merciful to the world. I put into my servants a hunger and longing for my honor and the salvation of souls so that I might be forced by their tears to soften the fury of my divine justice.

Bring, then, your tears and your sweat, you and my other servants. Draw them from the fountain of my divine love and use them to wash the face of my bride. I promise you that thus her beauty will be restored. Not by the sword or by war or by violence will she regain her beauty, but through peace and through the constant and humble prayers and sweat and tears poured out by my servants with eager desire.

And so I will fulfill your desire by giving you much to suffer, and your patience will spread light into the darkness in all the world's evil. Do not be afraid: Though the world may persecute you, I am at your side and never will my providence fail you.

Then that soul stood before the divine majesty deeply joyful and strengthened in her new knowledge. What hope she had found in the divine mercy! What

Have mercy, eternal God, on your little sheep, good
shepherd that you are!   Do not delay with your mercy
for the world, for already it almost seems they can no
longer survive! Everyone seems bereft of any oneness
in charity with you, eternal Truth, or even with each
other: I mean, whatever love they have for each other
has no grounding in you.

See how they all lash out at me! And I created them
with such burning love and gave them grace and gifts
without number--all freely, though I owed them nothing!
But see, daughter, how they strike back at me with
every sort of sin, but most of all with their wretched
and hateful selfishness, that breeding ground of every
evil, and with this selfish love they have poisoned the
whole world. I have shown you how love of me bears
every good that is brought to birth for others. By the
same principle this sensual selfishness (which is born
of pride just as my love is born of charity) is the
bearer of every evil.

This evil they do by means of other people. For love
of me and love of others are inseparable. And those

76

who have not loved me have cut themselves off as well from any love of their neighbors. This is why I said -- and I explained it to you -- that every good and every evil is done by means of your neighbors.

How many charges I could bring against humankind! For they have received nothing but good from me, and they repay me with every sort of hateful evil. But I have told you that my wrath would be softened by the tears of my servants, and I say it again: You, my servants, come into my presence laden with your prayers, your eager longing, your sorrow over their offense against me as well as their own damnation, and so you will soften my divinely just wrath.

Know that no one can escape my hands, for I am who I am, whereas you have no being at all of yourselves. What being you have is my doing; I am the Creator of everything that has any share in being. But sin is not of my making, for sin is nonbeing. Sin is unworthy of any love, then, because it has no part in me. Therefore, my creatures offend me when they love sin, which they should not love, and hate me, to whom they owe love because I am supremely good and gave them being with such burning love. But they cannot escape me: Either I will have them in justice because of their sin, or I will have them in mercy.

Open the eye of your understanding, then, and look at my hand, and you will see that what I have told you is true.

So in obedience to the most high Father, she raised her eyes, and she saw within his closed fist the entire world. And God said:

My daughter, see now and know that no one can be taken away from me. Everyone is here as I said, either in justice or in mercy. They are mine; I created them, and I love them ineffably. And so, in spite of their wickedness, I will be merciful to them because of my servants, and I will grant what you have asked of me with such love and sorrow.

The fire within that soul blazed higher and she was beside herself as if drunk, at once gloriously happy and grief-stricken. She was happy in her union with God, wholly submerged in his mercy and savoring his vast goodness; but to see such goodness offended brought her grief. She knew, though, that God had shown her his creatures' sinfulness to rouse her to intensify her concern and longing. And so she offered thanks to the divine majesty.

As she felt her emotions so renewed in the eternal Godhead, the force of her spirit made her body break into a sweat. (For her union with God was more intimate than was the union between her soul and her body.) The holy fire of love grew so fierce within her that its heat made her sweat water, but it was not enough. She longed to see her body sweat blood, so she said to herself:

Alas, my soul! You have frittered your whole life away, and for this have all these great and small evils come upon the world and holy Church! So I want you to heal them now with a sweat of blood.

Indeed, this soul remembered well what Truth had taught her: that she should always know herself and God's goodness at work in her, and that the medicine by which he willed to heal the whole world and to soothe his wrath and divine justice was humble, constant, holy prayer. So, spurred on by holy desire, she roused herself even more to open the eye of her understanding. She gazed into divine charity and there she saw and tasted how bound we are to love and seek the glory and praise of God's name through the salvation of souls. She saw that God's servants are called to this--and in particular eternal Truth had called and chosen her spiritual father, whom she brought before the divine goodness, asking God to light within him a lamp of grace by which he might in truth pursue this Truth.

Then, in answer to her third petition, which came from her hunger for her father's good, God said:

Daughter, this is what I want: that he seek to please me, Truth, by his deep hunger and concern for the salvation of souls. But neither he nor anyone else can achieve this without accepting whatever sufferings I grant.

As much as you long to see me honored in holy Church, just so much must you conceive the love it takes to suffer willingly and with true patience. By this will I know that he and you and my other servants are seeking my honor in truth.   Then will he be my very dear son, and he will rest, along with the others, on the breast of my only-begotten Son. And I will make of my Son a bridge by which you can all reach your goal and there receive the fruit of all the labors you have borne for my love. So carry on courageously!

I told you that I have made a bridge of the Word, my only-begotten Son, and such is the truth. I want you to realize, my children, that by Adam's sinful disobedience the road was so broken up that no one could reach everlasting life. Since they had no share in the good for which I had created them, they did not give me the return of glory they owed me, and so my truth was not fulfilled. What is this truth? That I had created them in my image and likeness so that they might have eternal life, sharing in my being and enjoying my supreme eternal tenderness and goodness. But because of their sin they never reached this goal and never fulfilled my truth, for sin closed heaven and the door of my mercy.

This sin sprouted thorns and troublesome vexations. My creatures found rebellion within themselves, for as soon as they rebelled against me, they became rebels against themselves. Their innocence lost, the flesh rebelled against the spirit and they became filthy beasts. All created things rebelled against them, whereas they would have been submissive if all had been kept as I had established it in the beginning. But they stepped outside my obedience and so deserved eternal death in both soul and body.

With sin there came at once the flood of a stormy river that beat against them constantly with its waves, bringing weariness and troubles from themselves as well as from the devil and the world.   You were all drowning, because not one of you, for all your righteousness, could reach eternal life.

But I wanted to undo these great troubles of yours. So I gave you a bridge, my Son, so that you could cross over the river, the stormy sea of this darksome life, without being drowned.

See how indebted to me my creatures are! And how foolish to choose to drown rather than accept the remedy I have given!

Open your mind's eye and you will see the blinded and the foolish, the imperfect, and the perfect ones who follow me in truth. Then weep for the damnation of the foolish and be glad for the perfection of my beloved children. Again, you will see the way of those who choose light and the way of those who choose darkness.

But first I want you to look at the bridge of my only-begotten Son, and notice its greatness. Look! It stretches from heaven to earth, joining the earth of your humanity with the greatness of the Godhead. This is what I mean when I say it stretches from heaven to earth--through my union with humanity.

This was necessary if I wanted to remake the road that had been broken up, so that you might pass over the bitterness of the world and reach life. From earth alone I could not have made it great enough to cross the river and bring you to eternal life. The earth of human nature by itself, as I have told you, was incapable of atoning for sin and draining off the pus from Adam's sin, for that stinking pus had infected the whole human race. Your nature had to be joined with the height of mine, the eternal Godhead, before it could make atonement for all of humanity. The human nature could endure the suffering, and the divine nature, joined with that humanity, would accept my Son's sacrifice on your behalf to release you from death and give you life.

So the height stooped to the earth of your humanity, bridging the chasm between us and rebuilding the road. And why should he have made of himself a roadway? So that you might in truth come to the same joy as the angels. But my Son's having made of himself a bridge for you could not bring you to life unless you make your way along that bridge.

You must all keep to this bridge, seeking the glory
and praise of my name through the salvation of souls,
bearing up under pain and weariness, following in the
footsteps of this gentle loving Word. There is no
other way you can come to me.

You are the workers I have hired for the vineyard of
holy Church. When I gave you the light of holy baptism
I sent you by my grace to work in the universal body of
Christianity. You received your baptism within the
mystic body of holy Church by the hands of my
ministers, and these ministers I have sent to work with
you. You are to work in the universal body. They,
however, have been placed within the mystic body to
shepherd your souls by administering the blood to you
through the sacraments you receive from them, and by
rooting out from you the thorns of deadly sin and
planting grace within you. They are my workers in the
vineyard of your souls, ambassadors for the vineyard of
holy Church.

Each of you has your own vineyard, your soul, in
which your free will is the appointed worker during
this life. Once the time of your life has passed, your
will can work neither for good nor for evil; but while
you live it can till the vineyard of your soul where I
have placed it. This tiller of your soul has been
given such power that neither the devil nor any other
creature can steal it without the will's consent, for
in holy baptism the will was armed with a knife that is
love of virtue and hatred of sin. This love and hatred
are to be found in the blood. For my only-begotten Son
gave his blood for you in death out of love for you and
hatred for sin, and through that blood you receive life
in holy baptism.

So you have this knife for your free will to use,
while you have time, to uproot the thorns of deadly sin
and to plant the virtues. This is the only way you can
receive the fruit of the blood from these workers I

have placed in holy Church.   For they are there, as I
have told you, to uproot deadly sin from the vineyard
of your soul and to give you grace by administering the
blood to you through the sacraments established in holy
Church.

So if you would receive the fruit of this blood, you
must first rouse yourself to heartfelt contrition,
contempt for sin, and love for virtue. Otherwise you
will not have done your part to be fit to be joined as
branches to the vine that is my only-begotten Son, who
said, "I am the true vine and you are the branches.
And my Father is the gardener."

Indeed I am the gardener, for all that exists comes
from me. With power and strength beyond imagining I
govern the whole world: Not a thing is made or kept in
order without me. I am the gardener, then, who planted
the vine of my only-begotten Son in the earth of your
humanity so that you, the branches, could be joined to
the vine and bear fruit.

Therefore, if you do not produce the fruit of good
and holy deeds you will be cut off from this vine and
you will dry up. For those who are cut off from this
vine lose the life of grace and are thrown into the
eternal fire, just as a branch that fails to bear fruit
is cut off the vine and thrown into the fire, since it
is good for nothing else.   So those who are cut off
because of their offenses, if they die still guilty of
deadly sin, will be thrown into the fire that lasts
forever, for they are good for nothing else.

Such people have not tilled their vineyards. They
have, in fact, destroyed them --yes, and other people's
as well. Not only did they fail to set out any good
plants of virtue, but they even dug out the seed of
grace that they had received with the light of holy
baptism, when they had drunk of the blood of my Son
--that wine poured out for you by this true vine. They
dug out this seed and fed it to beasts, that is, to
their countless sins.   And they trampled it underfoot
with their disordered will, and so offended me and
brought harm to their neighbors as well as to
themselves.

But that is not how my servants act, and you should
be like them, joined and engrafted to this vine. Then
you will produce much fruit, because you will share the
vital sap of the vine. And being in the Word, my Son,
you will be in me, for I am one with him and he with
me. If you are in him you will follow his teaching,
and if you follow his teaching you will share in the
very being of this Word --that is, you will share in
the eternal Godhead made one with humanity, whence you
will draw that divine love which inebriates the soul.
All this I mean when I say that you will share in the
very substance of the vine.

The Bridge

<u>Then God eternal, to stir up even more that soul's
love for the salvation of souls, responded to her</u>:

Before I show you what I want to show you, and what
you asked to see, I want to describe the bridge for
you. I have told you that it stretches from heaven to
earth by reason of my having joined myself with your
humanity, which I formed from the earth's clay.

This bridge, my only-begotten Son, has three stairs.
Two of them he built on the wood of the most holy
cross, and the third even as he tasted the great
bitterness of the gall and vinegar they gave him to
drink. You will recognize in these three stairs three
spiritual stages.

The first stair is the feet, which symbolize the
affections. For just as the feet carry the body, the
affections carry the soul. My Son's nailed feet are a
stair by which you can climb to his side, where you
will see revealed his inmost heart. For when the soul
has climbed up on the feet of affection and looked with
her mind's eye into my Son's opened heart, she begins
to feel the love of her own heart in his consummate and
unspeakable love. (I say consummate because it is not
for his own good that he loves you; you cannot do him
any good, since he is one with me.) Then the soul,
seeing how tremendously she is loved, is herself filled
to overflowing with love. So, having climbed the
second stair, she reaches the third. This is his

83

mouth, where she finds peace from the terrible war she
has had to wage because of her sins.

   At the first stair,   lifting   the feet of her
affections from the earth, she stripped herself of sin.
At the second she dressed herself in love for virtue.
And at the third she tasted peace.

   So the bridge has three stairs, and you can reach the
last by climbing the first two.   The last stair is so
high that the flooding waters cannot strike it--for the
venom of sin never touched my Son.

   But though this bridge has been raised so high, it
still is joined to the earth.   Do you know when it was
raised up? When my Son was lifted up on the wood of
the most holy cross he did not cut off his divinity
from the lowly earth of your humanity. So though he
was raised so high he was not raised off the earth. In
fact, his divinity is kneaded into the clay of your
humanity like one bread. Nor could anyone walk on that
bridge until my Son was raised up.   This is why he
said, "If I am lifted up high I will draw everything to
myself."

   When my goodness saw that you could be drawn in no
other way, I sent him to be lifted onto the wood of the
cross. I made of that cross an anvil where this child
of humankind could be hammered into an instrument to
release humankind from death and restore it to the life
of grace. In this way he drew everything to himself:
for he proved his unspeakable love, and the human heart
is always drawn by love.   You can hardly resist being
drawn by love, then, unless you foolishly refuse to be
drawn.

   I said that, having been raised up, he would draw
everything to himself.   This is true in two ways:
First, the human heart is drawn by love, as I said, and
with all its powers: memory, understanding, and will.
If these three powers are harmoniously united in my
name, everything else you do, in fact or in intention,
will be drawn to union with me in peace through the
movement of love, because all will be lifted up in the
pursuit of crucified love.   So my Truth indeed spoke

truly when he said, "If I am lifted up high, I will draw everything to myself." For everything you do will be drawn to him when he draws your heart and its powers.

What he said is true also in the sense that everything was created for your use, to serve your needs. But you who have the gift of reason were made not for yourselves but for me, to serve me with all your heart and all your love. So when you are drawn to me, everything is drawn with you, because everything was made for you.

It was necessary, then, that this bridge be raised high. And it had to have stairs so that you would be able to mount it more easily.

This bridge has walls of stone so that travelers will not be hindered when it rains. Do you know what stones these are? They are the stones of true solid virtue. These stones were not, however, built into walls before my Son's passion. So no one could get to the final destination, even though they walked along the pathway of virtue. For heaven had not yet been unlocked with the key of my Son's blood, and the rain of justice kept anyone from crossing over.

But after these stones were hewn on the body of the Word, my gentle Son (I have told you that he is the bridge), he built them into walls, tempering the mortar with his own blood. That is, his blood was mixed into the mortar of his divinity with the strong heat of burning love.

By my power the stones of virtue were built into walls on no less a foundation than himself, for all virtue draws life from him, nor is there any virtue that has not been tested in him. So no one can have any life-giving virtue but for him, that is, by following his example and his teaching. He perfected the virtues and planted them as living stones built into walls with his blood. So now all the faithful can walk without hindrance and with no cringing fear of the rain of divine justice, because they are sheltered by the mercy that came down from heaven through the incarnation of this Son of mine.

And how was heaven opened?   With the key of his
blood. So, you see, the bridge has walls and a roof of
mercy. And the hostelry of holy Church is there to
serve the bread of life and the blood, lest the
journeying pilgrims, my creatures, grow weary and faint
on the way. So has my love ordained that the blood and
body of my only-begotten Son, wholly God and wholly
human, be administered.

At the end of the bridge is the gate (which is, in
fact, one with the bridge), which is the only way you
can enter. This is why he said, "I am the Way and
Truth and Life; whoever walks with me walks not in
darkness but in light." And in another place my Truth
said that no one could come to me except through him,
and such is the truth.

I explained all this to you, you will recall, because
I wanted to let you see the way. So when he says that
he is the Way he is speaking the truth. And I have
already shown you that he is the Way, in the image of a
bridge. He says he is Truth, and so he is, and whoever
follows him goes the way of truth. And he is Life. If
you follow this truth you will have the life of grace
and never die of hunger, for the Word has himself
become your food. Nor will you ever fall into
darkness, for he is the light undimmed by any
falsehood. Indeed, with his truth he confounds and
destroys the lie with which the devil deceived Eve.
That lie broke up the road to heaven, but Truth
repaired it and walled it up with his blood.

Those who follow this way are children of the truth
because they follow the truth. They pass through the
gate of truth and find themselves in me. And I am one
with the gate and the way that is my Son, eternal
Truth, a sea of peace.

But those who do not keep to this way travel below
through the river --a way not of stones but of water.
And since there is no restraining the water, no one can
cross through it without drowning.

Such are the pleasures and conditions of the world.
Those whose love and desire are not grounded on the

rock but are set without order on created persons and things apart from me (and these, like water, are continually running on) run on just as they do. Though it seems to them that it is the created things they love that are running on by while they themselves remain firm, they are in fact continually running on to their end in death. They would like to preserve themselves (that is, their lives and the things they love) and not run away to nothingness. But they cannot. Either death makes them leave all behind, or by my decree these created things are taken away from them.

Such as these are following a lie by going the way of falsehood. They are children of the devil, who is the father of lies. And because they pass through the gate of falsehood they are eternally damned....

Then was that soul's longing stirred up. She considered her own and others' imperfection. She grieved to hear and see such blindness on the part of creatures, for she had seen how great was God's goodness. He had never ordained that anything in this life should be an obstacle to peoples' salvation, no matter what their situation, but that everything should serve the exercise and proving of virtue. But in spite of all this, because of their selfishness and disordered love, people still went the way of the river below, and if they did not reform, they would certainly end in eternal damnation. And many of those who began to reform turned back. She had learned the reason for this when he in his tender goodness had stooped to show himself to her. This made her bitterly sad, and, fixing her mind's eye on the eternal Father, she said:

O immeasurable love! How greatly are your creatures deluded! I wish you would explain to me more clearly --when it pleases your goodness --the three stairs imaged in the body of your only-begotten Son. Show me what people must do to escape completely from the flood and keep to the way of your Truth, and who are those who climb these stairs.

Then divine Goodness looked with the eye of his mercy upon that soul's hungry longing and said:

My dearest daughter, I am not scornful of desire.
No, I am the one who answers holy longings. Therefore
I want to explain to you what you ask.

You ask me to explain to you the image of the three
stairs, and to tell you how people must act to be able
to escape from the river and mount the bridge. I did
describe for you earlier people's delusion and
blindness, and how they taste even in this life the
pledge of hell and, like martyrs of the devil, reap
eternal damnation. I told you what fruit they harvest
from their evil actions. And when I told you these
things, I showed you how they ought to behave. Still,
to satisfy your longing, I will now explain it to you
more fully.

You know that every evil is grounded in selfish love
of oneself. This love is a cloud that blots out the
light of reason. It is in reason that the light of
faith is held, and one cannot lose the one without
losing the other.

I made the soul after my own image and likeness,
giving her memory, understanding, and will. The
understanding is the most noble aspect of the soul. It
is moved by affection, and it in turn nourishes
affection. Affection is love's hand, and this hand
fills the memory with thoughts of me and of the
blessings I have given. Such remembrance makes the
soul caring instead of indifferent, grateful instead of
thankless. So each power lends a hand to the other,
thus nourishing the soul in the life of grace.

The soul cannot live without love. She always wants
to love something because love is the stuff she is made
of, and through love I created her. This is why I said
that it is affection that moves the understanding,
saying, as it were, "I want to love, because the food I
feed on is love." And the understanding, feeling
itself awakened by affection, gets up, as it were, and
says, "If you want to love, I will give you something
good that you can love."...

Let me return now to the three stairs by which you
must go if you would escape from the river and not

drown, but reach the living water to which you are invited. By these stairs you must go if you would have me with you, for then I will dwell in your souls by grace and be with you on your journey.

If you would make progress, then, you must be thirsty, because only those who are thirsty are called: "Let anyone who is thirsty come to me and drink." Those who are not thirsty will never persevere in their journey. Either weariness or pleasure will make them stop. They cannot be bothered with carrying the vessel that would make it possible for them to draw the water. And though they cannot travel alone, they do not care for the company. So at the first sight of any prick of persecution (which they consider their enemy) they turn back. They are afraid because they are alone. If they were with the company they would not be afraid. And if they had climbed the three stairs they would be secure, because they would not be alone.

You must be thirsty, then, and you must gather together, as he said, either two or three or more. Why did he say "two or three"? Because there are not two without three nor three without two. One alone is excluded from my companionship, since I cannot be "in the midst" of someone who has no companion. Those who are wrapped up in selfish love of themselves are alone, mere nothings, because they are cut off from my grace and from charity for their neighbors. And once deprived of me through their own fault, they turn to nothingness--for I alone am who I am. So those who are alone, those who are wrapped up in selfish love of themselves, are neither taken account of by my Truth nor acceptable to me.

He says, then, "If two or three or more are gathered in my name, I shall be in their midst." I told you that two are not without three, nor three without two, and so it is. You know that all the commandments of the Law are comprised in two--to love me above all things and to love your neighbor as your very self--and without these two none of the commandments can be kept. This is the beginning, the middle, and the end of the commandments of the Law.

These two cannot be gathered together in my name
without three--that is, without the gathering of the
three powers of the soul: memory, understanding, and
will. The memory holds on to my blessings and my
goodness to the soul. Understanding contemplates the
unspeakable love I have shown you through the mediation
of my only-begotten Son, whom I have set before your
mind's eye for you to contemplate in him the fire of my
charity. The will, finally, is joined with them to
know and desire me, your final goal.

When these three powers of the soul are gathered
together, I am in their midst by grace. And as soon as
you are filled with my love and love of your neighbor,
you will fird yourself in the company of the multitude
of solid virtues. Then the soul's appetite is ready to
be thirsty--thirsty for virtue and my honor and the
salvation of souls. Every other thirst is now
exhausted and dead, and you travel securely, without
any slavish fear. You have climbed the first step,
that of desire. Once desire is stripped of selfish
love, you rise above yourself and above passing things.
What you decide to keep, you love and hold not apart
from me but with me, that is, with true holy fear and
love of virtue.

Then you find that you have climbed the second stair.
This is the enlightenment of the mind, which sees
itself reflected in the warmhearted love I have shown
you in Christ crucified, as in a mirror. Then you find
peace and quiet, for memory is filled with my love and
no longer empty. You know that when something is empty
it resounds if you strike it, but not so when it is
full. So when the memory is filled with light from
understanding and the overflowing love of the will,
even though troubles and the pleasures of the world
strike it, it will not resound with inordinate gladness
or impatience. For it is filled with me, and I am all
good.

After you have climbed you find that you are gathered
together. For once reason has taken possession of the
three stairs, which are the three powers of the soul,
they are gathered together in my name. When the
two--that is, love for me and love for your
neighbor--are gathered together, and the memory for
holding and understanding for seeing and the will for

loving are gathered together, you find that I am your companion, and I am your strength and your security. You discover the company of the virtues, and because I am in their midst you walk securely and are secure.

Then you are roused with eager longing, thirsty to follow the way of Truth that leads to the fountain of living water. Your thirst for my honor and for your own and your neighbors' salvation makes you long for the way, for without the way you could never reach what you thirst for. So walk on, carrying your heart like a vessel emptied of every desire and every disordered earthly love. But no sooner is your vessel emptied than it is filled. For nothing can remain empty. If it is not full of something material, it will fill up with air. Just so, the heart is a vessel that cannot remain empty. As soon as you have emptied it of all those transitory things you loved inordinately, it is filled with air--that is, with gentle heavenly divine love that brings you to the water of grace. And once you have arrived there you pass through the gate, Christ crucified, to enjoy that living water--for now you find yourself in me, the sea of peace....

PART II.

MAN IN A NATURE-CENTERED WORLD

10

FRANCESCO PETRARCH

Francesco Petrarch (1304-1374), born in Arezzo into an exiled Florentine family, lived most of his life at Avignon, seat of the Papacy during the greater part of his life. He returned to Italy in 1353, living in Milan, Venice, and Padua. where he died in 1374. His fame rests on his literary and scholarly works written both in Italian and Latin. He authored poems, orations, invectives. historical works, letters, as well as a few moral treatises. The most famous of his moral treatises is <u>On the Secret Conflict of My Worries,</u> which is more commonly referred to as <u>My Secret Book</u>.

Petrarch is generally regarded as the founder of Renaissance humanism, that is to say, the initiator of that intellectual attitude which stresses man's worth and dignity by emphasizing the purely secular value of man's achievements in this world. His writings exhibit the conflict between a world ruled in accordance with God's will and one governed by man's own search for personal glory and self-love. It is this conflict that is the theme of the ensuing selection taken from <u>My Secret Book</u>. The book, written in a dialogue form, reveals the struggle that Petrarch himself experienced as he sought to reconcile the dominant values of a theocentric world with those values emerging with the rebirth of interest in the human achievements of classical antiquity. Petrarch, who is represented by Franciscus in the dialogue, stresses those secular values that will eventually become realized in the writings of La Mettrie and Rousseau. By the eighteenth century, man will no longer live in a God-centered world but rather in a nature-centered world. God will still be judged as supreme artificer of nature, but God will stand outside the machine. Where Petrarch merely "defers" eternal concerns, the philosophers of the eighteenth century will no longer be concerned with man as one having a supernatural destiny.

MY SECRET BOOK:

Eternal concerns vs. earthly glory.

PROEM

Bemused, as is my frequent case, in reflections on
how I had come into this life and how I should leave
it, I was suddenly aware of a woman clothed in light
and beauty. She said to me: "Fear not. In pity for
your errors, I have descended from afar to bring you
timely aid. Enough, and more than enough, have you
gazed with clouded eyes at the ground. If hitherto
they have found pleasure in mortal things, what may you
not hope if you raise them to look at eternal matters?"
"Who are you?" I asked, trembling. "I am Truth."
Looking at her glorious face, I knew she could be none
other.

As I was gazing on her with ineffable delight I
perceived a venerable, majestic person by her side. I
did not need to ask his name; his religious aspect, his
modest air, his grave eyes, his sober bearing, his
African dress, his Roman style, identified that most
glorious Father, Augustine. His loving regard,
sweeter than that of any human, removed all doubt.
Truth turned to him and interrupted his profound
meditation with the words: "O Augustine, dearest to me
of all men, you know this man to be your devotee, and
you know how he has suffered, all unaware, a long,
dangerous illness. You must look to the life of this
wasting man. None better than you could do this work
of pity, since he has always worshiped your name, and
since his miseries are similar to those you suffered
when you were locked in the prison of the flesh." Said
he: "I shall obey you, who have ever been my guide."
And she: "I shall remain by your side during your
colloquy."

Then we sat down, all three. And with Truth sitting
in silent judgment by our side, the Saint and I engaged
in a conversation that lasted three days. That our
familiar talk might not be lost I have written it down
in the measure of a little book, not that I wish to
number it among my published works and attain glory

thereby, but that I may read it over whenever I wish
and taste again the sweetness of my experience. So, my
little book, you will flee all the concourse of men and
you will be happy to remain alone with me, and you will
never belie your name. For you are my _Secret Book_, and
that will be your name. And when I am busy with more
serious matters you will recall to me in secret what
you have recorded in secret.

To avoid the repetitions of "said he" and "said I" I
shall represent our words in the form of a dialogue. I
learned this style from my Cicero, and he in his turn
had learned it from Plato. But let us not digress.
Augustine then addressed me as follows....

BOOK III

AUG.: I haven't yet touched your deepest and most
persistent troubles. You are fastened by two mighty
chains. You are like a miser in prison shackled by
golden fetters; you would like to get free, but you
don't want to lose them. But there's a law in this
prison: if you don't throw off the chains you can't go
free. And you love them; you even boast of them.

FR.: What are these chains you're talking about?

AUG.: Love and glory.

FR.: Gods above, what's this I hear? So you call
love and glory chains, and if I permit it you'll take
them from me? You want to rob me of the loveliest
things in life, and condemn to darkness the fairest
part of my being?

AUG.: I'm going to try to, though I doubt if I
succeed. Tell me, don't you think love is the utmost
madness?

FR.: The fact is, love depends on its object. It
can be called either the ugliest passion of the spirit
or its noblest activity. If I adore a wicked,

contemptible woman, that is madness; but if a rare exemplar of virtue attracts me and I devote myself to loving and venerating her, what of that?

AUG.: There's no difference. In both cases you bid farewell to reason and to awareness of truth.

FR.: You're wasting your time. I've never loved anything foul, anything that was not very beautiful.

AUG.: Even beautiful things can be loved foully.

FR.: Do you know who it is you're talking about?

AUG.: I have thoroughly considered my subject. We are going to talk about a mortal woman, whom you have been admiring and celebrating during a large part of your life. I am amazed at your long insanity.

FR.: Don't be offensive. Do you realize that you are referring to a woman whose mind, ignoring earthly cares, burns with celestial desires? In whose aspect, as truth is truth, shines heavenly beauty? Whose behavior is an example of perfect virtue? Whose voice, whose eyes, are more than mortal, whose very walk seems no human action? Think of that, please, and you will realize what sort of language you must use.

AUG.: Poor fool! So for sixteen years you have fed your flame with false cajolements! How you have suffered! But in the end, when those eyes close in death, you will be ashamed that you tied your immortal soul to a mortal body and you will blush to recall what you have so exalted.

FR.: God forbid! I shall not live to see her death.

AUG.: How do you know? She is getting older; that splendid body, worn out with illness and with frequent childbirths, has already lost much of its old vigor. It is folly to submit your soul to any such mortal thing.

98

FR.: I have not done so.   I have never loved her
body so much as her soul.   My delight was in her
character, transcending mortality, resembling that of
the angels.   So if--the mere utterance makes me
shudder--if she should die first, I would appease my
grief by saying with Laelius, wisest of the Romans: "I
loved her virtue, which has not been spent."

AUG.: Well, pour all the praise you like on your
little woman. I won't contradict you. She's a queen,
a saint, if you like, or as Virgil said, a goddess, a
sister of Phoebus, a nymph. But her great virtue won't
help to excuse your errors.

FR.: I call Truth here by our side to witness that
in my love there has never been anything base, lewd, or
in any way culpable, except perhaps in its excess.
Nothing more wholly beautiful than my love can be
conceived.

AUG.: I'm sorry to hear such nonsense from one who
ought to think more clearly.

FR.: Whatever I am is due to her. I should never
have gained my present reputation, however one may
judge it, if she hadn't tended with her noble sympathy
that tiny little seed of virtue that nature sowed in my
breast. She recalled my youthful spirit from all
turpitude, pulled me back, as they say, with a hook,
and forced me to look upward.   How could I fail to be
transformed by her character? Never has any slanderer,
however scurrilous, attacked her good name or dared to
find anything reprehensible in her actions, words, or
even gestures. Even those who leave nothing unsoiled
spared her, in admiration and reverence.   It is not
strange that her good fame inspired in me the desire
for fame, and eased my labors to that end. From my
young manhood I longed for nothing else than to please
her, who alone had pleased me.   You know how, to gain
that end, I spurned the temptations of a myriad
pleasures and subjected myself prematurely to laborious
cares. And you order me to forget her or to love her
more temperately!

AUG.: You make me sick at my stomach.

FR.: Why, pray?

   AUG.:   Because to think falsely is a sign of
ignorance; but to proclaim the false impudently is a
sign both of ignorance and of vain glory.

   FR.: How can you prove that I have either thought or
said anything false?
.paragraph 5
AUG.: By everything you have said! First of all when
you say that she has made you what you are. The fact
is that she has prevented you from developing. What a
man you might have been, if she hadn't captured you
with her beauty!
It is kind nature that made you what you were; she
prevented you from becoming what you might have been,
or rather you threw it away for her, for she is
innocent.   Her beauty seemed to you so sweet and
attractive that you destroyed your native possibilities
in your longings and wailings.   And you boast that she
preserved you from all turpitudes!   Perhaps she did
save you from many, but she forced you into greater
calamities. For one who drives us to our downfall
while keeping us out of various filthy courses, or who
inflicts a mortal wound while healing some minor
scratches, can hardly be called our liberator, but
rather our murderer. So she whom you call your guide
has saved you from foul actions only to lay you out on
a splendid bier. And as for her teaching you to look
upward, to disdain the mass of men, what else is that
than making you slave to her alone, forgetful and
scornful of all else on earth? There is nothing worse
for a man among men. When you recall that she involved
you in innumerable labors you are certainly telling the
truth. But you got a good deal out of them! And as
for your boast that she made you seek for fame, well,
that is the worst burden on your soul. In short, this
woman you exalt so highly is ruining you.

   FR.: What do you mean?

   AUG.: She has distracted your mind from the love of
the Creator and has turned it to the love of the

creature. You have loved the Creator only as the
artificer who made that beautiful body.

   FR.: I protest to Truth here present and to my
conscience that I never loved her body more than her
soul! As she has grown older and her bodily beauty has
dwindled I have been the more constant. Although the
flower of youth visibly fades with the passage of time,
the beauty of her spirit kept increasing, and this has
kept me faithful.

   AUG.: Are you trying to fool me? If that spirit had
inhabited a squalid body, would you have loved it as
much?

   FR.: I don't dare to assert that, for the spirit is
invisible.   But if the spirit should make itself
manifest, no doubt I would love a beautiful spirit even
in an ugly habitation.

   AUG.: You are playing on words. For if you can love
only what is evident to the eyes, you love the body.
However, I won't deny that her spirit and her character
have added fuel to your flames, just as her very name
greatly increased your passion.   You loved body and
soul together, and both of them immoderately. And you
have fallen into great disasters because of this love.

   FR.: That I will never admit, even if you put me to
torture.

   AUG.: Do you remember your boyhood, your love of
God, your meditations on death, your religious feeling,
your love of virtue?

   FR.: I remember very well, and I grieve that as I
have grown older my merits have decreased.

   AUG.: When did you lose these good habits?

FR.: I came to a parting of the ways, and I took the downward path. And I have never been able to find the right way again.

AUG.: How old were you when this happened?

FR.: It was in the midst of youth's fevers. If you wait a moment, I can recollect the exact year.

AUG.: And when did this woman's beauty first appear to you?

FR.: Oh, that I'll never forget!

AUG.: How do those two times match?

FR.: Well, in fact her appearance in my life and my steps astray happened at about the same time.

AUG.: That's what I was after. And this glorious woman, this guide to heaven, why didn't she hold you by the hand and show you the right road?

FR.: She did all she could. Unmoved by my prayers and blandishments, in spite of her youth and mine and in spite of certain circumstances that might have moved a heart of stone, she kept her feminine purity and remained firm, impregnable. Isn't that something? She showed me my duty; and when I went my headstrong way she preferred to abandon me rather than to follow me.

AUG.: Ah, then you did sometimes have base desires! You denied that before.   Well, that's the familiar madness of lovers, always saying: "Will I, nill I, nill I, will I." You don't know what you want or what you don't want.

FR.: You've tricked me.   If perhaps I had such desires at the time, youthful ardor caused them. Now I know better.   But she never wavered in her womanly

virtue. If at the time I protested against it. now I
am glad of it, and I thank her.

   AUG.: It's hard to trust someone who has fallen
once. That flame of yours may be less intense, it
hasn't been extinguished.   And in ascribing so much
merit to your beloved, in absolving her, you are
condemning yourself.   Love has made you wretched;
that's what I began by saying.   Earthly love leads to
the forgetfulness of God; it has brought you to the
miserable state you have described. In your folly, you
were not even content with gazing on her living face,
the source of your woes, and you obtained from an
illustrious artist a painted image and carried it
around with you, to have something to cry over forever.
You sought out everything that would provoke and
irritate your emotion.   And--the final proof of an
unhinged mind--you were as much allured by her
beautiful name as by her body, and with incredible
folly you cultivated every punning significance of it!
You loved the laurel, whether of emperors or poets,
because it chimed with her name.   You could hardly
write a poem without dragging in the laurel. And since
you couldn't hope for the imperial wreath, you longed
for the laurel crown of poetry as immoderately as you
had loved the lady. You will be shocked some day when
you reflect how much effort you spent in obtaining it,
though I grant that you were often borne on the wings
of inspiration. Don't speak; I know what is in your
mind. I know that you were a poet before you fell in
love. But the difficulties and dangers in the way of
success would have delayed your effort, if the memory
of that sweetest of names hadn't spurned you on over
land and sea to Rome and Naples, where finally you
gained what you had lusted for so ardently. Anyone who
doesn't take this as an indication of notable madness
must be mad himself.

   FR.: What do you want me to do? Despair?

   AUG.: First we'll look for remedies. Cicero says
that many think of driving out an old love with a new
one, as a nail drives out a nail. That's good advice.
A mind dispersed on many objects has the more
difficulty in concentrating on one.   But the danger is
that if you cast off this passion, which I admit is one
of the nobler sort, you may get entangled in many, and

become, instead of a lover, a libertine. I won't
disapprove of your passing from one subjection to
another, for perhaps in such excursions you may find
your liberty, or a lighter servitude; but I would much
reprobate your bowing your neck to a series of sordid
involvements.

   FR.: May the patient interrupt the doctor for a
moment? Let me tell you this--I can never love anyone
else. My eyes are so used to gazing upon her, my mind
is so used to admiring her, that all that is not she
seems dark and ugly. So if you command me to love
another in order to free myself from love, you are
asking the impossible. It's all over; I am done for.

   AUG.: Then you must find some external remedy. Can
you persuade yourself to run away?

   FR.: Painful though it would be, I could do so.

   AUG.: If you can, you're saved. How can you be
secure in this place, where remain so many vestiges of
your old wounds, where you are oppressed by the present
and the past?

   FR.: I have often attempted flight, in search of
freedom. To obtain it I have wandered far and wide,
east and north, even to the edge of Ocean. But
wherever I went I bore my hurt within me.

   AUG.: As Socrates said, you were always traveling
with yourself. You must lay down that old burden of
care, and prepare your heart; then at least you will be
really fleeing.

   FR.: I don't see how that will cure me.

   AUG.: I didn't speak of curing or of getting well; I
said: "Prepare your heart." You must teach your heart
to cast off its burdens; you must go away without hope
of return, without a backward glance. But you must
beware of a relapse, in revisiting familiar scenes.

You yourself have often thought you were cured, and you
would have been cured if you had remained away. But
walking the well-known streets, recalling old vanities
at the mere sight of certain spots, you were struck
dumb, you sighed, you stood stock-still and barely
refrained from tears. Wounded once more, you fled,
murmuring: "I feel that here are still hidden some
traps of the old enemy; here remain some relics of
death." Is a man ever cured? A look at a comely body
arouses lust; a glance from lovely eyes may awaken
sleeping love. You must not only quit this
pestilential city, you must flee with all diligence
whatever recalls your mind to its past occupations.

    FR.: I have already been meditating flight, but I am
uncertain where to go.

    AUG.: Many ways, many harbors are open to you. I
know that you love above all Italy and your sweet
native soil, and rightfully enough. I therefore advise
Italy, for the manners of its people, for its skies and
surrounding seas and shores and Apennine hills. Go
surely and quickly, and do not turn back. Forget the
past, look to what is to come. Too long have you been
an exile from your fatherland and from yourself. It is
now time to return, for "evening is falling and night
is friend of the despoiler." But avoid solitude, until
you feel that no after-affects of your illness remain.
When you said that your rustications were of no benefit
to you, you were stating the obvious. What remedies
could you expect to find in a remote, solitary country
place? I admit that when you fled there alone and kept
sighing and looking back at the city, I often laughed
at you from on high, and I said to myself: "Love has
surrounded that poor fellow with a Lethean cloud, and
to flee from his disease he is running toward death!"

    FR.: Ovid advised forlorn lovers to avoid solitude.
I have known that passage from boyhood.

    AUG.: What is the use of knowing so much, if you
couldn't make the application to your own necessities?
I have been the more surprised at your error in seeking
solitude, in that you knew the wise verses of the
ancients against it, and you have added a few yourself.
You have often complained that solitude has done you no
good.

FR.:   Have you any other remedies to suggest?

AUG.:   To set forth everything one knows is rather
to show off than to really help a friend. But Cicero
says that three things distract the mind from love:
satiety, shame, and reflection. Well, satiety in your
case is impossible. As for shame--tell me, and excuse
me, have you looked in your mirror lately?

FR.:   What do you mean?   Yes, I suppose so, as
usual.

AUG.:   Haven't you noticed that your face is
changing, day by day?

FR.:   Now that you mention it, yes. Men seem to get
old faster now than they used to.   Of course I have
been white-haired since my youth, like Domitian, Numa
Pompilius, and Virgil.

AUG.:   If you had been bald you would have dragged
in Julius Caesar.   At any rate, shame should banish
passion. You are too old to play the passionate lover.
Most men don't reach your present age. Renounce the
follies of youth; extinguish the ardors of adolescence.
Don't be forever thinking of what you have been; look
around you to realize what you are now.

FR.:   Do you know what brings me a little comfort?
She is getting old along with me.

AUG.:   Perhaps you think it's more decent for you to
love her when you're both old than to fall in love with
a girl? As a matter of fact love is all the uglier as
there is less basis for love. You should therefore be
ashamed that your mind never changes, while the body is
continually changing.   That is a subject for
reflection, which, as I said, is Cicero's third cure of
love. Meditate on your manhood, on the nobility of the
human spirit, on the fragility and filth of the body,
on the brevity of life, on the flight of time, on the
certainty of death.   Think how revolting it is to be
the world's laughingstock, how improper your behavior

is for your clerical profession. Recall all your sufferings for her sake, all your lamentations and tears. Think, at the same time, of her ungrateful and supercilious bearing, how, if she was occasionally kind, it was more briefly than the blowing of a summer breeze. Think how you have added to her fame, and how much she has subtracted from your own life, and how you have protected her own fair name, while she has always been perfectly unconcerned about your state. Think how she has distracted you from the love of God, how she has interfered with the completion of the works you have in hand. And finally think of what she actually is! Few consider with a realizing sense the filthiness of the feminine body. Repel every recollection of your past preoccupations and all thought of the past. And besiege heaven with your prayers; tire the ears of the heavenly king. Let no night or day pass without tears and supplications. But we've talked enough about this. Now I come to your final fault, which I must undertake to cure. You are unduly desirous of worldly glory and of immortality for your name.

FR.: I must confess it. I cannot restrain this appetite.

AUG.: But it is to be feared that the longing for vain immortality may block the road to true immortality. Worldly fame is nothing but the diffuse gabble of many tongues. It is a gust of air, the breath of many men. You despise the vulgar mob; but you delight in the silly little words of the very men whose actions you condemn. Worse, you find the summit of your felicity therein! What is the purpose of your perpetual labors, your night vigils, the fervency of your studies? You may answer: "To learn something useful for my life;" but you already know all that is needful for life and death. It would be better for you to apply what you know to your conduct. And I notice that you have tried in most of your works to tickle the public taste, to please the very people you particularly dislike, plucking posies, in your poems, histories, and speeches, to enrapture your hearers. And not content with their ephemeral applause, you have lusted for fame among posterity. Thus you started a big history of Romans, from Romulus to Titus; and without finishing that, you dispatched a poetic craft to Africa. And so, writing of others, you forget yourself. And death may strike you down before you finish either task.

FR.: I have been afraid of that.   I once fell
seriously ill, and I thought I was going to die. And
what tortured me most was the thought that I was
leaving my _Africa_ half-finished.   As I didn't want
anyone else to edit it, I had determined to burn it
with my own hands. That is a bitter memory.

AUG.: You confirm me in my judgment. But suppose
you had plenty of time, leisure, tranquillity, without
dull periods or physical weakness, that you were spared
all those interruptions that have interfered with your
writing, that every condition was favorable.   What
great thing do you think you would accomplish?

FR.: No doubt some brilliant, rare, excellent book.

AUG.: The more excellent it might be, the more it
would detract from the care of your soul. And how vain
and transitory is earthly fame!

FR.:   Oh, I know   all that old stuff of the
philosophers about the vanity of human wishes and so
forth. But I don't expect to become a god and embrace
eternity. Human fame is enough for me. That's what I
long for. Being mortal, I desire only mortal rewards.

AUG.: What a calamity, if you are telling the truth!
If you don't want immortal rewards, if you don't look
to eternity, you are condemned to earth. Your fate is
sealed; there is no hope for you.

FR.: All I meant was this: I treat mortal things as
mortal, and I don't affront the nature of things by
vast, unreasonable desires.   I don't abandon eternal
concerns; I just defer them.

AUG.: Take care!   Death may strike at any moment.
Time is short; it is dangerous to make any
postponement.

FR.: Still, there is some reason in my stand. That
glory which it is permissible to hope for must be

sought while we are here below. The greater glory will
be enjoyed in heaven by those who will be admitted
there; they won't even think of earthly glory. So this
is the order: the care for mortal things must come
first in mortal minds; eternal concerns will succeed in
their turn to the transitory.

AUG.: What a foolish little man you are! You think
that all the joys of earth and heaven will shower upon
you at your summons!   What is earth in comparison with
heaven? I hate to hear you sneer at the "old stuff" of
the philosophers.   Is the geometrical proof that our
earth is tiny, just a long island of land, old stuff?
Is it old stuff that of the world's five so-called
zones the middle one is uninhabitable by men because of
the sun's heat, the extreme one to north and south
burdened by intolerable cold and perpetual ice, so that
only the two temperate zones are habitable?   It is
doubtful whether the antipodes are inhabited; I don't
think so myself. That leaves only the north temperate
zone, which according to some. is divided into two
parts, one reserved for our uses, the other cut off by
the northern Ocean, which forbids our access to it.   In
this tiny world glory is of small account.

FR.: Do you then order me to give up my studies and
live ingloriously?

AUG.: I will never advise you to live without glory,
but I admonish you not to prefer the quest of glory to
that of virtue. I will lay down this rule: take no
heed for glory; the less you long for it the more of it
you will gain.   A man would be mad who would bustle
about under the midday sun to show others his shadow,
and no less mad is he who, in the ardors of life, tries
to promote his own fame.   Go to your goal, and your
shadow will follow you.   You wear yourself out writing
books; you're making a great mistake, for you forget
your own advantage in trying to bring advantage to
others, and thus in the vain hope of glory you waste
unwitting this brief span of life.

FR.: What shall I do then: Shall I leave my books
unfinished? Wouldn't it be more sensible to hurry them
to a conclusion, if God grants it, and then, being
freed of these tasks, to give myself wholly to higher

things? I can't calmly leave half done works that have
cost me so much.

   AUG.: I know where the shoe pinches. You would
rather abandon yourself than your little books. Lay
down the burden of your histories; the deeds of the
Romans have been sufficiently celebrated by themselves
and by others.   Abandon Africa and leave it to its
inhabitants. You won't increase either Scipio's glory
or your own. He can't be any further exalted; you are
just creeping along behind him. So surrender all these
works, and at last give yourself back to yourself!
And, to return to the point from which we started,
begin to think deeply about death, which little by
little and all unconscious you are approaching. You
are part of the great procession; exulting in the prime
of your life, you are treading on the heels of others;
but others are treading on yours.   Remember Cicero:
"All the life of a philosopher is meditation on death."
You can find the right path by listening to your own
spirit, which tells you: "This is the way home." I
pray God that he may accompany you and bring your
wandering steps to safety.

   FR.: Oh, may your prayer be granted, and by God's
favor may I come safe out of the maze, free of my own
self-deceptions and delusions!   And   may the storms of
my spirit subside, and the world be silent, and fortune
molest me no more!

11

PICO DELLA MIRANDOLA

Giovanni Pico della Mirandola (1463-1494) pursued his studies at various intellectual centers, chief among which were Bologna, Padua, Pavia, Paris, and Florence. He learned to read Greek, Hebrew and Arabic with a view towards reading and translating original manuscripts that were inaccessible to most of his contemporaries. Pico's heritage to Western traditional thought, however, like Petrarch's, cannot be understood without taking into account the dissolution of the medieval world on the one hand, and the emergence of a new order on the other hand. In both worlds, as well as in the culture of the East, Pico sought the truth about the universe and man. In fact, while in Florence in 1484-1485, the young count della Mirandola became interested in the Platonic theology of Marsilio Ficino and in the hermetic mysteries of the cabalistic tradition, convinced that the latter contained the key to ultimate reality. Thus, he attempted to reconcile the faiths of the West and the East into one truth. His enthusiasm led him in December 1486 to publish in Rome nine hundred theses, which represented his basic views on matters of philosophy and theology, and to invite learned men from all parts of Europe to a public disputation. However, Pope Innocent VIII, upon finding some of the theses heretical, called for Pico's arrest.

Oration on the Dignity of Man was written as an introduction to the public disputation which never took place. Pico insists that man's dignity consists in the fact that he can move as high as God or as low as the beast, according to his own free will. In short, man can choose whatever he wills.

ORATION ON THE DIGNITY OF MAN:

Man empowered to be brutish or divine.

I have read in the records of the Arabians, reverend Fathers, that Abdala the Saracen, when questioned as to what on this stage of the world, as it were, could be seen most worthy of wonder, replied: "There is nothing to be seen more wonderful than man." In agreement with this opinion is the saying of Hermes Trismegistus: "A great miracle, Asclepius, is man." But when I weighed the reason for these maxims, the many grounds for the excellence of human nature reported by many men failed to satisfy me--that man is the intermediary between creatures, the intimate of the gods, the king of the lower beings, by the acuteness of his senses, by the discernment of his reason, and by the light of his intelligence the interpreter of nature, the interval between fixed eternity and fleeting time, and (as the Persians say) the bond, nay, rather, the marriage song of the world, on David's testimony but little lower than the angels. Admittedly great though these reasons be, they are not the principal grounds, that is, those which may rightfully claim for themselves the privilege of the highest admiration.   For why should we not admire more the angels themselves and the blessed choirs of heaven? At last it seems to me I have come to understand why man is the most fortunate of creatures and consequently worthy of all admiration and what precisely is that rank which is his lot in the universal chain of Being--a rank to be envied not only by brutes but even by the stars and by minds beyond this world. It is a matter past faith and a wondrous one. Why should it not be?   For it is on this very account that man is rightly called and judged a great miracle and a wonderful creature indeed.

2. But hear, Fathers, exactly what this rank is and, as friendly auditors, conformably to your kindness, do me this favor. God the Father, the supreme Architect, had already built this cosmic home we behold, the most sacred temple of His godhead, by the laws of His mysterious wisdom. The region above the heavens He had adorned with Intelligences, the heavenly spheres He had quickened with eternal souls, and the excrementary and filthy parts of the lower world He had filled with a multitude of animals of every kind. But, when the work

112

was finished, the Craftsman kept wishing that there were someone to ponder the plan of so great a work, to love its beauty, and to wonder at its vastness. Therefore, when everything was done (as Moses and Timaeus bear witness), He finally took thought concerning the creation of man. But there was not among His archetypes that from which He could fashion a new offspring, nor was there in His treasurehouses anything which He might bestow on His new son as an inheritance. nor was there in the seats of all the world a place where the latter might sit to contemplate the universe. All was now complete; all things had been assigned to the highest, the middle, and the lowest orders. But in its final creation it was not the part of the Father's power to fail as though exhausted. It was not the part of His wisdom to waver in a needful matter through poverty of counsel. It was not the part of His kindly love that he who was to praise God's divine generosity in regard to others should be compelled to condemn it in regard to himself.

3. At last the best of artisans ordained that that creature to whom He had been able to give nothing proper to himself should have joint possession of whatever had been peculiar to each of the different kinds of being. He therefore took man as a creature of indeterminate nature and, assigning him a place in the middle of the world, addressed him thus: "Neither a fixed abode nor a form that is thine alone nor any function peculiar to thyself have we given thee, Adam, to the end that according to thy longing and according to thy judgment thou mayest have and possess what abode, what form, and what functions thou thyself shalt desire. The nature of all other beings is limited and constrained within the bounds of laws prescribed by Us. Thou, constrained by no limits, in accordance with thine own free will, in whose hand We have placed thee, shalt ordain for thyself the limits of thy nature. We have set thee at the world's center that thou mayest from thence more easily observe whatever is in the world. We have made thee neither of heaven nor of earth, neither mortal nor immortal. so that with freedom of choice and with honor, as though the maker and molder of thyself, thou mayest fashion thyself in whatever shape thou shalt prefer. Thou shalt have the power to degenerate into the lower forms of life, which are brutish. Thou shalt have the power, out of thy soul's judgment, to be reborn into the higher forms, which are divine."

4. O supreme generosity of God the Father, O highest
and most marvelous felicity of man! To him it is
granted to have whatever he chooses, to be whatever he
wills. Beasts as soon as they are born (so says
Lucilius) bring with them from their mother's womb all
they will ever possess. Spiritual beings, either from
the beginning or soon thereafter, become what they are
to be for ever and ever. On man when he came into life
the Father conferred the seeds of all kinds and the
germs of every way of life. Whatever seeds each man
cultivates will grow to maturity and bear in him their
own fruit. If they be vegetative, he will be like a
plant. If sensitive, he will become brutish. If
rational, he will grow into a heavenly being. If
intellectual, he will be an angel and the son of God.
And if, happy in the lot of no created thing, he
withdraws into the center of his own unity, his spirit,
made one with God, in the solitary darkness of God, who
is set above all things, shall surpass them all. Who
would not admire this our chameleon? Or who could more
greatly admire aught else whatever? It is man who
Asclepius of Athens, arguing from his mutability of
character and from his self-transforming nature, on
just grounds says was symbolized by Proteus in the
mysteries....

6. Are there any who would not admire man, who is,
in the sacred writings of Moses and the Christians, not
without reason described sometimes by the name of "all
flesh," sometimes by that of "every creature," inasmuch
as he himself molds, fashions, and changes himself into
the form of all flesh and into the character of every
creature? For this reason the Persian Euanthes, in
describing the Chaldaean theology, writes that man has
no semblance that is inborn and his very own but many
that are external and foreign to him; whence this
saying of the Chaldaeans: "Hanorish tharah sharinas,"
that is, "Man is a being of varied, manifold, and
inconstant nature." But why do we emphasize this? To
the end that after we have been born to this
condition--that we can become what we will--we should
understand that we ought to have especial care to this,
that it should never be said against us that, although
born to a privileged position, we failed to recognize
it and became like unto wild animals and senseless
beasts of burden, but that rather the saying of Asaph
the prophet should apply: "Ye are all angels and sons
of the Most High," and that we may not, by abusing the
most indulgent generosity of the Father, make for

ourselves that freedom of choice He has given into something harmful instead of salutary. Let a certain holy ambition invade our souls, so that, not content with the mediocre. we shall pant after the highest and (since we may if we wish) toil with all our strength to obtain it.

7. Let us disdain earthly things, despise heavenly things, and, finally, esteeming less whatever is of the world, hasten to that court which is beyond the world and nearest to the Godhead. There, as the sacred mysteries relate, Seraphim, Cherubim, and Thrones hold the first places; let us, incapable of yielding to them. and intolerant of a lower place, emulate their dignity and their glory. If we have willed it, we shall be second to them in nothing.

8. But how shall we go about it, and what in the end shall we do? Let us consider what they do, what sort of life they lead. If we also come to lead that life (for we have the power), we shall then equal their good fortune. The Seraph burns with the fire of love. The Cherub glows with the splendor of intelligence. The Throne stands by the steadfastness of judgment. Therefore if, in giving ourselves over to the active life, we have after due consideration undertaken the care of the lower beings, we shall be strengthened with the firm stability of Thrones. If, unoccupied by deeds, we pass our time in the leisure of contemplation, considering the Creator in the creature and the creature in the Creator, we shall be all ablaze with Cherubic light. If we long with love for the Creator himself alone, we shall speedily flame up with His consuming fire into a Seraphic likeness. Above the Throne. that is, above the just judge, God sits as Judge of the ages. Above the Cherub, that is, above him who contemplates, God flies, and cherishes him, as it were, in watching over him. For the spirit of the Lord moves upon the waters, the waters, I say, which are above the firmament and which in Job praise the Lord with hymns before dawn. Who so is a Seraph, that is, a lover. is in God and God in him, nay, rather. God and himself are one. Great is the power of Thrones, which we attain in using judgment, and most high the exaltation of Seraphs, which we attain in loving....

9.   Let us also, therefore, by emulating the Cherubic
way of life on earth, by taming the impulses of our
passions with moral science, by dispelling the darkness
of reason with dialectic, and by, so to speak, washing
away the filth of ignorance and vice, cleanse our soul,
so that her passions may not rave at random nor her
reason through heedlessness ever be deranged.

10.   Then let us fill our well-prepared and purified
soul with the light of natural philosophy. so that we
may at last perfect her in the knowledge of things
divine. And lest we be satisfied with those of our
faith, let us consult the patriarch Jacob, whose form
gleams carved on the throne of glory. Sleeping in the
lower world but keeping watch in the upper, the wisest
of fathers will advise us.   But he will advise us
through a figure (in this way everything was wont to
come to those men) that there is a ladder extending
from the lowest earth to the highest heaven, divided in
a series of many steps, with the Lord seated at the
top, and angels in contemplation ascending and
descending over them alternately by turns.

12

NICCOLÒ MACHIAVELLI

Until July 1498 Niccolò Machiavelli (1469-1527) was relatively unknown to his fellow Florentines. But in that year he was appointed secretary to the Council of Ten, executing the functions of war and peace. During his tenure as secretary, Florence was at war with the various Italian principalities, as well as with the Papal states and the great European monarchies of France, Germany and Spain. As a representative of the Florentine Republic, Machiavelli served in various diplomatic capacities, visiting foreign and Italian princes.

From 1498 to 1512, Machiavelli enjoyed considerable political success. But because of his service to a free and republican Florence, he lost his position upon the return to power of the Medici in 1512. He was arrested for treason and exiled to San Casciano, a small estate just a few miles from the Florence that he loved so much.

It was at San Casciano that he turned to writing on war, history, and politics, completing his most famous literary productions <u>The Discourses</u> and <u>The Prince</u>. In the selection that follows, taken from his lesser known "The Golden Ass", written about 1517, Machiavelli paints a portrait of man as an ambitious, avaricious, and licentious being, in short, an irrational being. Born devoid of all protection from the forces of Fortune, man, according to Machiavelli, is more pathetic than an animal. At odds with his Creator, himself, and society, and as a result of his excessive desires, man is unable to fashion for himself a peaceful existence.

The poem tells in allegorical fashion the story of Machiavelli's own fall from power due to the irrational forces, both within man, (namely, his appetites), and outside man (Fortune), which cannot ever be totally controlled. In the poem, a man (representing

Machiavelli himself), lost in the forest (symbolic of
Machiavelli's world), encounters a beautiful lady who
is attending a herd of animals (they represent real
political figures with whom Machiavelli had dealings).
The lady, the visible manifestation of Fortune (Circe),
who is ultimately responsible for transforming men into
animals, attempts to console the man, who is despondent
over his life's many misfortunes, by showing him that
the life of an animal is preferable to the life of a
man. As a big fat porker covered with mud indicates to
the man, "in the mud I live more happily" than a man
for "here without anxiety I bathe and roll myself."

THE GOLDEN ASS:

    Man's insatiable and irrational appetites.

Chapter 7

...Though I was embarrassed by a thousand distresses,
yet I should have liked to speak with some of those
animals if I had found any interpreters there.

But my lady--who had observed my wish and my
longing--said: "Do not hesitate, your desire will be
fulfilled."

Look for a little there where I am pointing my finger,
without moving a pace farther on along the wall, in the
direction you have been taking."

Then I saw in a low place, when I had turned my eyes
toward it, a big fat porker covered with mud.

I shall by no means tell whom he resembled; let it be
enough for you that he would come to three hundred
pounds, yes more, if he were hung on the hook.

And my guide said: "Let us go down there close to that
hog, if you really are eager to hear his desires and
his words.

Because if you should try to draw him out of that
puddle, making him turn into a man, he would not desire
it, like a fish that lives in a river or a lake.

And because this seems incredible, in order that you
may convince yourself, you may ask him if he will come
out."

Thereupon my lady stepped along; and in order not to be
parted from her at all, I took her by the hand she
offered me.

Thus I came close to that hog.

Chapter 8

As we came near, that hog raised his snout all smeared
with turd and mud, such that to look at him made me
sick.

And because long before I had been known to him, he
turned toward me with a show of teeth, remaining
otherwise quiet and without motion.

So I said to him, in the most gracious tones: "May God
give you a better fate if it seems to you good; may God
support you if you desire support.

If you are willing to talk with me, I shall be pleased;
and in order that you may know for certain, if you
really wish to, you can satisfy yourself.

To speak to you freely and openly, I say it to you with
the permission of this lady, who has showed me this
desert path. The gods have granted me such great grace
that she has thought it no burden to rescue me and take
me from the afflictions you still suffer.

On her part she also wants me to tell you that she will
free you from such great evil, if you wish to return to
your early shape." Erect the boar stood on his feet
when he heard that, and in great excitement the muddy
beast made this reply:

"I know not whence you come or from what region, but if
you have come for nothing else than to get me away from
here, go off about your business.

I have no wish to live with you; I refuse. I see
clearly that you suffer from the error which for a long
time bound me too. So much your self love deceives you
that you do not believe there is any good apart from
human existence and its worth. But if on me you direct
your imagination, before you leave my presence I shall
see to it that in such an error you no longer remain.

I shall begin with prudence, an excellent virtue.
through which men magnify their excellence.

They know best how to apply this virtue who, without
instruction, for themselves see how to pursue their own
well-being and to avoid distress.

Without the least doubt I assert and affirm that
superior to yours is our condition, and even you will
not deny it soon. Who is that preceptor who explains
to us what any plant is, whether harmless or injurious?
Not any research, not your ignorance.

We change abode from shore to shore, and to leave one
dwelling gives us no pain, if only we are happy and
prosperous. One avoids the ice and another avoids the
sun, seeking the climate friendly to our way of life,
as Nature who teaches us commands.

You, much more hapless than I can tell, go exploring
one country and another, not to find a climate either
cool or sunny, but because your shameful greed for gain
does not confirm your spirit in a life sparing,
law-abiding and humble.

Often into an atmosphere rotten and sickly, leaving a
healthful climate, you shift yourselves--and not that
you may protect your livelihood.

We flee from the climate alone, you from poverty; in
dangers you seek wealth; this has blocked against you
the path of well-doing. And if we wish to speak of
strength, how much our condition surpasses yours is as
plain as the sun in its brightness.

The bull, the wild lion, the elephant and others of us
in countless numbers are found in the world whom a man
cannot confront.

If reflection about the spirit is good, you will see
that we have received a richer gift of hearts
invincible, noble and strong. Among us are done bold

121

deeds and exploits without hope of a triumph or other
fame, as once among those Romans who were famous. In
the lion you see great pride in a noble deed, and at a
shameful act a wish to blot out its memory.

Still among us some beasts live who to escape from
prison and chains, by dying gain both glory and
liberty; such valor they preserve in their breasts that
after they lose their liberty their hearts cannot
endure the life of slaves.

If on temperance you turn your gaze, you will plainly
see that in this game we have surpassed your side.

On Venus we spend but short and little time, but you
without measure follow her in every time and place.

Our species does not care for other food than the
product of the heavens without art; you wish that which
Nature cannot supply.

You are not content with one food only, as we are, but
better to fulfill your greedy desires, you journey for
such things to the kingdoms of the East.

That does not suffice which you can gather on land, for
you enter into the Ocean's bosom to glut yourselves
with his riches.

My talk would never come to an end if I should try to
show how hapless you are above all other earthly
creatures.

We are closer friends to Nature; to us she more freely
dispenses her vigor, making you only beggars for all
her good things. If you wish to see this, make use of
your senses; easily you will be convinced of a truth
opposed to what perhaps you now believe.

In the eagle's eye, in the dog's ear and nose and taste
as well we can show something better than you, though

touch is left as more your own; yet it is given not to
do you honor but only that Venus' appetite can bring
you greater affliction and trouble.

Every animal among us is born fully clad; this protects
him from weather cold and harsh under every sky and on
every shore.   Only   man   is born devoid of all
protection; he has neither hide nor spine nor feather
nor fleece nor bristles nor scales to make him a
shield.

In weeping he begins his life, with the sound of a cry
painful and choked, so that he is distressing to look
at.

Then as he grows up, his life is verily short when
compared with that of a stag, a raven, a goose.

Nature gave you hands and speech, and with them she
gave you also ambition and avarice, with which her
bounty is cancelled. To how many ills Nature subjects
you at starting! and afterwards

Fortune--how   much   good   she   promises   you without
fulfillment!

Yours are ambition, licentiousness, lamentation and
avarice, which bring on mange in the life you reckon so
high.

No animal can be found that has a frailer life, and has
for living a stronger desire, more disordered fear or
greater madness.

One hog to another hog causes no pain, one stag to
another; man by another man is slain, crucified and
plundered.

Consider now how you ask that I again become man, being
exempt from all miseries that I endured as long as I
was a man. And if any among men seems to you a god,

happy and rejoicing, do not believe him such, because
in this mud I live more happily; here without anxiety I
bathe and roll myself."

13

MICHEL EYQUEM DE MONTAIGNE

Born near Bordeaux, Montaigne (1533-1592) was raised a Catholic and after attending the College de Guyenne, completed his formal education at the University of Toulouse which was a center for humanism and unorthodox religious ideas. In 1568 he published a French translation of Raymond Sébond's <u>Natural Theology or The Book of Creatures</u>. In the preface to the translation Montaigne modified Sebond's rationalistic claims that unaided human reason could comprehend the universe and establish the existence and nature of God. Four years later, he began writing his <u>Essays</u> (the complete edition of all three volumes appeared in 1588). The "Apology for Raymond Sébond," the longest of the essays and by far the most important philosophical essay of Montaigne, was written about the same time that he was reading the writings of Sextus Empiricus and classical pyrrhonistic skepticism. Upon reading the entire essay, it is very apparent that the writings of the ancient Greek skeptics had an enormous impact on Montaigne. In turn, the essay had a significant influence on subsequent intellectual history. The case for skepticism which the essay puts forward stimulated philosophers like Descartes to meet the challenges it made. Descartes's rationalistic philosophy can be seen as a response to Montaigne's motto: What do I know?

In the selection that is provided, Montaigne argues that man is an arrogant and presumptuous being, who thinks himself to be better than he is, when in fact, as Montaigne views the matter, "man is the most vulnerable and frail of all creatures."

APOLOGY FOR RAYMOND SÉBOND:

Man - the most vulnerable and frail of creatures.

Let us then consider for the moment man alone, without outside assistance, armed solely with his own weapons, and deprived of divine grace and knowledge, which is his whole honor, his strength, and the foundation of his being. Let us see how much presence he has in this fine array. Let him help me to understand, by the force of his reason, on what foundations he has built these great advantages that he thinks he has over other creatures. Who has persuaded him that that admirable motion of the celestial vault, the eternal light of those torches rolling so proudly above his head, the fearful movements of that infinite sea, were established and have lasted so many centuries for his convenience and his service? Is it possible to imagine anything so ridiculous as that this miserable and puny creature, who is not even master of himself, exposed to the attacks of all things, should call himself master and emperor of the universe, the least part of which it is not in his power to know, much less to command? And this privilege that he attributes to himself of being the only one in this great edifice who has the capacity to recognize its beauty and its parts, the only one who can give thanks for it to the architect and keep an account of the receipts and expenses of the world: who has sealed him this privilege? Let him show us his letters patent for this great and splendid charge.

Have they been granted in favor of the wise only? Then they do not touch many people. Are the fools and the wicked worthy of such extraordinary favor, and, being the worst part of the world, of being preferred to all the rest?

Shall we believe this man? <u>For whom then shall a man say</u> that <u>the world was made</u>? <u>Naturally, for those souls who have the use of reason</u>. <u>These are gods and men, to whom certainly nothing is superior</u> [Cicero, quoting Balbus]. We shall never have flouted enough the impudence of this coupling.

But, poor wight, what has he in himself worthy of
such an advantage? When we consider the incorruptible
life of the celestial bodies, their beauty, their
greatness, their continual motion by so exact a rule;

> When the vaults of heaven meet our sight,
> Infinite worlds above, ether with stars alight;
> And when the course of sun and moon come to our
mind;

LUCRETIUS

when we consider the dominion and power that those
bodies have, not only over our lives and the conditions
of our fortune,

> For on the stars men's deeds and lives depend,

MANILIUS

but over our very inclinations, our reasonings, our
wills, which they govern, drive, and stir at the mercy
of their influences, as our reason finds and teaches
us;

> He learns that stars remotely seen
> Govern by silent laws, and intervene;
> To move the universe they alternate.
> And rule by certain signs the twists of fate;

MANILIUS

when we seek that not merely a man, nor a king, but
kingdoms, empires, and all this world below move in
step with the slightest movements of the heavens;

> How great a change the slightest motion brings: So
great this kingdom is that governs kings;

MANILIUS

127

if our virtue, our vices, our competence and knowledge,
and this very dissertation that we are making about the
power of the stars and this comparison of them to us,
comes, as our reason judges, by their medium and their
favor;

> One, in love's delirium,
> Can cross the sea and conquer Ilium;
> Another man is destined laws to build;
> Fathers kill sons, fathers by sons are killed,
> And brother wounds armed brother in the fray.
> This war is not of ours; Fate makes men stray,
> Punish themselves, their members lacerate.
>
> . . . .
> This too is fated, that I write of fate;

MANILIUS

if we hold by the dispensation of heaven this portion
of reason that we have, how can our reason make us
equal to heaven?   How   subject its essence and
conditions to our knowledge?   All that we see in those
bodies astonishes   us.   <u>What preparations, what
instruments, what levers, what machines, what workmen
performed so great a work</u>? [Cicero.]

Why do we deny them soul, and life, and reason? Have
we recognized in them some inert, insensible stupidity,
we who have no dealings with them except obedience?
Shall we say that we have seen in no other creature
than man the exercise of a rational soul? Well, have
we seen anything like the sun?   Does it fail to exist,
because we have seen nothing like it, and its movements
to exist, because there are none like them? If what we
have not seen does   not exist, our knowledge is
marvelously shrunk: <u>How narrow are the limits of our
mind</u>! [Cicero.]

Are these not dreams of human vanity, to make the
moon a celestial earth, to imagine mountains and
valleys there, like Anaxagoras; to plant habitations
and human dwellings there, and set up colonies for our
convenience, as Plato and Plutarch do; and to make our
earth a bright star lighting the moon? <u>Among other
human infirmities is this one also, mental fog, and not
so much the need to err as the love of errors</u> [Seneca].

128

<u>The corruptible body weighs down the soul, and the
earthy tabernacle oppresses the much pondering mind</u>.
[The Book of Wisdom. quoted by Saint Augustine].

Presumption is our natural and original malady. The
most vulnerable and frail of all creatures is man, and
at the same time the most arrogant. He feels and sees
himself lodged here, amid the mire and dung of the
world, nailed and riveted to the worst, the deadest.
and the most stagnant part of the universe, on the
lowest story of the house and the farthest from the
vault of heaven, with the animals of the worst
condition of the three; and in his imagination he goes
planting himself above the circle of the moon, and
bringing the sky down beneath his feet. It is by the
vanity of this same imagination that he equals himself
to God, attributes to himself divine characteristics,
picks himself out and separates himself from the horde
of other creatures, carves out their shares to his
fellows and companions the animals, and distributes
among them such portions of faculties and powers as he
sees fit. How does he know, by the force of his
intelligence, the secret internal stirrings of animals?
By what comparison between them and us does he infer
the stupidity that he attributes to them?

When I play with my cat, who knows if I am not a
pastime to her more than she is to me? Plato, in his
picture of the golden age under Saturn, counts among
the principal advantages of the man of that time the
communication he had with the beasts; inquiring of them
and learning from them, he knew the true qualities and
differences of each one of them; whereby he acquired a
very perfect intelligence and prudence. and conducted
his life far more happily that we could possibly do. Do
we need a better proof to judge man's impudence with
regard to the beasts? That great author opined that in
most of the bodily form that Nature gave them, she
considered solely the use of prognostications that were
derived from them in his time.

This defect that hinders communication between them
and us, why is it not just as much ours as theirs? It
is a matter of guesswork whose fault it is that we do
not understand one another; for we do not understand
them any more than they do us. By this same reasoning
they may consider us beasts, as we consider them. It

is no great wonder if we do not understand them;
neither do we understand the Basques and the
Troglodytes. However, some have boasted of
understanding them, like Apollonius of Tyana, Melampus,
Tiresias, Thales, and others. And since it is a fact.
as the cosmographers say, that there are nations that
accept a dog as their king, they must give a definite
interpretation to his voice and motions. We must
notice the parity there is between us. We have some
mediocre understanding of their meaning; so do they of
ours, in about the same degree. They flatter us,
threaten us, and implore us, and we them.

Furthermore, we discover very evidently that there is
full and complete communication between them and that
they understand each other, not only those of the same
species, but also those of different species.

    Even dumb cattle and the savage beasts
    Varied and different noises do employ
    When they feel fear or pain, or thrill with joy.

                                        LUCRETIUS

In a certain bark of the dog the horse knows there is
anger; at a certain other sound of his he is not
frightened. Even in the beasts that have no voice,
from the mutual services we see between them we easily
infer some other means of communication; their motions
converse and discuss:

    Likewise in children, the tongue's speechlessness
    Leads them to gesture what they would express.

                                        LUCRETIUS

Why not; just as well as our mutes dispute, argue, and
tell stories by signs? I have seen some so supple and
versed in this, that in truth they lacked nothing of
perfection in being able to make themselves understood.
Lovers grow angry, are reconciled, entreat, thank, make
assignations, and in fine say everything, with their
eyes:

And silence too records
Our prayers and our words.

TASSO

What of the hands? We beg, we promise. call,
dismiss, threaten, pray, entreat, deny, refuse.
question. admire, count, confess, repent. fear. blush,
doubt, instruct. command, incite, encourage, swear.
testify. accuse, condemn, absolve. insult, despise,
defy, vex, flatter. applaud, bless, humiliate. mock,
reconcile, commend, exalt, entertain, rejoice,
complain, grieve. mope. despair, wonder, exclaim. are
silent, and what not, with a variation and
multiplication that vie with the tongue. With the
head: we invite. send away, avow, disavow, give the
lie. welcome, honor, venerate. disdain. demand, show
out, cheer, lament, caress, scold, submit, brave.
exhort. menace, assure, inquire. What of the eyebrows?
What of the shoulders? There is no movement that does
not speak both a language intelligible without
instruction, and a public language; which means, seeing
the variety and particular use of other languages, that
this one must rather be judged the one proper to human
nature. I omit what necessity teaches privately and
promptly to those who need it, and the finger
alphabets. and the grammars in gestures, and the
sciences which are practiced and expressed only by
gestures, and the nations which Pliny says have no
other language.

An ambassador of the city of Abdera, after speaking
at length to King Agis of Sparta, asked him: "Well.
Sire, what answer do you wish me to take back to our
citizens?" "That I allowed you to say all you wanted,
and as much as you wanted, without ever saying a word."
Wasn't that an eloquent and thoroughly intelligible
silence?

Moreover, what sort of faculty of ours do we not
recognize in the actions of the animals? Is there a
society regulated with more order, diversified into
more charges and functions, and more consistently
maintained, than that of the honeybees? Can we imagine
so orderly an arrangement of actions and occupations as
this to be conducted without reason and foresight?

131

Some, by these signs and instances inclined,
Have said that bees share in the divine mind
And the ethereal spirit.

VIRGIL

Do the swallows that we see on the return of spring ferreting in all the corners of our houses search without judgment. and choose without discrimination, out of a thousand places, the one which is most suitable for them to dwell in? And in that beautiful and admirable texture of their buildings, can birds use a square rather than a round figure, an obtuse rather than a right angle, without knowing their properties and their effects? Do they take now water, now clay. without judging that hardness is softened by moistening? Do they floor their palace with moss or with down, without foreseeing that the tender limbs of their little ones will lie softer and more comfortably on it? Do they shelter themselves from the rainy wind and face their dwelling toward the orient without knowing the different conditions of these winds and considering that one is more salutary to them than the other? Why does the spider thicken her web in one place and slacken it in another, use now this sort of knot, now that one, unless she has the power of reflection. and thought. and inference?

We recognize easily enough, in most of their works, how much superiority the animals have over us and how feeble is our skill to imitate them. We see, however, in our cruder works, the faculties that we use, and that our soul applies itself with all its power; why do we not think the same thing of them? Why do we attribute to some sort of natural and servile inclination these works which surpass all that we can do by nature and by art? Wherein, without realizing it, we grant them a very great advantage over us, by making Nature, with maternal tenderness. accompany them and guide them as by the hand in all the actions and comforts of their life; while us she abandons to chance and to fortune. and to seek by art the things necessary for our preservation, and denies us at the same time the power to attain, by any education and mental straining, the natural resourcefulness of the animals: so that their brutish stupidity surpasses in all conveniences all that our divine intelligence can do.

132

Truly, by this reckoning, we should be quite right to call her a very unjust stepmother. But this is not so; our organization is not so deformed and disorderly. Nature has universally embraced all her creatures; and there is none that she has not very amply furnished with all powers necessary for the preservation of its being. For these vulgar complaints that I hear men make (as the license of their opinions now raises them above the clouds, and then sinks them to the antipodes) that we are the only animal abandoned naked on the naked earth, tied, bound, having nothing to arm and cover ourselves with except the spoils of others; whereas all other creatures Nature has clothed with shells, husks, bark, hair. wool, spikes, hide, down, feathers, scales, fleece, and silk, according to the need of their being; has armed them with claws, teeth, or horns for attack and defense; and has herself instructed them in what is fit for them--to swim, to run, to fly, to sing--whereas man can neither walk, nor speak, nor eat, nor do anything but cry, without apprenticeship--

> The infant. like a sailor tossed ashore
> By raging seas, lies naked on the earth.
> Speechless, helpless for life, when at his birth
> Nature from out the womb brings him to light.
> He fills the place with wailing, as his right
> For one who through so many woes must pass.
> Yet flocks, herds, savage beasts of every class
> Grow up without the need for any rattle,
> Or for a gentle nurse's soothing prattle;
> They seek no varied clothes against the sky;
> Lastly they need no arms, no ramparts high
> To guard their own--since earth itself and nature
> Amply bring forth all things for every creature.

LUCRETIUS

--those complaints are false, there is a greater equality and a more uniform relationship in the organization of the world. Our skin is provided as adequately as theirs with endurance against the assaults of the weather: witness so many nations who have not yet tried the use of any clothes. Our ancient Gauls wore hardly any clothes; nor do the Irish, our neighbors, under so cold a sky. But we may judge this better by ourselves; for all the parts of the body that we see fit to expose to the wind and air are found fit

to endure it: face,   feet,   hands, legs, shoulders,
head, according as custom invites us.   For if there is
a part of us that is tender and that seems as though it
should fear the cold,   it   should be the stomach, where
digestion takes place;   our   fathers left it uncovered,
and our ladies, soft   and   delicate as they are,
sometimes go half bare down to the navel.   Nor are the
bindings and swaddlings of   infants necessary either;
and the Lacedaemonian mothers raised their children in
complete freedom to move   their limbs, without wrapping
or binding them.   Our weeping is common to most of the
other animals; and there are   scarcely any who are not
observed to complain and wail   long after their birth,
since it is a   demeanor most appropriate to the
helplessness that they feel.   As for the habit of
eating, it is, in us as in them, natural and needing no
instruction:

For each one feels his powers and his needs.

LUCRETIUS

   Who doubts that a child, having attained the strength
to feed himself, would be able to seek his food? And
the earth produces and offers him enough of it for his
need, with no other cultivation or artifice; and if not
in all weather, neither does she for the beasts:
witness the provisions we see the ants and others make
for the sterile seasons of the year. These nations
that we have just discovered to be so abundantly
furnished with food and natural drink, without care or
preparation, have now taught us that bread is not our
only food, and that without plowing, our mother Nature
had provided us in plenty with all we needed; indeed,
as seems likely, more amply and richly than she does
now that we have interpolated our artifice:

    At first and of her own accord the earth
    Brought forth sleek fruits and vintages of worth.
    Herself gave harvests sweet and pastures fair,
    Which now scarce grow, despite our toil and care,
    And we exhaust our oxen and our men;

LUCRETIUS

134

the excess and unruliness of our appetite outstripping
all the inventions with which we seek to satisfy it.

   As for weapons, we have more that are natural than
most other animals, and more varied movements of our
limbs; and we get more service out of them. naturally
and without lessons.   Those who are trained to fight
naked are seen to throw themselves into dangers like
our own men.   If some animals surpass us in this
advantage, we surpass many others.   And the skill to
fortify and protect the body by acquired means, we
possess by a natural instinct and precept. As proof
that this is so, the elephant sharpens and whets the
teeth which he uses in war (for he has special ones for
this purpose. which he spares, and does not use at all
for his other functions).   When bulls go into combat,
they spread and toss the dust around them; boars whet
their tusks; and the ichneumon, when he is to come to
grips with the crocodile, arms his body, coats it, and
crusts it all over with mud, well pressed and well
kneaded, as with a cuirass.   Why shall we not say that
it is just as natural to arm ourselves with wood and
iron?

   As for speech, it is certain that if it is not
natural. it is not necessary. Nevertheless, I believe
that a child who had been brought up in complete
solitude, remote from all association (which would be a
hard experiment to make), would have some sort of
speech to express his ideas.   And it is not credible
that Nature has denied us this resource that she has
given to many other animals: for what is it but
speech, this faculty we see in them of complaining,
rejoicing, calling to each other for help, inviting
each other to love, as they do by the use of their
voice? How could they not speak to one another? They
certainly speak to us, and we to them. In how many
ways do we not speak to our dogs? And they answer us.
We talk to them in another language, with other names,
than to birds, hogs, oxen. horses; and we change the
idiom according to the species:

         So ants amidst their sable-colored band
         Greet one another, and inquire perchance
         The road each follows, and the prize in hand.

It seems to me that Lactantius attributes to beasts
not only speech but also laughter. And the difference
of language that is seen between us, according to the
difference of countries, is found also in animals of
the same species. Aristotle cites in this connection
the various calls of partridges according to the place
they are situated in,

> And various birds . . .
> Utter at different times far different cries . . .
> And some change with the changing of the skies
> Their raucous songs.

LUCRETIUS

But it is yet to be known what language this child
would speak; and what is said about it by conjecture
has not much appearance of truth. If they allege to
me, against this opinion, that men naturally deaf do
not speak at all, I reply that it is not only because
they could not be taught speech by ear, but rather
because the sense of hearing, of which they are
deprived, is related to that of speech, and they hold
together by a natural tie: so that what we speak we
must speak first to ourselves, and make it ring on our
own ears inwardly, before we send it to other ears.

I have said all this to maintain this resemblance
that exists to human things, and to bring us back and
join us to the majority. We are neither above nor
below the rest: all that is under heaven, says the
sage, incurs the same law and the same fortune,

> All things are bound by their own chains of fate.

LUCRETIUS

There is some difference, there are orders and degrees;
but it is under the aspect of one and the same nature:

And all things go their own way, nor forget
Distinctions by the law of nature set.

LUCRETIUS

Man must be constrained and forced into line inside the barriers of this order. The poor wretch is in no position really to step outside them; he is fettered and bound, he is subjected to the same obligation as the other creatures of his class, and in a very ordinary condition, without any real and essential prerogative or preeminence. That which he accords himself in his mind and in his fancy has neither body nor taste. And if it is true that he alone of all the animals has this freedom of imagination and this unruliness in thought that represents to him what is, what is not, what he wants, the false and the true, it is an advantage that is sold him very dear, and in which he has little cause to glory, for from it springs the principal source of the ills that oppress him: sin, disease, irresolution, confusion, despair.

So I say, to return to my subject, that there is no apparent reason to judge that the beasts do by natural and obligatory instinct the same things that we do by our choice and cleverness. We must infer from like results like faculties, and consequently confess that this same reason, this same method that we have for working, is also that of the animals. Why do we imagine in them this compulsion of nature, we who feel no similar effect? Besides, it is more honorable, and closer to divinity, to be guided and obliged to act lawfully by a natural and inevitable condition, than to act lawfully by accidental and fortuitous liberty; and safer to leave the reins of our conduct to nature than to ourselves. The vanity of our presumption makes us prefer to owe our ability to our powers than to nature's liberality; and we enrich the other animals with natural goods and renounce them in their favor, in order to honor and ennoble ourselves with goods acquired: a very simple notion, it seems to me, for I should prize just as highly graces that were all mine and inborn as those I had gone begging and seeking from education. It is not in our power to acquire a fairer recommendation than to be favored by God and nature.

137

14

MARTIN LUTHER

Martin Luther (1483-1546), an Augustinian monk with a training in law from the University of Erfurt. lectured on philosophy and New Testament theology at the University of Wittenberg where he received his doctorate in theology. After coming to a new understanding of the Gospel, Luther, in his <u>Ninety-five Theses</u> (1517), began to challenge the authority of the Catholic Church in the area of dogma and indulgences, charging that the Papacy was merely a creation of devils interested in preserving their own tyrannical and secular power with no concern for man's spiritual salvation. Appealing to the nobility of the German principalities, Luther called on the various rulers to dissociate themselves from the Papacy of Leo X of the Medici family and to accomplish a reform of the Church. Firmly convinced of the priesthood of all believers and the righteousness of God, Luther believed that the German nobility was truly interested in spiritual renewal from which political and social reforms of the German nation would follow.

We have selected the following passage taken from <u>The Bondage of the Will</u> (1525), a work written in response to Erasmus' <u>On Free Will</u>. to represent Luther's view of man, a view which portrays man as totally corrupt and, therefore. incapable of willing the good. From Luther's point of view, man is justified (saved) not by reason and good works, but by faith alone in the Scriptures and the preached Word. Luther repeatedly maintained that the philosophical tradition of medieval scholasticism which continues to permeate the Catholic Church with its emphasis on the rational aspect of man's nature, is nothing but a prostitute. a whore, a plague of man's soul. Basing his view on his reading of Scripture, Luther insisted that man can understand nothing of himself and that in moral and spiritual matters man is absolutely impotent.

THE BONDAGE OF THE WILL:

     The spiritual and moral impotence of man.

     For my own part, I frankly confess that even if it
were possible, I should not wish to have free choice
given to me. or to have anything left in my own hands
by which I might strive toward salvation. For, on the
one hand, I should be unable to stand firm and keep
hold of it amid so many adversities and perils and so
many assaults of demons, seeing that even one demon is
mightier than all men, and no man at all could be
saved; and on the other hand, even if there were no
perils or adversities or demons, I should nevertheless
have to labor under perpetual uncertainty and to fight
as one beating the air. since even if I lived, and
worked to eternity, my conscience would never be
assured and certain how much it ought to do to satisfy
God. For whatever work might be accomplished, there
would always remain an anxious doubt whether it pleased
God or whether he required something more. as the
experience of all self-justifiers proves, and as I
myself learned to my bitter cost through so many years.
But now, since God has taken my salvation out of my
hands into his, making it depend on his choice and not
mine. and has promised to save me, not by my own work
or exertion but by his grace and mercy, I am assured
and certain both that he is faithful and will not lie
to me, and also that he is too great and powerful for
any demons or any adversities to be able to break him
or to snatch me from him. "No one." he says, "shall
snatch them out of my hand, because my Father who has
given them to me is greater than all" (John 10:28 f.).
So it comes about that, if not all. some and indeed
many are saved, whereas by the power of free choice
none at all would be saved, but all would perish
together. Moreover, we are also certain and sure that
we please God, not by the merit of our own working, but
by the favor of his mercy promised to us, and that if
we do less than we should or do it badly, he does not
hold this against us, but in a fatherly way pardons and
corrects us. Hence the glorying of all the saints in
their God.

(<u>The Mercy and Justice of God in the Light of Nature,</u>

140

Now, if you are disturbed by the thought that it is difficult to defend the mercy and justice of God when he damns the undeserving, that is to say, ungodly men who are what they are because they were born in ungodliness and can in no way help being and remaining ungodly and damnable, but are compelled by a necessity of nature to sin and to perish (as Paul says: "We were all children of wrath like the rest," since they are created so by God himself from seed corrupted by the sin of the one man Adam)--rather must God be honored and revered as supremely merciful toward those whom he justifies and saves, supremely unworthy as they are, and there must be at least some acknowledgment of his divine wisdom so that he may be believed to be righteous where he seems to us to be unjust. For if his righteousness were such that it could be judged to be righteous by human standards, it would clearly not be divine and would in no way differ from human righteousness. But since he is the one true God, and is wholly incomprehensible and inaccessible to human reason, it is proper and indeed necessary that his righteousness also should be incomprehensible, as Paul also says where he exclaims: "O the depth of the riches of the wisdom and the knowledge of God! How incomprehensible are his judgments and how unsearchable his ways!" But they would not be incomprehensible if we were able in every instance to grasp how they are righteous. What is man, compared with God? How much is there within our power compared with his power? What is our strength in comparison with his resources? What is our knowledge compared with his wisdom? What is our substance over against his substance? In a word, what is our all compared with his?

If, therefore, we confess, as even nature teaches, that human power, strength, wisdom, substance, and everything we have. is simply nothing at all in comparison with divine power, strength. wisdom. knowledge, and substance, what is this perversity that makes us attack God's righteousness and judgment only, and make such claims for our own judgment as to wish to comprehend, judge, and evaluate the divine judgment? Why do we not take a similar line here too, and say, "Our judgment is nothing in comparison with the divine judgment"? Ask Reason herself whether she is not convinced and compelled to confess that she is foolish

and rash in not allowing the judgment of God to be
incomprehensible, when she admits that everything else
divine is incomprehensible.   In all other matters we
grant God his divine majesty, and only in respect of
his judgment are we prepared to deny it. We cannot for
a while believe that he is righteous, even though he
has promised us that when he reveals his glory we shall
all both see and feel that he has been and is
righteous.

I will give an example to confirm this faith and
console that evil eye which suspects God of injustice.
As you can see, God so orders this corporal world in
its external affairs that if you respect and follow the
judgment of human reason, you are bound to say either
that there is no God or that God is unjust. As the
poet says" "Oft I am moved to think there are no
gods!" For look at the prosperity the wicked enjoy and
the adversity the good endure, and note how both
proverbs and that parent of proverbs, experience,
testify that the bigger the scoundrel the greater his
luck. "The tents of the ungodly are at peace," says
Job (Job 12:6), and Psalm 72(73:12) complains that the
sinners of the world increase in riches. Tell me, is
it not in everyone's judgment most unjust that the
wicked should prosper and the good suffer? But that is
the way of the world.   Here even the greatest minds
have stumbled and fallen, denying the existence of God
and imagining that all things are moved at random by
blind Chance or Fortune.   So, for example, did the
Epicureans and Pliny; while Aristotle, in order to
preserve that Supreme Being of his from unhappiness,
never lets him look at anything but himself, because he
thinks it would be most unpleasant for him to see so
much suffering and so many injustices. The prophets,
however, who did believe in God, had more temptation to
regard him as unjust--Jeremiah, for instance, and Job,
David, Asaph, and others.   What do you suppose
Demosthenes and Cicero thought, when after doing all
they could they were rewarded with so tragic a death?

Yet all this, which looks so very like injustice in
God, and which has been represented as such with
arguments that no human reason or light of nature can
resist, is very easily dealt with in the light of the
gospel and the knowledge of grace, by which we are
taught that although the ungodly flourish in their
bodies, they lose their souls.   In fact, this whole

insoluble problem finds a quick solution in one short
sentence, namely, that there is a life after this life.
and whatever has not been punished and rewarded here
will be punished and rewarded there, since this life is
nothing but an anticipation, or rather, the beginning
of the life to come.

If, therefore, the light of the gospel, shining only
through the Word and faith, is so effective that this
question which has been discussed in all ages and never
solved is so easily settled and put aside, what do you
think it will be like when the light of the Word and of
faith comes to an end, and reality itself and the
Divine Majesty are revealed in their own light? Do you
not think that the light of glory will then with the
greatest of ease be able to solve the problem that is
insoluble in the light of the Word or of grace, seeing
that the light of grace has so easily solved the
problem that was insoluble in the light of nature?

Let us take it that there are three lights--the light
of nature, the light of grace, and the light of glory,
to use the common and valid distinction. By the light
of nature it is an insoluble problem how it can be just
that a good man should suffer and a bad man prosper;
but this problem is solved by the light of grace. By
the light of grace it is an insoluble problem how God
can damn one who is unable by any power of his own to
do anything but sin and be guilty. Here both the light
of nature and the light of grace tell us that it is not
the fault of the unhappy man, but of an unjust God; for
they cannot judge otherwise of a God who crowns one
ungodly man freely and apart from merits, yet damns
another who may well be less, or at least not more,
ungodly. But the light of glory tells us differently,
and it will show us hereafter that the God whose
judgment here is one of incomprehensible righteousness
is a God of most perfect and manifest righteousness.
In the meantime, we can only <u>believe</u> this, being
admonished and confirmed by the example of the light of
grace, which performs a similar miracle in relation to
the light of nature.

(CONCLUSION)

(<u>That the Case Against Free Choice is Unanswerable Let</u>

<u>Erasmus Be Willing to Admit</u>)

I will here bring this little book to an end, though I am prepared if need be to carry the debate farther. However, I think quite enough has been done here to satisfy the godly and anyone who is willing to admit the truth without being obstinate. For if we believe it to be true that God foreknows and predestines all things, that he can neither be mistaken in his foreknowledge nor hindered in his predestination, and that nothing takes place but as he wills it (as reason itself is forced to admit), then on the testimony of reason itself there cannot be any free choice in man or angel or any creature.

Similarly, if we believe that Satan is the ruler of this world, who is forever plotting and fighting against the Kingdom of Christ with all his powers, and that he will not let men go who are his captives unless he is forced to do so by the divine power of the Spirit, then again it is evident that there can be no such thing as free choice.

Similarly, if we believe that original sin has so ruined us that even in those who are led by the Spirit it causes a great deal of trouble by struggling against the good, it is clear that in a man devoid of the Spirit there is nothing left that can turn toward the good, but only toward evil.

Again, if the Jews, who pursued righteousness to the utmost of their powers, rather ran headlong into unrighteousness, while the Gentiles, who pursued ungodliness, attained righteousness freely and unexpectedly, then it is also manifest from this very fact and experience that man without grace can will nothing but evil.

To sum up: If we believe that Christ has redeemed men by his blood, we are bound to confess that the whole man was lost; otherwise, we should make Christ either superfluous or the redeemer of only the lowest part of man, which would be blasphemy and sacrilege.

144

15

JOHN CALVIN

John Calvin (1509-1564) was born and studied law and theology in France. During his studies he became acquainted with the scholastic and humanistic strains of his time. In 1532-1533, Calvin experienced a spiritual conversion, leading him away from his Catholic heritage to join the Protestant movement in France, spending his time advancing Church reform. However, he found France unreceptive to his brand of Lutheranism and, fearing for his life, he travelled first to Basel and then to Geneva where, in 1536, he wrote <u>The Institutes of The Christian Religion</u>, from which selected passages follow. This important theological treatise was addressed to King Francis I of France in defense of the French Protestants. While in Geneva, Calvin became the spokesman and leader for Protestant refugees; in short, he made Geneva the revolutionary center of reformed Christianity known as Calvinism which eventually spread throughout Europe and North America.

For Calvin, man is depraved enough as to merit salvation only within his newly founded and pure community of saints which alone interprets the Holy Scriptures according to God's authority. Man's corruption is the result of original sin from which the works of "concupiscence" flow. Hence, after the Fall, man's natural gifts (reason, understanding and will) became destitute of goodness so much so that not even God could purify them in this earthly life from the sins of the flesh. So, Calvin insisted, grace is needed to save man; but grace comes in degrees until death, thus making man always dependent on God for his perfection.

INSTITUTES OF THE CHRISTIAN RELIGION:

Original sin as root of man's utter depravity.

Book II, Chapter I, articles 8-9:

8. The nature of original sin

So that these remarks may not be made concerning an uncertain and unknown matter, let us define original sin. It is not my intention to investigate the several definitions proposed by various writers, but simply to bring forward the one that appears to me most in accordance with truth. Original sin, therefore, seems to be a hereditary depravity and corruption of our nature, diffused into all parts of the soul, which first makes us liable to God's wrath, then also brings forth in us those works which Scripture calls "works of the flesh" (Gal. 5:19). And that is properly what Paul often calls sin. The works that come forth from it --such as adulteries, fornications, thefts, hatreds, murders, carousings -- he accordingly calls "fruits of sin" (Gal. 5:19-21), although they are also commonly called "sins" in Scripture, and even by Paul himself.

We must, therefore, distinctly note these two things. First, we are so vitiated and perverted in every part of our nature that by this great corruption we stand justly condemned and convicted before God, to whom nothing is acceptable but righteousness, innocence, and purity. And this is not liability for another's transgression. For, since it is said that we became subject to God's judgment through Adam's sin, we are to understand it not as if we, guiltless and undeserving, bore the guilt of his offense but in the sense that, since we through his transgression have become entangled in the curse, he is said to have made us guilty. Yet not only has punishment fallen upon us from Adam, but a contagion imparted by him resides in us, which justly deserves punishment. For this reason, Augustine, though he often calls sin "another's" to show more clearly that it is distributed among us through propagation, nevertheless declares at the same time that it is peculiar to each. And the apostle himself most eloquently testifies that "death has spread to all because all have sinned" (Rom. 5:12).

That is, they have been enveloped in original sin and
defiled by its stains.   For that reason, even infants
themselves, while they carry their condemnation along
with them from the mother's womb, are guilty not of
another's fault but of their own. For, even though the
fruits of their iniquity have not yet come forth, they
have the seed enclosed within them.   Indeed, their
whole nature is a seed of sin; hence it can be only
hateful and abhorrent to God.   From this it follows
that it is rightly considered sin in God's sight, for
without guilt there would be no accusation.

Then comes the second consideration: that this
perversity never ceases in us, but continually bears
new fruits -- the works of the flesh that we have
already described -- just as a burning furnace gives
forth flame and sparks, or water ceaselessly bubbles up
from a spring.   Thus those who have defined original
sin as "the lack of the original righteousness, which
ought to reside in us," although they comprehend in
this definition the whole meaning of the term, have
still not expressed effectively enough its power and
energy. For our nature is not only destitute and empty
of good, but so fertile and fruitful of every evil that
it cannot be idle.   Those who have said that original
sin is "concupiscence" have used an appropriate word,
if only it be added --something that most will by no
means concede -- that whatever is in man, from the
understanding to the will, from the soul even to the
flesh, has been defiled and crammed with this
concupiscence. Or, to put it more briefly, the whole
man is of himself nothing but concupiscence.

9. Sin overturns the whole man

For this reason, I have said that all parts of the
soul were possessed by sin after Adam deserted the
fountain of righteousness.   For not only did a lower
appetite seduce him, but unspeakable impiety occupied
the very citadel of his mind, and pride penetrated to
the depths of his heart.   Thus it is pointless and
foolish to restrict the corruption that arises thence
only to what are called the impulses of the senses; or
to call it the "kindling wood" that attracts, arouses,
and drags into sin only that part which they term
"sensuality."   In this matter Peter Lombard has
betrayed his complete ignorance.   For, in seeking and
searching out its seat, he says that it lies in the

147

flesh, as Paul testifies; yet not intrinsically, but because it appears more in the flesh. As if Paul were indicating that only a part of the soul, and not its entire nature, is opposed to supernatural grace! Paul removes all doubt when he teaches that corruption subsists not in one part only, but that none of the soul remains pure or untouched by that mortal disease. For in his discussion of a corrupt nature Paul not only condemns the inordinate impulses of the appetites that are seen, but especially contends the mind is given over to blindness and the heart to depravity.

The whole third chapter of Romans is nothing but a description of original sin (vs. 1-20). From the "renewal" that fact appears more clearly. For the Spirit, who is opposed to the old man and to the flesh, not only marks the grace whereby the lower or sensual part of the soul is corrected, but embraces the full reformation of all the parts. Consequently, Paul not only enjoins that brute appetites be brought to nought but bids us "be renewed in the spirit of our mind" (Eph. 4:23); in another passage he similarly urges us to "be transformed in newness of mind" (Rom. 12:2). From this it follows that that part in which the excellence and nobility of the soul shine has not only been wounded, but so corrupted that it needs to be healed and to put on a new nature as well. We shall soon see to what extent sin occupies both mind and heart. Here I only want to suggest briefly that the whole man is overwhelmed --as by a deluge -- from head to foot, so that no part is immune from sin and all that proceeds from him is to be imputed to sin. As Paul says, all turnings of the thoughts to the flesh are enmities against God (Rom. 8:7), and are therefore death (Rom. 8:6).

Book II, Chapter II, articles 12 and 17

12.   <u>Supernatural gifts destroyed; natural gifts corrupted; but enough of reason remains to distinguish man from brute beasts</u>

And, indeed, that common opinion which they [ed. note, philosophers] have taken from Augustine pleases me: that the natural gifts were corrupted in man through sin, but that his supernatural gifts were stripped from him. For by the latter clause they understand the light of faith as well as righteousness, which would be sufficient to attain heavenly life and eternal bliss. Therefore, withdrawing from the Kingdom of God, he is at the same time deprived of spiritual gifts, with which he had been furnished for the hope of eternal salvation. From this is follows that he is so banished from the Kingdom of God that all qualities belonging to the blessed life of the soul have been extinguished in him, until he recovers them through the grace of regeneration. Among these are faith, love of God, charity toward neighbor, zeal for holiness and for righteousness. All these, since Christ restores them in us, are considered adventitious, and beyond nature: and for this reason we infer that they were taken away. On the other hand, soundness of mind and uprightness of heart were withdrawn at the same time. This is the corruption of the natural gifts. For even though something of understanding and judgment remains as a residue along with the will, yet we shall not call a mind whole and sound that is both weak and plunged into deep darkness. And depravity of the will is all too well known.

Since reason, therefore, by which man distinguishes between good and evil. and by which he understands and judges, is a natural gift, it could not be completely wiped out; but it was partly weakened and partly corrupted, so that its misshapen ruins appear. John speaks in this sense: "The light still shines in the darkness, but the darkness comprehends it not" (John 1:5). In these words both facts are clearly expressed. First, in man's perverted and degenerate nature some sparks still gleam. These show him to be a rational being, differing from brute beasts, because he is endowed with understanding. Yet, secondly, they show this light choked with dense ignorance, so that it cannot come forth effectively.

Similarly the will, because it is inseparable from man's nature, did not perish. but was so bound to wicked desires that it cannot strive after the right. This is, indeed, a complete definition, but one needing a fuller explanation.

Therefore, so that the order of discussion may proceed according to our original division of man's soul into understanding and will, let us first of all examine the power of the understanding.

When we so condemn human understanding for its perpetual blindness as to leave it no perception of any object whatever, we not only go against God's Word, but also run counter to the experience of common sense. For we see implanted in human nature some sort of desire to search out the truth to which man would not at all aspire if he had not already savored it. Human understanding then possesses some power of perception, since it is by nature captivated by love of truth. The lack of this endowment in brute animals proves their nature gross and irrational. Yet this longing for truth, such as it is, languishes before it enters upon its race because it soon falls into vanity. Indeed, man's mind, because of its dullness, cannot hold to the right path, but wanders through various errors and stumbles repeatedly, as if it were groping in darkness, until it strays away and finally disappears. Thus it betrays how incapable it is of seeking and finding truth.

Then it grievously labors under another sort of vanity: often it cannot discern those things which it ought to exert itself to know. For this reason, in investigating empty and worthless things, it torments itself in its absurd curiosity, while it carelessly pays little or no attention to matters that it should particularly understand. Indeed, it scarcely ever seriously applies itself to the study of them. Secular writers habitually complain of this perversity, yet they are almost all found to have entangled themselves in it. For this reason, Solomon, through the whole of his Ecclesiastes, after recounting all those studies in which men seem to themselves to be very wise, declares them to be vain and trifling (chs. 1:2, 14; 2:11; etc.).

17. <u>Summary of 12-16</u>

To sum up: We see among all mankind that reason is proper to our nature; it distinguishes us from brute beasts, just as they by possessing feeling differ from inanimate things. Now, because some are born fools or stupid, that defect does not obscure the general grace

of God. Rather, we are warned by that spectacle that
we ought to ascribe what is left in us to God's
kindness. For if he had not spared us, our fall would
have entailed the destruction of our whole nature.
Some men excel in keenness; others are superior in
judgment; still others have a readier wit to learn this
or that art. In this variety God commends his grace to
us, lest anyone should claim as his own what flowed
from the sheer bounty of God. For why is one person
more excellent than another? Is it not to display in
common nature God's special grace, which, in passing
many by, declares itself bound to none? Besides this,
God inspires special activities, in accordance with
each man's calling. Many examples of this occur in The
Book of Judges, where it is said that "the Spirit of
the Lord took possession" of those men whom he had
called to rule the people (ch. 6:34). In short, in
every extraordinary event there is some particular
impulsion. For this reason, Saul was followed by the
brave men "whose hearts God had touched" (I Sam.
10:26). And when Saul's consecration as king was
foretold, Samuel said: "Then the Spirit of the Lord
will come mightily upon you, and you shall be another
man" (I Sam. 10:6). And this was extended to the
whole course of government, as is said afterward of
David: "The Spirit of the Lord came upon him from that
day forward" (I Sam. 16:13). The same thing is taught
elsewhere with respect to particular actions. Even in
Homer, men are said to excel in natural ability not
only as Jupiter has bestowed it upon each, but "as he
leads them day by day." And surely experience shows
that, when those who were once especially ingenious and
skilled are struck dumb, men's minds are in God's hand
and under his will, so that he rules them at every
moment. For this reason it is said: "He takes
understanding away from the prudent (cf. Job 12:20) and
makes them wander in trackless wastes" (Job 12:24; cf.
Ps. 107:40). Still, we see in this diversity some
remaining traces of the image of God, which distinguish
the entire human race from the other creatures.

Book II, Chapter III, article 5

5. <u>Man sins of necessity, but without compulsion</u>

Because of the bondage of sin by which the will is
held bound, it cannot move toward good, much less apply

151

itself thereto; for a movement of this sort is the beginning of conversion to God, which in Scripture is ascribed entirely to God's grace. So Jeremiah prayed to the Lord to be "converted" if it were his will to "convert him" (Jer. 31:18, cf. Vg.). Hence the prophet in the same chapter, describing the spiritual redemption of the believing folk, speaks of them as "redeemed from the hand of one stronger than they" (v. 11 p.). By this he surely means the tight fetters with which the sinner is bound so long as, forsaken by the Lord, he lives under the devil's yoke. Nonetheless the will remains, with the most eager inclination disposed and hastening to sin. For man, when he gave himself over to this necessity, was not deprived of will, but of soundness of will. Not inappropriately Bernard teaches that to will is in us all: but to will good is gain; to will evil, loss. Therefore simply to will is of man; to will ill, of a corrupt nature; to will well, of grace.

Now, when I say that the will bereft of freedom is of necessity either drawn or led into evil, it is a wonder if this seems a hard saying to anyone, since it has nothing incongruous or alien to the usage of holy men. But it offends those who know not how to distinguish between necessity and compulsion. Suppose someone asks them: Is not God of necessity good? Is not the devil of necessity evil? What will they reply? God's goodness is so connected with his divinity that it is no more necessary for him to be God than for him to be good. But the devil by his fall was so cut off from participation in good that he can do nothing but evil. But suppose some blasphemer sneers that God deserves little praise for His own goodness, constrained as He is to preserve it. Will this not be a ready answer to him: not from violent impulsion. but from His boundless goodness comes God's inability to do evil? Therefore, if the fact that he must do good does not hinder God's free will in doing good; if the devil. who can do only evil. yet sins with his will -- who shall say that man therefore sins less willingly because he is subject to the necessity of sinning? Augustine everywhere speaks of this necessity; and even though Caelestius caviled against him invidiously. he did not hesitate to affirm it in these words: "Through freedom man came to be in sin, but the corruption which followed as punishment turned freedom into necessity." And whenever he makes mention of the matter. he does not hesitate to speak in this manner of the necessary bondage of sin.

The chief point of this distinction, then, must be
that man, as he was corrupted by the Fall, sinned
willingly, not unwillingly or by compulsion; by the
most eager inclination of his heart, not by forced
compulsion; by the prompting of his own lust, not by
compulsion from without. Yet so depraved is his nature
that he can be moved or impelled only to evil. But if
this is true, then it is clearly expressed that man is
surely subject to the necessity of sinning...

16

RENE DESCARTES

Born at La Haye, France, and educated at the Jesuit College of La Flèche, Rene Descartes (1596-1650) has come to be recognized as the father of modern philosophy because of his efforts to establish all knowledge on a solid foundation. Despite the high regard he had for the Jesuits and the education he received from them, Descartes came to the conclusion that the knowledge he acquired in every branch of learning, except mathematics, was lacking in absolute certitude. After leaving La Flèche, he first joined the army of Prince Maurice of Nassau during which time he still pursued mathematical study. He subsequently joined the army of Maximillian of Bavaria in 1619 and on Nov. 10 of that year, while stationed in Neuberg on the Danube, having been engaged in quiet reflection, he had a series of dreams which convinced him that his mission was to establish human knowledge on a sure footing. However, his efforts in this direction would not materialize until after a few more years of service in the army and a few relatively unproductive years in Paris.

Upon retiring to Holland in 1628, he wrote _Rules for the Direction of the Mind_, which would not be published until after his death, but which surely laid the groundwork for the momentous philosophy that later blossomed in _Discourse on the Method of rightfully conducting the Reason and seeking for Truth in the Sciences_ (1637), _Meditations on First Philosophy_ (1641), _Principles of Philosophy_ (1644), and _The Passions of the Soul_ (1649).

Descartes' ideal to establish all knowledge on a firm foundation was suggested to him in large part by the certitude he discovered in mathematics. He presupposed that the method of mathematics could be universally applied to all sciences. So just as mathematics begins with self-evident (axiomatic) truths, Descartes was intent on seeking the absolute truth upon which all truths could be based and from which all truths could be derived. In an effort to find an absolutely indubitable truth, he universally and methodically applied doubt to all previously held truths. Upon doing so, he came to intuit that there is a truth that survives all doubt: in doubting, I think. So _I think, therefore I am_ (a thinking thing). From this self-evident proposition. Descartes eventually came to demonstratively establish the existence of God and the existence of material things.

Descartes' view of human nature can be characterized as dualistic. Man is a combination of two separate substances (mind and body). His basis for arriving at this real distinction was rooted in the "clarity" and "distinctness" (these are recognized by Descartes as the criteria for truth) of the perceptions I have of mind and body. Yet, at the same time. Descartes emphasizes and tries to explain the interaction between the two substances. He maintains that there is empirical data which supports the feeling we have that the soul is influenced by the body and the body by the soul and that taken together they must constitute a unity.

Descartes' attempt to locate the point of interaction between mind and body in the pineal gland seems paradoxically to underline the distinction. but it is nevertheless clear that he was earnestly trying to explain the interaction between the two distinct substances. The readings that follow taken from _Meditations on First Philosophy. Principles of Philosophy,_ and _The Passions of the Soul_ reveal the tension in Descartes' philosophy of man between the recognition. by way of his method, of a real distinction between mind (unextended reality) and body (extended reality). on the one hand. and the felt need on the part of Descartes to speak of interaction. on the other hand. The readings also disclose the mechanistic view of the human body to which Descartes' principles led him.

PRINCIPLES OF PHILOSOPHY:

Man a composite of two really distinct substances.

...The real [distinction] is properly speaking found
between two or more substances; and we can conclude
that two substances are really distinct one from the
other from the sole fact that we can conceive the one
clearly and distinctly without the other. For in
accordance with the knowledge which we have of God, we
are certain that He can carry into effect all that of
which we have a distinct idea. That is why from the
fact that we now have, e.g. the idea of an extended or
corporeal substance, although we do not yet know
certainly whether such really exists at all, we may yet
conclude that it may exist; and if it does exist. any
one portion of it which we can demarcate in our thought
must be distinct from every other part of the same
substance. Similarly because each one of us is
conscious that he thinks, and that in thinking he can
shut off from himself all other substance. either
thinking or extended, we may conclude that each of us,
similarly regarded, is really distinct from every other
thinking substance and from every corporeal substance.
And even if we suppose that God has united a body to a
soul so closely that it was impossible to bring them
together more closely, and made a single thing out of
two, they would yet remain really distinct one from the
other notwithstanding the union; because however
closely God connected them He could not set aside the
power which He possessed of separating them. or
conserving them one apart from the other. and those
things which God can separate, or conceive in
separation, are really distinct.

MEDITATIONS:

The relation of mind and body.

But now that I begin to know myself better. and to
discover more clearly the author of my being, I do not
in truth think that I should rashly admit all the
matters which the senses seem to teach us. but, on the
other hand, I do not think that I should doubt them all
universally.

And first of all, because I know that all things
which I apprehend clearly and distinctly can be created
by God as I apprehend them. it suffices that I am able
to apprehend one thing apart from another clearly and
distinctly in order to be certain that the one is
different from the other, since they may be made to
exist in separation at least by the omnipotence of God;
and it does not signify by what power this separation
is made in order to compel me to judge them to be
different: and, therefore. just because I know
certainly that I exist, and that meanwhile I do not
remark that any other thing necessarily pertains to my
nature or essence. excepting that I am a thinking
thing, I rightly conclude that my essence consists
solely in the fact that I am a thinking thing [or a
substance whose whole essence or nature is to think].
And although possibly (or rather certainly, as I shall
say in a moment) I possess a body with which I am very
intimately conjoined, yet because, on the one side, I
have a clear and distinct idea of myself inasmuch as I
am only a thinking and unextended thing, and as, on the
other, I possess a distinct idea of body, inasmuch as
it is only an extended and unthinking thing, it is
certain that this I [that is to say, my soul by which I
am what I am]. is entirely and absolutely distinct from
my body, and can exist without it....

But there is nothing which this nature teaches me
more expressly [nor more sensibly] than that I have a
body which is adversely affected when I feel pain,
which has need of food or drink when I experience the
feelings of hunger and thirst. and so on; nor can I
doubt there being some truth in all this.

Nature also teaches me by these sensations of pain,
hunger, thirst, etc., that I am not only lodged in my
body as a pilot in a vessel, but that I am very closely
united to it, and so to speak so intermingled with it
that I seem to compose with it one whole. For if that
were not the case, when my body is hurt. I, who am
merely a thinking thing, should not feel pain, for I
should perceive this wound by the understanding only,
just as the sailor perceives by sight when something is
damaged in his vessel; and when my body has need of
drink or food, I should clearly understand the fact
without being warned of it by confused feelings of
hunger and thirst. For all these sensations of hunger.
thirst, pain, etc. are in truth none other than certain

confused modes of thought which are produced by the union and apparent intermingling of mind and body....

...And thus it still remains to inquire how the goodness of God does not prevent the nature of man so regarded from being fallacious.

In order to begin this examination, then, I here say. in the first place, that there is a great difference between mind and body, inasmuch as body is by nature always divisible, and the mind is entirely indivisible. For, as a matter of fact, when I consider the mind, that is to say. myself inasmuch as I am only a thinking thing, I cannot distinguish in myself any parts, but apprehend myself to be clearly one and entire; and although the whole mind seems to be united to the whole body, yet if a foot, or an arm, or some other part, is separated from my body, I am aware that nothing has been taken away from my mind. And the faculties of willing, feeling, conceiving, etc. cannot be properly speaking said to be its parts. for it is one and the same mind which employs itself in willing and in feeling and understanding. But it is quite otherwise with corporeal or extended objects. for there is not one of these imaginable by me which my mind cannot easily divide into parts, and which consequently I do not recognise as being divisible; this would be sufficient to teach me that the mind or soul of man is entirely different from the body, if I had not already learned it from other sources.

I further notice that the mind does not receive the impressions from all parts of the body immediately. but only from the brain, or perhaps even from one of its smallest parts. to wit. from that in which the common sense is said to reside, which, whenever it is disposed in the same particular way. conveys the same thing to the mind, although meanwhile the other portions of the body may be differently disposed, as is testified by innumerable experiments which it is unnecessary here to recount.

I notice, also, that the nature of body is such that none of its parts can be moved by another part a little way off which cannot also be moved in the same way by each one of the parts which are between the two,

although this more remote part does not act at all.
As, for example, in the cord ABCD [which is in tension]
if we pull the last part D, the first part A will not
be moved in any way differently from what would be the
case if one of the intervening parts B or C were
pulled, and the last part D were to remain unmoved.
And in the same way, when I feel pain in my foot. my
knowledge of physics teaches me that this sensation is
communicated by means of nerves dispersed through the
foot, which, being extended like cords from there to
the brain. when they are contracted in the foot. at the
same time contract the inmost portions of the brain
which is their extremity and place of origin, and then
excite a certain movement which nature has established
in order to cause the mind to be affected by a
sensation of pain represented as existing in the foot.
But because these nerves must pass through the tibia.
the thigh, the loins, the back and the neck, in order
to reach from the leg to the brain. it may happen that
although their extremities which are in the foot are
not affected, but only certain ones of their
intervening parts [which pass by the loins or the
neck], this action will excite the same movement in the
brain that might have been excited there by a hurt
received in the foot, in consequence of which the mind
will necessarily feel in the foot the same pain as if
it had received a hurt. And the same holds good of all
the other perceptions of our senses.

I notice finally that since each of the movements
which are in the portion of the brain by which the mind
is immediately affected brings about one particular
sensation only. we cannot under the circumstances
imagine anything more likely than that this movement,
amongst all the sensations which it is capable of
impressing on it, causes mind to be affected by that
one which is best fitted and most generally useful for
the conservation of the human body when it is in
health. But experience makes us aware that all the
feelings with which nature inspires us are such as I
have just spoken of; and there is therefore nothing in
them which does not give testimony to the power and
goodness of the God [who has produced them]. Thus, for
example, when the nerves which are in the feet are
violently or more than usually moved, their movement.
passing through the medulla of the spine to the inmost
parts of the brain, gives a sign to the mind which
makes it feel somewhat, to wit, pain, as though in the
foot, by which the mind is excited to do its utmost to

remove the cause of the evil as dangerous and hurtful to the foot. It is true that God could have constituted the nature of man in such a way that this same movement in the brain would have conveyed something quite different to the mind; for example, it might have produced consciousness of itself either in so far as it is in the brain, or as it is in the foot, or as it is in some other place between the foot and the brain, or it might finally have produced consciousness of anything else whatsoever; but none of all this would have contributed so well to the conservation of the body. Similarly, when we desire to drink, a certain dryness of the throat is produced which moves its nerves, and by their means the internal portions of the brain; and this movement causes in the mind the sensation of thirst, because in this case there is nothing more useful to us than to become aware that we have need to drink for the conservation of our health; and the same holds good in other instances.

From this it is quite clear that, notwithstanding the supreme goodness of God, the nature of man, inasmuch as it is composed of mind and body, cannot be otherwise than sometimes a source of deception. For if there is any cause which excites, not in the foot but in some part of the nerves which are extended between the foot and the brain, or even in the brain itself, the same movement which usually is produced when the foot is detrimentally affected, pain will be experienced as though it were in the foot, and the sense will thus naturally be deceived; for since the same movement in the brain is capable of causing but one sensation in the mind, and this sensation is much more frequently excited by a cause which hurts the foot than by another existing in some other quarter, it is reasonable that it should convey to the mind pain in the foot rather than in any other part of the body. And although the parchedness of the throat does not always proceed, as it usually does, from the fact that drinking is necessary for the health of the body, but sometimes comes from quite a different cause, as is the case with dropsical patients, it is yet much better that it should mislead on this occasion than if, on the other hand, it were always to deceive us when the body is in good health; and so on in similar cases.

And certainly this consideration is of great service to me, not only in enabling me to recognise all the

errors to which my nature is subject, but also in
enabling me to avoid them or to correct them more
easily. For knowing that all my senses more frequently
indicate to me truth than falsehood respecting the
things which concern that which is beneficial to the
body, and being able almost always to avail myself of
many of them in order to examine one particular thing,
and, besides that, being able to make use of my memory
in order to connect the present with the past, and of
my understanding which already has discovered all the
causes of my errors, I ought no longer to fear that
falsity may be found in matters every day presented to
me by my senses. And I ought to set aside all the
doubts of these past days as hyperbolical and
ridiculous, particularly that very common uncertainty
respecting sleep, which I could not distinguish from
the waking state; for at present I find a very notable
difference between the two, inasmuch as our memory can
never connect our dreams one with the other. or with
the whole course of our lives, as it unites events
which happen to us while we are awake. And, as a
matter of fact, if someone, while I was awake, quite
suddenly appeared to me and disappeared as fast as do
the images which I see in sleep, so that I could not
know from whence the form came nor whither it went, it
would not be without reason that I should deem it a
spectre or a phantom formed by my brain [and similar to
those which I form in sleep], rather than a real man.
But when I perceive things as to which I know
distinctly both the place from which they proceed, and
that in which they are. and the time at which they
appeared to me; and when, without any interruption. I
can connect the perceptions which I have of them with
the whole course of my life, I am perfectly assured
that these perceptions occur while I am waking and not
during sleep. And I ought in no wise to doubt the
truth of such matters, if, after having called up all
my senses, my memory. and my understanding, to examine
them. nothing is brought to evidence by any one of them
which is repugnant to what is set forth by the others.
For because God is in no wise a deceiver, it follows
that I am not deceived in this. But because the
exigencies of action often oblige us to make up our
minds before having leisure to examine matters
carefully. we must confess that the life of man is very
frequently subject to error in respect to individual
objects, and we must in the end acknowledge the
infirmity of our nature.

THE PASSIONS OF THE SOUL:

The interaction of mind (soul) and body.

Article XXX.

<u>That the soul is united to all the portions of the body conjointly</u>.

But in order to understand all these things more perfectly, we must know that the soul is really joined to the whole body, and that we cannot, properly speaking, say that it exists in any one of its parts to the exclusion of the others, because it is one and in some manner indivisible, owing to the disposition of its organs, which are so related to one another that when any one of them is removed, that renders the whole body defective; and because it is of a nature which has no relation to extension, nor dimensions, nor other properties of the matter of which the body is composed, but only to the whole conglomerate of its organs, as appears from the fact that we could not in any way conceive of the half or the third of a soul, nor of the space it occupies, and because it does not become smaller owing to the cutting off of some portion of the body, but separates itself from it entirely when the union of its assembled organs is dissolved.

Article XXXIV.

<u>How the soul and the body act on one another</u>.

Let us then conceive here that the soul has its principal seat in the little gland which exists in the middle of the brain, from whence it radiates forth through all the remainder of the body by means of the animal spirits, nerves, and even the blood, which, participating in the impressions of the spirits, can carry them by the arteries into all the members. And recollecting what has been said above about the machine of our body, i.e. that the little filaments of our nerves are so distributed in all its parts, that on the occasion of the diverse movements which are there

excited by sensible objects, they open in diverse ways
the pores of the brain, which causes the animal spirits
contained in these cavities to enter in diverse ways
into the muscles, by which means they can move the
members in all the different ways in which they are
capable of being moved; and also that all the other
causes which are capable of moving the spirits in
diverse ways suffice to conduct them into diverse
muscles; let us here add that the small gland which is
the main seat of the soul is so suspended between the
cavities which contain the spirits that it can be moved
by them in as many different ways as there are sensible
diversities in the object, but that it may also be
moved in diverse ways by the soul, whose nature is such
that it receives in itself as many diverse impressions,
that is to say, that it possesses as many diverse
perceptions as there are diverse movements in this
gland. Reciprocally, likewise, the machine of the body
is so formed that from the simple fact that this gland
is diversely moved by the soul, or by such other cause,
whatever it is, it thrusts the spirits which surround
it towards the pores of the brain, which conduct them
by the nerves into the muscles, by which means it
causes them to move the limbs.

17

BLAISE PASCAL

Born into an upper middle class family at Clermont, in Auvergne, Blaise Pascal (1623-1662), exceedingly precocious as a child, was educated entirely by his father at home. Pascal's achievements in both mathematics and science are well-documented and need not be recounted here. But these accomplishments have come to be overshadowed by the penetrating religious and philosophical views contained in his two most important philosophical works: <u>Pensées</u> and <u>De l'esprit géometrique</u>.

Convinced that the method of geometry was the most perfect method of acquiring knowledge known to mankind, Pascal, nevertheless, recognized that such a method still was dependent on first principles which cannot be demonstrated as true by the geometrical method. Like Descartes before him, Pascal insisted that man is a thinking being. However, unlike Descartes, Pascal argued that unaided reason is incapable of knowing the first principles of knowledge. As Pascal observes in the selection that follows, the nature of our existence hides from us the knowledge of first beginnings which are born of the Nothing, and the littleness of our being conceals from us the sight of the Infinite. In short, Pascal contends that first principles are known not by reason, but by instinct and revelation. Consequently, feeling and submission to God must be recognized as essential vehicles in man's quest for truth.

PENSÉES:

> Man - a Nothing in comparison with the Infinite,
> an All in comparison with the Nothing.

72

...Let man then contemplate the whole of nature in her full and grand majesty, and turn his vision from the low objects which surround him. Let him gaze on that brilliant light, set like an eternal lamp to illumine the universe; let the earth appear to him a point in comparison with the vast circle described by the sun; and let him wonder at the fact that this vast circle is itself but a very fine point in comparison with that described by the stars in their revolution round the firmament. But if our view be arrested there, let our imagination pass beyond; it will sooner exhaust the power of conception than nature that of supplying material for conception. The whole visible world is only an imperceptible atom in the ample bosom of nature. No idea approaches it. We may enlarge our conceptions beyond all imaginable space; we only produce atoms in comparison with the reality of things. It is an infinite sphere, the centre of which is everywhere, the circumference nowhere. In short it is the greatest sensible mark of the almighty power of God, that imagination loses itself in that thought.

Returning to himself, let man consider what he is in comparison with all existence; let him regard himself as lost in this remote corner of nature; and from the little cell in which he finds himself lodged, I mean the universe, let him estimate at their true value the earth, kingdoms, cities, and himself. What is a man in the Infinite?

But to show him another prodigy equally astonishing, let him examine the most delicate things he knows. Let a mite be given him, with its minute body and parts incomparably more minute, limbs with their joints, veins in the limbs, blood in the veins, humours in the blood, drops in the humours, vapours in the drops. Dividing these last things again, let him exhaust his powers of conception, and let the last object at which

he can arrive be now that of our discourse. Perhaps he
will think that here is the smallest point in nature.
I will let him see therein a new abyss. I will paint
for him not only the visible universe, but all that he
can conceive of nature's immensity in the womb of this
abridged atom. Let him see therein an infinity of
universes, each of which has its firmament, its
planets, its earth, in the same proportion as in the
visible world; in each earth animals, and in the last
mites, in which he will find again all that the first
had, finding still in these others the same thing
without end and without cessation.   Let him lose
himself in wonders as amazing in their littleness as
the others in their vastness.   For who will not be
astounded at the fact that our body, which a little
while ago was imperceptible in the universe, itself
imperceptible in the bosom of the whole, is now a
colossus, a world, or rather a whole, in respect of the
nothingness which we cannot reach?   He who regards
himself in this light will be afraid of himself, and
observing himself sustained in the body given him by
nature between those two abysses of the Infinite and
Nothing, will tremble at the sight of these marvels;
and I think that, as his curiosity changes into
admiration, he will be more disposed to contemplate
them in silence than to examine them with presumption.

   For in fact what is man in nature?   A Nothing in
comparison with the Infinite, an All in comparison with
the Nothing, a mean between nothing and everything.
Since he is infinitely removed from comprehending the
extremes, the end of things and their beginning are
hopelessly hidden from him in an impenetrable secret;
he is equally incapable of seeing the Nothing from
which he was made, and the Infinite in which he is
swallowed up.

   What will he do then, but perceive the appearance of
the middle of things, in an eternal despair of knowing
either their beginning or their end.   All things
proceed from the Nothing, and are borne towards the
Infinite. Who will follow these marvellous processes?
The Author of these wonders understands them. None
other can do so.

   Through failure to contemplate these Infinites, men
have rashly rushed into the examination of nature, as

though they bore some proportion to her. It is strange that they have wished to understand the beginnings of things, and thence to arrive at the knowledge of the whole, with a presumption as infinite as their object. For surely this design cannot be formed with presumption or without a capacity infinite like nature.

If we are well informed, we understand that, as nature has graven her image and that of her Author on all things, they almost all partake of her double infinity. Thus we see that all the sciences are infinite in the extent of their researches. For who doubts that geometry, for instance, has an infinite infinity of problems to solve? They are also infinite in the multitude and fineness of their premises; for it is clear that those which are put forward as ultimate are not self-supporting, but are based on others which, again having others for their support, do not permit of finality. But we represent some as ultimate for reason, in the same way as in regard to material objects we call that an indivisible point beyond which our senses can no longer perceive anything, although by its nature it is infinitely divisible.

Of these two Infinites of science, that of greatness is the most palpable, and hence a few persons have pretended to know all things. "I will speak of the whole," said Democritus.

But the infinitely little is the least obvious. Philosophers have much oftener claimed to have reached it, and it is here they have all stumbled. This has given rise to such common titles as <u>First Principles</u>, <u>Principles of Philosophy</u>, and the like, as ostentatious in fact, though not in appearance, as that one which blinds us, <u>De omni scibili</u>.

We naturally believe ourselves far more capable of reaching the centre of things than of embracing their circumference. The visible extent of the world visibly exceeds us; but as we exceed little things, we think ourselves more capable of knowing them. And yet we need no less capacity for attaining the Nothing than the All. Infinite capacity is required for both, and it seems to me that whoever shall have understood the ultimate principles of being might also attain to the knowledge of the Infinite. The one depends on the other, and one leads to the other. These extremes meet and reunite by force of distance, and find each other in God, and in God alone.

Let us then take our compass; we are something, and we are not everything. The nature of our existence hides from us the knowledge of first beginnings which are born of the Nothing; and the littleness of our being conceals from us the sight of the Infinite.

Our intellect holds the same position in the world of thought as our body occupies in the expanse of nature.

Limited as we are in every way, this state which holds the mean between two extremes is present in all our impotence. Our senses perceive no extreme. Too much sound deafens us; too much light dazzles us; too great distance or proximity hinders our view. Too great length and too great brevity of discourse tend to obscurity; too much truth is paralysing (I know some who cannot understand that to take four from nothing leaves nothing). First principles are too self-evident for us; too much pleasure disagrees with us. Too many concords are annoying in music; too many benefits irritate us; we wish to have the wherewithal to over-pay our debts. _Beneficia eo usque laeta sunt dum videntur exsolvi posse; ubi multum antevenere, pro gratia odium redditur._ We feel neither extreme heat nor extreme cold. Excessive qualities are prejudicial to us and not perceptible by the senses; we do not feel but suffer them. Extreme youth and extreme age hinder the mind, as also too much and too little education. In short, extremes are for us as though they were not, and we are not within their notice. They escape us, or we them.

This is our true state; this is what makes us incapable of certain knowledge and of absolute ignorance. We sail within a vast sphere, ever drifting in uncertainty, driven from end to end. When we think to attach ourselves to any point and to fasten to it, it wavers and leaves us; and if we follow it, it eludes our grasp, slips past us, and vanishes for ever. Nothing stays for us. This is our natural condition, and yet most contrary to our inclination; we burn with desire to find solid ground and an ultimate sure foundation whereon to build a tower reaching to the Infinite. But our whole groundwork cracks, and the earth opens to abysses.

Let us therefore not look for certainty and stability. Our reason is always deceived by fickle shadows; nothing can fix the finite between the two Infinites, which both enclose and fly from it.

If this be well understood, I think that we shall remain at rest, each in the state wherein nature has placed him. As this sphere which has fallen to us as our lot is always distant from either extreme, what matters it that man should have a little more knowledge of the universe? If he has it, he but gets a little higher. Is he not always infinitely removed from the end, and is not the duration of our life equally removed from eternity, even if it lasts ten years longer?

In comparison with these Infinites all finites are equal, and I see no reason for fixing our imagination on one more than on another. The only comparison which we make of ourselves to the finite is painful to us.

If man made himself the first object of study, he would see how incapable he is of going further. How can a part know the whole? But he may perhaps aspire to know at least the parts to which he bears some proportion. But the parts of the world are all so related and linked to one another, that I believe it impossible to know one without the other and without the whole.

Man, for instance, is related to all he knows. He needs a place wherein to abide, time through which to live, motion in order to live, elements to compose him, warmth and food to nourish him, air to breathe. He sees light; he feels bodies; in short, he is in a dependent alliance with everything. To know man, then, it is necessary to know how it happens that he needs air to live, and, to know the air, we must know how it is thus related to the life of man, etc. Flame cannot exist without air; therefore to understand the one, we must understand the other.

Since everything then is cause and effect, dependent and supporting, mediate and immediate, and all is held together by a natural though imperceptible chain, which binds together things most distant and most different, I hold it equally impossible to know the parts without knowing the whole, and to know the whole without knowing the parts in detail.

(The eternity of things in itself or in God must also astonish our brief duration. The fixed and constant immobility of nature, in comparison with the continual change which goes on within us, must have the same effect.)

And what completes our incapability of knowing things, is the fact that they are simple, and that we are composed of two opposite natures, different in kind, soul and body. For it is impossible that our rational part should be other than spiritual; and if any one maintain that we are simply corporeal, this would far more exclude us from the knowledge of things, there being nothing so inconceivable as to say that matter knows itself. It is impossible to imagine how it should know itself.

So if we are simply material, we can know nothing at all; and if we are composed of mind and matter, we cannot know perfectly things which are simple, whether spiritual or corporeal. Hence it comes that almost all philosophers have confused ideas of things, and speak of material things in spiritual terms, and of spiritual things in material terms. For they say boldly that bodies have a tendency to fall, that they seek after their centre, that they fly from destruction, that they fear the void, that they have inclinations, sympathies, antipathies, all of which attributes pertain only to mind. And in speaking of minds, they consider them as in a place, and attribute to them movement from one place to another; and these are qualities which belong only to bodies.

Instead of receiving the ideas of these things in their purity, we colour them with our own qualities, and stamp with our composite being all the simple things which we contemplate.

Who would not think, seeing us compose all things of
mind and body, but that this mixture would be quite
intelligible to us? Yet it is the very thing we least
understand. Man is to himself the most wonderful
object in nature; for he cannot conceive what the body
is, still less what the mind is, and least of all how a
body should be united to a mind. This is the
consummation of his difficulties, and yet it is his
very being....

146

Man is obviously made to think. It is his whole
dignity and his whole merit; and his whole duty is to
think as he ought. Now, the order of thought is to
begin with self, and with its Author and its end.

Now, of what does the world think? Never of this,
but of dancing, playing the lute, singing, making
verses, running at the ring, etc., fighting, making
oneself king, without thinking what it is to be a king
and what to be a man.

147

We do not content ourselves with the life we have in
ourselves and in our own being; we desire to live an
imaginary life in the mind of others, and for this
purpose we endeavour to shine. We labour unceasingly
to adorn and preserve this imaginary existence, and
neglect the real. And if we possess calmness, or
generosity, or truthfulness, we are eager to make it
known, so as to attach these virtues to that imaginary
existence. We would rather separate them from
ourselves to join them to it; and we would willingly be
cowards in order to acquire the reputation of being
brave. A great proof of the nothingness of our being,
not to be satisfied with the one without the other, and
to renounce the one for the other! For he would be
infamous who would not die to preserve his honour.

172

DAVID HUME

Following the lead of John Locke, David Hume (1711-1776) adopted the principle that all ideas arise ultimately from experience. Using the word "perceptions" to cover the mind's contents in general, he divides perceptions into impressions and ideas. Impressions, for Hume, are the immediate data of experience, for example, sensations. He describes ideas as the copies or faint images of impressions in thinking and reasoning. Unlike Locke, who in Hume's estimation still retained a metaphysics of substance inherited from Rene Descartes, Hume endeavored to develop a consistent empiricist philosophy.

Born at Edinburgh, Hume early on in his life decided against becoming a lawyer despite the wishes of his family. To quote Hume, he felt "an insurmountable aversion to everything but the pursuits of philosophy and general learning." As a philosopher and a man of letters, his career began inauspiciously. His first publication, _A Treatise of Human Nature_, to use his own words, "fell dead-born from the press." Despite this troubling set-back, he published _Essays, Moral and Political_ in 1741, a work which was very well received by the public. This successful effort, consequently stimulated him to revise the _Treatise_ and, in 1748, published it anew under the title _Philosophical Essays Concerning Human Understanding_, and when a second edition appeared in 1751, the book had still a new title, namely, the now famous _An Enquiry Concerning Human Understanding_. In that same year he published _An Enquiry Concerning the Principles of Morals_ and, one year later, he authored still another book - _Political Discourses_ - which earned for him a considerable reputation. After writing a comprehensive history of England, and after spending a few years in France as secretary to the British Ambassador to France and another two years in London as Under-secretary of State, he returned to Edinburgh where he died in 1776.

     In the selection that follows, David Hume takes issue
with those philosophers "who imagine we are every
moment internally conscious of what we call our SELF;
that we feel its existence and its continuance in
existence; and are certain, beyond the evidence of
demonstration, both of its perfect identity and
simplicity." Hume contends that such a view of the
self is contrary to our "experience". We have no such
idea of the self. Rather, he maintains that the self
is "nothing but a bundle or collection of different
perceptions." The mind is "a kind of theatre, where
several perceptions successively make their
appearance,..."

A TREATISE OF HUMAN NATURE:

The self as nothing but a bundle of perceptions.

There are some philosophers, who imagine we are every
moment intimately conscious of what we call our SELF;
that we feel its existence and its continuance in
existence; and are certain, beyond the evidence of a
demonstration, both of its perfect identity and
simplicity. The strongest sensation, the most violent
passion, say they, instead of distracting us from this
view, only fix it the more intensely, and make us
consider their influence on _self_ either by their pain
or pleasure. To attempt a farther proof of this were
to weaken its evidence; since no proof can be deriv'd
from any fact, of which we are so intimately conscious;
nor is there any thing, of which we can be certain, if
we doubt of this.

Unluckily all these positive assertions are contrary
to that very experience, which is pleaded for them, nor
have we any idea of _self_, after the manner it is here
explain'd. For from what impression cou'd this idea be
deriv'd? This question 'tis impossible to answer
without a manifest contradiction and absurdity; and yet
'tis a question, which must necessarily be answer'd, if
we wou'd have the idea of self pass for clear and
intelligible. It must be some one impression, that
gives rise to every real idea. But self or person is
not any one impression, but that to which our several
impressions and ideas are suppos'd to have a reference.
If any impression gives rise to the idea of self, that
impression must continue invariably the same, thro' the
whole course of our lives; since self is suppos'd to
exist after that manner. But there is no impression
constant and invariable. Pain and pleasure, grief and
joy, passions and sensations succeed each other, and
never all exist at the same time. It cannot,
therefore, be from any of these impressions, or from
any other, that the idea of self is deriv'd; and
consequently there is no such idea.

But farther, what must become of all our particular
perceptions upon this hypothesis? All these are
different, and distinguishable, and separable from each
other, and may be separately consider'd, and may exist

separately, and have no need of any thing to support
their existence. After what manner, therefore, do they
belong to self; and how are they connected with it?
For my part, when I enter most intimately into what I
call _myself_, I always stumble on some particular
perception or other, of heat or cold, light or shade,
love or hatred, pain or pleasure. I never can catch
myself at any time without a perception, and never can
observe any 'thing but the perception. When my
perceptions are remov'd for any time, as by sound
sleep; so long am I insensible of _myself_, and may truly
be said not to exist. And were all my perceptions
remov'd by death, and cou'd I neither think, nor feel,
nor see, nor love, nor hate after the dissolution of my
body, I shou'd be entirely annihilated, nor do I
conceive what is farther requisite to make me a perfect
non-entity. If any one, upon serious and unprejudic'd
reflection, thinks he has a different notion of
himself, I must confess I can reason no longer with
him. All I can allow him is, that he may be in the
right as well as I, and that we are essentially
different in this particular. He may, perhaps,
perceive something simple and continu'd, which he calls
himself; tho' I am certain there is no such principle
in me.

But setting aside some metaphysicians of this kind, I
may venture to affirm of the rest of mankind, that they
are nothing but a bundle or collection of different
perceptions, which succeed each other with an
inconceivable rapidity, and are in a perpetual flux and
movement. Our eyes cannot turn in their sockets
without varying our perceptions. Our thought is still
more variable than our sight; and all our other senses
and faculties contribute to this change; nor is there
any single power of the soul, which remains unalterably
the same, perhaps for one moment. The mind is a kind
of theatre, where several perceptions successively make
their appearance; pass, re-pass, glide away, and mingle
in an infinite variety of postures and situations.
There is properly no _simplicity_ in it at one time, nor
identity in different; whatever natural propension we
may have to imagine that simplicity and identity. The
comparison of the theatre must not mislead us. They
are the successive perceptions only, that constitute
the mind; nor have we the most distant notion of the
place, where these scenes are represented, or of the
materials, of which it is compos'd.

What then gives us so great a propension to ascribe an identity to these successive perceptions, and to suppose ourselves possest of an invariable and uninterrupted existence thro' the whole course of our lives? In order to answer this question, we must distinguish betwixt personal identity, as it regards our thought or imagination, and as it regards our passions or the concern we take in ourselves. The first is our present subject; and to explain it perfectly we must take the matter pretty deep, and account for that identity, which we attribute to plants and animals; there being a great analogy betwixt it, and the identity of a self or person.

We have a distinct idea of an object, that remains invariable and uninterrupted thro' a suppos'd variation of time; and this idea we call that of _identity_ or _sameness_. We have also a distinct idea of several different objects existing in succession, and connected together by a close relation; and this to an accurate view affords as perfect a notion of _diversity_, as if there was no manner of relation among the objects. But tho' these two ideas of identity, and a succession of related objects be in themselves perfectly distinct, and even contrary, yet 'tis certain, that in our common way of thinking they are generally confounded with each other. That action of the imagination, by which we consider the uninterrupted and invariable object, and that by which we reflect on the succession of related objects, are almost the same to the feeling, nor is there much more effort of thought requir'd in the latter case than in the former. The relation facilitates the transition of the mind from one object to another, and renders its passage as smooth as if it contemplated one continu'd object. This resemblance is the cause of the confusion and mistake, and makes us substitute the notion of identity, instead of that of related objects. However at one instant we may consider the related succession as variable or interrupted, we are sure the next to ascribe to it a perfect identity, and regard it as invariable and uninterrupted. Our propensity to this mistake is so great from the resemblance above-mention'd, that we fall into it before we are aware; and tho' we incessantly correct ourselves by reflection, and return to a more accurate method of thinking, yet we cannot long sustain our philosophy, or take off this biass from the imagination. Our last resource is to yield to it, and boldly assert that these different related objects are in effect the same, however interrupted and variable. In order to justify to ourselves this absurdity, we often feign some new and unintelligible principle, that connects the objects together, and prevents their interruption or variation. Thus we feign the continu'd existence of the perceptions of our senses, to remove the interruption; and run into the notion of a <u>soul</u>, and <u>self</u>, and <u>substance</u>, to disguise the variation. But we may farther observe, that where we do not give rise to such a fiction, our propension to confound identity with relation is so great, that we are apt to imagine something unknown and mysterious, connecting the parts, beside their relation; and this I take to be the case with regard to the identity we ascribe to plants and vegetables. And even when this does not take place, we still feel a propensity to confound these ideas, tho' we are not able fully to satisfy ourselves in that particular, nor find any thing invariable and uninterrupted to justify our notion of identity.

Thus the controversy concerning identity is not merely a dispute of words. For when we attribute identity, in an improper sense, to variable or interrupted objects, our mistake is not confin'd to the expression, but is commonly attended with a fiction, either of something invariable and uninterrupted, or of something mysterious and inexplicable, or at least with a propensity to such fictions. What will suffice to prove this hypothesis to the satisfaction of every fair enquirer, is to shew from daily experience and observation, that the objects, which are variable or interrupted, and yet are suppos'd to continue the same, are such only as consist of a succession of parts, connected together by resemblance, contiguity, or causation. For as such a succession answers evidently to our notion of diversity, it can only be by mistake we ascribe to it an identity; and as the relation of parts, which leads us into this mistake, is really nothing but a quality, which produces an association of ideas, and an easy transition of the imagination from one to another, it can only be from the resemblance, which this act of the mind bears to that, by which we contemplate one continu'd object, that the error arises. Our chief business, then, must be to prove, that all objects, to which we ascribe identity, without observing their invariableness and uninterruptedness, are such as consist of a succession of related objects.

In order to this, suppose any mass of matter, of which the parts are contiguous and connected, to be plac'd before us; 'tis plain we must attribute a perfect identity to this mass, provided all the parts continue uninterruptedly and invariably the same, whatever motion or change of place we may observe either in the whole or in any of the parts. But supposing some very <u>small</u> or <u>inconsiderable</u> part to be added to the mass, or substracted from it; tho' this absolutely destroys the identity of the whole, strictly speaking; yet as we seldom think so accurately, we scruple not to pronounce a mass of matter the same, where we find so trivial an alteration. The passage of the thought from the object before the change to the object after it, is so smooth and easy, that we scarce perceive the transition, and are apt to imagine, that 'tis nothing but a continu'd survey of the same object.

There is a very remarkable circumstance, that attends this experiment; which is, that tho' the change of any considerable part in a mass of matter destroys the identity of the whole, yet we must measure the greatness of the part, not absolutely, but by its <u>proportion</u> to the whole. The addition or diminution of a mountain wou'd not be sufficient to produce a diversity in a planet; tho' the change of a very few inches wou'd be able to destroy the identity of some bodies. 'Twill be impossible to account for this, but by reflecting that objects operate upon the mind, and break or interrupt the continuity of its actions not according to their real greatness, but according to their proportions to each other: And therefore, since this interruption makes an object cease to appear the same, it must be the uninterrupted progress of the thought, which constitutes the imperfect identity.

This may be confirm'd by another phaenomenon. A change in any considerable part of a body destroys its identity; but 'tis remarkable, that where the change is produc'd <u>gradually</u> and <u>insensibly</u> we are less apt to ascribe to it the same effect. The reason can plainly be no other, than that the mind, in following the successive changes of the body, feels an easy passage from the surveying its condition in one moment to the viewing of it in another, and at no particular time perceives any interruption in its actions. From which continu'd perception, it ascribes a continu'd existence and identity to the object.

179

But whatever precaution we may use in introducing the
changes gradually, and making them proportionable to
the whole, 'tis certain that where the changes are at
last observ'd to become considerable, we make a scruple
of ascribing identity to such different objects. There
is, however, another artifice, by which we may induce
the imagination to advance a step farther; and that is,
by producing a reference of the parts to each other,
and a combination to some <u>common end</u> or purpose. A
ship, of which a considerable part has been chang'd by
frequent reparations, is still consider'd as the same;
nor does the difference of the materials hinder us from
ascribing an identity to it. The common end, in which
the parts conspire, is the same under all their
variations, and affords an easy transition of the
imagination from one situation of the body to another.

But this is still more remarkable, when we add a
<u>sympathy</u> of parts to their <u>common end</u>, and suppose that
they bear to each other, the reciprocal relation of
cause and effect in all their actions and operations.
This is the case with all animals and vegetables; where
not only the several parts have a reference to some
general purpose, but also a mutual dependance on, and
connexion with each other. The effect of so strong a
relation is, that tho' every one must allow, that in a
very few years both vegetables and animals endure a
<u>total</u> change, yet we still attribute identity to them,
while their form, size, and substance are entirely
alter'd. An oak, that grows from a small plant to a
large tree, is still the same oak; tho' there be not
one particle of matter, or figure of its parts the
same. An infant becomes a man, and is sometimes fat,
sometimes lean, without any change in his identity.

We may also consider the two following phaenomena,
which are remarkable in their kind. The first is, that
tho' we commonly be able to distinguish pretty exactly
betwixt numerical and specific identity, yet it
sometimes happens, that we confound them, and in our
thinking and reasoning employ the one for the other.
Thus a man, who hears a noise, that is frequently
interrupted and renew'd, says, it is still the same
noise; tho' 'tis evident the sounds have only a
specific identity or resemblance, and there is nothing
numerically the same, but the cause, which produc'd
them. In like manner it may be said without breach of
the propriety of language, that such a church, which

was formerly of brick, fell to ruin, and that the parish rebuilt the same church of free-stone, and according to modern architecture. Here neither the form nor materials are the same, nor is there any thing common to the two objects, but their relation to the inhabitants of the parish; and yet this alone is sufficient to make us denominate them the same. But we must observe, that in these cases the first object is in a manner annihilated before the second comes into existence; by which means, we are never presented in any one point of time with the idea of difference and multiplicity; and for that reason are less scrupulous in calling them the same.

Secondly, We may remark, that tho' in a succession of related objects, it be in a manner requisite, that the change of parts be not sudden nor entire, in order to preserve the identity, yet where the objects are in their nature changeable and inconstant, we admit of a more sudden transition, than wou'd otherwise be consistent with that relation. Thus as the nature of a river consists in the motion and change of parts; tho' in less than four and twenty hours these be totally alter'd; this hinders not the river from continuing the same during several ages. What is natural and essential to any thing is, in a manner, expected; and what is expected makes less impression, and appears of less moment, than what is unusual and extraordinary. A considerable change of the former kind seems really less to the imagination, than the most trivial alteration of the latter; and by breaking less the continuity of the thought, has less influence in destroying the identity.

We now proceed to explain the nature of _personal identity_, which has become so great a question in philosophy, especially of late years in _England_, where all the abstruser sciences are study'd with a peculiar ardour and application. And here 'tis evident, the same method of reasoning must be continu'd, which has so successfully explain'd the identity of plants, and animals, and ships, and houses, and of all the compounded and changeable productions either of art or nature. The identity, which we ascribe to the mind of man, is only a fictitious one, and of a like kind with that which we ascribe to vegetables and animal bodies. It cannot, therefore, have a different origin, but must proceed from a like operation of the imagination upon like objects.

181

But lest this argument shou'd not convince the reader; tho' in my opinion perfectly decisive; let him weigh the following reasoning, which is still closer and more immediate. 'Tis evident, that the identity, which we attribute to the human mind, however perfect we may imagine it to be, is not able to run the several different perceptions into one, and make them lose their characters of distinction and difference, which are essential to them. 'Tis still true, that every distinct perception, which enters into the composition of the mind, is a distinct existence, and is different, and distinguishable, and separable from every other perception, either contemporary or successive. But, as, notwithstanding this distinction and separability, we suppose the whole train of perceptions to be united by identity, a question naturally arises concerning this relation of identity; whether it be something that really binds our several perceptions together, or only associates their ideas in the imagination. That is, in other words, whether in pronouncing concerning the identity of a person, we observe some real bond among his perceptions, or only feel one among the ideas we form of them. This question we might easily decide, if we wou'd recollect what has been already prov'd at large, that the understanding never observes any real connexion among objects, and that even the union of cause and effect, when strictly examin'd, resolves itself into a customary association of ideas. For from thence it evidently follows, that identity is nothing really belonging to these different perceptions, and uniting them together; but is merely a quality, which we attribute to them, because of the union of their ideas in the imagination, when we reflect upon them. Now the only qualities, which can give ideas an union in the imagination, are these three relations above-mention'd. These are the uniting principles in the ideal world, and without them every distinct object is separable by the mind, and may be separately consider'd, and appears not to have any more connexion with any other object, than if disjoin'd by the greatest difference and remoteness. 'Tis, therefore, on some of these three relations of resemblance, contiguity and causation, that identity depends; and as the very essence of these relations consists in their producing an easy transition of ideas; it follows, that our notions of personal identity, proceed entirely from the smooth and uninterrupted progress of the thought along a train of connected ideas, according to the principles above-explain'd.

The only question, therefore, which remains, is, by what relations this uninterrupted progress of our thought is produc'd, when we consider the successive existence of a mind or thinking person. And here 'tis evident we must confine ourselves to resemblance and causation, and must drop contiguity, which has little or no influence in the present case.

To begin with <u>resemblance</u>; suppose we cou'd see clearly into the breast of another, and observe that succession of perceptions, which constitutes his mind or thinking principle, and suppose that he always preserves the memory of a considerable part of past perceptions; 'tis evident that nothing cou'd more contribute to the bestowing a relation on this succession amidst all its variations. For what is the memory but a faculty, by which we raise up the images of past perceptions? And as an image necessarily resembles its object, must not the frequent placing of these resembling perceptions in the chain of thought, convey the imagination more easily from one link to another, and make the whole seem like the continuance of one object? In this particular, then, the memory not only discovers the identity, but also contributes to its production, by producing the relation of resemblance among the perceptions. The case is the same whether we consider ourselves or others.

As to <u>causation</u>; we may observe, that the true idea of the human mind, is to consider it as a system of different perceptions or different existences, which are link'd together by the relation of cause and effect, and mutually produce, destroy, influence, and modify each other. Our impressions give rise to their correspondent ideas; and these ideas in their turn produce other impressions. One thought chaces another, and draws after it a third, by which it is expell'd in its turn. In this respect, I cannot compare the soul more properly to any thing than to a republic or commonwealth, in which the several members are united by the reciprocal ties of government and subordination, and give rise to other persons, who propagate the same republic in the incessant changes of its parts. And as the same individual republic may not only change its members, but also its laws and constitutions; in like manner the same person may vary his character and disposition, as well as his impressions and ideas, without losing his identity. Whatever changes he endures, his several parts are still connected by the relation of causation. And in this view our identity with regard to the passions serves to corroborate that with regard to the imagination, by the making our distant perceptions influence each other, and by giving us a present concern for our past or future pains or pleasures.

As a memory alone acquaints us with the continuance and extent of this succession of perceptions, 'tis to be considered, upon that account chiefly, as the source of personal identity. Had we no memory, we never shou'd have any notion of causation, nor consequently of that chain of causes and effects, which constitute our self or person. But having once acquir'd this notion of causation from the memory, we can extend the same chain of causes, and consequently the identity of our persons beyond our memory, and can comprehend times, and circumstances, and actions, which we have entirely forgot, but suppose in general to have existed. For how few of our past actions are there, of which we have any memory? Who can tell me, for instance, what were his thoughts and actions on the 1st of <u>January</u> 1715, the 11th of <u>March</u> 1719, and the 3rd of <u>August</u> 1733? Or will he affirm, because he has entirely forgot the incidents of these days, that the present self is not the same person with the self of that time; and by that means overturn all the most establish'd notions of personal identity? In this view, therefore memory does not so much <u>produce</u> as <u>discover</u> personal identity, by showing us the relation of cause and effect among our different perceptions. 'Twill be incumbent on those, who affirm that memory produces entirely our personal identity, to give a reason why we can thus extend our identity beyond our memory.

The whole of this doctrine leads us to a conclusion, which is of great importance in the present affair, <u>viz</u>. that all the nice and subtile questions concerning personal identity can never possibly be decided, and are to be regarded rather as grammatical than as philosophical difficulties. Identity depends on the relations of ideas; and these relations produce identity, by means of that easy transition they occasion. But as the relations, and the easiness of the transition may diminish by insensible degrees, we have no just standard, by which we can decide any dispute concerning the time, when they acquire or lose a title to the name of identity. All the disputes concerning the identity of connected objects are merely verbal, except so far as the relation of parts gives rise to some fiction or imaginary principle of union, as we have already observ'd.

What I have said concerning the first origin and uncertainty of our notion of identity, as apply'd to the human mind, may be extended with little or no variation to that of <u>simplicity</u> bound together by a close relation, operates upon the imagination after much the same manner as one perfectly simple and indivisible, and requires not a much greater stretch of thought in order to its conception. From this similarity of operation we attribute a simplicity to it, and feign a principle of union as the support of this simplicity, and the center of all the different parts and qualities of the object.

Thus we have finish'd our examination of the several systems of philosophy, both of the intellectual and natural world; and in our miscellaneous way of reasoning have been led into several topics; which will either illustrate and confirm some preceding part of this discourse, or prepare the way for our following opinions. 'Tis now time to return to a more close examination of our subject, and to proceed in the accurate anatomy of human nature, having fully explain'd the nature of our judgment and understanding.

ALEXANDER POPE

Despite his Catholicism in a Protestant England, and his ill health, Alexander Pope (1688-1744), nevertheless, achieved great literary success. In fact, he may be seen as the true representative, with Leibniz and Locke, of what is known as the Age of Enlightenment. Rooting his views on the scientific vision of his day, Pope sees man and the world as rational structures created by God. Although rational and hierarchical, the world is not totally intelligible. Man, according to Pope, can find his place in the chain of being only if he remains within his own sphere, avoiding pride.

An Essay on Man, written in 1734, is a poem in four epistles (only the first epistle is reprinted below) addressed to Henry St. John and Lord Bolingbroke, both of whom were deists who believed in matter as the principle of motion and held that God is nothing but Reason or universal Mind. Thus Pope's essay fluctuates, in language and in structure, between Nature's Reason or the ordering principle of this whole universe, and human reason as the source of man's essential nature. And, while it is true that Pope admits God as a creator of Nature, he nevertheless subjects God, as well as nature and society, to the laws of nature which are the laws of the physical world, or science. Voicing the philosophy of a deistic world where natural religion, as opposed to revealed religion, rules, Pope gives us an image of man based on reason and science.

AN ESSAY ON MAN:

Man, God, and Nature subject to the laws of nature.

Epistle I

Awake, my St. John! leave all meaner things
To low ambition, and the pride of Kings.
Let us (since Life can little more supply
Than just to look about us and to die)
Expatiate free o'er all this scene of Man;
A mighty maze! but not without a plan;
A Wild, where weeds and flow'rs promiscuous shoot,
Or Garden, tempting with forbidden fruit.
Together let us beat this ample field,
Try what the open, what the covert yield;
The latent tracts, the giddy heights explore
Of all who blindly creep, or sightless soar;
Eye Nature's walks, shoot Folly as it flies,
And catch the Manners living as they rise;
Laugh where we must, be candid where we can;
But vindicate the ways of God to Man.

    I. Say first, of God above, or Man below,
What can we reason, but from what we know?
Of Man what see we, but his station here,
From which to reason, or to which refer?
Thro' worlds unnumber'd tho' the God be known,
'Tis ours to trace him only in our own.
He, who thro' vast immensity can pierce,
See worlds on worlds compose one universe,
Observe how system into system runs,
What other planets circle other suns,
What vary'd being peoples ev'ry star,
May tell why Heav'n has made us as we are.
But of this frame the bearings, and the ties,
The strong connections, nice dependencies,
Gradations just, has thy pervading soul
Look'd thro'? or can a part contain the whole?

    Is the great chain, that draws all to agree,
And drawn supports, upheld by God, or thee?

    II. Presumptuous Man! the reason wouldst
thou find,
Why form'd so weak, so little, and so blind!

First, if thou canst, the harder reason guess,
Why form'd no weaker, blinder, and no less!
Ask of thy mother earth, why oaks are made
Taller or stronger than the weeds they shade?
Or ask of yonder argent fields above,
Why JOVE's Satellites are less than JOVE?

    Of Systems possible, if 'tis confest
That Wisdom infinite must form the best,
Where all must full or not coherent be,
And all that rises, rise in due degree;
Then, in the scale of reas'ning life, 'tis plain
There must be, somewhere, such a rank as Man
And all the question (wrangle e'er so long)
Is only this, if God has plac'd him wrong?

    Respecting Man, whatever wrong we call,
May, must be right, as relative to all.
In human works, tho' labour'd on with pain,
A thousand movements scarce one purpose gain;
In God's, one single can its end produce;
Yet serves to second too some other use.
So Man, who here seems principal alone,
Perhaps acts second to some sphere unknown,
Touches some wheel, or verges to some goal;
'Tis but a part we see, and not a whole.

    When the proud steed shall know why Man
restrains
His fiery course, or drives him o'er the plains;
When the dull Ox, why now he breaks the clod,
Is now a victim, and now Egypt's God:
Then shall Man's pride and dulness comprehend
His actions', passions', being's, use and end;
Why doing, suff'ring, check'd, impell'd; and why
This hour a slave, the next a deity.

    Then say not Man's imperfect, Heav'n in fault;
Say rather. Man's as perfect as he ought;
His knowledge measur'd to his state and place,
His time a moment, and a point his space.
If to be perfect in a certain sphere,
What matter, soon or late, or here or there?
The blest today is as completely so,
As who began a thousand years ago.

    III.   Heav'n from all creatures hides the book
of Fate,
All but the page prescrib'd, their present state;

From brutes what men, from men what spirits know:
Or who could suffer Being here below?
The lamb thy riot dooms to bleed to-day,
Had he thy Reason, would he skip and play?
Pleas'd to the last, he crops the flow'ry food,
And licks the hand just rais'd to shed his blood.
Oh blindness to the future! kindly giv'n,
That each man fill the circle mark'd by Heav'n;
Who sees with equal eye, as God of all,
A hero perish, or a sparrow fall,
Atoms or systems into ruin hurl'd,
And now a bubble burst, and now a world.

    Hope humbly then; with trembling pinions soar;
Wait the great teacher Death, and God adore!
What future bliss, he gives not thee to know,
But gives that Hope to be thy blessing now.
Hope springs eternal in the human breast:
Man never Is, but always To be blest:
The soul, uneasy and confin'd from home,
Rests and expatiates in a life to come.

    Lo! the poor Indian, whose untutor'd mind
Sees God in clouds, or hears him in the wind;
His soul proud Science never taught to stray
Far as the solar walk, or milky way;
Yet simple Nature to his hope has giv'n,
Behind the cloud-topt hill, an humbler heav'n;
Some safer world in depth of woods embrac'd,
Some happier island in the watry waste,
Where slaves once more their native land behold,
No fiends torment, no Christians thirst for gold!
To be, contents his natural desire,
He asks no Angel's wing, no Seraph's fire;
But thinks, admitted to that equal sky,
His faithful dog shall bear him company.

    IV. Go, wiser thou! and in they scale of
sense
Weigh thy Opinion against Providence;
Call Imperfection what thou fancy'st such,
Say, here he gives too little, there too much;
Destroy all creatures for thy sport or gust,
Yet cry, If Man's unhappy, God's unjust;
If Man alone ingross not Heav'n's high care,
Alone made perfect here, immortal there:
Snatch from his hand the balance and the rod,
Re-judge his justice, be the God of God!

In Pride, in reas'ning Pride, our error lies;
All quit their sphere, and rush into the skies.
Pride still is aiming at the blest abodes,
Men would be Angels, Angels would be Gods.
Aspiring to be Gods, if Angels fell,
Aspiring to be Angels, Men rebel;
And who but wishes to invert the laws
Of ORDER, sins against th' Eternal Cause.

    V.   Ask for what end the heav'nly bodies
shine,
Earth for whose use? Pride answers, "'Tis for
mine:
"For me kind Nature waker her genial pow'r,
"Suckles each herb, and spreads out ev'ry flow'r;
"Annual for me, the grape, the rose renew
"The juice nectarious, and the balmy dew;
"For me, the mine a thousand treasures brings;
"For me, health gushes from a thousand springs;
"Seas roll to waft me, suns to light me rise;
"My foot-stool earth, my canopy the skies."

    But errs not Nature from this gracious end,
From burning suns when livid deaths descend,
When earthquakes swallow, or when tempests sweep
Towns to one grave, whole nations to the deep?
"No ('tis reply'd) the first Almighty Cause
"Acts not by partial, but by gen'ral laws;
"Th' exceptions few; some change since all began,
"And what created perfect?" --Why then Man?
If the great end be human Happiness,
Then Nature deviates; and can Man do less?
As much that end a constant course requires
Of show'rs and sun-shine, as of Man's desires;
As much eternal springs and cloudless skies,
As Men for ever temp'rate, calm, and wise.
If plagues or earthquakes break not Heav'n's
design,
Why then a Borgia, or a Catiline?
Who knows but he, whose hand the light'ning forms,
Who heaves old Ocean, and who wings the storms,
Pours fierce Ambition in a Caesar's mind,
Or turns young Ammon loose to scourge mankind?
From pride, from pride, our very reas'ning
springs;
Account for moral as for nat'ral things:
Why charge we Heav'n in those, in these acquit?
In both, to reason right is to submit.

Better for Us, perhaps, it might appear,
Where there all harmony, all virtue here;
That never air or ocean felt the wind;
That never passion discompos'd the mind:
But ALL subsists by elemental strife;
And Passions are the elements of Life.
The gen'ral ORDER, since the whole began,
Is kept in Nature, and is kept in Man.

    VI. What would this Man? Now upward will he
soar,
And little less than Angel, would be more;
Now looking downwards, just as griev'd appears
To want the strength of bulls, the fur of bears.
Made for his use all creatures if he call,
Say what their use, had he the pow'rs of all?
Nature to these, without profusion kind,
The proper organs, proper pow'rs assign'd;
Each seeming want compensated of course,
Here with degrees of swiftness, there of force;
All in exact proportion to the state;
Nothing to add, and nothing to abate.
Each beast, each insect, happy in its own;
Is Heav'n unkind to Man, and Man alone?
Shall he alone, whom rational we call,
Be pleas'd with nothing, if not bless'd with all?

    The bliss of Man (could Pride that blessing
find)
Is not to act or think beyond mankind;
No pow'rs of body or of soul to share,
But what his nature and his state can bear.
Why has not Man a microscopic eye?
For this plain reason, Man is not a Fly.
Say what the use, were finer optics giv'n,
T' inspect a mite, not comprehend the heav'n?
Or touch, if tremblingly alive all o'er,
To smart and agonize at ev'ry pore?
Or quick effluvia darting thro' the brain,
Die of a rose in aromatic pain?
If nature thunder'd in his op'ning ears,
And stunn'd him with the music of the spheres,
How would he wish that Heav'n had left him still
The whisp'ring Zephyr, and the purling rill?
Who finds not Providence all good and wise,
Alike in what it gives, and what denies?

    VII. Far as Creation's ample range extends,
The scale of sensual, mental pow'rs ascends:

Mark how it mounts, to man's imperial race,
From the green myriads in the peopled grass:
What modes of sight betwixt each wide extreme,
The mole's dim curtain, and the lynx's beam:
Of smell, the headlong lioness between,
And hound sagacious on the tainted green:
Of hearing, from the life that fills the flood,
To that which warbles thro' the vernal wood:
The spider's touch, how exquisitely fine!
Feels at each thread, and lives along the line:
In the nice bee, what sense so subtly true
From pois'nous herbs extracts the healing dew:
How Instinct varies in the grov'ling swine,
Compar'd, half-reas'ning elephant, with thine:
'Twixt that, and Reason, what a nice barrier;
For ever sep'rate, yet for ever near!
Remembrance and Reflection how ally'd;
What thin partitions Sense from Thought divide:
And Middle natures, how they long to join,
Yet never pass th' insuperable line!
Without this just gradation, could they be
Subjected these to those, or all to thee?
The pow'rs of all subdu'd by thee alone,
Is not thy Reason all these pow'rs in one?

    VIII. See, thro' this air, this ocean, and this earth,
All matter quick, and bursting into birth.
Above, how high progressive life may go!
Around, how wide! how deep extend below!
Vast chain of being, which from God began,
Natures aethereal, human, angel, man,
Beast, bird, fish, insect! what no eye can see,
No glass can reach! from Infinite to thee,
From thee to Nothing! --On superior pow'rs
Were we to press, inferior might on ours:
On in the full creation leave a void,
Where, one step broken, the great scale's destroy'd:
From Nature's chain whatever link you strike,
Tenth or ten thousandth, breaks the chain alike.

    And if each system in gradation roll,
Alike essential to th' amazing whole;
The least confusion but in one, not all
That system only, but the whole must fall.
Let Earth unbalanc'd from her orbit fly,
Planets and Suns run lawless thro' the sky,
Let ruling Angels from their spheres be hurl'd,

Being on being wreck'd, and world on world,
Heav'ns whole foundations to their centre nod,
And Nature tremble to the throne of God:
All this dread ORDER break --for whom? for thee?
Vile worm! --oh Madness, Pride, Impiety!

    IX. What if the foot, ordain'd the dust to
tread,
Or hand to toil, aspir'd to be the head?
What if the head, the eye, or ear repin'd
To serve mere engines to the ruling Mind?
Just as absurd for any part to claim
To be another, in this gen'ral frame:
Just as absurd, to mourn the tasks or pains
The great directing MIND of ALL ordains.

    All are but parts of one stupendous whole,
Whose body Nature is, and God the soul;
That, chang'd thro' all, and yet in all the same,
Great in the earth, as in th' aethereal frame,
Warms in the sun, refreshes in the breeze,
Glows in the stars, and blossoms in the trees,
Lives thro' all life, extends thro' all extent,
Spreads undivided, operates unspent,
Breathes in our soul, informs our mortal part,
As full, as perfect, in a hair as heart;
As full, as perfect, in vile Man that mourns,
As the rapt Seraph that adores and burns;
To him no high, no low, no great, no small;
He fills, he bounds, connects, and equals all.

    X. Cease then, nor ORDER Imperfection name:
Our proper bliss depends on what we blame.
Know thy own point: This kind, this due degree
Of blindness, weakness, Heav'n bestows on thee.
Submit --In this, or any other sphere,
Secure to be as blest as thou canst bear:
Safe in the hand of one disposing Pow'r,
Or in the natal, or the mortal hour.
All Nature is but Art, unknown to thee;
All Chance, Direction, which thou canst not see;
All Discord, Harmony, not understood;
All partial Evil, universal Good:
And, spite of Pride, in erring Reason's spite,
One truth is clear, "Whatever is, is RIGHT."

JULIEN OFFRAY DE LA METTRIE

Julien Offray de La Mettrie (1709-1751) was born in Brittany of a wealthy family. His advanced formal education was in the field of medicine, studying first at the University of Paris but receiving his doctorate at Reims and completing his training at Leiden. After medical school, he joined the French Army in which he served from 1743-1745 in the capacity of surgeon. During his military tour, he wrote satires directed primarily against the medical profession and the clergy. In 1745, he published his first philosophical work <u>The Natural History of the Soul</u>, a work which brought him under severe official censure because of its materialistic views. The enemies made as a result of his satirical writing and, more importantly, from his philosophical treatise, forced La Mettrie to exile himself to Holland. It was there that he published <u>Man A Machine</u> (1747), a work whose atheistic and materialistic perspective caused even the liberal-minded Dutch to protest vehemently. Accordingly, when he received an invitation from Frederick the Great of Prussia to join his court and also serve as a member of the Royal Academy of Sciences, he availed himself of this opportunity to acquire the necessary security to continue developing his views. During the next few years he published such works as <u>Discourse on Happiness</u> and <u>The System of Epicurus</u>. He died in 1751 and some of his critics insisted that the fact that he died of overeating clearly established the dangers associated with the materialistic views that he had defended.

<u>Man A Machine</u> maintains that states of the soul are materially dependent on corresponding states of the body. In fact, La Mettrie argues that the soul is but "an empty word," of which no one has any idea. In addition to the mechanistic view of man so clearly and unequivocally articulated in the selection that follows, La Mettrie's essay ends by rejecting the <u>a priori</u> method of establishing principles of psychology. He proposes in its place an experimental-inductive method from which his own theory of man emerged.

MAN A MACHINE:

The soul an "empty word" and the body a machine whose
mainspring is the brain.

   Man is so complicated a machine that it is impossible
to get a clear idea of the machine beforehand, and
hence impossible to define it.   For this reason, all
the investigations have been vain, which the greatest
philosophers have made _a priori_, that is to say, in so
far as they use, as it were, the wings of the spirit.
Thus it is only <u>a posteriori</u> or by trying to
disentangle the soul from the organs of the body, so to
speak, that one can reach the highest probability
concerning man's own nature, even though one can not
discover with certainty what his nature is.

   Let us then take in our hands the staff of
experience, paying no heed to the accounts of all the
idle theories of philosophers.   To be blind and to
think that one can do without this staff is the worst
kind of blindness.   How truly a contemporary writer
says that only vanity fails to gather from secondary
causes the same lessons as from primary causes! One
can and one even ought to admire all these fine
geniuses in their most useless works, such men as
Descartes, Malebranche, Leibniz, Wolff and the rest,
but what profit, I ask, has any one gained from their
profound meditations, and from all their works? Let us
start out then to discover not what has been thought,
but what must be thought for the sake of repose in
life....

   The human body is a machine which winds its own
springs. It is the living image of perpetual movement.
Nourishment keeps up the movements which fever excites.
Without food, the soul pines away, goes mad, and dies
exhausted. The soul is a taper whose light flares up
the moment before it goes out. But nourish the body,
pour into its veins life-giving juices and strong
liquors, and then the soul grows strong like them, as
if arming itself with a proud courage, and the soldier
whom water would have made flee, grows bold and runs
joyously to death to the sound of drums. Thus a hot
drink sets into stormy movement the blood which a cold
drink would have calmed.

What power there is in a meal! Joy revives in a sad
heart, and infects the souls of comrades, who express
their delight in the friendly songs in which the
Frenchman excels.   The   melancholy man alone is
dejected, and the studious man is equally out of place
in such company.

Raw meat makes animals fierce, and it would have the
same effect on man.   This is so true that the English
who eat meat red and bloody, and not as well done as
ours, seem to share more or less in the savagery due to
this kind of food, and to other causes which can be
rendered ineffective by education only. This savagery
creates in the soul, pride, hatred, scorn of other
nations, indocility and other sentiments which degrade
the character, just as heavy food makes a dull and
heavy mind whose usual traits are laziness and
indolence....

Words, languages, laws, sciences, and the fine arts
have come, and by them finally the rough diamond of our
mind has been polished.   Man has been trained in the
same way as animals. He has become an author, as they
became beasts of burden. A geometrician has learned to
perform   the   most   difficult   demonstrations   and
calculations, as a monkey has learned to take his
little hat off and on, and to mount his tame dog. All
has been accomplished through signs, every species has
learned what it could understand, and in this way men
have acquired symbolic knowledge, still so called by
our German philosophers.

Nothing, as any one can see, is so simple as the
mechanism of our education.   Everything may be reduced
to sounds or words that pass from the mouth of one
through the ears of another into his brain. At the
same moment, he perceives through his eyes the shape of
the bodies of which these words are the arbitrary
signs.

But who was the first to speak?   Who was the first
teacher of the human race?   Who invented the means of
utilizing the plasticity of our organism?   I can not
answer: the names of these first splendid geniuses
have been lost in the night of time. But art is the
child of nature, so nature must have long preceded it.

197

We must think that the men who were the most highly
organized, those on whom nature had lavished her
richest gifts, taught the others. They could not have
heard a new sound for instance, nor experienced new
sensations, nor been struck by all the varied and
beautiful objects that compose the ravishing spectacle
of nature without finding themselves in the state of
mind of the deaf man of Chartres, whose experience was
first related by the great Fontenelle, when, at forty
years, he heard for the first time, the astonishing
sound of bells.

Would it be absurd to conclude from this that the
first mortals tried after the manner of this deaf man,
or like animals and like mutes (another kind of
animals), to express their new feelings by motions
depending on the nature of their imagination, and
therefore afterwards by spontaneous sounds, distinctive
of each animal, as the natural expression of their
surprise, their joy, their ecstasies and their needs?
For doubtless those whom nature endowed with finer
feeling had also greater facility in expression.

That is the way in which, I think, men have used
their feeling and their instinct to gain intelligence
and then have employed their intelligence to gain
knowledge. Those are the ways, so far as I can
understand them, in which men have filled the brain
with the ideas, for the reception of which nature made
it. Nature and man have helped each other; and the
smallest beginnings have, little by little, increased,
until everything in the universe could be as easily
described as a circle.

As a violin string or a harpsichord key vibrates and
gives forth sound, so the cerebral fibres, struck by
waves of sound, are stimulated to render or repeat the
words that strike them. And as the structure of the
brain is such that when eyes well formed for seeing,
have once perceived the image of objects, the brain can
not help seeing their images and their differences, as
when the signs of these differences have been traced or
imprinted in the brain, the soul necessarily examines
their relations--an examination that would have been
impossible without the discovery of signs or the
invention of language. At the time when the universe
was almost dumb, the soul's attitude toward all objects

was that of a man without any idea of proportion toward a picture or a piece of sculpture, in which he could distinguish nothing; or the soul was like a little child (for the soul was then in its infancy) who, holding in his hand small bits of straw or wood, sees them in a vague and superficial way without being able to count or distinguish them. But let some one attach a kind of banner or standard, to this bit of wood (which perhaps is called a mast), and another banner to another similar object; let the first be known by the symbol 1, and the second by the symbol or number 2, then the child will be able to count the objects, and in this way he will learn all of arithmetic. As soon as one figure seems equal to another in its numerical sign, he will decide without difficulty that they are two different bodies, that 1 + 1 make 2, and 2 + 2 make 4, etc.

This real or apparent likeness of figures is the fundamental basis of all truths and of all we know. Among these sciences, evidently those whose signs are less simple and less sensible are harder to understand than the others, because more talent is required to comprehend and combine the immense number of words by which such sciences express the truths in their province. On the other hand, the sciences that are expressed by numbers or by other small signs, are easily learned; and without doubt this facility rather than its demonstrability is what has made the fortune of algebra.

All this knowledge, with which vanity fills the balloon-like brains of our proud pedants, is therefore but a huge mass of words and figures, which form in the brain all the marks by which we distinguish and recall objects. All our ideas are awakened after the fashion in which the gardener who knows plants recalls all stages of their growth at sight of them. These words and the objects designated by them are so connected in the brain that it is comparatively rare to imagine a thing without the name or sign that is attached to it.

But since all the faculties of the soul depend to such a degree on the proper organization of the brain and of the whole body, that apparently they are but this organization itself, the soul is clearly an enlightened machine. For finally, even if man alone had received a share of natural law, would he be any less a machine for that? A few more wheels, a few more springs than in the most perfect animals, the brain proportionally nearer the heart and for this very reason receiving more blood--any one of a number of unknown causes might always produce this delicate conscience so easily wounded, this remorse which is no more foreign to matter than to thought, and in a word all the differences that are supposed to exist here. Could the organism then suffice for everything? Once more, yes; since thought visibly develops with our organs, why should not the matter of which they are composed be susceptible of remorse also, when once it has acquired, with time, the faculty of feeling?

The soul is therefore but an empty word, of which no one has any idea, and which an enlightened man should use only to signify the part in us that thinks. Given the least principle of motion, animated bodies will have all that is necessary for moving, feeling, thinking, repeating, or in a word for conducting themselves in the physical realm, and in the moral realm which depends upon it.

Let us now go into some detail concerning these springs of the human machine. All the vital, animal, natural, and automatic motions are carried on by their action. Is it not in a purely mechanical way that the body shrinks back when it is struck with terror at the sight of an unforeseen precipice, that the eyelids are lowered at the menace of a blow, as some have remarked, and that the pupil contracts in broad daylight to save the retina, and dilates to see objects in darkness? Is it not by mechanical means that the pores of the skin close in winter so that the cold can not penetrate to the interior of the blood vessels, and that the stomach vomits when it is irritated by poison, by a certain quantity of opium and by all emetics, etc.? that the heart, the arteries and the muscles contract in sleep as well as in waking hours, that the lungs serve as bellows continually in exercise....that the heart contracts more strongly than any other muscle?...

I shall not go into any more detail concerning all these little subordinate forces, well known to all. But there is another more subtle and marvelous force, which animates them all; it is the source of all our

feelings, of all our pleasures, of all our passions,
and of all our thoughts: for the brain has its muscles
for thinking, as the legs have muscles for walking. I
wish to speak of this impetuous principle that
Hippocrates calls (soul). This principle exists and
has its seat in the brain at the origin of the nerves,
by which it exercises its control over all the rest of
the body. By this fact is explained all that can be
explained, even to the surprising effects of maladies
of the imagination....

Look at the portrait of the famous Pope who is, to
say the least, the Voltaire of the English. The
effort, the energy of his genius are imprinted upon his
countenance. It is convulsed. His eyes protrude from
their sockets, the eyebrows are raised with the muscles
of the forehead. Why? Because the brain is in travail
and all the body must share in such a laborious
deliverance. If there were not an internal cord which
pulled the external ones, whence would come all these
phenomena? To admit a soul as explanation of them, is
to be reduced to explaining phenomena by the operations
of the Holy Spirit.

In fact, if what thinks in my brain is not a part of
this organ and therefore of the whole body, why does my
blood boil, and the fever of my mind pass into my
veins, when lying quietly in bed, I am forming the plan
of some work or carrying on an abstract calculation?
Put this question to men of imagination, to great
poets, to men who are enraptured by the felicitous
expression of sentiment, and transported by an
exquisite fancy or by the charms of nature, of truth,
or of virtue! By their enthusiasm, by what they will
tell you they have experienced, you will judge the
cause by its effects: by that harmony which Borelli, a
mere anatomist, understood better than all the
Leibnizians, you will comprehend the material unity of
man. In short, if the nerve-tension which causes pain
occasions also the fever by which the distracted mind
loses its will-power, and if, conversely, the mind too
much excited, disturbs the body (and kindles that inner
fire which killed Bayle while he was still so young);
if an agitation rouses my desire and my ardent wish for
what, a moment ago, I cared nothing about, and if in
their turn certain brain impressions excite the same
longing and the same desires, then why should we regard
as double what is manifestly one being? In vain you

fall back on the power of the will, since for one order
that the will gives, it bows a hundred times to the
yoke. And what wonder that in health the body obeys,
since a torrent of blood and of animal spirits forces
its obedience, and since the will has as ministers an
invisible legion of fluids swifter than lightning and
ever ready to do its bidding! But as the power of the
will is exercised by means of the nerves, it is
likewise limited by them....

Does the result of jaundice surprise you? Do you not
know that the color of bodies depends on the color of
the glasses through which we look at them, and that
whatever is the color of the humors, such is the color
of objects, at least for us, vain playthings of a
thousand illusions? But remove this color from the
aqueous humor of the eye, let the bile flow through its
natural filter, then the soul having new eyes, will no
longer see yellow. Again, is it not thus, by removing
cataract, or by injecting the Eustachian canal, that
sight is restored to the blind, or hearing to the deaf?
How many people, who were perhaps only clever
charlatans, passed for miracle workers in the dark
ages! Beautiful the soul, and powerful the will which
can not act save by permission of the bodily
conditions, and whose tastes change with age and fever!
Should we, then, be astonished that philosophers have
always had in mind the health of the body, to preserve
the health of the soul, that Pythagoras gave rules for
the diet as carefully as Plato forbade wine? The
regime suited to the body is always the one with which
sane physicians think they must begin, when it is a
question of forming the mind, and of instructing it in
the knowledge of truth and virtue; but these are vain
words in the disorder of illness, and in the tumult of
the senses. Without the precepts of hygiene,
Epictetus, Socrates, Plato, and the rest preach in
vain: all ethics is fruitless for one who lacks his
share of temperance; it is the source of all virtues,
as intemperance is the source of all vices.

Is more needed...to prove that man is but an animal,
or a collection of springs which wind each other up,
without our being able to tell at what point in this
human circle, nature has begun? If these springs
differ among themselves, these differences consist only
in their position and in their degrees of strength, and
never in their nature; wherefore the soul is but a

principle of motion or a material and sensible part of
the brain, which can be regarded, without fear of
error, as the mainspring of the whole machine, having a
visible influence on all the parts. The soul seems
even to have been made for the brain, so that all the
other parts of the system are but a kind of emanation
from the brain....

The human body is a watch, a large watch constructed
with such skill and ingenuity, that if the wheel which
marks the seconds happens to stop, the minute wheel
turns and keeps on going its round, and in the same way
the quarter-hour wheel, and all the others go on
running when the first wheels have stopped because
rusty or, for any reason, out of order. Is it not for
a similar reason that the stoppage of a few blood
vessels is not enough to destroy or suspend the
strength of the movement which is in the heart as in
the mainspring of the machine; since, on the contrary,
the fluids whose volume is diminished, having a shorter
road to travel, cover the ground more quickly, borne on
as by a fresh current which the energy of the heart
increases in proportion to the resistance it encounters
at the ends of the blood-vessels? And is not this the
reason why the loss of sight (caused by the compression
of the optic nerve and by its ceasing to convey the
images of objects) no more hinders hearing, than the
loss of hearing (caused by obstruction of the functions
of the auditory nerve) implies the loss of sight? In
the same way, finally, does not one man hear (except
immediately after the attack) without being able to say
that he hears, while another who hears nothing, but
whose lingual nerves are uninjured in the brain,
mechanically tells of all the dreams which pass through
his mind? These phenomena do not surprise enlightened
physicians at all. They know what to think about man's
nature, and (more accurately to express myself in
passing) of two physicians, the better one and the one
who deserves more confidence is always, in my opinion,
the one who is more versed in the physique or mechanism
of the human body, and who, leaving aside the soul and
all the anxieties which this chimera gives to fools and
to ignorant men, is seriously occupied in pure
naturalism....

To be a machine, to feel, to think, to know how to
distinguish good from bad, as well as blue from yellow,
in a word, to be born with an intelligence and a sure

moral instinct, and to be but an animal, are therefore
characters which are no more contradictory, than to be
an ape or a parrot and to be able to give oneself
pleasure.... I believe that thought is so little
incompatible with organized matter, that it seems to be
one of its properties on a par with electricity, the
faculty of motion, impenetrability, extension, etc.

Do you ask for further observations? Here are some
which are incontestable and which all prove that man
resembles animals perfectly, in his origin as well as
in all the points in which we have thought it essential
to make the comparison....

Let us observe man both in and out of his shell, let
us examine young embryos of four, six, eight or fifteen
days with a microscope; after that time our eyes are
sufficient. What do we see?   The head alone; a little
round egg with two black points which mark the eyes.
Before that, everything is formless, and one sees only
a medullary pulp, which is the brain, in which are
formed first the roots of the nerves, that is, the
principle of feeling, and the heart, which already
within this substance has the power of beating of
itself; it is the <u>punctum saliens</u> of Malpighi, which
perhaps already owes a part of its excitability to the
influence of the nerves.   Then little by little, one
sees the head lengthen from the neck, which, in
dilating, forms first the thorax inside which the heart
has already sunk, there to become stationary; below
that is the abdomen which is divided by a partition
(the diaphragm). One of these enlargements of the body
forms the arms, the hands, the fingers, the nails, and
the hair; the other forms the thighs, the legs, the
feet, etc., which differ only in their observed
situation, and which constitute the support and the
balancing pole of the body.   The whole process is a
strange sort of growth, like that of plants. On the
tops of our heads is hair in place of which the plants
have leaves and flowers; everywhere is shown the same
luxury of nature, and finally the directing principle
of plants is placed where we have our soul, that other
quintessence of man.

Such is the uniformity of nature, which we are
beginning to realize; and the analogy of the animal
with the vegetable kingdom, of man with plant. Perhaps

there even are animal plants, which in vegetating, either fight as polyps do, or perform other functions characteristic of animals....

Let us not say that every machine or every animal perishes altogether or assumes another form after death, for we know absolutely nothing about the subject. On the other hand, to assert that an immortal machine is a chimera or a logical fiction, is to reason as absurdly as caterpillars would reason if, seeing the cast-off skins of their fellow-caterpillars, they should bitterly deplore the fate of their species, which to them would seem to come to nothing. The soul of these insects (for each animal has his own) is too limited to comprehend the metamorphoses of nature. Never one of the most skilful among them could have imagined that it was destined to become a butterfly. It is the same with us. What more do we know of our destiny than of our origin? Let us then submit to an invincible ignorance on which our happiness depends.

He who so thinks will be wise, just, tranquil about his fate, and therefore happy. He will await death without either fear or desire, and will cherish life (hardly understanding how disgust can corrupt a heart in this place of many delights); he will be filled with reverence, gratitude, affection, and tenderness for nature, in proportion to his feeling of the benefits he has received from nature; he will be happy, in short, in feeling nature, and in being present at the enchanting spectacle of the universe, and he will surely never destroy nature either in himself or in others. More than that! Full of humanity, this man will love human character even in his enemies. Judge how he will treat others. He will pity the wicked without hating them; in his eyes, they will be mis-made men. But in pardoning the faults of the structure of mind and body, he will none the less admire the beauties and the virtues of both. Those whom nature shall have favored will seem to him to deserve more respect than those whom she has treated in stepmotherly fashion. Thus, as we have seen, natural gifts, the source of all acquirements gain from the lips and heart of the materialist, the homage which every other thinker unjustly refuses them. In short, the materialist, convinced, in spite of the protests of his vanity, that he is but a machine or an animal, will not maltreat his kind, for he will know too well the nature of those actions, whose humanity is always in proportion to the degree of the analogy proved above (between human beings and animals); and following the natural law given to all animals, he will not wish to do to others what he would not wish them to do to him.

Let us then conclude boldly that man is a machine, and that in the whole universe there is but a single substance differently modified. This is no hypothesis set forth by dint of a number of postulates and assumptions; it is not the work of prejudice, nor even of my reason alone; I should have disdained a guide which I think to be so untrustworthy, had not my senses, bearing a torch, so to speak, induced me to follow reason by lighting the way themselves. Experience has thus spoken to me in behalf of reason; and in this way I have combined the two....

III.

MAN IN A HUMAN-CENTERED WORLD

LUDWIG FEUERBACH

Ludwig Andreas Feuerbach (1804-1872), born in Landshut, Bavaria, began his formal studies as a student of theology at both Heidelberg and Berlin. However, in 1825, under the influence of Hegel, he transferred to the faculty of philosophy and three years later received his doctorate at Erlangen where he remained to teach until 1832. After being forced to resign because of a controversial work he published in which he claimed that Christianity is an egoistic and inhumane religion, Feuerbach spent the next ten to fifteen years writing extensively on religion and philosophy. The two most important works of this period were The Essence of Christianity (1841) and The Essence of Religion (1846). In his later life, he devoted much of his time to the study of the natural sciences as well as to the composition of the monumental work Théogonie (1857) and to voluminous correspondence with friends.

In The Essence of Christianity, as well as in The Essence of Religion, Feuerbach maintains that man's ideas about God are simply reflections of the modes of man's existence. In other words, all so-called knowledge of God is really man's knowledge of himself. Religion, then, is judged by Feuerbach to be nothing else but a projection of man himself. Consequently, Feuerbach insists that the question of the essential nature of man is the fundamental question to be resolved before one can take up the question of the essence of religion and, more particularly, the essence of Christianity.

In the opening pages of the first chapter of The Essence of Christianity, sections of which are reprinted below, Feuerbach considers the question of man's essential nature, observing that his distinctive feature lies in the fact that he possesses a two-fold life: "an inner and an outer life". His outer life is very much like the life of other animals who can engage in conscious activity. The brute, Feuerbach contends,

is indeed conscious of himself as an individual.
However, man's inner life is "the life which has
relation to his species, to his general, as
distinguished from his individual, nature." Feuerbach
then raises the question - What is the nature of man of
which man is conscious?   Feuerbach's response is that
Reason, Will, and Affection are the defining powers of
man's essence.   These powers are the basis of his
existence, "the constituent elements of his nature,"
and they are further characterized as "divine, absolute
powers".

THE ESSENCE OF CHRISTIANITY:

The divine and absolute powers of man's nature.

Chapter I.

Introduction

1. <u>The Essential Nature of Man</u>

Religion has its basis in the essential difference
between man and the brute--the brutes have no religion.

But what is this essential difference between man
and the brute? The most simple, general, and also the
most popular answer to this question is--
consciousness:--but consciousness in the strict sense;
for the consciousness implied in the feeling of self as
an individual, in discrimination by the senses, in the
perception and even judgment of outward things
according to definite sensible signs, cannot be denied
to the brutes. Consciousness in the strictest sense is
present only in a being to whom his species, his
essential nature, is an object of thought. The brute
is indeed conscious of himself as an individual--and he
has accordingly the feeling of self as the common
centre of successive sensations--but not as a species:
hence, he is without that consciousness which in its
nature, as in its name, is akin to science. Where
there is this higher consciousness there is a
capability of science. Science is the cognisance of
species. In practical life we have to do with
individuals; in science, with species. But only a
being to whom his own species, his own nature, is an
object of thought, can make the essential nature of
other things or beings an object of thought.

Hence the brute has only a simple, man a twofold
life: in the brute, the inner life is one with the
outer; man has both an inner and an outer life. The
inner life of man is the life which has relation to his
species, to his general, as distinguished from his
individual, nature. Man thinks--that is, he converses

211

with himself. The brute can exercise no function which
has relation to its species without another individual
external to itself; but man can perform the functions
of thought and speech, which strictly imply such a
relation, apart from another individual.   Man is
himself at once I and thou; he can put himself in the
place of another, for this reason, that to him his
species, his essential nature, and not merely his
individuality, is an object of thought....

     ...The consciousness of the caterpillar, whose
life is confined to a particular species of plant, does
not extend itself beyond this narrow domain. It does,
indeed, discriminate between this plant and other
plants, but more it knows not.   A consciousness so
limited, but on account of that very limitation so
infallible, we do not call consciousness, but instinct.
Consciousness, in the strict or proper sense, is
identical with consciousness of the infinite; a limited
consciousness is no consciousness; consciousness is
essentially infinite in its nature. The consciousness
of the infinite is nothing else than the consciousness
of the infinity of the consciousness; or, in the
consciousness of the infinite, the conscious subject
has for his object the infinity of his own nature.

     What, then, _is_ the nature of man, of which he is
conscious,   or   what   constitutes   the   specific
distinction, the proper humanity of man? Reason, Will,
Affection.   To a complete man belong the power of
thought, the power of will, the power of affection.
The power of thought is the light of the intellect, the
power of will is energy of character, the power of
affection is love.   Reason, love, force of will, are
perfections--the perfections of the human being--nay,
more, they are absolute perfections of being. To will,
to love, to think, are the highest powers, are the
absolute nature of man as man, and the basis of his
existence. Man exists to think, to love, to will. Now
that which is the end, the ultimate aim, is also the
true basis and principle of a being. But what is the
end of reason?   Reason.   Of love? Love. Of will?
Freedom of the Will.   We think for the sake of
thinking; love for the sake of loving; will for the
sake of willing--i.e., that we may be free. True
existence is thinking, loving, willing existence. That
alone is true, perfect, divine, which exists for its
own sake. But such is love, such is reason, such is

212

will. The divine trinity in man, above the individual
man, is the unity of reason, love, will. Reason, Will,
Love, are not powers which man possesses, for he is
nothing without them, he is what he is only by them;
they are the constituent elements of his nature, which
he neither has nor makes, the animating, determining,
governing powers--divine, absolute powers--to which he
can oppose no resistance....

     Man is nothing without an object. The great
models of humanity, such men as reveal to us what man
is capable of, have attested the truth of this
proposition by their lives. They had only one dominant
passion--the realisation of the aim which was the
essential object of their activity. But the object to
which a subject essentially, necessarily relates, is
nothing else than this subject's own, but objective,
nature.   If it be an object common to several
individuals of the same species, but under various
conditions, it is still, at least as to the form under
which it presents itself to each of them according to
their respective modifications, their own, but
objective, nature....

     In the object which he contemplates, therefore,
man becomes acquainted with himself; consciousness of
the objective is the self-consciousness of man. We
know the man by the object, by his conception of what
is external to himself; in it his nature becomes
evident; this object is his manifested nature, his true
objective _ego_. And this is true not merely of
spiritual, but also of sensuous objects. Even the
objects which are the most remote from man, _because_
they are objects to him, and to the extent to which
they are so, are revelations of human nature.... Man
alone has purely intellectual, disinterested joys and
passions; the eye of man alone keeps theoretic
festivals. The eye which looks into the starry
heavens, which gazes at that light, alike useless and
harmless, having nothing in common with the earth and
its necessities--this eye sees in that light its own
nature, its own origin. The eye is heavenly in its
nature. Hence man elevates himself above the earth
only with the eye; hence theory begins with the
contemplation of the heavens....

     The _absolute_ to man is his own nature. The power
of the object over him is therefore the power of his
own nature. Thus the power of the object of feeling is
the power of feeling itself; the power of the object of
the intellect is the power of the intellect itself; the
power of the object of the will is the power of the
will itself.

     Every limitation of the reason, or in general of
the nature of man, rests on a delusion, an error. It
is true that the human being, as an individual, can and
must--herein consists his distinction from the
brute--feel and recognise himself to be limited; but he
can become conscious of his limits, his finiteness,
only because the perfection, the infinitude of his
species, is perceived by him, whether as an object of
feeling, of conscience, or of the thinking
consciousness. If he makes his own limitations the
limitations of the species, this arises from the
mistake that he identifies himself immediately with the
species--a mistake which is intimately connected with
the individual's love of ease, sloth, vanity, and
egoism. For a limitation which I know to be merely
mine humiliates, shames, and perturbs me. Hence to
free myself from this feeling of shame, from this state
of dissatisfaction, I convert the limits of my
individuality into the limits of human nature in
general. What is incomprehensible to me is
incomprehensible to others; why should I trouble myself
further? It is no fault of mine; my understanding is
not to blame, but the understanding of the race. But
it is a ludicrous and even culpable error to define as
finite and limited what constitutes the essence of man,
the nature of the species, which is the absolute nature
of the individual. Every being is sufficient to
itself. No being can deny itself, i.e., its own
nature; no being is a limited one to itself. Rather,
every being is in and by itself infinite--has its God,
its highest conceivable being, in itself....

22

CHARLES DARWIN

A native of Shrewsbury, England, Charles Robert Darwin (1809-1882), renowned biologist and naturalist, affected a scientific revolution of comparable magnitude to that affected by Copernicus. Like the Copernican revolution, the effects of Darwin's famed theory of evolution extended beyond the domain of science to the fields of philosophy and theology. Both the general theory of evolution which he defended in his <u>Origin of Species</u> (1859) and the more specific theory explaining man's evolutionary development which is articulated in <u>The Descent of Man</u> (1871) sent shock waves that are still being felt within philosophical and theological circles.

Attending the universities of Edinburg and Cambridge, where he initially pursued medical and theological studies, Darwin came under the decided influence of J. T. Henslow, his professor of botany at Cambridge. This association inspired Darwin to seek a career as a natural scientist. In fact, Professor Henslow arranged for Darwin to serve on the surveying ship, the H.M.S. Beagle, in the capacity of naturalist. From 1831-1836, Darwin sailed to South America and to many of the Pacific islands, where he made detailed observations of various species of plants and animals as well as various geological formations. This experience, as it turned out, was the springboard for many of the ideas that he developed in his aforementioned revolutionary works.

In the concluding chapter of <u>The Descent of Man</u>, which is reprinted below, Darwin pointedly remarks that anyone who carefully examines the facts presented in this study, cannot any longer believe that man is the work of a separate act of creation. Rather man must be seen as the co-descendant with other mammals of a common progenitor. After reviewing the manner of man's development, his genealogy, his intellectual and moral faculties, and the issue of sexual selection, Darwin concludes the treatise by admitting that its principal thesis will be "highly distasteful to many." However, he goes on to insist that it is nevertheless necessary to acknowledge that man, with all his exalted powers, "still bears in his bodily frame the indelible stamp of his lowly origin."

THE DESCENT OF MAN:

The natural origins of man and his faculties.

Chapter XXI

<u>General Summary and Conclusion</u>

A brief summary will be sufficient to recall to the
reader's mind the more salient points in this work.
Many of the views which have been advanced are highly
speculative, and some no doubt will prove erroneous;
but I have in every case given the reasons which have
led me to one view rather than to another. It seemed
worth while to try how far the principle of evolution
would throw light on some of the more complex problems
in the natural history of man. False facts are highly
injurious to the progress of science, for they often
endure long; but false views, if supported by some
evidence, do little harm, for every one takes a
salutary pleasure in proving their falseness: and when
this is done, one path towards error is closed and the
road to truth is often at the same time opened.

The main conclusion here arrived at, and now held
by many naturalists who are well competent to form a
sound judgment is that man is descended from some less
highly organised form. The grounds upon which this
conclusion rests will never be shaken, for the close
similarity between man and the lower animals in
embryonic development, as well as in innumerable points
of structure and constitution, both of high and of the
most trifling importance,--the rudiments which he
retains, and the abnormal reversions to which he is
occasionally liable,--are facts which cannot be
disputed. They have long been known, but until
recently they told us nothing with respect to the
origin of man. Now when viewed by the light of our
knowledge of the whole organic world, their meaning is
unmistakable. The great principle of evolution stands
up clear and firm, when these groups or facts are
considered in connection with others, such as the
mutual affinities of the members of the same group,
their geographical distribution in past and present
times, and their geological succession. It is

incredible that all these facts should speak falsely. He who is not content to look, like a savage, at the phenomena of nature as disconnected, cannot any longer believe that man is the work of a separate act of creation. He will be forced to admit that the close resemblance of the embryo of man to that, for instance, of a dog--the construction of his skull, limbs and whole frame on the same plan with that of other mammals, independently of the uses to which the parts may be put--the occasional re-appearance of various structures, for instance of several muscles, which man does not normally possess, but which are common to the Quadrumana--and a crowd of analogous facts--all point in the plainest manner to the conclusion that man is the co-descendant with other mammals of a common progenitor.

We have seen that man incessantly presents individual differences in all parts of his body and in his mental faculties. These differences or variations seem to be induced by the same general causes, and to obey the same laws as with the lower animals. In both cases similar laws of inheritance prevail. Man tends to increase at a greater rate than his means of subsistence; consequently he is occasionally subjected to a severe struggle for existence, and natural selection will have effected whatever lies within its scope. A succession of strongly-marked variations of a similar nature is by no means requisite; slight fluctuating differences in the individual suffice for the work of natural selection; not that we have any reason to suppose that in the same species, all parts of the organisation tend to vary to the same degree. We may feel assured that the inherited effects of the long-continued use or disuse of parts will have done much in the same direction with natural selection. Modifications formerly of importance, though no longer of any special use, are long-inherited. When one part is modified, other parts change through the principle of correlation, of which we have instances in many curious cases of correlated monstrosities. Something may be attributed to the direct and definite action of the surrounding conditions of life, such as abundant food, heat or moisture; and lastly, many characters of slight physiological importance, some indeed of considerable importance, have been gained through sexual selection.

No doubt man, as well as every other animal, presents structures, which seem to our limited knowledge, not to be now of any service to him, nor to have been so formerly, either for the general conditions of life, or in the relations of one sex to the other. Such structures cannot be accounted for by any form of selection, or by the inherited effects of the use and disuse of parts. We know, however, that many strange and strongly-marked peculiarities of structure occasionally appear in our domesticated productions, and if their unknown causes were to act more uniformly, they would probably become common to all the individuals of the species. We may hope hereafter to understand something about the causes of such occasional modifications, especially through the study of monstrosities: hence the labours of experimentalists such as those of M. Camille Dareste, are full of promise for the future. In general we can only say that the cause of each slight variation and of each monstrosity lies much more in the constitution of the organism, than in the nature of the surrounding conditions; though new and changed conditions certainly play an important part in exciting organic changes of many kinds.

Through the means just specified, aided perhaps by others as yet undiscovered, man has been raised to his present state. But since he attained to the rank of manhood, he has diverged into distinct races, or as they may be more fitly called, sub-species. Some of these, such as the Negro and European, are so distinct that, if specimens had been brought to a naturalist without any further information, they would undoubtedly have been considered by him as good and true species. Nevertheless all the races agree in so many unimportant details of structure and in so many mental peculiarities that these can be accounted for only by inheritance from a common progenitor; and a progenitor thus characterised would probably deserve to rank as man.

It must not be supposed that the divergence of each race from the other races, and of all from a common stock, can be traced back to any one pair of progenitors. On the contrary, at every stage in the process of modification, all the individuals which were in any way better fitted for their conditions of life, though in different degrees, would have survived in

greater numbers than the less well-fitted. The process
would have been like that followed by man, when he does
not intentionally select particular individuals, but
breeds from all the superior individuals, and neglects
the inferior. He thus slowly but surely modifies his
stock, and unconsciously forms a new strain. So with
respect to modifications acquired independently of
selection, and due to variations arising from the
nature of the organism and the action of the
surrounding conditions, or from changed habits of life,
no single pair will have been modified much more than
the other pairs inhabiting the same country, for all
will have been continually blended through free
intercrossing....

     The high standard of our intellectual powers and
moral disposition is the greatest difficulty which
presents itself, after we have been driven to this
conclusion on the origin of man. But every one who
admits the principle of evolution, must see that the
mental powers of the higher animals, which are the same
in kind with those of man, though so different in
degree, are capable of advancement. Thus the interval
between the mental powers of one of the higher apes and
of a fish, or between those of an ant and scale-insect,
is immense; yet their development does not offer any
special difficulty; for with our domesticated animals,
the mental faculties are certainly variable, and the
variations are inherited. No one doubts that they are
of the utmost importance to animals in a state of
nature. Therefore the conditions are favourable for
their development through natural selection. The same
conclusion may be extended to man; the intellect must
have been all-important to him, even at a very remote
period, as enabling him to invent and use language, to
make weapons, tools, traps, etc., whereby with the aid
of his social habits, he long ago became the most
dominant of all living creatures.

     A great stride in the development of the intellect
will have followed, as soon as the half-art and
half-instinct of language came into use; for the
continued use of language will have reacted on the
brain and produced an inherited effect; and this again
will have reacted on the improvement of language. As
Mr. Chauncey Wright has well remarked, the largeness of
the brain in man relatively to his body, compared with
the lower animals, may be attributed in chief part to

the early use of some simple form of language,--that
wonderful engine which affixes signs to all sorts of
objects and qualities, and excites trains of thought
which would never arise from the mere impression of the
senses, or if they did arise could not be followed out.
The higher intellectual powers of man, such as those of
ratiocination, abstraction, self-consciousness, etc.,
probably follow from the continued improvement and
exercise of the other mental faculties.

The development of the moral qualities is a more
interesting problem. The foundation lies in the social
instincts, including under this term the family ties.
These instincts are highly complex, and in the case of
the lower animals give special tendencies towards
certain definite actions; but the more important
elements are love, and the distinct emotion of
sympathy. Animals endowed with the social instincts
take pleasure in one another's company, warn one
another of danger, defend and aid one another in many
ways. These instincts do not extend to all the
individuals of the species, but only to those of the
same community. As they are highly beneficial to the
species, they have in all prabability been acquired
through natural selection.

A moral being is one who is capable of reflecting
on his past actions and their motives--of approving of
some and disapproving of others; and the fact that man
is the one being who certainly deserves this
designation, is the greatest of all distinctions
between him and the lower animals. But in the fourth
chapter I have endeavoured to show that the moral sense
follows, firstly, from the enduring and ever-present
nature of the social instincts; secondly, from man's
appreciation of the approbation and disapprobation of
his fellows; and thirdly, from the high activity of his
mental faculties, with past impressions extremely
vivid; and in these latter respects he differs from the
lower animals. Owing to this condition of mind, man
cannot avoid looking both backwards and forwards, and
comparing past impressions. Hence after some temporary
desire or passion has mastered his social instincts, he
reflects and compares the now weakened impression of
such past impulses with the ever-present social
instincts; and he then feels that sense of
dissatisfaction which all unsatisfied instincts leave
behind them, he therefore resolves to act differently

for the future,--and this is conscience. Any instinct, permanently stronger or more enduring than another, gives rise to a feeling which we express by saying that it ought to be obeyed. A pointer dog, if able to reflect on his past conduct, would say to himself, I ought (as indeed we may say of him) to have pointed at that hare and not have yielded to the passing temptation of hunting it....

The moral nature of man has reached its present standard, partly through the advancement of his reasoning powers and consequently of a just public opinion, but especially from his sympathies having been rendered more tender and widely diffused through the effects of habit, example, instruction, and reflection. It is not improbable that after long practice virtuous tendencies may be inherited. With the more civilised races, the conviction of the existence of an all-seeing Deity has had a potent influence on the advance of morality. Ultimately man does not accept the praise or blame of his fellows as his sole guide, though few escape this influence, but his habitual convictions, controlled by reason, afford him the safest rule. His conscience then becomes the supreme judge and monitor. Nevertheless the first foundation or origin of the moral sense lies in the social instincts, including sympathy; and these instincts no doubt were primarily gained, as in the case of the lower animals, through natural selection.

The belief in God has often been advanced as not only the greatest, but the most complete of all the distinctions between man and the lower animals. It is however impossible, as we have seen, to maintain that this belief is innate or instinctive in man. On the other hand a belief in all-pervading spiritual agencies seems to be universal; and apparently follows from a considerable advance in man's reason, and from a still greater advance in his faculties of imagination, curiosity and wonder. I am aware that the assumed instinctive belief in God has been used by many persons as an argument for His existence. But this is a rash argument, as we should thus be compelled to believe in the existence of many cruel and malignant spirits, only a little more powerful than man; for the belief in them is far more general than in a beneficent Deity. The idea of a universal and beneficent Creator does not seem to arise in the mind of man, until he has been elevated by long-continued culture.

222

He who believes in the advancement of man from
some low organised form, will naturally ask how does
this bear on the belief in the immortality of the soul.
The barbarous races of man, as Sir J. Lubbock has
shown, possess no clear belief of this kind; but
arguments derived from the primeval beliefs of savages
are, as we have just seen, of little or no avail. Few
persons feel any anxiety from the impossibility of
determining at what precise period in the development
of the individual, from the first trace of a minute
germinal vesicle, man becomes an immortal being; and
there is no greater cause for anxiety because the
period cannot possibly be determined in the gradually
ascending organic scale....

Sexual selection has been treated at great length
in this work; for, as I have attempted to shew, it has
played an important part in the history of the organic
world....

Sexual selection depends on the success of certain
individuals over others of the same sex, in relation to
the propagation of the species; whilst natural
selection depends on the success of both sexes, at all
ages, in relation to the general conditions of life.
The sexual struggle is of two kinds; in the one it is
between individuals of the same sex, generally the
males, in order to drive away or kill their rivals, the
females remaining passive; whilst in the other, the
struggle is likewise between the individuals of the
same sex, in order to excite or charm those of the
opposite sex, generally the females, which no longer
remain passive, but select the more agreeable partners.
This latter kind of selection is closely analogous to
that which man unintentionally, yet effectually, brings
to bear on his domesticated productions, when he
preserves during a long period the most pleasing or
useful individuals, without any wish to modify the
breed.

The laws of inheritance determine whether
characters gained through sexual selection by either
sex shall be transmitted to the same sex, or to both;
as well as the age at which they shall be developed.
It appears that variations arising late in life are
commonly transmitted to one and the same sex.
Variability is the necessary basis for the action of

selection, and is wholly independent of it. It follows
from this, that variations of the same general nature
have often been taken advantage of and accumulated
through sexual selection in relation to the propagation
of the species, as well as through natural selection in
relation to the general purposes of life. Hence
secondary sexual characters, when equally transmitted
to both sexes can be distinguished from ordinary
specific characters only by the light of analogy. The
modifications acquired through sexual selection are
often so strongly pronounced that the two sexes have
frequently been ranked as distinct species, or even as
distinct genera. Such strongly-marked differences must
be in some manner highly important; and we know that
they have been acquired in some instances at the cost
not only of inconvenience, but of exposure to actual
danger.

The belief in the power of sexual selection rests
chiefly on the following considerations. Certain
characters are confined to one sex; and this alone
renders it probable that in most cases they are
connected with the act of reproduction. In innumerable
instances these characters are fully developed only at
maturity, and often during only a part of the year,
which is always the breeding-season. The males
(passing over a few exceptional cases) are the more
active in courtship; they are the better armed, and are
rendered the more attractive in various ways. It is to
be especially observed that the males display their
attractions with elaborate care in the presence of the
females; and that they rarely or never display them
excepting during the season of love. It is incredible
that all this should be purposeless. Lastly we have
distinct evidence with some quadrupeds and birds, that
the individuals of one sex are capable of feeling a
strong antipathy or preference for certain individuals
of the other sex....

He who admits the principle of sexual selection
will be led to the remarkable conclusion that the
nervous system not only regulates most of the existing
functions of the body, but has indirectly influenced
the progressive development of various bodily
structures and of certain mental qualities. Courage,
pugnacity, perseverance, strength and size of body,
weapons of all kinds, musical organs, both vocal and
instrumental, bright colours and ornamental appendages,

have all been indirectly gained by the one sex or the other, through the exertion of choice, the influence of love and jealousy, and the appreciation of the beautiful in sound, colour or form; and these powers of the mind manifestly depend on the development of the brain.

Man scans with scrupulous care the character and pedigree of his horses, cattle, and dogs before he matches them; but when he comes to his own marriage he rarely, or never, takes any such care. He is impelled by nearly the same motives as the lower animals, when they are left to their own free choice, though he is in so far superior to them that he highly values mental charms and virtues. On the other hand he is strongly attracted by mere wealth or rank. Yet he might by selection do something not only for the bodily constitution and frame of his offspring, but for their intellectual and moral qualities. Both sexes ought to refrain from marriage if they are in any marked degree inferior in body or mind; but such hopes are Utopian and will never be even partially realised until the laws of inheritance are thoroughly known. Everyone does good service, who aids towards this end. When the principles of breeding and inheritance are better understood, we shall not hear ignorant members of our legislature rejecting with scorn a plan for ascertaining whether or not consanguineous marriages are injurious to man.

The advancement of the welfare of mankind is a most intricate problem: all ought to refrain from marriage who cannot avoid abject poverty for their children; for poverty is not only a great evil, but tends to its own increase by leading to recklessness in marriage. On the other hand, as Mr. Galton has remarked, if the prudent avoid marriage, whilst the reckless marry, the inferior members tend to supplant the better members of society. Man, like every other animal, has no doubt advanced to his present high condition through a struggle for existence consequent on his rapid multiplication; and if he is to advance still higher, it is to be feared that he must remain subject to a severe struggle. Otherwise he would sink into indolence, and the more gifted men would not be more successful in the battle of life than the less gifted. Hence our natural rate of increase, though leading to many and obvious evils, must not be greatly

diminished by any means.   There should be open
competition for all men; and the most able should not
be prevented by laws or customs from succeeding best
and rearing the largest number of offspring. Important
as the struggle for existence has been and even still
is, yet as far as the highest part of man's nature is
concerned there are other agencies more important. For
the moral qualities are advanced, either directly or
indirectly, much more through the effects of habit, the
reasoning powers, instruction, religion, etc., than
through natural selection, though to this latter agency
may be safely attributed the social instincts, which
afforded the basis for the development of the moral
sense.

     The main conclusion arrived at in this work,
namely, that man is descended from some lowly organised
form, will, I regret to think, be highly distasteful to
many. But there can hardly be a doubt that we are
descended from barbarians.   The astonishment which I
felt on first seeing a party of Fuegians on a wild and
broken shore will never be forgotten by me, for the
reflection at once rushed into my mind--such were our
ancestors.   These men were absolutely naked and
bedaubed with paint, their long hair was tangled, their
mouths frothed with excitement, and their expression
was wild, startled, and distrustful.   They possessed
hardly any arts, and like wild animals lived on what
they could catch; they had no government, and were
merciless to every one not of their own small tribe.
He who has seen a savage in his native land will not
feel much shame, if forced to acknowledge that the
blood of some more humble creature flows in his veins.
For my own part I would as soon be descended from that
heroic little monkey, who braved his dreaded enemy in
order to save the life of his keeper, or from that old
baboon, who descending from the mountains, carried away
in triumph his young comrade from a crowd of astonished
dogs--as from a savage who delights to torture his
enemies, offers up bloody sacrifices, practices
infanticide without remorse, treats his wives like
slaves, knows no decency, and is haunted by the
grossest superstitions.

     Man may be excused for feeling some pride at
having risen, though not through his own exertions, to
the very summit of the organic scale; and the fact of
his having thus risen, instead of having been

aboriginally placed there, may give him hope for a still higher destiny in the distant future. But we are not here concerned with hopes or fears, only with the truth as far as our reason permits us to discover it; and I have given the evidence to the best of my ability. We must, however, acknowledge, as it seems to me, that man with all his noble qualities, with sympathy which feels for the most debased, with benevolence which extends not only to other men but to the humblest living creature, with his god-like intellect which has penetrated into the movements and constitution of the solar system--with all these exalted powers--Man still bears in his bodily frame the indelible stamp of his lowly origin.

23

FRIEDRICH NIETZSCHE

Born in Rocken, Germany, Friedrich Nietzsche (1844-1900), after acquiring an excellent classical education at Schulpforta, a famous monastery school near Naumber, attended the universities of Bonn and Leipzig where he studied classical philosophy. He made such an impression on some of his professors, that on their recommendation, he was named to fill the vacant chair of classical philology at the University of Basel in Switzerland despite the fact that he did not yet possess the doctorate (which University of Leipzig hurriedly conferred on him before he left for Basel). After serving only one year at Basel, in 1870, he volunteered to serve as a medical orderly in the Prussian army but because he contracted dysentery and diphtheria. he returned to Basel. There he resumed his teaching duties despite the fact that he had not fully recovered from his ailments. In fact, he would be plagued by ill-health for the remainder of his life. In 1872, he published his first book, <u>The Birth of Tragedy from the Spirit of Music</u> and over the next four years published four <u>Untimely Meditations</u>. The titles of the four meditations were: <u>David Strauss, The Confessor and Writer</u>; <u>Of the Use and Disadvantage of History for Life</u>; <u>Schopenhauer as Educator</u>; and <u>Richard Wagner in Bayreuth</u>. During his first years at Basel, Nietzsche was very much influenced by Schopenhauer's book, <u>The World as Will and Idea</u>, and by Richard Wagner, the brilliant German composer. However, in 1876, Nietzsche became very disillusioned with Wagner, a man in whom he had hoped to find an innovator of European thought and art. Furthermore, already in 1876, Nietzsche was weary of his teaching of classical philology and longed to engage in the writing of his philosophical views. In 1879, he resigned from the university and, with the modest pension he received, spent the next ten years writing at a furious pace, publishing such renowned and controversial works as: <u>The Gay Science</u> (1882), <u>Thus Spake Zarathustra</u> (written in four parts between 1882-1885), <u>Beyond Good and Evil</u> (1886), <u>Toward a Genealogy of Morals</u> (1887), <u>The Twilight of the Idols</u> (1888), <u>The Anti-Christ</u> (1888), and <u>Nietzsche Contra Wagner</u> (1888).

Suddenly, in January 1889, Nietzsche became insane (one theory is that he suffered this fate due to syphilis which he may have contracted while ministering to soldiers during his brief stint as a medical orderly during the Franco-Prussian War). He was initially committed to an asylum but was then released to the care of his mother and, upon her death in 1897, to the care of his sister. He died of pneumonia in 1900 and subsequent to his death, his sister proceeded to publish an edited collection of his notes under the title _The Will to Power_ and later published _Ecce Home_ (1908), a work that had been written in 1888.

Nietzsche's philosophical significance lies in both his role as critic and as oracle. As critic, Nietzsche unmercifully attacks Western European thought from Plato to modern science to Christianity, as well as various modern ideologies such as nationalism, liberalism, and socialism. He decries what he identifies as the advent of nihilism and he claims that, paradoxically, even though heretofore philosophy, science, Christianity, etc., had developed value systems intended to overcome nihilism, they were, in fact, accelerating its coming. In the first selection from _The Gay Science_, Nietzsche proclaims in the parable of the madman the death of God. He announces that God is dead (for the majority of Europeans of the 19th century) despite the fact that they were unaware of this event. His proclamation was meant to signal the challenge that this fact poses to Europeans. In the selection from _Thus Spake Zarathustra_, we find Nietzsche expressing his will to power theory. By the will to power, he means the will to create, man's most distinctive act. According to Nietzsche, man must overcome himself in order to become what he is. In so doing, the "higher Man' (the Superman or Overman) will emerge as man's last hope in the face of the onslaught of nihilism. However, this new species of man (Higher Man) does not represent the emergence of a Golden Age. For Nietzsche, the world has no aim. Higher Man can bring meaning to the world by his creative activity and not by his creations which will themselves eventually run into nothingness. So Nietzsche postulates the doctrine of "eternal recurrence": everything that has happened happens again and again an infinite number of times. This doctrine can be found in aphorisms 285 and 341 of _The Gay Science_.

THE GAY SCIENCE:

The death of God and man doomed to eternal recurrence.

[125]

    The Madman. Have you not heard of that madman who
lit a lantern in the bright morning hours, ran to the
market place, and cried incessantly, "I seek God! I
seek God!" As many of   those who do not believe in God
were standing around just then, he provoked much
laughter. Why, did he get lost? said one. Did he lose
his way like a child? said another. Or is he hiding?
Is he afraid of us?   Has he gone on a voyage? or
emigrated? Thus they yelled and laughed. The madman
jumped into their midst and pierced them with his
glances.

    "Whither is God" he cried. "I shall tell you. We
have killed him--you and I.   All of us are his
murderers. But how   have we done this? How were we
able to drink up the sea?   Who gave us the sponge to
wipe away the entire horizon?   What did we do when we
unchained this earth from its sun?   Whither is it
moving now? Whither are we moving now? Away from all
suns?   Are we not plunging continually? Backward,
sideward, forward, in all directions?   Is there any up
or down left?   Are we not straying as through an
infinite nothing?   Do we not feel the breath of empty
space? Has it not become colder?   Is not night and
more night coming on all the while? Must not lanterns
be lit in the morning?   Do we not hear anything yet of
the noise of the gravediggers who are burying God?   Do
we not smell anything yet of God's decomposition?
Gods too decompose.   God is dead.   God remains dead.
And we have killed him.   How shall we, the murderers of
all murderers, comfort ourselves? What was holiest and
most powerful of all that the world has yet owned has
bled to death under our knives.   Who will wipe this
blood off us?   What water is there for us to clean
ourselves? What festivals of atonement, what sacred
games shall we have to invent? Is not the greatness of
this deed too great for us?   Must not we ourselves
become gods simply to seem worthy of it? There has
never been a greater deed; and whoever will be born
after us--for the sake of this deed he will be part of
a higher history than all history hitherto."
231

Here the madman fell silent and looked again at
his listeners; and they too were silent and stared at
him in astonishment. At last he threw his lantern on
the ground, and it broke and went out. "I come too
early," he said then; "my time has not come yet. This
tremendous event is still on its way, still
wandering--it has not yet reached the ears of man.
Lightning and thunder require time, the light of the
stars requires time, deeds require time even after they
are done, before they can be seen and heard. This deed
is still more distant from them than the most distant
stars--<u>and yet they have done it themselves</u>."

    It has been related further than on that same day
the madman entered divers churches and there sang his
<u>requiem aeternam deo</u>. Led out and called to account,
he is said to have replied each time, "What are these
churches now if they are not the tombs and sepulchers
of God?"

[285]

    <u>Excelsior</u>! "You will never pray again, never adore
again, never again rest in endless trust; you deny
yourself any stopping before ultimate wisdom, ultimate
goodness, ultimate power, while unharnessing your
thoughts; you have no perpetual guardian and friend for
your seven solitudes; you live without a view of
mountains with snow on their peaks and fire in their
hearts; there is no avenger for you, no eventual
improver; there is no reason any more in what happens,
no love in what will happen to you; no resting place is
any longer open to your heart, where it has only to
find and no longer to seek; you resist any ultimate
peace, you want the eternal recurrence of war and
peace. Man of renunciation, do you want to renounce
all this? Who will give you the necessary strength?
Nobody yet has had this strength."   There is a lake
which one day refused to flow off and erected a dam
where it had hitherto flowed off: ever since, this
lake has been rising higher and higher. Perhaps that
very renunciation will also lend us the strength to
bear the renunciation itself; perhaps man will rise
ever higher when he once ceases to <u>flow out</u> into a god.

232

<u>The greatest stress</u>. How, if some day or night a demon were to sneak after you into your loneliest loneliness and say to you, "This   life as you now live it and have lived it, you will have to live once more and innumerable times more; and there will be nothing new in it, but every pain and every joy and every thought and sigh and everything immeasurably small or great in your life must return to you--all in the same succession and sequence--even this spider and this moonlight between the trees, and even this moment and I myself. The eternal hourglass of existence is turned over and over, and you with it, a dust grain of dust." Would you not throw yourself down and gnash your teeth and curse the demon who spoke thus?   Or did you once experience a tremendous moment when you would have answered him. "You are a god, and never have I heard anything more godly." If this thought were to gain possession of you, it would change you, as you are, or perhaps crush you.   The question in each and every thing.   "Do you want this once more and innumerable times more?" would weigh upon your actions as the greatest stress. Or how well disposed would you have to become to yourself and to life to <u>crave nothing more fervently</u> than this ultimate eternal confirmation and seal?

THUS SPAKE ZARATHUSTRA:

Man as bridge to the Superman

Part I

<u>3</u>

When Zarathustra arrived at the nearest town which
adjoineth the forest, he found many people assembled in
the market-place; for it had been announced that a
rope-dancer would give a performance. And Zarathustra
spake thus unto the people:

<u>I teach you the Superman</u>. Man is something that
is to be
 surpassed. What have ye done to surpass man?

All beings hitherto have created something beyond
themselves: and ye want to be the ebb of that great
tide, and would rather go back to the beast than
surpass man? What is the ape to man? A
laughing-stock, a thing of shame. And just the same
shall man be to the Superman: a laughing-stock, a
thing of shame.

Ye have made your way from the worm to man, and
much within you is still worm. Once were ye apes, and
even yet man is more of an ape than any of the apes.

Even the wisest among you is only a disharmony and
hybrid of plant and phantom. But do I bid you become
phantoms or plants?

Lo, I teach you the Superman!

The Superman is the meaning of the earth. Let
your will say: The Superman <u>shall be</u> the meaning of
the earth!

I conjure you, my brethren, <u>remain true to the earth</u>, and believe not those who speak unto you of superearthly hopes! Poisoners are they, whether you know it or not.

Despisers of life are they, decaying ones and poisoned ones themselves, of whom the earth is weary: so away with them!

Once blasphemy against God was the greatest blasphemy; but God died, and therewith also those blasphemers. To blaspheme the earth is now the dreadfulest sin, and to rate the heart of the unknowable higher than the meaning of the earth!

Once the soul looked contemptuously on the body, and then that contempt was the supreme thing:--the soul wished the body meagre, ghastly, and famished. Thus is thought to escape from the body and the earth.

Oh, that soul was itself meagre, ghastly, and famished; and cruelty was the delight of that soul!

But ye, also, my brethren, tell me: What doth your body say about your soul? Is your soul not poverty and pollution and wretched self-complacency?

Verily, a polluted stream is man. One must be a sea, to receive a polluted stream without becoming impure.

Lo, I teach you the Superman: he is that sea; in him can your great contempt be submerged.

What is the greatest thing ye can experience? It is the hour of great contempt. The hour in which even your happiness becometh loathsome unto you, and so also your reason and virtue.

The hour when ye say: "What good is my happiness! It is poverty and pollution and wretched

self-complacency.   But   my   happiness should justify
existence itself!"

     The hour when ye   say: "What good is my reason!
Doth it long for   knowledge   as   the lion for his food?
It   is   poverty   and   pollution   and   wretched
self-complacency!"

     The hour when ye say: What good is my virtue! As
yet it hath not made me   passionate. How weary I am of
my good and   my   bad!   It   is   all   poverty   and
pollution and wretched self-complacency!"

     The hour when ye say: "What good is my justice! I
do not see   that   I   am   fervour   and   fuel. The just,
however, are fervour and fuel!"

     The hour when we say: "What good is my pity! Is
not pity the cross   on   which   he   is nailed who loveth
man? But my pity is not a crucifixion."

     Have ye ever   spoken   thus?   Have   ye ever cried
thus? Ah! would that I had heard you crying thus!

     It is not   your   sin--it is your self-satisfaction
that crieth unto heaven;   your   very sparingness in sin
crieth unto heaven!

     Where   is   the   lightning   to   lick   you   with its
tongue? Where is the   frenzy   with which ye should be
inoculated?

     Lo,   I   teach   you   the   Superman: he   is that
lightning, he is that frenzy!--

     When   Zarathustra   had   thus   spoken,   one   of the
people called out: "We   have   now heard enough of the
rope-dancer; it is time now   for   us   to see him!" And
all   the   people   laughed   at   Zarathustra.   But   the
rope-dancer, who thought   the   words   applied   to him,
began his performance.

4

Zarathustra, however, looked at the people and wondered. Then he spake thus:

Man is a rope stretched between the animal and the Superman--a rope over an abyss.

A dangerous crossing, a dangerous wayfaring, a dangerous looking-back, a dangerous trembling and halting.

What is great in man is that he is a bridge and not a goal: what is lovable in man is that he is an <u>over-going</u> and a <u>down-going</u>.

I love those that know now how to live except as down-goers, for they are the over-goers.

I love the great despisers, because they are the great adorers, and arrows of longing for the other shore.

I love those who do not first seek a reason beyond the stars for going down and being sacrifices, but sacrifice themselves to the earth, that the earth of the Superman may hereafter arrive.

I love him who liveth in order to know, and seeketh to know in order that the Superman may hereafter live. Thus seeketh he his own down-going.

I love him who laboureth and inventeth. that he may build the house for the Superman, and prepare for him earth. animal, and plant: for thus seeketh he his own down-going.

I love him who loveth his virtue: for virtue is the will to down-going, and an arrow of longing.

I love him who reserveth no share of spirit for himself, but wanteth to be wholly the spirit of his virtue: thus walketh he as spirit over the bridge.

I love him who maketh his virtue his inclination and destiny: thus, for the sake of his virtue, he is willing to live on, or live no more.

I love him who desireth not too many virtues. One virtue is more of a virtue than two, because it is more of a knot for one's destiny to cling to.

I love him whose soul is lavish, who wanteth no thanks and doth not give back: for he always bestoweth, and desireth not to keep for himself.

I love him who is ashamed when the dice fall in his favour, and who then asketh: "Am I a dishonest player?" --for he is willing to succumb.

I love him who scattereth golden words in advance of his deeds, and always doeth more than he promiseth: for he seeketh his own down-going.

I love him who justifieth the future ones, and redeemeth the past ones: for he is willing to succumb through the present ones.

I love him who chasteneth his God, because he loveth his God: for he must succumb through the wrath of his God.

I love him whose soul is deep even in the wounding, and may succumb through a small matter: thus goeth he willingly over the bridge.

I love him whose soul is so overfull that he forgetteth himself, and all things are in him: thus all things become his down-going.

I love him who is of a free spirit and a free heart: thus is his head only the bowels of his heart; his heart, however, causeth his down-going.

I love all who are like heavy drops falling one by one out of the dark cloud that lowereth over man: they herald the coming of the lightning, and succumb as heralds.

Lo, I am a herald of the lightning, and a heavy drop out of the cloud: the lightning, however, is the _Superman_.--

_5_

When Zarathustra had spoken these words, he again looked at the people, and was silent. "There they stand," said he to his heart; "there they laugh: they understand me not; I am not the mouth for these ears.

Must one first batter their ears, that they may learn to
hear with their eyes? Must one clatter like kettledrums and penitential preachers? Or do they only believe the stammerer?

They have something whereof they are proud. What do they call it, that which maketh them proud? Culture, they call it; it distinguisheth them from the goatherds.

They dislike, therefore, to hear of 'contempt' of themselves. So I will appeal to their pride.

I will speak unto them of the most contemptible thing: that however, is _the last man_!"

And thus spake Zarathustra unto the people.

239

It is time for man to fix his goal. It is time for man to   plant the germ of his highest hope.

Still is his soil rich enough for it. But that soil will one day be poor and exhausted, and no lofty tree will any longer be able to grow thereon.

Alas! there cometh the time when man will no longer launch   the arrow of his longing beyond man--and the string of his bow   will have unlearned to whizz!

I tell you: one must still have chaos in one, to give birth   to a dancing star. I tell you: ye have still chaos in you.

Alas! There cometh the time when man will no longer give   birth to any star. Alas! There cometh the time of the most   despicable man, who can no longer despise himself.

Lo! I show you <u>the last man</u>.

"What is love?   What is creation?   What is longing? What is   a star?"-so asketh the last man and blinketh.

The earth hath then become small, and on it there hoppeth the last man who maketh everything small. His species is   ineradicable like that of the ground-flea; the last man liveth   longest.

"We have discovered happiness"--say the last men, and blink   thereby.

They have left the regions where it is hard to live; for they need warmth.   One still loveth one's neighbour and rubbeth against him; for one needeth warmth.

Turning ill and being distrustful, they consider sinful: they walk warily. He is a fool who still stumbleth over stones or men!

A little poison now and then: that maketh pleasant dreams. And much poison at last for a pleasant death.

One still worketh, for work is a pastime. But one is careful lest the pastime should hurt one.

One no longer becometh poor or rich; both are too burdensome. Who still wanteth to rule? Who still wanteth to obey? Both are too burdensome.

No shepherd, and one herd! Everyone wanteth the same; everyone is equal: he who hath other sentiments goeth voluntarily into the madhouse.

"Formerly all the world was insane,"--say the subtlest of them, and blink thereby.

They are clever and know all that hath happened: so there is no end to their raillery. People still fall out, but are soon reconciled--otherwise it spoileth their stomachs.

They have their little pleasures for the day, and their little pleasures for the night, but they have a regard for health.

"We have discovered happiness,"--say the last men, and blink thereby.--

And here ended the first discourse of Zarathustra, which is also called "The Prologue", for at this point the shouting and mirth of the multitude interrupted him. "Give us this last man, O Zarathustra,"--they called out--"make us into these last men! Then will we make thee a present of the Superman!" And all the people exulted and smacked

their lips. Zarathustra, however, turned sad, and said
to his heart:

     "They understand me not: I am not the mouth for
these ears.

     Too long, perhaps, have I lived in the mountains;
too much have I hearkened unto the brooks and trees:
now do I speak unto them as unto the goatherds.

     Calm is my soul, and clear, like the mountains in
the morning. But they think me cold, and mocker with
terrible jests.

     And now do they look at me and laugh: and while
they laugh they hate me too.   There is ice in their
laughter."

...

Part IV

73. The Higher Man

1

     When I came unto men for the first time, then did
I commit   the anchorite folly, the great folly: I
appeared on the market-place.

     And when I spake unto all, I spake unto none. In
the evening, however, rope-dancers were my companions,
and corpses; and I myself almost a corpse.

     With the new morning, however, there came unto me
a new truth: then did I learn to say: "Of what
account to me are   market-place and populace and
populace-noise and long populace-cars!"

Ye higher men, learn _this_ from me: On the
market-place no one believeth in higher men. But if ye
will speak there, very well! The populace, however,
blinketh: "We are all equal."

"Ye higher men,"--so blinketh the populace--"there
are no higher men, we are all equal; man is man,
before God--we are all equal!"

Before God!--Now, however, this God hath died.
Before the populace, however, we will not be equal.
Ye higher men, away from the market-place!

2

Before God!--Now however this God hath died! Ye
higher men, this God was your greatest danger.

Only since he lay in the grave have ye again
arisen. Now only cometh the great noontide, now only
doth the higher man become--master!

Have ye understood this word, O my brethren? Ye
are frightened: do your hearts turn giddy? Doth the
abyss here yawn for you?   Doth the hell-hound here
yelp at you?

Well! Take heart! Ye higher men! Now only
travaileth the mountain of the human future. God hath
died: now do _we_ desire--the Superman to live.

3

The most careful ask today: "How is man to be
maintained?" Zarathustra however asketh, as the first
and only one: "How is man to be _surpassed_?

The Superman, I have at heart; _that_ is the first
and only thing to me--and _not_ man: not the neighbour,
not the poorest, not the sorriest, not the best.--

O my brethren, what I can love in man is that he
is an   over-going and a down-going. And also in
you there is much   that maketh me love and hope.

In that ye have despised, ye higher men, that
maketh me hope. For the great despisers are the great
reverers.

In that ye have despaired, there is much to
honour. For ye   have not learned to submit
yourselves, ye have not learned   petty policy....

GEORGE HERBERT MEAD

After receiving his baccalaureate degree from Oberlin College in 1883, George Herbert Mead (1863-1931), a native of South Hadley, Massachusetts, pursued graduate work at Harvard University where he came under the influence of Josiah Royce and William James. Subsequently, he spent three years in Europe studying philosophy and psychology and upon his return from abroad, was appointed instructor at the University of Michigan. In 1892, he joined the staff of the University of Chicago eventually becoming chairman of the philosophy department. After John Dewey, Mead was the most prominent of the group of thinkers who gathered at the university about the turn of the century and who soon came to be known as the "Chicago School". In fact, Dewey, in 1931, described Mead as the most original mind in philosophy in America of the previous generation and admitted that he hated to think what his own thinking might have been were it not for the seminal ideas he derived from him. Mead's influence was felt by a whole generation of psychologists, social scientists, and philosophers and the primary vehicle used to transmit his ideas was his classroom. Indeed, Mead was not as prolific a writer as Dewey had become; nevertheless, as Charles Morris had occasion to remark in the introduction to <u>Mind, Self, and Society from the Standpoint of a Social Behaviorist</u>: "If Dewey gives range and vision, Mead gave analytical depth and scientific precision. If Dewey is at once the rolling rim and many of the radiating spokes of the contemporary pragmatist wheel, Mead is the hub."

In addition to the aforementioned <u>Mind, Self, and Society</u> which was published posthumously in 1934, and which consists primarily of notes from his lectures in his course in social psychology, three other works were published posthumously: <u>The Philosophy of the Present</u> (1932), <u>Movements of Thought in the Nineteenth Century</u> (1936), and <u>The Philosophy of the Act</u> (1938).

In the selection from <u>Mind, Self, and Society</u> reprinted below, Mead, after initially discussing the social foundations of the self and suggesting that the self does not consist simply in the bare organization of social attitudes, proceeds to raise the question of the nature of the "I" which is aware of the social "me". He observes that he is not interested in raising the metaphysical question of how a person can be both "I" and "me", but that his primary concern is to consider the significance of the distinction from the point of view of conduct itself.

The social foundations of the self and the
nature of the "I" as distinct from the
social "me".

21. The Self and the Subjective

The process out of which the self arises is a
social process which implies interaction of individuals
in the group, implies the pre-existence of the group.
It implies also certain co-operative activities in
which the different members of the group are involved.
It implies, further, that out of this process there may
in turn develop a more elaborate organization than that
out of which the self has arisen, and that the selves
may be the organs, the essential parts at least, of
this more elaborate social organization within which
these selves arise and exist. Thus, there is a social
process out of which selves arise and within which
further differentiation, further evolution, further
organization, take place.

It has been the tendency of psychology to deal
with the self as a more or less isolated and
independent element, a sort of entity that could
conceivably exist by itself. It is possible that there
might be a single self in the universe if we start off
by identifying the self with a certain
feeling-consciousness. If we speak of this feeling as
objective, then we can think of that self as existing
by itself. We can think of a separate physical body
existing by itself, we can assume that it has these
feelings or conscious states in question, and so we can
set up that sort of a self in thought as existing
simply by itself.

Then there is another use of "consciousness" with
which we have been particularly occupied, denoting that
which we term thinking or reflective intelligence, a
use of consciousness which always has, implicitly at
least, the reference to an "I" in it. This use of
consciousness has no necessary connection with the
other; it is an entirely different conception. One

usage has to do with a certain mechanism, a certain way in which an organism acts. If an organism is endowed with sense organs then there are objects in its environment, and among those objects will be parts of its own body. It is true that if the organism did not have a retina and a central nervous system there would not be any objects of vision. For such objects to exist there have to be certain physiological conditions, but these objects are not in themselves necessarily related to a self. When we reach a self we reach a certain sort of conduct, a certain type of social process which involves the interaction of different individuals and yet implies individuals engaged in some sort of co-operative activity. In that process a self, as such, can arise.

We want to distinguish the self as a certain sort of structural process in the conduct of the form, from what we term consciousness of objects that are experienced. The two have no necessary relationship. The aching tooth is a very important element. We have to pay attention to it. It is identified in a certain sense with the self in order that we may control that sort of experience. Occasionally we have experiences which we say belong to the atmosphere. The whole world seems to be depressed, the sky is dark, the weather is unpleasant, values that we are interested in are sinking. We do not necessarily identify such a situation with the self; we simply feel a certain atmosphere about us. We come to remember that we are subject to such sorts of depression, and find that kind of an experience in our past. And then we get some sort of relief, we take aspirin, or we take a rest, and the result is that the world changes its character. There are other experiences which we may at all times identify with selves. We can distinguish, I think, very clearly between certain types of experience, which we call subjective because we alone have access to them, and that experience which we call reflective.

It is true that reflection taken by itself is something to which we alone have access. One thinks out his own demonstration of a proposition, we will say in Euclid, and the thinking is something that takes place within his own conduct. For the time being it is a demonstration which exists only in his thought. Then he publishes it and it becomes common property. For the time being it was accessible only to him. There

are other contents of this sort, such as memory images
and the play of the imagination, which are accessible
only to the individual.   There is a common character
that belongs to these types of objects which we
generally identify with consciousness and this process
which we call that of thinking, in that both are, at
least in certain phases, accessible only to the
individual. But, as I have said, the two sets of
phenomena stand on entirely different levels. This
common feature of accessibility does not necessarily
give them the same metaphysical status.   I do not now
want to discuss metaphysical problems, but I do want to
insist that the self has a sort of structure that
arises in social conduct that is entirely
distinguishable from this so-called subjective
experience of these particular sets of objects to which
the organism alone has access--the common character of
privacy of access does not fuse them together.

The self to which we have been referring arises
when the conversation of gestures is taken over into
the conduct of the individual form.   When this
conversation of gestures can be taken over into the
individual's conduct so that the attitude of the other
forms can affect the organism, and the organism can
reply with its corresponding gesture and thus arouse
the attitude of the other in its own process, then a
self arises.   Even the bare conversation of gestures
that can be carried out in lower forms is to be
explained by the fact that this conversation of
gestures has an intelligent function. Even there it is
a part of social process. If it is taken over into the
conduct of the individual it not only maintains that
function but acquires still greater capacity. If I can
take the attitude of a friend with whom I am going to
carry on a discussion, in taking that attitude I can
apply it to myself and reply as he replies, and I can
have things in very much better shape than if I had not
employed that conversation of gestures in my own
conduct. The same is true of him. It is good for both
to think out the situation in advance. Each individual
has to take also the attitude of the community, the
generalized attitude. He has to be ready to act with
reference to his own conditions just as any individual
in the community would act.

One of the greatest advances in the development of
the community arises when this reaction of the

community on the individual takes on what we call an institutional form. What we mean by that is that the whole community acts toward the individual under certain circumstances in an identical way. It makes no difference, over against a person who is stealing your property, whether it is Tom, Dick, or Harry. There is an identical response on the part of the whole community under these conditions. We call that the formation of the institution.

There is one other matter which I wish briefly to refer to now. The only way in which we can react against the disapproval of the entire community is by setting up a higher sort of community which in a certain sense out-votes the one we find. A person may reach a point of going against the whole world about him; he may stand out by himself over against it. But to do that he has to speak with the voice of reason to himself. He has to comprehend the voices of the past and of the future. That is the only way in which the self can get a voice which is more than the voice of the community. As a rule we assume that this general voice of the community is identical with the larger community of the past and the future; we assume that an organized custom represents what we call morality. The things one cannot do are those which everybody would condemn. If we take the attitude of the community over against our own responses, that is a true statement, but we must not forget this other capacity, that of replying to the community and insisting on the gesture of the community changing. We can reform the order of things; we can insist on making the community standards better standards. We are not simply bound by the community. We are engaged in a conversation in which what we say is listened to by the community and its response is one which is affected by what we have to say.... The process of conversation is one in which the individual has not only the right but the duty of talking to the community of which he is a part, and bringing about those changes which take place through the interaction of individuals. That is the way, of course, in which society gets ahead, by just such interactions as those in which some person thinks a thing out. We are continually changing our social system in some respects, and we are able to do that intelligently because we can think.

Such is the reflective process within which a self arises; and what I have been trying to do is to distinguish this kind of consciousness from consciousness as a set of characters determined by the accessibility to the organism of certain sorts of objects. It is true that our thinking is also, while it is just thinking, accessible only to the organism. But that common character of being accessible only to the organism does not make either thought or the self something which we are to identify with a group of objects which simply are accessible. We cannot identify the self with what is commonly called consciousness, that is, which the private or subjective thereness of the characters of objects.

There is, of course, a current distinction between consciousness and self-consciousness: consciousness answering to certain experiences such as those of pain or pleasure, self-consciousness referring to a recognition or appearance of a self as an object. It is, however, very generally assumed that these other conscious contents carry with them also a self-consciousness--that a pain is always somebody's pain, and that if there were not this reference to some individual it would not be pain. There is a very definite element of truth in this, but it is far from the whole story. The pain does have to belong to an individual; it has to be your pain if it is going to belong to you. Pain can belong to anybody, but if it did belong to everybody it would be comparatively unimportant. I suppose it is conceivable that under an anesthetic what takes place is the dissociation of experiences so that the suffering, so to speak, is no longer your suffering. We have illustrations of that, short of the anesthetic dissociation, in an experience of a disagreeable thing which loses its power over us because we give our attention to something else. If we can get, so to speak, outside of the thing, dissociating it from the eye that is regarding it, we may find that it has lost a great deal of its unendurable character. The unendurableness of pain is a reaction against it. If you can actually keep yourself from reacting against suffering you get rid of a certain content in the suffering itself. What takes place in effect is that it ceases to be your pain. You simply regard it objectively. Such is the point of view we are continually impressing on a person when he is apt to be swept away by emotion. In that case what we get rid of is not the offense itself, but the reaction against the offense. The objective character of the judge is that of a person who is neutral, who can simply stand outside of a situation and assess it. If we can get that judicial attitude in regard to the offenses of a person against ourselves, we reach the point where we do not resent them but understand them, we get the situation where to understand is to forgive. We remove much of experience outside of our own self by this attitude. The distinctive and natural attitude against another is a resentment of an offense, but we now have in a certain sense passed beyond that self and become a self with other attitudes. There is a certain technique, then, to which we subject ourselves in enduring suffering or any emotional situation, and which consists in partially separating one's self from the experience so that it is no longer the experience of the individual in question.

If, now, we could separate the experience entirely, so that we should not remember it, so that we should not have to take it up continually into the self from day to day, from moment to moment, then it would not exist any longer so far as we are concerned. If we had no memory which identifies experiences with the self, then they would certainly disappear so far as their relation to the self is concerned, and yet they might continue as sensuous or sensible experiences without being taken up into a self. That sort of situation is presented in the pathological case of a multiple personality in which an individual loses the memory of a certain phase of his existence. Everything connected with that phase of his existence is gone and he becomes a different personality. The past has a reality whether in the experience or not, but here it is not identified with the self--it does not go to make up the self. We take an attitude of that sort, for example, with reference to others when a person has committed some sort of an offense which leads to a statement of the situation, an admission, and perhaps regret, and then is dropped. A person who forgives but does not forget is an unpleasant companion; what goes with forgiving is forgetting, getting rid of the memory of it.

There are many illustrations which can be brought up of the loose relationship of given contents to a self in defense of our recognition of them as having a certain value outside of the self. At the least, it

must be granted that we can approach the point where
something which we recognize as a content is less and
less essential to the self, is held off from the
present self, and no longer has the value for that self
which it had for the former self. Extreme cases seem
to support the view that a certain portion of such
contents can be entirely cut off from the self. While
in some sense it is there ready to appear under
specific conditions, for the time being it is
dissociated and does not get in above the threshold of
our self-consciousness.

Self-consciousness, on the other hand, is
definitely organized about the social individual, and
that, as we have seen, is not simply because one is in
a social group and affected by others and affects them,
but because (and this is a point I have been
emphasizing) his own experience as a self is one which
he takes over from his action upon others. He becomes
a self in so far as he can take the attitude of another
and act toward himself as others act. In so far as the
conversation of gestures can become part of conduct in
the direction and control of experience, then a self
can arise. It is the social process of influencing
others in a social act and then taking the attitude of
the others aroused by the stimulus, and then reacting
in turn to this response, which constitutes a self.

Our bodies are parts of our environment; and it is
possible for the individual to experience and be
conscious of his body, and of bodily sensations,
without being conscious or aware of himself--without,
in other words, taking the attitude of the other toward
himself. According to the social theory of
consciousness, what we mean by consciousness is that
peculiar character and aspect of the environment of
individual human experience which is due to human
society, a society of other individual selves who take
the attitude of the other toward themselves. The
physiological conception or theory of consciousness is
by itself inadequate; it requires supplementation from
the socio-psychological point of view. The taking or
feeling of the attitude of the other toward yourself is
what constitutes self-consciousness, and not mere
organic sensations of which the individual is aware and
which he experiences. Until the rise of his
self-consciousness in the process of social experience,
the individual experiences his body--its feelings and

sensations--merely as an immediate part of his
environment, not as his own, not in terms of
self-consciousness. The self and self-consciousness
have first to arise, and then these experiences can be
identified peculiarly with the self, or appropriated by
the self; to enter, so to speak, into this heritage of
experience, the self has first to develop within the
social process in which this heritage is involved.

Through self-consciousness the individual organism
enters in some sense into its own environmental field;
its own body becomes a part of the set of environmental
stimuli to which it responds or reacts. Apart from the
context of the social process at its higher
levels--those at which it involves conscious
communication, conscious conversations of gestures,
among the individual organisms interacting with it--the
individual organism does not set itself as a whole over
against its environment; it does not as a whole become
an object to itself (and hence is not self-conscious);
it is not as a whole a stimulus to which it reacts. On
the contrary, it responds only to parts or separate
aspects of itself, and regards them, not as parts or
aspects of itself at all, but simply as parts or
aspects of its environment in general. Only within the
social process at its higher levels, only in terms of
the more developed forms of the social environment or
social situation, does the total individual organism
become an object to itself, and hence self-conscious;
in the social process at its lower, non-conscious
levels, and also in the merely psycho-physiological
environment or situation which is logically antecedent
to and presupposed by the social process of experience
and behavior, it does not thus become an object to
itself. In such experience or behavior as may be
called self-conscious, we act and react particularly
with reference to ourselves, though also with reference
to other individuals; and to be self-conscious is
essentially to become an object to one's self in virtue
of one's social relations to other individuals.

Emphasis should be laid on the central position of
thinking when considering the nature of the self.
Self-consciousness, rather than affective experience
with its motor accompaniments, provides the core and
primary structure of the self, which is thus
essentially a cognitive rather than an emotional
phenomenon. The thinking or intellectual process--the

internalization and inner dramatization, by the individual, of the external conversation of significant gestures which constitutes his chief mode of interaction with other individuals belonging to the same society--is the earliest experiential phase in the genesis and development of the self.... The essence of the self, as we have said, is cognitive: it lies in the internalized conversation of gestures which constitutes thinking, or in terms of which thought or reflection proceeds. And hence the origin and foundation of the self, like those of thinking, are social.

22. The "I" and the "Me"

We have discussed at length the social foundations of the self, and hinted that the self does not consist simply in the bare organization of social attitudes. We may now explicitly raise the question as to the nature of the "I" which is aware of the social "me." I do not mean to raise the metaphysical question of how a person can be both "I" and "me," but to ask for the significance of this distinction from the point of view of conduct itself. Where in conduct does the "I" come in as over against the "me"? If one determines what his position is in society and feels himself as having a certain function and privilege, these are all defined with reference to an "I," but the "I" is not a "me" and cannot become a "me." We may have a better self and a worse self, but that again is not the "I" as over against the "me," because they are both selves. We approve of one and disapprove of the other, but when we bring up one or the other they are there for such approval as "me's." The "I" does not get into the limelight; we talk to ourselves, but do not see ourselves. The "I" reacts to the self which arises through the taking of the attitudes of others. Through taking those attitudes we have introduced the "me" and we react to it as an "I."

The simplest way of handling the problem would be in terms of memory. I talk to myself, and I remember what I said and perhaps the emotional content that went with it. The "I" of this moment is present in the "me" of the next moment. There again I cannot turn around quick enough to catch myself. I become a "me" in so far as I remember what I said. The "I" can be given,

255

however, this functional relationship. It is because
of the "I" that we say that we are never fully aware of
what we are, that we surprise ourselves by our own
action. It is as we act that we are aware of
ourselves. It is in memory that the "I" is constantly
present in experience. We can go back directly a few
moments in our experience, and then we are dependent
upon memory images for the rest. So that the "I" in
memory is there as the spokesman of the self of the
second, or minute, or day ago. As given, it is a "me,"
but it is a "me" which was the "I" at the earlier time.
If you ask, then, where directly in your own experience
the "I" comes in, the answer is that it comes in as a
historical figure. It is what you were a second ago
that is the "I" of the "me." It is another "me" that
has to take that role. You cannot get the immediate
response of the "I" in the process. The "I" is in a
certain sense that with which we do identify ourselves.
The getting of it into experience constitutes one of
the problems of most of our conscious experience; it is
not directly given in experience.

     The "I" is the response of the organism to the
attitudes of the others; the "me" is the organized set
of attitudes of others which one himself assumes. The
attitudes of the others constitute the organized "me,"
and then one reacts toward that as an "I." I now wish
to examine these concepts in greater detail.

     There is neither "I" nor "me" in the conversation
of gestures; the whole act is not yet carried out, but
the preparation takes place in this field of gesture.
Now, in so far as the individual arouses in himself the
attitudes of the others, there arises an organized
group of responses. And it is due to the individual's
ability to take the attitudes of these others in so far
as they can be organized that he gets
self-consciousness. The taking of all of those
organized sets of attitudes gives him his "me"; that is
the self he is aware of. He can throw the ball to some
other member because of the demand made upon him from
other members of the team. That is the self that
immediately exists for him in his consciousness. He
has their attitudes, knows what they want and what the
consequence of any act of his will be, and he has
assumed responsibility for the situation. Now, it is
the presence of those organized sets of attitudes that
constitutes that "me" to which he as an "I" is

responding. But what that response will be he does not
know and nobody else knows.   Perhaps he will make a
brilliant play or an error.   The response to that
situation as it appears in his immediate experience is
uncertain, and it is that which constitutes the "I."

     The "I" is his action over against that social
situation within his own conduct, and it gets into his
experience only after he has carried out the act.   Then
he is aware of it.   He had to do such a thing and he
did it. He fulfills his duty and he may look with
pride at the throw which he made. The "me" arises to
do that duty--that is the way in which it arises in his
experience. He had in him all the attitudes of others,
calling for a certain response; that was the "me" of
that situation, and his response is the "I."

     I want to call attention particularly to the fact
that this response of the "I" is something that is more
or less uncertain.   The attitudes of others which one
assumes as affecting his own conduct constitute the
"me," and that is something that is there, but the
response to it is as yet not given. When one sits down
to think anything out, he has certain data that are
there. Suppose that it is a social situation which he
has to straighten out.   He sees himself from the point
of view of one individual or another in the group.
These individuals, related all together, give him a
certain self. Well, what is he going to do? He does
not know and nobody else knows.   He can get the
situation into his experience because he can assume the
attitudes of the various individuals involved in it.
He knows how they feel about it by the assumption of
their attitudes.   He says, in effect, "I have done
certain things that seem to commit me to a certain
course of conduct." Perhaps if he does so act it will
place him in a false position with another group. The
"I" as a response to this situation, in contrast to the
"me" which is involved in the attitudes which he takes,
is uncertain. And when the response takes place, then
it appears in the field of experience largely as a
memory image....

     The "I," then, in this relation of the "I" and the
"me," is something that is, so to speak, responding to
a social situation which is within the experience of
the individual. It is the answer which the individual

257

makes to the attitude which others take toward him when
he assumes an attitude toward them. Now, the attitudes
he is taking toward them are present in his own
experience, but his response to them will contain a
novel element. The "I" gives the sense of freedom, of
initiative. The situation is there for us to act in a
self-conscious fashion. We are aware of ourselves, and
of what the situation is, but exactly how we will act
never gets into experience until after the action takes
place....

     ...Taken together they [the "I" and "me"]
constitute a personality as it appears in social
experience. The self is essentially a social process
going on with these two distinguishable phases. If it
did not have these two phases there could not be
conscious responsibility, and there would be nothing
novel in experience.

     23.   Social Attitudes and the Physical World

     The self is not so much a substance as a process
in which the conversation of gestures has been
internalized within an organic form. This process does
not exist for itself, but is simply a phase of the
whole social organization of which the individual is a
part. The organization of the social act has been
imported into the organism and becomes then the mind of
the individual. It still includes the attitudes of
others, but now highly organized, so that they become
what we call social attitudes rather than roles of
separate individuals. This process of relating one's
own organism to the others in the interactions that are
going on, in so far as it is imported into the conduct
of the individual with the conversation of the "I" and
the "me," constitutes the self....

JOHN DEWEY

Along with William James, John Dewey (1859-1952) substantially contributed to bringing philosophy to the attention of the educated public of America. Although his thinking was primarily known by way of his novel philosophy of education, his impact has been felt in psychology, logic, epistemology, philosophy of science, aesthetics, and many other areas as well. Born in Burlington, Vermont, he attended the University of Vermont where, under the influence of H. A. P. Torrey, he developed an interest in both philosophy and social thought. After graduation, he taught for two years in a one room school house in Oil City, Pennsylvania before returning to Burlington where he continued to teach high school. While there, he availed himself of further tutorial instruction in philosophy from Professor Torrey who, along with W. T. Harris, the editor of <u>The Journal of Speculative Philosophy</u>, encouraged him to apply for graduate study at Johns Hopkins University. While a student there, he came under the influence of Charles Sanders Peirce, generally recognized as the father of pragmatism in America, G. S. Hall, one of the first experimental psychologists in America, and George S. Morris, a philosopher in the tradition of Hegel. In the early part of Dewey's career, Dewey was particularly drawn to Morris' idealism and organismic approach to most philosophical problems.

Upon completing his studies, Dewey received a teaching appointment in philosophy at the University of Michigan where he remained until 1894, except for one year as visiting professor at the University of Minnesota. He then accepted an invitation to head the philosophy department at the University of Chicago and while there, founded his Laboratory School which gave him the opportunity to effect a union of theory and practice for many of his psychological and pedagogical ideas. In 1904, he left Chicago because of problems he was encountering with the school administration regarding his Laboratory School and proceeded to Columbia University, where he remained until his retirement in 1929. Through Columbia University's Teachers College, a training center for teachers from many foreign countries as well as for Americans, Dewey's educational philosophy spread both nationally and world-wide.

The range and quantity of Dewey's publications can only be described as awesome. Among the most important and most well-known of his writings are: <u>The School and Society</u> (1900), <u>Studies in Logical Theory</u> (1903), <u>Ethics</u> (1908), <u>How We Think</u> (1910), <u>The Influence of Darwin and Other Essays in Contemporary Thought</u> (1910), <u>Democracy and Education</u> (1916), <u>Essays in Experimental Logic</u> (1916), <u>Reconstruction in Philosophy</u> (1920), <u>Human Nature and Conduct</u> (1922), <u>Experience and Nature</u> (1925), <u>The Quest for Certainty</u> (1929), <u>Art as Experience</u> (1934), and <u>Logic: The Theory of Inquiry</u> (1939).

In the Foreword to the Modern Library edition to <u>Human Nature and Conduct</u>, Dewey makes it very clear that his philosophy of man is based on "anthropology and the allied sciences." He admits that he is in the tradition of David Hume, but unlike Hume, he has come to recognize "the pervasive and powerful influence of what anthropologists call culture in shaping the concrete manifestations of every human nature subject to its influence." In the body of the work, Dewey argues that the moral life (the life of man) is a process in which impulses, habit, and intelligence play a role in modifying or reinforcing each other to bring about an ever-widening and deepening harmony among themselves, with a corresponding integration of conduct.

In addition to the very revealing Foreword to the Modern Library edition of <u>Human Nature and Conduct</u>, portions of chapter 3, and all of chapter 4 of Section Two which take up the issues of the plasticity of human nature and the subjects of impulse and conflict of habits respectively, are reprinted below.

HUMAN NATURE AND CONDUCT:

 The identity of human nature and the influence of cult
ure.

        Foreword to the Modern Library Edition

     In the eighteenth century, the word Morals was
used in English literature with a meaning of broad
sweep. It included all the subjects of distinctively
humane import, all of the social disciplines as far as
they are intimately connected with the life of man and
as they bear upon the interests of humanity. The pages
that follow are intended as a contribution, from one
point of view, to Morals thus conceived.   The
particular point of view taken is that of the structure
and workings of human nature, of psychology when that
term is used also in its wider sense.

     Were it not for one consideration, the volume
might be said to be an essay in continuing the
tradition of David Hume.   But it happens that in the
usual interpretation of Hume, he is treated simply as a
writer who carried philosophical skepticism to its
limit. There is sufficient ground in Hume for this way
of looking at his work.   But it is one-sided. No one
can read the introductory remarks with which he
prefaced his two chief philosophical writings without
realizing that he had also a constructive aim. To a
considerable extent local and temporal controversies
incident to the period in which he wrote led to an
excessive emphasis on the skeptical import of his
conclusions. He was so anxious to oppose certain views
current and influential in his own day that his
original positive aim got obscured and overlaid as he
proceeded. In a period in which these other views were
themselves dim and unimportant his thought might well
have taken a happier turn.

     His constructive idea is that a knowledge of human
nature provides a map or chart of all humane and social
subjects, and that with this chart in our possession we
can find our way intelligently about through all the
complexities of the phenomena of economics, politics,
religious beliefs, etc.   Indeed, he went further, and
                          261

held that human nature gives also the key to the
sciences of the physical world, since when all is said
and done they are also the products of the workings of
the human mind. It is likely that in enthusiasm for a
new idea, Hume carried it too far. But there is to my
mind an inexpugnable element of truth in his teachings.
Human nature is at least a contributing factor to the
form which even natural science takes, although it may
not give the key to its _content_ in the degree which
Hume supposed.

But in the social subjects, he was on safer
ground. Here at least we are in the presence of facts
in which human nature is truly central and where a
knowledge of human nature is necessary to enable us to
thread our way through the tangled scene. If Hume
erred in his use of his key, it was because he failed
to note the reaction of social institutions and
conditions upon the ways in which human nature
expresses itself. He saw the part played by the
structure and operations of our common nature in
shaping social life. He failed to see with equal
clearness the reflex influence of the latter upon the
shape which a plastic human nature takes because of its
social environment. He emphasized habit and custom,
but he failed to see that custom is essentially a fact
of associated living whose force is dominant in forming
the habits of individuals.

To point out this relative failure is only to say
that he thought and wrote before the rise of
anthropology and allied sciences. There was in his day
little intimation of the pervasive and powerful
influence of what anthropologists call culture in
shaping the concrete manifestations of every human
nature subject to its influence. It was a great
achievement to insist upon the uniform workings of a
common human structure amid the diversity of social
conditions and institutions. What the growth of
knowledge since his time enables us to add is that this
diversity operates to create different attitudes and
dispositions in the play of ultimately identical human
factors.

It is not easy to keep a balance between the two
sides of the scene. There always tend to be two
schools, one emphasizing original and native human

nature; the other depending upon the influence of the social environment. Even in anthropology, there are those who carry back social phenomena to processes of diffusion, those who whenever they find common beliefs and institutions in different parts of the world assume some earlier contact and intercourse in which borrowing took place. Then there are those who prefer to dwell upon the identity of human nature at all times and places and to carry back the interpretation of cultural phenomena to this inherent unity of human nature. When this volume was first produced, there was a tendency, especially among psychologists, to insist upon native human nature untouched by social influences and to explain social phenomena by reference to traits of original nature called "instincts." Since that date (1922), the pendulum has undoubtedly swung in the opposite direction. The importance of culture as a formative medium is more generally recognized. Perhaps the tendency to-day in many quarters is to overlook the basic identity of human nature amid its different manifestations.

At all events, difficulty persists in securing and maintaining an equilibrium with reference to intrinsic human nature on one side and social customs and institutions on the other. There are doubtless many shortcomings in the pages which follow, but they are to be interpreted in the light of an endeavor to keep the two forces in balance. There is, I hope, due emphasis upon the power of cultural habitude and trend in diversifying the forms assumed by human nature. But there is also an attempt to make clear that there are always intrinsic forces of a common human nature at work; forces which are sometimes stifled by the encompassing social medium but which also in the long course of history are always striving to liberate themselves and to make over social institutions so that the latter may form a freer, more transparent and more congenial medium for their operation. "Morals" in its broad sense is a function of the interaction of these two forces.

Part 2, III

Changing Human Nature

263

Incidentally we have touched upon a most far-reaching problem: The alterability of human nature. Early reformers, following John Locke, were inclined to minimize the significance of native activities, and to emphasize the possibilities inherent in practice and habit-acquisition. There was a political slant to this denial of the native and a priori, this magnifying of the accomplishments of acquired experience. It held out a prospect of continuous development, of improvement without end. Thus writers like Helvetius made the idea of the complete malleability of a human nature which originally is wholly empty and passive, the basis for asserting the omnipotence of education to shape human society, and the ground of proclaiming the infinite perfectibility of mankind.

Wary, experienced men of the world have always been skeptical of schemes of unlimited improvement. They tend to regard plans for social change with an eye of suspicion. They find in them evidences of the proneness of youth to illusion, or of incapacity on the part of those who have grown old to learn anything from experience. This type of conservative has thought to find in the doctrine of native instincts a scientific support for asserting the practical unalterability of human nature. Circumstances may change, but human nature remains from age to age the same. Heredity is more potent than environment, and human heredity is untouched by human intent. Effort for a serious alteration of human institutions is utopian. As things have been so they will be. The more they change the more they remain the same.

Curiously enough both parties rest their case upon just the factor which when it is analyzed weakens their respective conclusions. That is to say, the radical reformer rests his contention in behalf of easy and rapid change upon the psychology of habits, of institutions in shaping raw nature, and the conservative grounds his counter-assertion upon the psychology of instincts. As matter of fact, it is precisely custom which has greatest inertia, which is least susceptible of alteration; while instincts are most readily modifiable through use, most subject to educative direction. The conservative who begs scientific support from the psychology of instincts is the victim of an outgrown psychology which derived its

notion of instinct from an exaggeration of the fixity
and certainty of the operation of instincts among the
lower animals. He is a victim of a popular zoology of
the bird, bee and beaver, which was largely framed to
the greater glory of God. He is ignorant that
instincts in the animals are less infallible and
definite than is supposed, and also that the human
being differs from the lower animals in precisely the
fact that his native activities lack the complex
ready-made organization of the animals' original
abilities.

But the short-cut revolutionist fails to realize
the full force of the things about which he talks most,
namely institutions as embodied habits. Any one with
knowledge of the stability and force of habit will
hesitate to propose or prophesy rapid and sweeping
social changes. A social revolution may effect abrupt
and deep alterations in external customs, in legal and
political institutions. But the habits that are behind
these institutions and that have, willy-nilly, been
shaped by objective conditions, the habits of thought
and feeling, are not so easily modified. They persist
and insensibly assimilate to themselves the outer
innovations--much as American judges nullify the
intended changes of statute law by interpreting
legislation in the light of common law. The force of
lag in human life is enormous.

Actual social change is never so great as is
apparent change. Ways of belief, of expectation, of
judgment and attendant emotional dispositions of like
and dislike, are not easily modified after they have
once taken shape. Political and legal institutions may
be altered, even abolished; but the bulk of popular
thought which has been shaped to their pattern
persists. This is why glowing predictions of the
immediate coming of a social millennium terminate so
uniformly in disappointment, which gives point to the
standing suspicion of the cynical conservative about
radical changes. Habits of thought outlive
modifications in habits of overt action. The former
are vital, the latter, without the sustaining life of
the former, are muscular tricks. Consequently as a
rule the moral effects of even great political
revolutions, after a few years of outwardly conspicuous
alterations, do not show themselves till after the
lapse of years. A new generation must come upon the

scene whose habits of mind have been formed under the new conditions. There is pith in the saying that important reforms cannot take real effect until after a number of influential persons have died. Where general and enduring moral changes do accompany an external revolution it is because appropriate habits of thought have previously been insensibly matured. The external change merely registers the removal of an external superficial barrier to the operation of existing intellectual tendencies.

Those who argue that social and moral reform is impossible on the ground that the Old Adam of human nature remains forever the same, attribute however to native activities the permanence and inertia that in truth belong only to acquired customs. To Aristotle slavery was rooted in aboriginal human nature. Native distinctions of quality exist such that some persons are by nature gifted with power to plan, command and supervise, and others possess merely capacity to obey and execute. Hence slavery is natural and inevitable. There is error in supposing that because domestic and chattel slavery has been legally abolished, therefore slavery as conceived by Aristotle has disappeared. But matters have at least progressed to a point where it is clear that slavery is a social state not a psychological necessity. Nevertheless the worldlywise Aristotles of today assert that the institutions of war and the present wage-system are so grounded in immutable human nature that effort to change them is foolish.

Like Greek slavery or feudal serfdom, war and the existing economic regime are social patterns woven out of the stuff of instinctive activities. Native human nature supplies the raw materials, but custom furnishes the machinery and the designs. War would not be possible without anger, pugnacity, rivalry, self-display, and such like native tendencies. Activity inheres in them and will persist under every condition of life. To imagine they can be eradicated is like supposing that society can go on without eating and without union of the sexes. But to fancy that they must eventuate in war is as if a savage were to believe that because he uses fibers having fixed natural properties in order to weave baskets, therefore his immemorial tribal patterns are also natural necessities and immutable forms.

266

From a humane standpoint our study of history is still all too primitive. It is possible to study a multitude of histories, and yet permit history, the record of the transitions and transformations of human activities, to escape us. Taking history in separate doses of this country and that, we take it as a succession of isolated finalities, each one in due season giving way to another, as supernumeraries succeed one another in a march across the stage. We thus miss the fact of history and also its lesson; the diversity of institutional forms and customs which the same human nature may produce and employ. An infantile logic, now happily expelled from physical science, taught that opium put men to sleep because of its dormitive potency. We follow the same logic in social matters when we believe that war exists because of bellicose instincts; or that a particular economic regime is necessary because of acquisitive and competitive impulses which must find expression.

Pugnacity and fear are no more native than are pity and sympathy. The important thing morally is the way these native tendencies interact, for their interaction may give a chemical transformation not a mechanical combination. Similarly, no social institution stands alone as a product of one dominant force. It is a phenomenon or function of a multitude of social factors in their mutual inhibitions and reinforcements. If we follow an infantile logic we shall reduplicate the unity of result in an assumption of unity of force behind it--as men once did with natural events, employing teleology as an exhibition of causal efficiency. We thus take the same social custom twice over: once as an existing fact and then as an original force which produced the fact, and utter sage platitudes about the unalterable workings of human nature or of race. As we account for war by pugnacity, for the capitalistic system by the necessity of an incentive of gain to stir ambition and effort, so we account for Greece by power of esthetic observation, Rome by administrative ability, the middle ages by interest in religion and so on. We have constructed an elaborate political zoology as mythological and not nearly as poetic as the other zoology of phoenixes, griffins and unicorns. Native racial spirit, the spirit of the people or of the time, national destiny are familiar figures in this social zoo. As names for effects, for existing customs, they are sometimes useful. As names for explanatory forces they work havoc with intelligence.

An immense debt is due William James for the mere
title of his essay: The Moral Equivalents of War. It
reveals with a flash of light the true psychology.
Clans, tribes, races, cities, empires, nations, states
have made war. The argument that this fact proves an
ineradicable belligerent instinct which makes war
forever inevitable is much more respectable than many
arguments about the immutability of this and that
social tradition. For it has the weight of a certain
empirical generality back of it. Yet the suggestion of
an <u>equivalent</u> for war calls attention to the medley of
impulses which are casually bunched together under the
caption of belligerent impulse; and it calls attention
to the fact that the elements of this medley may be
woven together into many differing types of activity,
some of which may function the native impulses in much
better ways than war has ever done.

     Pugnacity, rivalry, vainglory, love of booty,
fear, suspicion, anger, desire for freedom from the
conventions and restrictions of peace, love of power
and hatred of oppression, opportunity for novel
displays, love of home and soil, attachment to one's
people and to the altar and the hearth, courage,
loyalty, opportunity to make a name, money or a career,
affection, piety to ancestors and ancestral gods--all
of these things and many more make up the war-like
force. To suppose there is some one unchanging native
force which generates war is as naive as the usual
assumption that our enemy is actuated solely by the
meaner of the tendencies named and we only by the
nobler. In earlier days there was something more than
a verbal connection between pugnacity and fighting;
anger and fear moved promptly through the fists. But
between a loosely organized pugilism and the highly
organized warfare of today there intervenes a long
economic, scientific and political history. Social
conditions rather than an old and unchangeable Adam
have generated wars; the ineradicable impulses that are
utilized in them are capable of being drafted into many
other channels....

                    Part 2, IV

              Impulse and Conflict of Habits

                        268

War and the existing economic regime have not been
discussed primarily on their own account. They are
crucial cases of the relation existing between original
impulse and acquired habit. They are so fraught with
evil consequences that any one who is disposed can heap
up criticisms without end. Nevertheless they persist.
This persistence constitutes the case for the
conservative who argues that such institutions are
rooted in an unalterable human nature. A truer
psychology locates the difficulty elsewhere. It shows
that the trouble lies in the inertness of established
habit. No matter how accidental and irrational the
circumstances of its origin, no matter how different
the conditions which now exist to those under which the
habit was formed, the latter persists until the
environment obstinately rejects it. Habits once formed
perpetuate themselves by acting unremittingly upon the
native stock of activities. They stimulate, inhibit,
intensify, weaken, select, concentrate and organize the
latter into their own likeness. They create out of the
formless void of impulses a world made in their own
image. Man is a creature of habit, not of reason nor
yet of instinct.

Recognition of the correct psychology locates the
problem but does not guarantee its solution. Indeed,
at first sight it seems to indicate that every attempt
to solve the problem and secure fundamental
reorganizations is caught in a vicious circle. For the
direction of native activity depends upon acquired
habits, and yet acquired habits can be modified only by
redirection of impulses. Existing institutions impose
their stamp, their superscription, upon impulse and
instinct. They embody the modifications the latter
have undergone. How then can we get leverage for
changing institutions? How shall impulse exercise that
re-adjusting office which has been claimed for it?
Shall we not have to depend in the future as in the
past upon upheaval and accident to dislocate customs so
as to release impulses to serve as points of departure
for new habits?

The existing psychology of the industrial worker
for example is slack, irresponsible, combining a
maximum of mechanical routine with a maximum of
explosive, unregulated impulsiveness. These things
have been bred by the existing economic system. But
they exist, and are formidable obstacles to social

change. We cannot breed in men the desire to get something for as nearly nothing as possible and in the end not pay the price. We satisfy ourselves cheaply by preaching the charm of productivity and by blaming the inherent selfishness of human nature, and urging some great moral and religious revival. The evils point in reality to the necessity of a change in economic institutions, but meantime they offer serious obstacles to the change. At the same time, the existing economic system has enlisted in behalf of its own perpetuity the managerial and the technological abilities which must serve the cause of the laborer if he is to be emancipated. In the face of these difficulties other persons seek an equally cheap satisfaction in the thought of universal civil war and revolution.

Is there any way out of the vicious circle? In the first place, there are possibilities resident in the education of the young which have never yet been taken advantage of. The idea of universal education is as yet hardly a century old, and it is still much more of an idea than a fact, when we take into account the early age at which it terminates for the mass. Also, thus far schooling has been largely utilized as a convenient tool of the existing nationalistic and economic regimes. Hence it is easy to point out defects and perversions in every existing school system. It is easy for a critic to ridicule the religious devotion to education which has characterized for example the American republic. It is easy to represent it as zeal without knowledge, fanatical faith apart from understanding. And yet the cold fact of the situation is that the chief means of continuous, graded, economical improvement and social rectification lies in utilizing the opportunities of educating the young to modify prevailing types of thought and desire.

The young are not as yet as subject to the full impact of established customs. Their life of impulsive activity is vivid, flexible, experimenting, curious. Adults have their habits formed, fixed, at least comparatively. They are the subjects, not to say victims, of an environment which they can directly change only by a maximum of effort and disturbance. They may not be able to perceive clearly the needed changes, or be willing to pay the price of effecting them. Yet they wish a different life for the generation to come. In order to realize that wish they may create a special environment whose main function is education. In order that education of the young be efficacious in inducing an improved society, it is not necessary for adults to have a formulated definite ideal of some better state. An educational enterprise conducted in this spirit would probably end merely in substituting one rigidity for another. What is necessary is that habits be formed which are more intelligent, more sensitively percipient, more informed with foresight, more aware of what they are about, more direct and sincere, more flexibly responsive than those now current. Then they will meet their own problems and propose their own improvements.

Educative development of the young is not the only way in which the life of impulse may be employed to effect social ameliorations, though it is the least expensive and most orderly. No adult environment is all of one piece. The more complex a culture is, the more certain it is to include habits formed on differing, even conflicting patterns. Each custom may be rigid, unintelligent in itself, and yet this rigidity may cause it to wear upon others. The resulting attrition may release impulse for new adventures. The present time is conspicuously a time of such internal frictions and liberations. Social life seems chaotic, unorganized, rather than too fixedly regimented. Political and legal institutions are now inconsistent with the habits that dominate friendly intercourse, science and art. Different institutions foster antagonistic impulses and form contrary dispositions.

If we had to wait upon exhortations and unembodied "ideals" to effect social alterations, we should indeed wait long. But the conflict of patterns involved in institutions which are inharmonious with one another is already producing great changes. The significant point is not whether modifications shall continue to occur, but whether they shall be characterized chiefly by uneasiness, discontent and blind antagonistic struggles, or whether intelligent direction may modulate the harshness of conflict, and turn the elements of disintegration into a constructive synthesis. At all events, the social situation in "advanced" countries is such as to impart an air of absurdity to our insistence upon the rigidity of customs. There are plenty of persons to tell us that

the real trouble lies in lack of fixity of habit and
principle; in departure from immutable standards and
structures constituted once for all. We are told that
we are suffering from an excess of instinct, and from
laxity of habit due to surrender to impulse as a law of
life.   The remedy is said to be to return from
contemporary fluidity to the stable and spacious
patterns of a classic antiquity that observed law and
proportion: for somehow antiquity is always classic.
When instability, uncertainty, erratic change are
diffused throughout the situation, why dwell upon the
evils of fixed habit and the need of release of impulse
as an initiator of reorganizations? Why not rather
condemn impulse and exalt habits of reverencing order
and fixed truth?

     The question is natural, but the remedy suggested
is futile. It is not easy to exaggerate the extent to
which we now pass from one kind of nurture to another
as we go from business to church, from science to the
newspaper, from business to art, from companionship to
politics, from home to school. An individual is now
subjected to many conflicting schemes of education.
Hence habits are divided against one another,
personality is disrupted, the scheme of conduct is
confused and disintegrated. But the remedy lies in the
development of a new morale which can be attained only
as released impulses are intelligently employed to form
harmonious habits adapted to one another in a new
situation. A laxity due to decadence of old habits
cannot be corrected by exhortations to restore old
habits in their former rigidity. Even though it were
abstractly desirable it is impossible. And it is not
desirable because the inflexibility of old habits is
precisely the chief cause of their decay and
disintegration. Plaintive lamentations at the
prevalence of change and abstract appeals for
restoration of senile authority are signs of personal
feebleness, of inability to cope with change. It is a
"defense reaction."

ERNST CASSIRER

Ernst Cassirer (1874-1945) has contributed significantly to the dominant contemporary view of man which places the human person precisely at the center of the world. Born in Breslau, Silesia, he studied at the universities of Berlin, Leipzig, Heidelberg, and Marburg. After his studies, he was named professor of philosophy and rector of the University of Hamburg, positions he held from 1919 to 1933. However, being of Jewish descent, he was forced to resign his post due to the rise to power of the Nazis in Germany. So, he moved first to England where he taught at Oxford from 1933-1935 and then to Sweden where he held a professorial post at Goteborg until 1941. Finally, he came to America and taught at Yale University. In 1945, while at Columbia University as visiting professor, he died. Renowned as a prolific historian of philosophy and an original thinker, his major philosophical works include <u>The Philosophy of Symbolic Forms</u> (1923) and <u>An Essay on Man</u> (1944).

In <u>An Essay on Man</u>, Cassirer observes that the human world forms no exception to those biological rules which govern the life of all other organisms. Yet Cassirer also insists that the distinctive mark of human life is that man has developed a symbolic system, namely, language, myth, art, and religion, by which he adapts himself to his environment. Consequently, no longer does man deal with things themselves, rather "man is in a sense conversing with himself." In short, man should not be defined as a rational animal, but as an <u>animal symbolicum</u> (a symbolic animal). As such, man is constantly creating and uncreating culture which fundamentally points to man's power to create an ideal or symbolic world of his own.

AN ESSAY ON MAN:

Man - a symbolic animal.

II

<u>A Clue to the Nature of Man</u>:   <u>the Symbol</u>

The biologist Johannes von Uexkull has written a book in which he undertakes a critical revision of the principles of biology. Biology, according to Uexkull, is a natural science which has to be developed by the usual empirical methods--the methods of observation and experimentation. Biological thought, on the other hand, does not belong to the same type as physical or chemical thought. Uexkull is a resolute champion of vitalism; he is a defender of the principle of the autonomy of life. Life is an ultimate and self-dependent reality. It cannot be described or explained in terms of physics or chemistry. From this point of view Uexkull evolves a new general scheme of biological research. As a philosopher he is an idealist or phenomenalist. But his phenomenalism is not based upon metaphysical or epistemological considerations; it is founded rather on empirical principles. As he points out, it would be a very naive sort of dogmatism to assume that there exists an absolute reality of things which is the same for all living beings. Reality is not a unique and homogeneous thing; it is immensely diversified, having as many different schemes and patterns as there are different organisms. Every organism is, so to speak, a monadic being. It has a world of its own because it has an experience of its own. The phenomena that we find in the life of a certain biological species are not transferable to any other species. The experiences--and therefore the realities--of two different organisms are incommensurable with one another. In the world of a fly, says Uexkull, we find only "fly things"; in the world of a sea urchin we find only "sea urchin things."

From this general presupposition Uexkull develops a very ingenious and original scheme of the biological world. Wishing to avoid all psychological

274

interpretations, he follows an entirely objective or behavioristic method. The only clue to animal life, he maintains, is given us in the facts of comparative anatomy. If we know the anatomical structure of an animal species, we possess all the necessary data for reconstructing its special mode of experience. A careful study of the structure of the animal body, of the number, the quality, and the distribution of the various sense organs, and the conditions of the nervous system, gives us a perfect image of the inner and outer world of the organism. Uexkull began his investigations with a study of the lowest organisms; he extended them gradually to all the forms of organic life. In a certain sense he refuses to speak of lower or higher forms of life. Life is perfect everywhere; it is the same in the smallest as in the largest circle. Every organism, even the lowest, is not only in a vague sense adapted to (_angepasst_) but entirely fitted into (_eingepasst_) its environment. According to its anatomical structure it possesses a certain _Merknetz_ and a certain _Wirknetz_--a receptor system and an effector system. Without the cooperation and equilibrium of these two systems the organism could not survive. The receptor system by which a biological species receives outward stimuli and the effector system by which it reacts to them are in all cases closely interwoven. They are links in one and the same chain which is described by Uexkull as the _functional circle_ (_Funktionskreis_) of the animal.

I cannot enter here upon a discussion of Uexkull's biological principles. I have merely referred to his concepts and terminology in order to pose a general question. Is it possible to make use of the scheme proposed by Uexkull for a description and characterization of the _human world_? Obviously this world forms no exception to those biological rules which govern the life of all the other organisms. Yet in the human world we find a new characteristic which appears to be the distinctive mark of human life. The functional circle of man is not only quantitatively enlarged; it has also undergone a qualitative change. Man has, as it were, discovered a new method of adapting himself to his environment. Between the receptor system and the effector system, which are to be found in all animal species, we find in man a third link which we may describe as the _symbolic system_. This new acquisition transforms the whole of human life. As compared with the other animals man lives not merely in a broader reality; he lives, so to speak, in a new <u>dimension</u> of reality. There is an unmistakable difference between organic reactions and human responses. In the first case a direct and immediate answer is given to an outward stimulus; in the second case the answer is delayed. It is interrupted and retarded by a slow and complicated process of thought. At first sight such a delay may appear to be a very questionable gain. Many philosophers have warned man against this pretended progress....

Yet there is no remedy against this reversal of the natural order. Man cannot escape from his own achievement. He cannot but adopt the conditions of his own life. No longer in a merely physical universe, man lives in a symbolic universe. Language, myth, art, and religion are parts of this universe. They are the varied threads which weave the symbolic net, the tangled web of human experience. All human progress in thought and experience refines upon and strengthens this net. No longer can man confront reality immediately; he cannot see it, as it were, face to face. Physical reality seems to recede in proportion as man's symbolic activity advances. Instead of dealing with the things themselves man is in a sense constantly conversing with himself. He has so enveloped himself in linguistic forms, in artistic images, in mythical symbols or religious rites that he cannot see or know anything except by the interposition of this artificial medium. His situation is the same in the theoretical as in the practical sphere. Even here man does not live in a world of hard facts, or according to his immediate needs and desires. He lives rather in the midst of imaginary emotions, in hopes and fears, in illusions and disillusions, in his fantasies and dreams. "What disturbs and alarms man," said Epictetus, "are not the things, but his opinions and fancies about the things."

From the point of view at which we have just arrived we may correct and enlarge the classical definition of man. In spite of all the efforts of modern irrationalism this definition of man as an <u>animal rationale</u> has not lost its force. Rationality is indeed an inherent feature of all human activities. Mythology itself is not simply a crude mass of superstitions or gross delusions. It is not merely chaotic, for it possesses a systematic or conceptual

form. But, on the other hand, it would be impossible
to characterize the structure of myth as rational.
Language has often been identified with reason, or with
the very source of reason.   But it is easy to see that
this definition fails to cover the whole field.   It is
a <u>pars pro toto</u>; it offers us a part for the whole.
For side by side with conceptual language there is an
emotional language; side by side with logical or
scientific language there is a language of poetic
imagination.   Primarily language does not express
thoughts or ideas, but feelings and affections.... The
great thinkers who have defined man as an <u>animal
rationale</u> were not empiricists, nor did they ever
intend to give an empirical account of human nature.
By this definition they were expressing rather a
fundamental moral imperative.   Reason is a very
inadequate term with which to comprehend the forms of
man's cultural life in all their richness and variety.
But all these forms are symbolic forms. Hence, instead
of defining man as an <u>animal rationale</u>, we should
define him as an <u>animal symbolicum</u>. By so doing we can
designate his specific difference, and we can
understand the new way open to man--the way to
civilization....

VI

<u>The Definition of Man in Terms of Human Culture</u>

     It was a turning point in Greek culture and Greek
thought when Plato interpreted the maxim "Know thyself"
in an entirely new sense.   This interpretation
introduced a problem which was not only alien to
pre-Socratic thought but also went far beyond the
limits of the Socratic method.   In order to obey the
demand of the Delphic god, in order to fulfill the
religious duty of self-examination and self-knowledge,
Socrates had approached the individual man.   Plato
recognized the limitations of the Socratic way of
inquiry. In order to solve the problem, he declared,
we must project it upon a larger plan. The phenomena
we encounter in our individual experience are so
various, so complicated and contradictory that we can
scarcely disentangle them. Man is to be studied not in
his individual life but in his political and social
life. Human nature, according to Plato, is like a
difficult text, the meaning of which has to be

277

deciphered by philosophy. But in our personal experience this text is written in such small characters that it becomes illegible. The first labor of philosophy must be to enlarge these characters. Philosophy cannot give us a satisfactory theory of man until it has developed a theory of the state. The nature of man is written in capital letters in the nature of the state. Here the hidden meaning of the text suddenly emerges, and what seemed obscure and confused becomes clear and legible.

But political life is not the only form of a communal human existence. In the history of mankind the state, in its present form, is a late product of the civilizing process. Long before man had discovered this form of social organization he had made other attempts to organize his feelings, desires, and thoughts. Such organizations and systematizations are contained in language, in myth, in religion, and in art. We must accept this broader basis if we wish to develop a theory of man. The state, however important, is not all. It cannot express or absorb all the other activities of man. To be sure these activities in their historical evolution are closely connected with the development of the state; in many respects they are dependent upon the forms of political life. But, while not possessing a separate historical existence, they have nevertheless a purport and value of their own.

In modern philosophy Comte was one of the first to approach this problem and to formulate it in a clear and systematic way. It is something of a paradox that in this respect we must regard the positivism of Comte as a modern parallel to the Platonic theory of man. Comte was of course never a Platonist. He could not accept the logical and metaphysical presuppositions upon which Plato's theory of ideas is based. Yet, on the other hand, he was strongly opposed to the views of the French ideologists. In his hierarchy of human knowledge two new sciences, the science of social ethics and that of social dynamics, occupy the highest rank. From this sociological viewpoint Comte attacks the psychologism of his age. One of the fundamental maxims of his philosophy is that our method of studying man must, indeed, be subjective, but that it cannot be individual. For the subject we wish to know is not the individual consciousness but the universal subject. If we refer to this subject by the term "humanity," then we must affirm that humanity is not to be explained by man, but man by humanity. The problem must be reformulated and re-examined; it must be put on a broader and sounder basis. Such a basis we have discovered in sociological and historical thought. "To know yourself," says Comte, "know history." Henceforth historical psychology supplements and supersedes all previous forms of individual psychology. "The so-called observations made on the mind, considered in itself and _a priori_," wrote Comte in a letter, "are pure illusions. All that we call _logic_, _metaphysics_, _ideology_, is an idle fancy and a dream when it is not an absurdity."

In Comte's _Cours de philosophie positive_ we can trace step by step the nineteenth-century transition in methodological ideals. Comte began merely as a scientist, his interest being apparently wholly absorbed in mathematical, physical, and chemical problems. In his hierarchy of human knowledge the scale goes from astronomy through mathematics, physics, and chemistry to biology. Then comes what looks like a sudden reversal of this order. As we approach the human world the principles of mathematics or of the natural sciences do not become invalid, but they are no longer sufficient. Social phenomena are subject to the same rules as physical phenomena, yet they are of a different and much more complicated character. They are not to be described merely in terms of physics, chemistry, and biology. "In all social phenomena," says Comte,

we perceive the working of the physiological laws of the individual; and moreover something which modifies their effects, and which belongs to the influence of individuals over each other--singularly complicated in the case of the human race by the influence of generations on their successors. Thus it is clear that our social science must issue from that which relates to the life of the individual. On the other hand, there is no occasion to suppose, as some eminent physiologists have done, that Social Physics is only an appendage to Physiology. The phenomena of the two are not identical, though they are homogeneous; and it is of high importance to hold the two sciences separate. As social conditions modify the operation of physiological laws, Social Physics must have a set of observations of its own.

The disciples and followers of Comte were not, however, inclined to accept this distinction. They denied the difference between physiology and sociology because they feared that acknowledging it would lead back to a metaphysical dualism. Their ambition was to establish a purely naturalistic theory of the social and cultural world. To this end they found it necessary to negate and destroy all those barriers which seem to separate the human from the animal world. The theory of evolution had evidently effaced all these differences. Even before Darwin the progress of natural history had frustrated all attempts at such differentiation. In the earlier stages of empirical observation it was still possible for the scientist to cherish the hope of finding eventually an anatomical character reserved for man. As late as the eighteenth century it was still a generally accepted theory that there is a marked difference, in some respects a sharp contrast, between the anatomical structure of man and that of the other animals. It was one of Goethe's great merits in the field of comparative anatomy that he vigorously combated this theory. The same homogeneity, not merely in the anatomical and physiological but also in the mental structure of man, remained to be demonstrated. For this purpose all the attacks on the older way of thinking had to be concentrated upon one point. The thing to be proved was that what we call the intelligence of man is by no means a self-dependent, original faculty. Proponents of the naturalistic theories could appeal for proof to the principles of psychology established by the older schools of sensationalism. Taine developed the psychological basis for his general theory of human culture in a work on the intelligence of man. According to Taine, what we call "intelligent behavior" is not a special principle or privilege of human nature; it is only a more refined and complicated play of the same associative mechanism and automatism which we find in all animal reactions. If we accept this explanation the difference between intelligence and instinct becomes negligible; it is a mere difference of degree, not of quality. Intelligence itself becomes a useless and scientifically meaningless term.

The most surprising and paradoxical feature of the theories of this type is the striking contrast between what they promise and what they actually give us. The thinkers who built up these theories were very severe with respect to their methodological principles. They

were not content to speak of human nature in terms of
our common experience, for they were striving after a
much higher ideal, an ideal of absolute scientific
exactness. But if we compare their results with this
standard we cannot help being greatly disappointed.
"Instinct" is a very vague term. It may have a certain
descriptive value but it has obviously no explanatory
value. By reducing some classes of organic or human
phenomena to certain fundamental instincts, we have not
alleged a new cause; we have only introduced a new
name. We have put a question, not answered one. The
term "instinct" gives us at best an _idem per idem_, and
in most cases it is an _obscurum per obscurius_. Even in
the description of animal behavior most modern
biologists and psycho-biologists have become very
cautious about using it. They warn us against the
fallacies which appear to be inextricably connected
with it. They try rather to avoid or to abandon "the
error-freighted concept of instinct and the oversimple
concept of intelligence." In one of his most recent
publications Robert M. Yerkes declares that the terms
"instinct" and "intelligence" are outmoded and that the
concepts for which they stand are sadly in need of
redefining. But in the field of anthropological
philosophy we are still, apparently, far from any such
redefinition. Here these terms are very often accepted
quite naively without critical analysis. When used in
this way the concept of instinct becomes an example of
that typical methodological error which was described
by William James as the psychologist's fallacy. The
word "instinct," which may be useful for the
description of animal or human behavior, is
hypostatized into a sort of natural power. Curiously
enough this error was often committed by thinkers who,
in all other respects, felt secure against relapses
into scholastic realism or "faculty-psychology." A
very clear and impressive criticism of this mode of
thinking is contained in John Dewey's _Human Nature and
Conduct_. "It is unscientific," writes Dewey,

> to try to restrict original activities to a
> definite number of sharply demarcated classes of
> instincts. And the practical result of this
> attempt is injurious. To classify is, indeed, as
> useful as it is natural. The indefinite multitude
> of particular and changing events is met by the
> mind with acts of defining, inventorying, and
> listing, reducing to common heads and tying up in
> bunches....But when we assume that our lists and

bunches represent fixed separations and collections _in rerum natura_, we obstruct rather than aid our transactions with things. We are guilty of a presumption which nature promptly punishes. We are rendered incompetent to deal effectively with the delicacies and novelties of nature and life....The tendency to forget the office of distinctions and classifications, and to take them as marking things in themselves is the current fallacy of scientific specialism....This attitude which once flourished in physical science now governs theorizing about human nature. Man has been resolved into a definite collection of primary instincts which may be numbered, catalogued and exhaustively described one by one. Theorists differ only or chiefly as to their number and ranking. Some say one, self-love; some two, egoism and altruism; some three, greed, fear and glory; while today writers of a more empirical turn run the number up to fifty and sixty. But in fact there are as many specific reactions to differing stimulating conditions as there is time for, and our lists are only classifications for a purpose.

After this brief survey of the different methods that have hitherto been employed in answering the question: What is man? we now come to our central issue. Are these methods sufficient and exhaustive? Or is there still another approach to an anthropological philosophy? Is any other way left open besides that of psychological introspection, biological observation and experiment, and of historical investigation? I have endeavored to discover such an alternative approach in my _Philosophy of Symbolic Forms_. The method of this work is by no means a radical innovation. It is not designed to abrogate but to complement former views. The philosophy of symbolic forms starts from the presupposition that, if there is any definition of the nature or "essence" of man, this definition can only be understood as a functional one, not a substantial one. We cannot define man by any inherent principle which constitutes his metaphysical essence--nor can we define him by any inborn faculty or instinct that may be ascertained by empirical observation. Man's outstanding characteristic, his distinguishing mark, is not his metaphysical or physical nature--but his work. It is this work, it is the system of human activities, which defines and determines the circle of "humanity." Language, myth, religion, art, science, history are the constituents, the various sectors of this circle. A "philosophy of man" would therefore be a philosophy which would give us insight into the fundamental structure of each of these human activities, and which at the same time would enable us to understand them as an organic whole. Language, art, myth, religion are no isolated, random creations. They are held together by a common bond. But this bond is not a _vinculum substantiale_, as it was conceived and described in scholastic thought; it is rather a _vinculum functionale_. It is the basic function of speech, of myth, of art, of religion that we must seek far behind their innumerable shapes and utterances, and that in the last analysis we must attempt to trace back to a common origin.

It is obvious that in the performance of this task we cannot neglect any possible source of information. We must examine all the available empirical evidence, and utilize all the methods of introspection, biological observation, and historical inquiry. These older methods are not to be eliminated but referred to a new intellectual center, and hence seen from a new angle. In describing the structure of language, myth, religion, art, and science, we feel the constant need of a psychological terminology. We speak of religious "feeling," of artistic or mythical "imagination," of logical or rational thought. And we cannot enter into all these worlds without a sound scientific psychological method. Child psychology gives us valuable clues for the study of the general development of human speech. Even more valuable seems to be the help we get from the study of general sociology. We cannot understand the form of primitive mythical thought without taking into consideration the forms of primitive society. And more urgent still is the use of historical methods. The question as to what language, myth, and religion "are" cannot be answered without a penetrating study of their historical development.

But even if it were possible to answer all these psychological, sociological, and historical questions, we should still be in the precincts of the properly "human" world; we should not have passed its threshold. All human works arise under particular historical and sociological conditions. But we could never understand these special conditions unless we were able to grasp the general structural principles underlying these works. In our study of language, art, and myth the problem of meaning takes precedence over the problem of historical development. And here too we can ascertain a slow and continuous change in the methodological concepts and ideals of empirical science. In linguistics, for instance, the conception that the history of language covers the whole field of linguistic studies was for a long time an accepted dogma. This dogma left its mark upon the whole development of linguistics during the nineteenth century. Nowadays, however, this one-sidedness appears to have been definitely overcome.

The necessity of independent methods of descriptive analysis is generally recognized. We cannot hope to measure the depth of a special branch of human culture unless such measurement is preceded by a descriptive analysis. This structural view of culture must precede the merely historical view. History itself would be lost in the boundless mass of disconnected facts if it did not have a general structural scheme by means of which it can classify, order, and organize these facts. In the field of the history of art such a scheme was developed, for instance, by Heinrich Wolfflin. As Wolfflin insists, the historian of art would be unable to characterize the art of different epochs or of different individual artists if he were not in possession of some fundamental <u>categories</u> of artistic description. He finds these categories by studying and analyzing the different modes and possibilities of artistic expression. These possibilities are not unlimited; as a matter of fact they may be reduced to a small number. It was from this point of view that Wolfflin gave his famous description of classic and baroque. Here the terms "classic" and "baroque" were not used as names for definite historical phases. They were intended to designate some general structural patterns not restricted to a particular age. "It is not the art of the sixteenth and seventeenth centuries," says Wolfflin at the end of his <u>Principles of Art History,</u>

which was to be analyzed--only the schema and the visual and creative possibilities within which art remained in both cases. To illustrate this, we could naturally only proceed by referring to the individual work of art, but everything which was said of Raphael and Titian, of Rembrandt and

Velasquez, was only intended to elucidate the general course of things.... Everything is transition and it is hard to answer the man who regards history as an endless flow. For us, intellectual self-preservation demands that we should classify the infinity of events with reference to a few results.

If the linguist and the historian of art require fundamental structural categories for their "intellectual self-preservation," such categories are even more necessary to a philosophical description of human civilization. Philosophy cannot be content with analyzing the individual forms of human culture. It seeks a universal synthetic view which includes all individual forms. But is not such an all-embracing view an impossible task, a mere chimera? In human experience we by no means find the various activities which constitute the world of culture existing in harmony. On the contrary, we find the perpetual strife of diverse conflicting forces. Scientific thought contradicts and suppresses mythical thought. Religion in its highest theoretical and ethical development is under the necessity of defending the purity of its own ideal against the extravagant fancies of myth or art. Thus the unity and harmony of human culture appear to be little more than a <u>pium desiderium</u>--a pious fraud--which is constantly frustrated by the real course of events.

But here we must make a sharp distinction between a material and a formal point of view. Undoubtedly human culture is divided into various activities proceeding along different lines and pursuing different ends. If we content ourselves with contemplating the results of these activities--the creations of myth, religious rites or creeds, works of art, scientific theories--it seems impossible to reduce them to a common denominator. But a philosophic synthesis means something different. Here we seek not a unity of effects but a unity of action; not a unity of products but a unity of the <u>creative process</u>. If the term "humanity" means anything at all it means that, in spite of all the differences and oppositions existing among its various forms, these are, nevertheless, all working toward a common end. In the long run there must be found an outstanding feature, a universal character, in which they all agree and harmonize. If

we can determine this character the divergent rays may
be assembled and brought into a focus of thought. As
has been pointed out, such an organization of the facts
of human culture is already getting under way in the
particular sciences--in linguistics, in the comparative
study of myth and religion, in the history of art. All
of these sciences are striving for certain principles,
for definite "categories," by virtue of which to bring
the phenomena of religion, of art, of language into a
systematic order. Were it not for this previous
synthesis effected by the sciences themselves
philosophy would have no starting point. Philosophy
cannot, on the other hand, stop here. It must seek to
achieve an even greater condensation and
centralization. In the boundless multiplicity and
variety of mythical images, of religious dogmas, of
linguistic forms, of works of art, philosophic thought
reveals the unity of a general function by which all
these creations are held together. Myth, religion,
art, language, even science, are now looked upon as so
many variations on a common theme--and it is the task
of philosophy to make this theme audible and
understandable.

XII

<u>Summary and Conclusion</u>

...

Aristotle's definition of a man as a "social animal"
is not sufficiently comprehensive. It gives us a
generic concept but not the specific difference.
Sociability as such is not an exclusive characteristic
of man, nor is it the privilege of man alone. In the
so-called animal states, among bees and ants, we find a
clear-cut division of labor and a surprisingly
complicated social organization. But in the case of
man we find not only, as among animals, a society of
action but also a society of thought and feeling.
Language, myth, art, religion, science are the elements
and the constitutive conditions of this higher form of
society. They are the means by which the forms of
social life that we find in organic nature develop into
a new state, that of social consciousness. Man's
social consciousness depends upon a double act, of

286

identification and discrimination.   Man cannot find
himself, he cannot become aware of his individuality,
save through the medium of social life.   But to him
this medium signifies more than an external determining
force. Man, like the animals, submits to the rules of
society but, in addition, he has an active share in
bringing about, and an active power to change, the
forms of social life.   In the rudimentary stages of
human society   such   activity   is   still scarcely
perceptible; it appears to be at a minimum. But the
farther we proceed the more explicit and significant
this feature becomes.   This slow development can be
traced in almost all forms of human culture....

...Every perfection that an organism can gain in the
course of its individual life is confined to its own
existence and does not influence the life of the
species. Even man is no exception to this general
biological rule. But man has discovered a new way to
stabilize and propagate his works.   He cannot live his
life without expressing his life. The various modes of
this expression constitute a new sphere. They have a
life of their own, a sort of eternity by which they
survive man's individual and ephemeral existence. In
all human activities we find a fundamental polarity,
which may be described in various ways. We may speak
of a tension between stabilization and evolution,
between a tendency that leads to fixed and stable forms
of life and another tendency to break up this rigid
scheme. Man is torn between these two tendencies, one
of which seeks to preserve old forms whereas the other
strives to produce new ones.   There is a ceaseless
struggle between tradition and innovation, between
reproductive and creative forces.   This dualism is to
be found in all the domains of cultural life. What
varies is the proportion of the opposing factors. Now
the one factor, now the other, seems to preponderate.
This preponderance to a high degree determines the
character of the single forms and gives to each of them
its particular physiognomy....

Human culture taken as a whole may be described as
the process of man's progressive self-liberation.
Language, art, religion, science, are various phases in
this process. In all of them man discovers and proves
a new power--the power to build up a world of his own,
an "ideal" world. Philosophy cannot give up its search
for a fundamental unity in this ideal world. But it

does not confound this unity with simplicity. It does
not overlook the tensions and frictions, the strong
contrasts and deep conflicts between the various powers
of man. These cannot be reduced to a common
denominator. They tend in different directions and
obey different principles. But this multiplicity and
disparateness does not denote discord or disharmony.
All these functions complete and complement one
another. Each one opens a new horizon and shows us a
new aspect of humanity. The dissonant is in harmony
with itself; the contraries are not mutually exclusive,
but inter-dependent: "harmony in contrariety, as in
the case of the bow and the lyre."

27

CARL GUSTAV JUNG

Carl Jung (1875-1961), next to Sigmund Freud, is probably the best known modern psychologist. Born in Switzerland into a well-educated Protestant family, his original interests were in philosophy and ancient history which contributed to his desire to become an archeologist. However, since the University of Basel offered no curriculum in archeology, and since he was not in a financial position to study elsewhere, he decided to pursue a career in medicine and by 1900 earned his medical degree. His first clinical appointment was to the Psychiatric Clinic of the University of Zurich and its hospital, known as Burgholzi, both of which were under the directorship of Eugene Bleuler, the best known psychiatrist in Switzerland at the time. Initially, Jung was assigned as Bleuler's assistant but, by 1905, he became a lecturer in psychiatry at the university and was also promoted to physician at the clinic, a position he held until 1909. In 1913, he resigned his university appointment in order to devote his efforts to private practice, research and writing.

Upon reading Freud's _The Interpretation of Dreams_ (1900) shortly after he arrived at Zurich, Jung became fascinated with the concept of repression and its effect in the formation of dreams. After meeting Freud in Vienna in 1907, a friendship developed between the two men based on mutual respect. In fact, at one point, Freud considered Jung to be the heir of the psychoanalytic movement. However, because of differences of opinion with Freud's postulation of the role of the sexual drive in the life of an individual, Jung broke with his master. In 1912, he published _The Psychology of the Unconscious_, a work which served to bring their differences about libido into sharp focus. Two years later, Jung officially severed his connection with psychoanalysis by resigning his post as president of the _International Psychoanalytic Society_ and eventually giving up membership in the organization altogether. Although he retained admiration for Freud, Jung thereafter referred to his own theory under the label "Analytical Psychology."

After his resignation from the University of Zurich, his research was primarily directed at trying to understand the notion of the unconscious and, more specifically, the significance of myths, legends, and cultural history for the unconscious life of the individual. After twenty years of research and travel for the purpose of studying the mental processes of primitive peoples, he returned to teaching at the Federal Polytechnical University in Zurich where he remained until ill-health forced him to give up his teaching duties in 1942 and his private practice in 1945.

As a result of his research, Jung maintained that the mind (psyche) consists of three levels: the conscious, the personal unconscious, and the collective unconscious. He was convinced that the unconscious aspect of the psyche is much more important than consciousness. The personal unconscious, he claimed, consists of all the impulses, wishes and, generally, experiences in an individual's life that have been suppressed or forgotten. However, existing on a deeper level than the personal unconscious is the collective unconscious which contains, unknown to the individual, the cumulative experiences of all previous generations, including our animal ancestors. Jung theorized that the collective unconscious forms the basis of personality. He referred to the contents of the collective unconscious as archetypes--universal cultural symbols--the most common of which are the persona, the anima and the animus, and the shadow (the dark self).

In the first of the following selections which was originally published in 1934, Jung focuses on the meaning of the collective unconscious. The second selection, which was originally written in English in 1939, addresses the relation between the conscious and the unconscious, on the one hand, and the process whereby a person becomes a psychological individual or whole--the process of integration of the personality, on the other hand.

ARCHETYPES OF THE COLLECTIVE UNCONSCIOUS:

The meaning of the collective unconscious.

The hypothesis of a collective unconscious belongs to
the class of ideas that people at first find strange
but soon come to possess and use as familiar
conceptions. This has been the case with the concept
of the unconscious in general. After the philosophical
idea of the unconscious, in the form presented chiefly
by Carus and von Hartmann, had gone down under the
overwhelming wave of materialism and empiricism,
leaving hardly a ripple behind it, it gradually
reappeared in the scientific domain of medical
psychology.

At first the concept of the unconscious was limited
to denoting the state of repressed or forgotten
contents. Even with Freud, who makes the unconscious--
at least metaphorically--take the stage as the acting
subject, it is really nothing but the gathering place
of forgotten and repressed contents, and has a
functional significance thanks only to these. For
Freud, accordingly, the unconscious is of an
exclusively personal nature, although he was aware of
its archaic and mythological thought-forms.

A more or less superficial layer of the unconscious
is undoubtedly personal. I call it the _personal
unconscious_. But this personal unconscious rests upon
a deeper layer, which does not derive from personal
experience and is not a personal acquisition but is
inborn. This deeper layer I call the _collective
unconscious_. I have chosen the term "collective"
because this part of the unconscious is not individual
but universal; in contrast to the personal psyche, it
has contents and modes of behaviour that are more or
less the same everywhere and in all individuals. It
is, in other words, identical in all men and thus
constitutes a common psychic substrate of a
suprapersonal nature which is present in every one of
us.

Psychic existence can be recognized only by the
presence of contents that are _capable of consciousness_.

291

We can therefore speak of an unconscious only in so far as we are able to demonstrate its contents. The contents of the personal unconscious are chiefly the _feeling-toned complexes_, as they are called; they constitute the personal and private side of psychic life. The contents of the collective unconscious, on the other hand, are known as _archetypes_.

The term "archetype" occurs as early as Philo Judaeus, with reference to the _Imago Dei_ (God-image) in man. It can also be found in Irenaeus, who says: "The creator of the world did not fashion these things directly from himself but copied them from archetypes outside himself." ...For our purposes this term is apposite and helpful, because it tells us that so far as the collective unconscious contents are concerned we are dealing with archaic or--I would say--primordial types, that is, with universal images that have existed since the remotest times. The term "representations collectives," used by Levy-Bruhl to denote the symbolic figures in the primitive view of the world, could easily be applied to unconscious contents as well, since it means practically the same thing. Primitive tribal lore is concerned with archetypes that have been modified in a special way. They are no longer contents of the unconscious, but have already been changed into conscious formulae taught according to tradition, generally in the form of esoteric teaching. This last is a typical means of expression for the transmission of collective contents originally derived from the unconscious.

Another well-known expression of the archetypes is myth and fairytale. But here too we are dealing with forms that have received a specific stamp and have been handed down through long periods of time. The term "archetype" thus applies only indirectly to the "representations collectives," since it designates only those psychic contents which have not yet been submitted to conscious elaboration and are therefore an immediate datum of psychic experience. In this sense there is a considerable difference between the archetype and the historical formula that has evolved. Especially on the higher levels of esoteric teaching the archetypes appear in a form that reveals quite unmistakably the critical and evaluating influence of conscious elaboration. Their immediate manifestation, as we encounter it in dreams and vision, is much more individual, less understandable, and more naive than in myths, for example. The archetype is essentially an unconscious content that is altered by becoming conscious and by being perceived, and it takes its colour from the individual consciousness in which it happens to appear.

What the word "archetype" means in the nominal sense is clear enough, then, from its relations with myth, esoteric teaching, and fairytale. But if we try to establish what an archetype is <u>psychologically</u>, the matter becomes more complicated. So far mythologists have always helped themselves out with solar, lunar, meteorological, vegetal, and other ideas of the kind. The fact that myths are first and foremost psychic phenomena that reveal the nature of the soul is something they have absolutely refused to see until now. Primitive man is not much interested in objective explanations of the obvious, but he has an imperative need--or rather, his unconscious psyche has an irresistible urge--to assimilate all outer sense experiences to inner, psychic events. It is not enough for the primitive to see the sun rise and set; this external observation must at the same time be a psychic happening: the sun in its course must represent the fate of a god or hero who, in the last analysis, dwells nowhere except in the soul of man. All the mythologized processes of nature, such as summer and winter, the phases of the moon, the rainy seasons, and so forth, are in no sense allegories of these objective occurrences; rather they are symbolic expressions of the inner, unconscious drama of the psyche which becomes accessible to man's consciousness by way of projection-- that is, mirrored in the events of nature. The projection is so fundamental that it has taken several thousand years of civilization to detach it in some measure from its outer object. In the case of astrology, for instance, this age-old "scientia intuitiva" came to be branded as rank heresy because man had not yet succeeded in making the psychological description of character independent of the stars. Even today, people who still believe in astrology fall almost without exception for the old superstitious assumption of the influence of the stars. And yet anyone who can calculate a horoscope should know that, since the days of Hipparchus of Alexandria, the spring-point has been fixed at 0° Aries, and that the zodiac on which every horoscope is based is therefore quite arbitrary, the spring-point having gradually advanced, since then, into the first degrees of Pisces, owing to the precession of the equinoxes.

Primitive man impresses us so strongly with his subjectivity that we should really have guessed long ago that myths refer to something psychic. His knowledge of nature is essentially the language and outer dress of an unconscious psychic process. But the very fact that this process is unconscious gives us the reason why man has thought of everything except the psyche in his attempts to explain myths. He simply didn't know that the psyche contains all the images that have ever given rise to myths, and that our unconscious is an acting and suffering subject with an inner drama which primitive man rediscovers, by means of analogy, in the processes of nature both great and small.

CONSCIOUS, UNCONSCIOUS, AND INDIVIDUATION:

The importance of integrating consciousness and the unconscious.

The relation between the conscious and the unconscious on the one hand, and the individuation process on the other, are problems that arise almost regularly during the later stages of analytical treatment. By "analytical" I mean a procedure that takes account of the existence of the unconscious. These problems do not arise in a procedure based on suggestion. A few preliminary words may not be out of place in order to explain what is meant by "individuation."

I use the term "individuation" to denote the process by which a person becomes a psychological "in-dividual," that is, a separate, indivisible unity or "whole." It is generally assumed that consciousness is the whole of the psychological individual. But knowledge of the phenomena that can only be explained on the hypothesis of unconscious psychic processes makes it doubtful whether the ego and its contents are in fact identical with the "whole." If unconscious processes exist at all, they must surely belong to the

totality of the individual, even though they are not
components of the conscious ego.   If they were part of
the ego they would necessarily be conscious, because
everything that is directly related to the ego is
conscious. Consciousness can even be equated with the
relation between the ego and the psychic contents.   But
unconscious phenomena are so little related to the ego
that most people do not hesitate to deny their
existence outright.   Nevertheless, they manifest
themselves in an individual's behaviour. An attentive
observer can detect them without difficulty, while the
observed person remains quite unaware of the fact that
he is betraying his most secret thoughts or even things
he has never thought consciously.   It is, however, a
great prejudice to suppose that something we have never
thought consciously does not exist in the psyche.
There is plenty of evidence to show that consciousness
is very far from covering the psyche in its totality.
Many things occur semiconsciously, and a great many
more remain entirely unconscious.   Thorough
investigation of the phenomena of dual and multiple
personalities, for instance, has brought to light a
mass of material with observations to prove this point.
(I would refer the reader to the writings of Pierre
Janet, Theodore Flournoy, Morton Prince, and others.)

The importance of such phenomena has made a deep
impression on medical psychology, because they give
rise to all sorts of psychic and physiological
symptoms. In these circumstances, the assumption that
the ego expresses the totality of the psyche has become
untenable. It is, on the contrary, evident that the
whole must necessarily include not only consciousness
but the illimitable field of unconscious occurrences as
well, and that the ego can be no more than the centre
of the field of consciousness.

You will naturally ask whether the unconscious
possesses a centre too.   I would hardly venture to
assume that there is in the unconscious a ruling
principle analogous to the ego.   As a matter of fact,
everything points to the contrary.   If there were such
a centre, we could expect almost regular signs of its
existence. Cases of dual personality would then be
frequent occurrences instead of rare curiosities. As a
rule, unconscious phenomena manifest themselves in
fairly chaotic and unsystematic form.   Dreams, for
instance, show no apparent order and no tendency to

systematization, as they would have to do if there were
a personal consciousness at the back of them. The
philosophers Carus and von Hartmann treat the
unconscious as a metaphysical principle, a sort of
universal mind, without any trace of personality or
ego-consciousness, and similarly Schopenhauer's "Will"
is without an ego. Modern psychologists, too, regard
the unconscious as an egoless function below the
threshold of consciousness. Unlike the philosophers,
they tend to derive its subliminal functions from the
conscious mind. Janet thinks that there is a certain
weakness of consciousness which is unable to hold all
the psychic processes together. Freud, on the other
hand, favours the idea of conscious factors that
suppress certain incompatible tendencies. Much can be
said for both theories, since there are numerous cases
where a weakness of consciousness actually causes
certain contents to fall below the threshold, or where
disagreeable contents are repressed. It is obvious
that such careful observers as Janet and Freud would
not have constructed theories deriving the unconscious
mainly from conscious sources had they been able to
discover traces of an independent personality or of an
autonomous will in the manifestations of the
unconscious.

If it were true that the unconscious consists of
nothing but contents accidentally deprived of
consciousness but otherwise indistinguishable from the
conscious material, then one could identify the ego
more or less with the totality of the psyche. But
actually the situation is not quite so simple. Both
theories are based mainly on observations in the field
of neurosis. Neither Janet nor Freud had any
specifically psychiatric experience. If they had, they
would surely have been struck by the fact that the
unconscious displays contents that are utterly
different from conscious ones, so strange, indeed, that
nobody can understand them, neither the patient himself
nor his doctors. The patient is inundated by a flood
of thoughts that are as strange to him as they are to a
normal person. That is why we call him "crazy": we
cannot understand his ideas. We understand something
only if we have the necessary premises for doing so.
But here the premises are just as remote from our
consciousness as they were from the mind of the patient
before he went mad. Otherwise he would never have
become insane.

There is, in fact, no field directly known to us from which we could derive certain pathological ideas. It is not a question of more or less normal contents that became unconscious just by accident. They are, on the contrary, products whose nature is at first completely baffling. They differ in every respect from neurotic material, which cannot be said to be at all bizarre. The material of a neurosis is understandable in human terms, but that of a psychosis is not.

This peculiar psychotic material cannot be derived from the conscious mind, because the latter lacks the premises which would help to explain the strangeness of the ideas. Neurotic contents can be integrated without appreciable injury to the ego, but psychotic ideas cannot. They remain inaccessible, and ego-consciousness is more or less swamped by them. They even show a distinct tendency to draw the ego into their "system."

Such cases indicate that under certain conditions the unconscious is capable of taking over the role of the ego. The consequence of this exchange is insanity and confusion, because the unconscious is not a second personality with organized and centralized functions but in all probability a decentralized congeries of psychic processes. However, nothing produced by the human mind lies absolutely outside the psychic realm. Even the craziest idea must correspond to something in the psyche. We cannot suppose that certain minds contain elements that do not exist at all in other minds. Nor can we assume that the unconscious is capable of becoming autonomous only in certain people, namely in those predisposed to insanity. It is very much more likely that the tendency to autonomy is a more or less general peculiarity of the unconscious. Mental disorder is, in a sense, only one outstanding example of a hidden but none the less general condition. This tendency to autonomy shows itself above all in affective states, including those of normal people. When in a state of violent affect one says or does things which exceed the ordinary. Not much is needed: love and hate, joy and grief, are often enough to make the ego and the unconscious change places. Very strange ideas indeed can take possession of otherwise healthy people on such occasions. Groups, communities, and even whole nations can be seized in this way by psychic epidemics.

The autonomy of the unconscious therefore begins where emotions are generated. Emotions are instinctive, involuntary reactions which upset the rational order of consciousness by their elemental outbursts. Affects are not "made" or wilfully produced; they simply happen. In a state of affect a trait of character sometimes appears which is strange even to the person concerned, or hidden contents may irrupt involuntarily. The more violent an affect the closer it comes to the pathological, to a condition in which the ego-consciousness is thrust aside by autonomous contents that were unconscious before. So long as the unconscious is in a dormant condition, it seems as if there were absolutely nothing in this hidden region. Hence we are continually surprised when something unknown suddenly appears "from nowhere." Afterwards, of course, the psychologist comes along and shows that things had to happen as they did for this or that reason. But who could have said so beforehand?

We call the unconscious "nothing," and yet it is a reality _in potentia_. The thought we shall think, the deed we shall do, even the fate we shall lament tomorrow, all lie unconscious in our today. The unknown in us which the affect uncovers was always there and sooner or later would have presented itself to consciousness. Hence we must always reckon with the presence of things not yet discovered. These, as I have said, may be unknown quirks of character. But possibilities of future development may also come to light in this way, perhaps in just such an outburst of affect which sometimes radically alters the whole situation. The unconscious has a Janus-face: on one side its contents point back to a preconscious, prehistoric world of instinct, while on the other side it potentially anticipates the future--precisely because of the instinctive readiness for action of the factors that determine man's fate. If we had complete knowledge of the ground plan lying dormant in an individual from the beginning, his fate would be in large measure predictable.

Now, to the extent that unconscious tendencies--be they backward-looking images or forward-looking anticipations--appear in dreams, dreams have been regarded, in all previous ages, less as historical regressions than as anticipations of the future, and rightly so. For everything that will be happens on the basis of what has been, and of what--consciously or unconsciously--still exists as a memory-trace. In so far as no man is born totally new, but continually repeats the stage of development last reached by the species, he contains unconsciously, as an _a priori_ datum, the entire psychic structure developed both upwards and downwards by his ancestors in the course of the ages. That is what gives the unconscious its characteristic "historical" aspect, but it is at the same time the _sine qua non_ for shaping the future. For this reason it is often very difficult to decide whether an autonomous manifestation of the unconscious should be interpreted as an _effect_ (and therefore historical) or as an _aim_ (and therefore teleological and anticipatory). The conscious mind thinks as a rule without regard to ancestral preconditions and without taking into account the influence this _a priori_ factor has on the shaping of the individual's fate. Whereas we think in periods of years, the unconscious thinks and lives in terms of millennia. So when something happens that seems to us an unexampled novelty, it is generally a very old story indeed. We still forget, like children, what happened yesterday. We are still living in a wonderful new world where man thinks himself astonishingly new and "modern." This is unmistakable proof of the youthfulness of human consciousness, which has not yet grown aware of its historical antecedents.

As a matter of fact, the "normal" person convinces me far more of the autonomy of the unconscious than does the insane person. Psychiatric theory can always take refuge behind real or alleged organic disorders of the brain and thus detract from the importance of the unconscious. But such a view is no longer applicable when it comes to normal humanity. What one sees happening in the world is not just a "shadowy vestige of activities that were once conscious," but the expression of a living psychic condition that still exists and always will exist. Were that not so, one might well be astonished. But it is precisely those who give least credence to the autonomy of the unconscious who are the most surprised by it. Because of its youthfulness and vulnerability, our consciousness tends to make light of the unconscious. This is understandable enough, for a young man should not let himself be overawed by the authority of his parents if he wants to start something on his own account. Historically as well as individually, our consciousness has developed out of the darkness and somnolence of primordial unconsciousness. There were psychic processes and functions long before any ego-consciousness existed. "Thinking" existed long before man was able to say: "I am conscious of thinking."

The primitive "perils of the soul" consist mainly of dangers to consciousness. Fascination, bewitchment, "loss of soul," possession, etc. are obviously phenomena of the dissociation and suppression of consciousness caused by unconscious contents. Even civilized man is not yet entirely free of the darkness of primeval times. The unconscious is the mother of consciousness. Where there is a mother there is also a father. yet he seems to be unknown. Consciousness, in the pride of its youth, may deny its father, but it cannot deny its mother. That would be too unnatural, for one can see in every child how hesitantly and slowly its ego-consciousness evolves out of a fragmentary consciousness lasting for single moments only, and how these islands gradually emerge from the total darkness of mere instinctuality.

Consciousness grows out of an unconscious psyche which is older than it, and which goes on functioning together with it or even in spite of it. Although there are numerous cases of conscious contents becoming unconscious again (through being repressed, for instance), the unconscious as a whole is far from being a mere remnant of consciousness. Or are the psychic functions of animals remnants of consciousness?

As I have said, there is little hope of our finding in the unconscious an order equivalent to that of the ego. It certainly does not look as if we were likely to discover an unconscious ego-personality, something in the nature of a Pythagorean "counter-earth." Nevertheless, we cannot overlook the fact that, just as consciousness arises from the unconscious, the ego-centre, too, crystallizes out of a dark depth in which it was somehow contained <u>in potentia</u>. Just as a human mother can only produce a human child, whose deepest nature lay hidden during its potential existence within her, so we are practically compelled to believe that the unconscious cannot be an entirely chaotic accumulation of instincts and images. There must be something to hold it together and give expression to the whole. Its centre cannot possibly be the ego, since the ego was born out of it into consciousness and turns its back on the unconscious, seeking to shut it out as much as possible. Or can it be that the unconscious loses its centre with the birth of the ego? In that case we would expect the ego to be far superior to the unconscious in influence and importance. The unconscious would then follow meekly in the footsteps of the conscious, and that would be just what we wish.

Unfortunately, the facts show the exact opposite: consciousness succumbs all too easily to unconscious influences, and these are often truer and wiser than our conscious thinking. Also, it frequently happens that unconscious motives overrule our conscious decisions, especially in matters of vital importance. Indeed, the fate of the individual is largely dependent on unconscious factors. Careful investigation shows how very much our conscious decisions depend on the undisturbed functioning of memory. But memory often suffers from the disturbing interference of unconscious contents. Moreover, it functions as a rule automatically. Ordinarily it uses the bridges of association, but often in such an extraordinary way that another thorough investigation of the whole process of memory-reproduction is needed in order to find out how certain memories managed to reach consciousness at all. And sometimes these bridges cannot be found. In such cases it is impossible to dismiss the hypothesis of the spontaneous activity of the unconscious. Another example is intuition, which is chiefly dependent on unconscious processes of a very complex nature. Because of this peculiarity, I have defined intuition as "perception via the unconscious."

Normally the unconscious collaborates with the conscious without friction or disturbance, so that one is not even aware of its existence. But when an individual or a social group deviates too far from their instinctual foundations, they then experience the full impact of unconscious forces. The collaboration of the unconscious is intelligent and purposive, and even when it acts in opposition to consciousness its expression is still compensatory in an intelligent way, as if it were trying to restore the lost balance.

There are dreams and visions of such an impressive
character that some people refuse to admit that they
could have originated in an unconscious psyche. They
prefer to assume that such phenomena derive from a sort
of "superconsciousness." Such people make a
distinction between a quasi-physiological or
instinctive unconscious and a psychic sphere or layer
"above" consciousness, which they style the
"superconscious." As a matter of fact, this psyche,
which in Indian philosophy is called the "higher"
consciousness, corresponds to what we in the West call
the "unconscious." Certain dreams, visions, and
mystical experiences do, however, suggest the existence
of a consciousness in the unconscious. But, if we
assume a consciousness in the unconscious, we are at
once faced with the difficulty that no consciousness
can exist without a subject, that is, an ego to which
the contents are related. Consciousness needs a
centre, an ego to which something is conscious. We
know of no other kind of consciousness, nor can we
imagine a consciousness without an ego. There can be
no consciousness when there is no one to say: "I am
conscious."

It is unprofitable to speculate about things we
cannot know. I therefore refrain from making
assertions that go beyond the bounds of science. It
was never possible for me to discover in the
unconscious anything like a personality comparable with
the ego. But although a "second ego" cannot be
discovered (except in the rare cases of dual
personality), the manifestations of the unconscious do
at least show <u>traces of personalities</u>. A simple
example is the dream, where a number of real or
imaginary people represent the dream-thoughts. In
nearly all the important types of dissociation, the
manifestations of the unconscious assume a strikingly
personal form. Careful examination of the behaviour
and mental content of these personifications, however,
reveals their fragmentary character. They seem to
represent complexes that have split off from a greater
whole, and are the very reverse of a personal centre of
the unconscious.

I have always been greatly impressed by the character
of dissociated fragments as personalities. Hence I
have often asked myself whether we are not justified in
assuming that, if such fragments have personality, the

whole from which they were broken off must have
personality to an even higher degree. The inference
seemed logical, since it does not depend on whether the
fragments are large or small. Why, then, should not
the whole have personality too? <u>Personality need not
imply consciousness</u>. <u>It can just as easily be dormant
or dreaming</u>.

The general aspect of unconscious manifestations is
in the main chaotic and irrational, despite certain
symptoms of intelligence and purposiveness. The
unconscious produces dreams, visions, fantasies,
emotions, grotesque ideas, and so forth. This is
exactly what we would expect a dreaming personality to
do. It seems to be a personality that was never awake
and was never conscious of the life it had lived and of
its own continuity. The only question is whether the
hypothesis of a dormant and hidden personality is
possible or not. It may be that all of the personality
to be found in the unconscious is contained in the
fragmentary personifications mentioned before. Since
this is very possible, all my conjectures would be in
vain--unless there were evidence of much less
fragmentary and more complete personalities, even
though they are hidden.

I am convinced that such evidence exists.
Unfortunately, the material to prove this belongs to
the subtleties of psychological analysis. It is
therefore not exactly easy to give the reader a simple
and convincing idea of it.

I shall begin with a brief statement: in the
unconscious of every man there is hidden a feminine
personality, and in that of every woman a masculine
personality.

It is a well-known fact that sex is determined by a
majority of male or female genes, as the case may be.
But the minority of genes belonging to the other sex
does not simply disappear. A man therefore has in him
a feminine side, an unconscious feminine figure--a fact
of which he is generally quite unaware. I may take it
as known that I have called this figure the "anima,"
and its counterpart in a woman the "animus.".... This
figure frequently appears in dreams, where one can

observe all the attributes I have mentioned in earlier
publications.

   Another, no less important and clearly defined figure
is the "shadow." Like the anima, it appears either in
projection on suitable persons, or personified as such
in dreams.   The shadow coincides with the "personal"
unconscious (which corresponds to Freud's conception of
the unconscious).   Again like the anima, this figure
has often been portrayed by poets and writers.   I would
mention the Faust-Mephistopheles relationship and E. T.
A. Hoffmann's tale <u>The Devil's Elixir</u> as two especially
typical   descriptions.   The   shadow   personifies
everything that the subject refuses to acknowledge
about himself and yet is always thrusting itself upon
him directly or indirectly--for instance, inferior
traits of character and other incompatible tendencies.

   The   fact   that   the   unconscious   spontaneously
personifies certain affectively   toned   contents   in
dreams is the reason why I have taken over these
personifications in my terminology and formulated them
as names.

   Besides these figures there are still a few others,
less frequent and less striking, which have likewise
undergone poetic as well as mythological formulation.
I would mention, for instance, the figure of the hero
and of the wise old man, to name only two of the best
known.

When one studies the archetypal personalities and
their behaviour with the help of the dreams, fantasies,
and delusions of patients, one is profoundly impressed
by their manifold and unmistakable connections with
mythological ideas completely unknown to the layman.
They form a species of singular beings whom one would
like to endow with ego-consciousness; indeed, they
almost seem capable of it.   And yet this idea is not
borne out by the facts.   There is nothing in their
behaviour to suggest that they have an
ego-consciousness as we know it.   They show, on the
contrary, all the marks of fragmentary personalities.
They are masklike, wraithlike, without problems,
lacking self-reflection, with no conflicts, no doubts,
no sufferings; like gods, perhaps, who have no

philosophy, such as the Brahma-gods of the
Samyutta-nikaya, whose erroneous views needed
correction by the Buddha. Unlike other contents, they
always remain strangers in the world of consciousness,
unwelcome intruders saturating the atmosphere with
uncanny forebodings or even with the fear of madness.

If we examine their content, i.e., the fantasy
material constituting their phenomenology, we find
countless archaic and "historical" associations and
images of an archetypal nature. This peculiar fact
permits us to draw conclusions about the "localization"
of anima and animus in the psychic structure. They
evidently live and function in the deeper layers of the
unconscious, especially in that phylogenetic substratum
which I have called the collective unconscious. This
localization explains a good deal of their strangeness:
they bring into our ephemeral consciousness an unknown
psychic life belonging to a remote past. It is the
mind of our unknown ancestors, their way of thinking
and feeling, their way of experiencing life and the
world, gods and men. The existence of these archaic
strata is presumably the source of man's belief in
reincarnations and in memories of "previous
existences." Just as the human body is a museum, so to
speak, of its phylogenetic history, so too is the
psyche. We have no reason to suppose that the specific
structure of the psyche is the only thing in the world
that has no history outside its individual
manifestations. Even the conscious mind cannot be
denied a history reaching back at least five thousand
years. It is only our ego-consciousness that has
forever a new beginning and an early end. The
unconscious psyche is not only immensely old, it is
also capable of growing into an equally remote future.
It moulds the human species and is just as much a part
of it as the human body, which, though ephemeral in the
individual, is collectively of immense age.

The anima and animus live in a world quite different
from the world outside--in a world where the pulse of
time beats infinitely slowly, where the birth and death
of individuals count for little. No wonder their
nature is strange, so strange that their irruption into
consciousness often amounts to a psychosis. They
undoubtedly belong to the material that comes to light
in schizophrenia.

  What I have said about the collective unconscious may
give you a more or less adequate idea of what I mean by
this term.   If we now turn back to the problem of
individuation, we shall see ourselves faced with a
rather extraordinary task: the psyche consists of two
incongruous halves which together should form a whole.
One is inclined to think that ego-consciousness is
capable of assimilating the unconscious, at least one
hopes that such a solution is possible.   But
unfortunately the unconscious really is unconscious; in
other words, it is unknown. And how can you assimilate
something unknown?   Even if you can form a fairly
complete picture of the anima and animus, this does not
mean that you have plumbed the depths of the
unconscious....

  For this reason we must look for a different
solution. We believe in ego-consciousness and in what
we call reality.... For us it makes sense to concern
ourselves with reality. Our European ego-consciousness
is therefore inclined to swallow up the unconscious,
and if this should not prove feasible we try to
suppress it.   But if we understand anything of the
unconscious, we know that it cannot be swallowed. We
also know that it is dangerous to suppress it, because
the unconscious is life and this life turns against us
if suppressed, as happens in neurosis.

  Conscious and unconscious do not make a whole when
one of them is suppressed and injured by the other. If
they must contend, let it at least be a fair fight with
equal rights on both sides.   Both are aspects of life.
Consciousness should defend its reason and protect
itself, and the chaotic life of the unconscious should
be given the chance of having its way too--as much of
it as we can stand.   This means open conflict and open
collaboration at once.   That, evidently, is the way
human life should be. It is the old game of hammer and
anvil: between them the patient iron is forged into an
indestructible whole, an "individual."

  This, roughly, is what I mean by the individuation
process. As the name shows, it is a process or course
of development arising out of the conflict between the
two fundamental psychic facts....

How the harmonizing of conscious and unconscious data
is to be undertaken cannot be indicated in the form of
a recipe.   It is an irrational life-process which
expresses itself in definite symbols.   It may be the
task of the analyst to stand by this process with all
the help he can give.   In this case, knowledge of the
symbols is indispensable, for it is in them that the
union of conscious and unconscious is consummated. Out
of this union emerge new situations and new conscious
attitudes.   I have therefore called the union of
opposites the "transcendent function."   This rounding
out of the personality into a whole may well be the
goal of any psychotherapy that claims to be more than a
mere cure of symptoms.

28

B. F. SKINNER

Burrhus Frederic Skinner (1904-   ), a psychologist whose application of radical behaviorism to a variety of social problems has made him the most controversial figure in psychology today, was born and raised in Susquehanna, Pennsylvania.   He attended Hamilton College where he majored in English and developed an interest in writing.   As a result of encouragement he received from Robert Frost while attending the Summer School of English in Vermont, he decided to embark on a career as a writer after graduation.   But, after spending a year writing fiction, he realized that this venture was going nowhere.   As he observed much later: "I discovered the unhappy fact that I had nothing to say." So, in 1928, after having read about the work of Pavlov, he entered Harvard University to study psychology.   He earned his doctorate in 1931 and remained at Harvard doing research in experimental psychology before accepting a teaching appointment at the University of Minnesota in 1936. Nine years later, he proceeded to Indiana University where he served as chairman of the psychology department. Subsequently, he returned to Harvard in 1948 where he taught until his retirement in 1974.   His major publications include: The Behavior of Organisms (1938), Walden II (1948), Science and Human Behavior (1953), Schedules of Reinforcement (1957), Verbal Behavior (1957), The Analysis of Behavior: A Program for Self-Instruction (1961), The Techniques of Teaching (1968), Contingencies of Reinforcement (1969), Beyond Freedom and Dignity (1971), and About Behaviorism (1974).

Skinner maintains that human beings, and, more particularly, their behaviors, are essentially shaped and determined by their sociocultural environment. Accordingly, he opposes any attempt to explain behavior by way of reference to internal entities within man or within any organism for that matter.   In fact, he contends that the function of psychological science is limited to describing behavior, not explaining it.

Despite the fact that Skinner follows in the Pavlovian tradition in maintaining that behavior is conditioned by environmental stimuli, he differs with the classical theory of conditioning inasmuch as it portrays the responding organism in essentially a passive mode. According to this view, the environment initiates behavior and the organism responds. In contrast to this theory, Skinner proposes the idea of operant conditioning, a process of behavior wherein the organism acts on its environment. How the environment reacts to the behavior of the organism, positively or negatively, rewarding or not, largely determines whether the behavior will be repeated. In short, if a behavior is positively or negatively reinforced, then the reinforcement determines whether the behavior will be duplicated or not. Skinner concludes that man can shape his destiny because he knows what must be done and how to do it.

Within the context of his behaviorist theory, Skinner draws certain conclusions about the self in chapter XVIII of <u>Science and Human Behavior</u>, which was written as a text book for his behaviorist psychology. The first part of that chapter is reprinted as the initial selection. In the second selection, taken from <u>Beyond Freedom and Dignity</u>, Skinner argues that man himself may be controlled by his environment, but it is an environment which is almost wholly of his own making. So, Skinner concludes that man "is what man has made of man."

SCIENCE AND HUMAN BEHAVIOR:

   The self as an organized system of responses.

   What is meant by the "self" in self-control or
self-knowledge? When a man jams his hands into his
pockets to keep himself from biting his nails, <u>who</u> is
controlling <u>whom</u>? When he discovers that a sudden mood
must be due to a glimpse of an unpleasant person, <u>who</u>
discovers <u>whose</u> mood to be due to <u>whose</u> visual
response? Is the self which works to facilitate the
recall of a name the same as the self which recalls it?
When a thinker teases out an idea, is it the teaser who
also eventually has the idea?

   The self is most commonly used as a hypothetical
cause of action. So long as external variables go
unnoticed or are ignored, their function is assigned to
an originating agent within the organism. If we cannot
show what is responsible for a man's behavior, we say
that he himself is responsible for it.... Perhaps it is
because the notion of personification is so close to a
conception of a behaving individual that it has been
difficult to dispense with similar explanations of
behavior. The practice resolves our anxiety with
respect to unexplained phenomena and is perpetuated
because it does so.

   Whatever the self may be, it is apparently not
identical with the physical organism. The organism
behaves, while the self initiates or directs behavior.
Moreover, more than one self is needed to explain the
behavior of one organism. A mere inconsistency in
conduct from one moment to the next is perhaps no
problem, for a single self could dictate different
kinds of behavior from time to time. But there appear
to be two selves acting simultaneously and in different
ways when one self controls another or is aware of the
activity of another.

   The same facts are commonly expressed in terms of
"personalities." The personality, like the self, is
said to be responsible for features of behavior. For
example, delinquent behavior is sometimes attributed to
a psychopathic personality. Personalities may also be

311

multiple. Two or more personalities may appear in
alternation or concurrently.   They are often in
conflict with each other, and one may or may not be
aware of what the other is doing.

   Multiple selves or personalities are often said to be
systematically related to each other. Freud conceived
of the ego, super-ego, and id as distinguishable agents
within the organism.   The id was responsible for
behavior which was ultimately reinforced with food,
water, sexual contact, and other primary biological
reinforcers.   It was not unlike the selfish, aggressive
"Old Adam" of Judeo-Christian theology, preoccupied
with the basic deprivations and untouched by similar
requirements on the parts of others. The superego--the
"conscience" of Judeo-Christian theology--was
responsible for the behavior which controlled the id.
It used techniques of self-control acquired from the
group. When these were verbal, they constituted "the
still small voice of conscience." The superego and the
id were inevitably opposed to each other, and Freud
conceived of them as often in violent conflict. He
appealed to a third agent--the ego--which, besides
attempting to reach a compromise between the id and the
superego, also dealt with the practical exigencies of
the environment.

   We may quarrel with any analysis which appeals to a
self or personality as an inner determiner of action,
but the facts which have been represented with such
devices cannot be ignored.   The three selves or
personalities in the Freudian scheme represent
important characteristics of behavior in a social
milieu.   Multiple personalities which are less
systematically related to each other serve a similar
function. A concept of self is not essential in an
analysis of behavior, but what is the alternative way
of treating the data?

THE SELF AS AN ORGANIZED SYSTEM OF RESPONSES

   The best way to dispose of any explanatory fiction is
to examine the facts upon which it is based. These
usually prove to be, or suggest, variables which are
acceptable from the point of view of scientific method.
In the present case it appears that a self is simply a

device for representing <u>a functionally unified system
of responses</u>. In dealing with the data, we have to
explain the functional unity of such systems and the
various relationships which exist among them.

<u>The unity of a self</u>. A self may refer to a common
<u>mode of action</u>. Such expressions as "The scholar is
Man Thinking" or "He was a better talker than plumber"
suggest personalities identified with <u>topographical
subdivisions</u> of behavior. In a single skin we find the
man of action and the dreamer, the solitary and the
social spirit.

On the other hand, a personality may be tied to a
particular type of occasion--when a system of responses
is organized around a given <u>discriminative stimulus</u>.
Types of behavior which are effective in achieving
reinforcement upon occasion A are held together and
distinguished from those effective upon occasion B.
Thus one's personality in the bosom of one's family may
be quite different from that in the presence of
intimate friends.

Responses which lead to a common reinforcement,
regardless of the situation, may also comprise a
functional system. Here the principal variable is
<u>deprivation</u>. A motion to adjourn a meeting which has
run through the lunch hour may show "the hungry man
speaking." One's personality may be very different
before and after a satisfying meal. The libertine is
very different from the ascetic who achieves his
reinforcement from the ethical group, but the two may
exist side by side in the same organism.

<u>Emotional</u> variables also establish personalities.
Under the proper circumstances the timid soul may give
way to the aggressive man. The hero may struggle to
conceal the coward who inhabits the same skin.

The effects of <u>drugs</u> upon personality are well known.
The euphoria of the morphine addict represents a
special repertoire of responses the strength of which
is attributable to an obvious variable. The alcoholic
wakes on the morrow a sadder and wiser man.

It is easy to overestimate the unity of a group of responses, and unfortunately personification encourages us to do so. The concept of a self may have an early advantage in representing a relatively coherent response system, but it may lead us to expect consistencies and functional integrities which do not exist. The alternative to the use of the concept is simply to deal with demonstrated covariations in the strength of responses.

   <u>Relations among selves</u>. Organized systems of responses may be related to each other in the same way as are single responses and for the same reasons (Chapter XIV, XV, XVI). For example, two response systems may be incompatible. If the relevant variables are never present at the same time, the incompatibility is unimportant. If the environment of which behavior is a function is not consistent from moment to moment, there is no reason to expect consistency in behavior. The pious churchgoer on Sunday may become an aggressive, unscrupulous businessman on Monday. He possesses two response systems appropriate to different sets of circumstances, and his inconsistency is no greater than that of the environment which takes him to church on Sunday and to work on Monday. But the controlling variables may come together; during a sermon, the churchgoer may be asked to examine his business practices, or the businessman may engage in commercial transactions with his clergyman or his church. Trouble may then arise. Similarly, if an individual has developed different repertoires with family and friends, the two personalities come into conflict when he is with both at the same time. Many of the dramatic struggles which flood the literature on multiple personalities can be accounted for in the same way.

   More systematic relations among personalities arise from the controlling relations discussed in Chapters XV and XVI. In self-control, for example, the responses to be controlled are organized around certain immediate primary reinforcements. To the extent that competition for reinforcement makes this behavior aversive to others--and to this extent only--we may refer to an anti-social personality, the id or Old Adam. On the other hand, the controlling behavior engendered by the community consists of a selected group of practices evolved in the history of a particular culture because

of their effect upon antisocial behavior. To the
extent that this behavior works to the advantage of the
community--and again to this extent only--we may speak
of a unitary conscience, social conscience, or
superego. These two sets of variables account, not
only for the membership of each group of responses, but
for the relation between them which we describe when we
say that one personality is engaged in controlling the
other. Other kinds of relations between personalities
are evident in the processes of making a decision,
solving a problem, or creating a work of art.

An important relation between selves is the
self-knowledge of Chapter XVII. The behavior which we
call knowing is due to a particular kind of
differential reinforcement. In even the most
rudimentary community such questions as "What did you
do?" or "What are you doing?" compel the individual to
respond to his own overt behavior. Probably no one is
completely unselfconscious in this sense. At the other
extreme an advanced and relatively nonpractical society
produces the highly introspective or introverted
individual, whose repertoire of self-knowledge extends
to his covert behavior--a repertoire which in some
cultures may be almost nonexistent. An extensive
development of self-knowledge is common in certain
Eastern cultures and is emphasized from time to time in
those of the West--for example, in the _culte du moi_ of
French literature. An efficient repertoire of this
sort is sometimes set up in the individual for purposes
of therapy. The patient under psychoanalysis may
become highly skilled in observing his own covert
behavior.

When an occasion arises upon which a report of the
organism's own behavior, particularly at the covert
level, is likely to be reinforced, the personality
which makes the report is a specialist trained by a
special set of contingencies. The self which is
concerned with self-knowing functions concurrently with
the behavioral system which it describes. But it is
sometimes important to ask whether the selves generated
by other contingencies "know about each other." The
literature on multiple personalities raises the
question as one of "continuity of memory." It is also
an important consideration in the Freudian scheme: to
what extent, for example, is the superego aware of the
behavior of the id? The contingencies which set up the

315

superego as a controlling system involve stimulation
from the behavior of the id, but they do not
necessarily establish responses of knowing about the
behavior of the id.   It is perhaps even less likely
that the id will know about the superego. The ego can
scarcely deal with conflicts between the other selves
without responding to the behavior attributed to them,
but this does not mean that the ego possesses a
repertoire of knowing about such behavior in any other
sense....

BEYOND FREEDOM AND DIGNITY:

          Man is what man has made of man.

A scientific analysis of behavior dispossesses
autonomous man and turns the control he has been said
to exert over to the environment. The individual may
then seem particularly vulnerable. He is henceforth to
be controlled by the world around him, and in large
part by other men.   Is he not then simply a victim?
Certainly men have been victims, as they been
victimizers, but the word is too strong. It implies
despoliation, which is by no means an essential
consequence of interpersonal control.   But even under
benevolent control is the individual not at best a
spectator who may watch what happens but is helpless to
do anything about it? Is he not "at a dead end in his
long struggle to control his own destiny"?

It is only autonomous man who has reached a dead end.
Man himself may be controlled by his environment, but
it is an environment which is almost wholly of his own
making. The physical environment of most people is
largely man-made. The surfaces a person walks on, the
walls which shelter him, the clothing he wears, many of
the foods he eats, the tools he uses, the vehicles he
moves about in, most of the things he listens to and
looks at are human products. The social environment is
obviously man-made--it generates the language a person
speaks, the customs he follows, and the behavior he
exhibits with respect to the ethical, religious,
governmental, economic, educational, and
psychotherapeutic institutions which control him.   The
evolution of a culture is in fact a kind of gigantic

exercise in self-control.   As the individual controls
himself by manipulating the world in which he lives, so
the human species has constructed an environment in
which its members behave in a highly effective way.
Mistakes have been made, and we have no assurance that
the environment man has constructed will continue to
provide gains which outstrip the losses, but man as we
know him, for better or for worse, is what man has made
of man.

    This will not satisfy those who cry "Victim!" C. S.
Lewis protested: "...the power of man to make himself
what he pleases...means...the power of some men to make
other men what they please." This is inevitable in the
nature of cultural evolution.   The controlling _self_
must be distinguished from the controlled self, even
when they are both inside the same skin, and when
control is exercised through the design of an external
environment, the selves are, with minor exceptions,
distinct.   The person who unintentionally or
intentionally introduces a new cultural practice is
only one among possibly billions who will be affected
by it.   If this does not seem like an act of
self-control, it is only because we have misunderstood
the nature of self-control in the individual.

    When a person changes his physical or social
environment "intentionally"--that is, in order to
change human behavior, possibly including his own--he
plays two roles: one as a controller, as the designer
of a controlling culture, and another as the
controlled, as the product of a culture. There is
nothing inconsistent about this; it follows from the
nature of the evolution of a culture, with or without
intentional design.

    The human species has probably not undergone much
genetic change in recorded time.   We have only to go
back a thousand generations to reach the artists of the
caves of Lascaux.   Features which bear directly on
survival (such as resistance to disease) change
substantially in a thousand generations, but the child
of one of the Lascaux artists transplanted to the world
of today might be almost indistinguishable from a
modern child. It is possible that he would learn more
slowly than his modern counterpart, that he could
maintain only a smaller repertoire without confusion,

or that he would forget more quickly; we cannot be
sure. But we can be sure that a twentieth-century
child transplanted to the civilization of Lascaux would
not be very different from the children he met there,
for we have seen what happens when a modern child is
raised in an impoverished environment.

Man has greatly changed himself as a person in the
same period of time by changing the world in which he
lives. Something of the order of a hundred generations
will cover the development of modern religious
practices, and something of the same order of magnitude
modern government and law. Perhaps no more than twenty
generations will account for modern industrial
practices, and possibly no more than four or five for
education and psychotherapy. The physical and
biological technologies which have increased man's
sensitivity to the world around him and his power to
change that world have taken no more than four or five
generations.

Man has "controlled his own destiny," if that
expression means anything at all. The man that man has
made is the product of the culture man has devised. He
has emerged from two quite different processes of
evolution: the biological evolution responsible for
the human species and the cultural evolution carried
out by that species. Both of these processes of
evolution may now accelerate because they are both
subject to intentional design. Men have already
changed their genetic endowment by breeding selectively
and by changing contingencies of survival, and they may
now begin to introduce mutations directly related to
survival. For a long time men have introduced new
practices which serve as cultural mutations, and they
have changed the conditions under which practices are
selected. They may now begin to do both with a clearer
eye to the consequences.

Man will presumably continue to change, but we cannot
say in what direction. No one could have predicted the
evolution of the human species at any point in its
early history, and the direction of intentional genetic
design will depend upon the evolution of a culture
which is itself unpredictable for similar reasons.
"The limits of perfection of the human species," said
Etienne Cabet in _Voyage en Icarie_, "are as yet

unknown." But, of course, there are no limits. The human species will never reach a final state of perfection before it is exterminated--"some say in fire, some in ice," and some in radiation.

29

JEAN-PAUL SARTRE

Whereas Ludwig Feuerbach had maintained that both God and religion were but projections of man, and whereas Friedrich Nietzsche had proclaimed that God is dead, it was Jean-Paul Sartre (1905-1980) who thought out the implications of God's non-existence. In carrying out this task, Sartre became the most vigorous spokesperson for atheistic existentialism.

Born in Paris, the young Sartre impressed his professors with his intelligence and eagerness to learn. He attended the École Normalle Supérieure (1924-1928) and, after failing the agrégation (an examination that admits one to the body of Professors who teach in the lycées and universities), he proceeded to pass the examination as first in his class in 1929. After two years of military service as an army nurse, he was appointed professor of philosophy at the lycée of Le Havre where he remained until 1933, at which time he received a grant to do research at the Institut Français in Berlin and at the University of Freiburg. After a year of study, he returned to France to teach over the next few years at lycées in Le Havre, Laon, and Paris. With the outbreak of World War II, he was drafted into the army and within a few months was taken prisoner. When the armistice was declared, he was released from prison and returned to Paris teaching for a while at Lycée Pasteur and then at the Lycée Condorcet. Throughout the German occupation, Sartre was actively involved in the French Resistance, contributing to a French underground newspaper and writing plays which stressed liberation themes. With the end of the war, Sartre gave up his teaching career but remained in Paris concerning himself primarily with issues of political significance.

As a young man, Sartre had ambitions to be a writer. However, gradually his attention shifted to philosophical study and analysis but never to the point where he would give up his literary work. In fact, Sartre cleverly used his novels, short stories and plays as vehicles to communicate his philosophical observations and insights. Among his most important works are his best-selling novel <u>Nausea</u> (1938), a number of plays including <u>The Flies</u> (1943) and <u>No Exit</u> (1944), his philosophical masterpiece - <u>Being and Nothingness</u> (1943) which attempts to penetrate the mystery of man, and <u>Critique of Dialectical Reason</u> (1960) in which Sartre tries to show how Marxism and existentialism are in harmony with one another.

Apart from some of his plays, perhaps the most widely read of all of Sartre's writings is <u>Existentialism is a Humanism</u> (1946) which was written for the purpose of supplying a simplified statement of the central doctrines of <u>Being and Nothingness</u>. Despite the fact that even Sartre recognized the inadequacies of his summary, the first selection presents an edited version of this very readable presentation of the implications of atheistic existentialism. The second selection is taken from the end of Act III of <u>The Flies</u>. The play, which is an adaptation of Aeschylus' <u>Oresteia</u>, not only symbolically portrays the spirit of the resistance movement against German oppression but also conveys the spirit of modern man whose life "begins on the far side of despair". Modern man has come to realize that there is no God to rely on and that the universe is meaningless but that nevertheless he is the source of meaning by his creative actions. In many respects, Orestes is the embodiment of the superman about whom Nietzsche had prophetically spoken in <u>Thus Spake Zarathustra</u>.

THE HUMANISM OF EXISTENTIALISM:

Man, the maker of himself.

...What is meant by the term <u>existentialism</u>?

Most people who use the word would be rather
embarrassed if they had to explain it, since, now that
the word is all the rage, even the work of a musician
or painter is being called existentialist. A gossip
columnist in <u>Clartes</u> signs himself <u>The Existentialist</u>,
so that by this time the word has been so stretched and
has taken on so broad a meaning, that it no longer
means anything at all. It seems that for want of an
advanced-guard doctrine analogous to surrealism, the
kind of people who are eager for scandal and flurry
turn to this philosophy which in other respects does
not at all serve their purposes in this sphere.

Actually, it is the least scandalous, the most
austere of doctrines. It is intended strictly for
specialists and philosophers. Yet it can be defined
easily. What complicates matters is that there are two
kinds of existentialists; first, those who are
Christian, among whom I would include Jaspers and
Gabriel Marcel, both Catholic; and on the other hand
the atheistic existentialists among whom I class
Heidegger, and then the French existentialists and
myself. What they have in common is that they think
that existence precedes essence, or, if you prefer,
that subjectivity must be the starting point.

Just what does that mean? Let us consider some
object that is manufactured, for example, a book or a
paper-cutter: here is an object which has been made by
an artisan whose inspiration came from a concept. He
referred to the concept of what a paper-cutter is and
likewise to a known method of production, which is part
of the concept, something which is, by and large, a
routine. Thus, the paper-cutter is at once an object
produced in a certain way and, on the other hand, one
having a specific use; and one can not postulate a man
who produced a paper-cutter but does not know what it
is used for. Therefore, let us say that, for the
paper-cutter, essence--that is, the ensemble of both

the production routines and the properties which enable
it to be both produced and defined--precedes existence.
Thus, the presence of the paper-cutter or book in front
of me is determined. Therefore, we have here a
technical view of the world whereby it can be said that
production precedes existence.

When we conceive God as the Creator, He is generally
thought of as a superior sort of artisan. Whatever
doctrine we may be considering, whether one like that
of Descartes or that of Leibniz, we always grant that
will more or less follows understanding or, at the very
least, accompanies it, and that when God creates He
knows exactly what He is creating. Thus, the concept
of man in the mind of God is comparable to the concept
of a paper-cutter in the mind of the manufacturer, and,
following certain techniques and a conception, God
produces man, just as the artisan, following a
definition and a technique, makes a paper-cutter.
Thus, the individual man is the realization of a
certain concept in the divine intelligence.

In the eighteenth century, the atheism of the
philosophers discarded the idea of God, but not so much
for the notion that essence precedes existence. To a
certain extent, this idea is found everywhere; we find
it in Diderot, in Voltaire, and even in Kant. Man has
a human nature; this human nature, which is the concept
of the human, is found in all men, which means that
each man is a particular example of a universal
concept, man. In Kant, the result of this universality
is that the wild-man, the natural man, as well as the
bourgeois, are circumscribed by the same definition and
have the same basic qualities. Thus, here too the
essence of man precedes the historical existence that
we find in nature.

Atheistic existentialism, which I represent, is more
coherent. It states that if God does not exist, there
is at least one being in whom existence precedes
essence, a being who exists before he can be defined by
any concept, and that this being is man, or, as
Heidegger says, human reality. What is meant here by
saying that existence precedes essence? It means that,
first of all, man exists, turns up, appears on the
scene, and, only afterwards, defines himself. If man,
as the existentialist conceives him, is indefinable, it

is because at first he is nothing. Only afterward will
he be something, and he himself will have made what he
will be. Thus, there is no human nature, since there
is no God to conceive it.   Not only is man what he
conceives himself to be, but he is also only what he
wills himself to be after this thrust toward existence.

     Man is nothing else but what he makes of himself.
Such is the first principle of existentialism. It is
also what is called subjectivity, the name we are
labeled with when charges are brought against us. But
what do we mean by this, if not that man has a greater
dignity than a stone or table?   For we mean that man
first exists, that is, that man first of all is the
being who hurls himself toward a future and who is
conscious of imagining himself as being in the future.
Man is at the start a plan which is aware of itself,
rather than a patch of moss, a piece of garbage, or a
cauliflower; nothing exists prior to this plan; there
is nothing in heaven; man will be what he will have
planned to be. Not what he will want to be. Because
by the word "will" we generally mean a conscious
decision, which is subsequent to what we have already
made of ourselves. I may want to belong to a political
party, write a book, get married; but all that is only
a manifestation of an earlier, more spontaneous choice
that is called "will."   But if existence really does
precede essence, man is responsible for what he is.
Thus, existentialism's first move is to make every man
aware of what he is and to make the full responsibility
of his existence rest on him.   And when we say that a
man is responsible for himself, we do not only mean
that he is responsible for his own individuality, but
that he is responsible for all men.

     The word subjectivism has two meanings, and our
opponents play on the two.   Subjectivism means, on the
one hand, that an individual chooses and makes himself;
and, on the other, that it is impossible for man to
transcend human subjectivity.   The second of these is
the essential meaning of existentialism.   When we say
that man chooses his own self, we mean that every one
of us does likewise; but we also mean by that that in
making this choice he also chooses all men. In fact,
in creating the man that we want to be, there is not a
single one of our acts which does not at the same time
create an image of man as we think he ought to be. To
choose to be this or that is to affirm at the same time

the value of what we choose, because we can never choose evil. We always choose the good, and nothing can be good for us without being good for all.

If, on the other hand, existence precedes essence, and if we grant that we exist and fashion our image at one and the same time, the image is valid for everybody and for our whole age. Thus, our responsibility is much greater than we might have supposed, because it involves all mankind. If I am a workingman and choose to join a Christian trade-union rather than be a communist, and if by being a member I want to show that the best thing for man is resignation, that the kingdom of man is not of this world, I am not only involving my own case--I want to be resigned for everyone. As a result, my action has involved all humanity. To take a more individual matter. if I want to marry, to have children; even if this marriage depends solely on my own circumstances or passion or wish, I am involving all humanity in monogamy and not merely myself. I am creating a certain image of man of my own choosing. In choosing myself, I choose man....

If existence really does precede essence, there is no explaining things away by reference to a fixed and given human nature. In other words, there is no determinism, man is free, man is freedom. On the other hand, if God does not exist, we find no values or commands to turn to which legitimize our conduct. So, in the bright realm of values, we have no excuse behind us, nor justification before us. We are alone, with no excuses.

That is the idea I shall try to convey when I say that man is condemned to be free. Condemned, because he did not create himself, yet, in other respects is free; because, once thrown into the world, he is responsible for everything he does. The existentialist does not believe in the power of passion. He will never agree that a sweeping passion is a ravaging torrent which fatally leads a man to certain acts and is therefore an excuse. He thinks that man is responsible for his passion....

"After all, these people are so spineless, how are you going to make heroes out of them?" This objection almost makes me laugh, for it assumes that people are born heroes. That's what people really want to think. If you're born cowardly, you may set your mind perfectly at rest; there's nothing you can do about it; you will be cowardly all your life, whatever you may do. If you're born a hero, you may set your mind just as much at rest; you'll be a hero all your life; you'll drink like a hero and eat like a hero. What the existentialist says is that the coward makes himself cowardly, that the hero makes himself heroic. There's always a possibility for the coward not to be cowardly any more and for the hero to stop being heroic. What counts is total involvement; some one particular action or set of circumstances is not total involvement....

...If it is impossible to find in every man some universal essence which would be human nature, yet there does exist a universal human condition. It's not by chance that today's thinkers speak more readily of man's condition than of his nature. By condition they mean, more or less definitely, the _a priori_ limits which outline man's fundamental situation in the universe. Historical situations vary; a man may be born a slave in a pagan society or a feudal lord or a proletarian. What does not vary is the necessity for him to exist in the world, to be at work there, to be there in the midst of other people, and to be mortal there. The limits are neither subjective nor objective, or, rather, they have an objective and a subjective side. Objective because they are to be found everywhere and are recognizable everywhere; subjective because they are _lived_ and are nothing if man does not live them, that is, freely determine his existence with reference to them. And though the configurations may differ, at least none of them are completely strange to me, because they all appear as attempts either to pass beyond these limits or recede from them or deny them or adapt to them. Consequently, every configuration, however individual it may be, has a universal value....

In this sense we may say that there is a universality of man; but it is not given, it is perpetually being made. I build the universal in choosing myself; I build it in understanding the configuration of every other man, whatever age he might have lived in. This absoluteness of choice does not do away with the relativeness of each epoch. At heart, what

327

existentialism shows is the connection between the
absolute character of free involvement, by virtue of
which every man realizes himself in realizing a type of
mankind, an involvement always comprehensible in any
age whatsoever and by any person whosoever, and the
relativeness of the cultural ensemble which may result
from such a choice; it must be stressed that the
relativity of Cartesianism and the absolute character
of Cartesian involvement go together. In this sense,
you may, if you like, say that each of us performs an
absolute act in breathing, eating, sleeping, or
behaving in any way whatever. There is no difference
between being free, like a configuration, like an
existence which chooses its essence, and being
absolute. There is no difference between being an
absolute temporarily localized, that is, localized in
history, and being universally comprehensible.

THE FLIES:

Human life begins on the far side of despair.

ZEUS: Orestes, I created you, and I created all
    things. Now see! [The walls of the temple draw
    apart, revealing the firmament, spangled with
    wheeling stars. ZEUS is standing in the background.
    His voice becomes huge--amplified by
    loud-speakers--but his form is shadowy.] See those
    planets wheeling on their appointed ways, never
    swerving, never clashing. It was I who ordained
    their courses, according to the law of justice.
    Hear the music of the spheres, that vast, mineral
    hymn of praise, sounding and resounding to the
    limits of the firmament. [Sounds of music.] It is
    my work that living things increase and multiply,
    each according to his kind. I have ordained that
    man shall always beget man, and dog give birth to
    dog. It is my work that the tides with their
    innumerable tongues creep up to lap the sand and
    draw back at the appointed hour. I make the plants
    grow, and my breath fans round the earth the yellow
    clouds of pollen. You are not in your own home,
    intruder; you are a foreign body in the world, like
    a splinter in flesh, or a poacher in his lordship's
    forest. For the world is good; I made it according
    to my will, and I am Goodness. But you, Orestes, you

328

have done evil. the very rocks and stones cry out
against you. The Good is everywhere, it is the
coolness of the wellspring, the pith of the reed,
the grain of flint, the weight of stone. Yes, you
will find it even in the heart of fire and light;
even your own body plays you false, for it abides
perforce by my law. Good is everywhere, in you and
about you; sweeping through you like a scythe,
crushing you like a mountain. Like an ocean it
buoys you up and rocks you to and fro, and it
enabled the success of your evil plan, for it was in
the brightness of the torches, the temper of your
blade, the strength of your right arm. And that of
which you are so vain, the Evil that you think is
your creation, what is it but a reflection in a
mocking mirror, a phantom thing that would have no
being but for Goodness. No, Orestes, return to your
saner self; the universe refutes you, you are a mite
in the scheme of things. Return to Nature, Nature's
thankless son. Know your sin, abhor it, and tear it
from you as one tears out a rotten, noisome tooth.
Or else--beware lest the very seas shrink back at
your approach, springs dry up when you pass by,
stones and rocks roll from your path, and the earth
crumbles under your feet.

ORESTES: Let it crumble! Let the rocks revile me, and
flowers wilt at my coming. Your whole universe is
not enough to prove me wrong. You are the king of
gods, king of stones and stars, king of the waves of
the sea. But you are not the king of man.

[The walls draw together. ZEUS comes into view,
tired and dejected, and he now speaks in his normal
voice.]

ZEUS: Impudent spawn! So I am not your king? Who,
then, made you?

ORESTES: You. But you blundered; you should not have
made me free.

ZEUS: I gave you freedom so that you might serve me.

ORESTES: Perhaps. But now it has turned against its
     giver. And neither you nor I can undo what has been
     done.

ZEUS: Ah, at last! So this is your excuse?

ORESTES: I am not excusing myself.

ZEUS: No?   Let me tell you it sounds much like an
     excuse, this freedom whose slave you claim to be.

ORESTES: Neither slave nor master. I _am_ my freedom.
     No sooner had you created me than I ceased to be
     yours.

ELECTRA: Oh, Orestes!   By all you hold most holy, by
     our father's memory, I beg you do not add blasphemy
     to your crime!

ZEUS: Mark her words, young man. And hope no more to
     win her back by arguments like these. Such language
     is somewhat new to her ears--and somewhat shocking.

ORESTES: To my ears, too.   And to my lungs, which
     breathe the words, and to my tongue, which shapes
     them. In fact, I can hardly understand myself.
     Only yesterday you were still a veil on my eyes, a
     clot of wax in my ears; yesterday, indeed, I had an
     excuse. _You_ were my excuse for being alive, for you
     had put me in the world to fulfill your purpose, and
     the world was an old pandar prating to me about your
     goodness, day in, day out. And then you forsook me.

ZEUS: _I_ forsook you? How?

ORESTES: Yesterday, when I was with Electra, I felt at
     one with Nature, this Nature of your making. It
     sang the praises of the Good--_your_ Good--in siren
     tones, and lavished intimations.   To lull me into
     gentleness, the fierce light mellowed and grew
     tender as a lover's eyes.   And, to teach me the

forgiveness of offenses, the sky grew bland as a pardoner's face. Obedient to your will, my youth rose up before me and pleaded with me like a girl who fears her lover will forsake her. That was the last time, the last, I saw my youth. Suddenly, out of the blue, freedom crashed down on me and swept me off my feet. Nature sprang back, my youth went with the wind, and I knew myself alone, utterly alone in the midst of this well-meaning little universe of yours. I was like a man who's lost his shadow. And there was nothing left in heaven, no right or wrong, nor anyone to give me orders.

ZEUS: What of it? Do you want me to admire a scabby sheep that has to be kept apart; or the leper mewed in a lazar-house? Remember, Orestes, you once were of my flock, you fed in my pastures among my sheep. Your vaunted freedom isolates you from the fold; it means exile.

ORESTES: Yes, exile.

ZEUS: But the disease can't be deeply rooted yet; it began only yesterday. Come back to the fold. Think of your loneliness; even your sister is forsaking you. Your eyes are big with anguish, your face is pale and drawn. The disease you're suffering from is inhuman, foreign to my nature, foreign to yourself. Come back, I am forgetfulness, I am peace.

ORESTES: Foreign to myself--I know it. Outside nature, against nature, without excuse, beyond remedy, except what remedy I find within myself. But I shall not return under your law; I am doomed to have no other law but mine. Nor shall I come back to nature, the nature you found good; in it are a thousand beaten paths all leading up to you--but I must blaze my trail. For I, Zeus, am a man, and every man must find out his own way. Nature abhors man, and you too, god of gods, abhor mankind.

ZEUS: That is true; men like you I hold in abhorrence.

ORESTES: Take care; those words were a confession of your weakness. As for me, I do not hate you. What have I to do with you, or you with me? We shall glide past each other, like ships in a river, without touching. You are God and I am free; each of us is alone, and our anguish is akin. How can you know I did not try to feel remorse in the long night that has gone by? And to sleep? But no longer can I feel remorse, and I can sleep no more. [<u>A short silence</u>.]

ZEUS: What do you propose to do?

ORESTES: The folk of Argos are my folk. I must open their eyes.

ZEUS: Poor people! Your gift to them will be a sad one; of loneliness and shame. You will tear from their eyes the veils I had laid on them, and they will see their lives as they are, foul and futile, a barren boon.

ORESTES: Why, since it is their lot, should I deny them the despair I have in me?

ZEUS: What will they make of it?

ORESTES: What they choose. They're free; and human life begins on the far side of despair.

[<u>A short silence</u>.]

ZEUS: Well, Orestes, all this was foreknown. In the fullness of time a man was to come, to announce my decline. And you're that man, it seems. But seeing you yesterday--you with your girlish face--who'd have believed it?

ORESTES: Could I myself have believed it?... The words I speak are too big for my mouth, they tear it; the load of destiny I bear is too heavy for my youth and has shattered it.

ZEUS: I have little love for you, yet I am sorry for
   you.

ORESTES: And I, too, am sorry for you.

ZEUS: Good-by, Orestes.   [<u>He takes some steps
   forward</u>.] As for you, Electra, bear this in mind.
   My reign is not yet over--far from it!--and I shall
   not give up the struggle. So choose if you are with
   me or against me. Farewell.

ORESTES: Farewell. [<u>Zeus goes out</u>.   <u>Electra slowly
   rises to her feet</u>.] Where are you going?

ELECTRA: Leave me alone. I'm done with you.

ORESTES: I have known you only for a day, and must I
   lose you now forever?

ELECTRA: Would to God that I had never known you!

ORESTES: Electra! My sister. dear Electra! My only
   love, the one joy of my life, do not leave me. Stay
   with me.

ELECTRA: Thief! I had so little, so very little to
   call mine; only a few weak dreams, a morsel of
   peace. And now you've taken my all; you've robbed a
   pauper of her mite!   You were my brother, the head
   of our house. and it was your duty to protect me.
   But no, you needs must drag me into carnage; I am
   red as a flayed ox, these loathsome flies are
   swarming after me, and my heart is buzzing like an
   angry hive.

ORESTES: Yes, my beloved, it's true, I have taken all
   from you, and I have nothing to offer in return;
   nothing but my crime.   But think how vast a gift
   that is! Believe me, it weighs on my heart like
   lead. We were too light, Electra; now our feet sink
   into the soil. like chariot-wheels in turf. So come

with me; we will tread heavily on our way, bowed
     beneath our precious load. You shall give me your
     hand, and we will go--

ELECTRA: Where?

ORESTES: I don't know. Towards ourselves. Beyond the
     rivers and mountains are an Orestes and an Electra
     waiting for us, and we must make our patient way
     towards them.

ELECTRA: I won't hear any more from you. All you have
     to offer me is misery and squalor. [_She rushes out
     into the center of the stage.   The FURIES slowly
     close in on her_.] Help! Zeus, king of gods and men,
     my king, take me in your arms, carry me from this
     place, and shelter me. I will obey your law. I will
     be your creature and your slave, I will embrace your
     knees. Save me from the flies, from my brother.
     from myself! Do not leave me lonely and I will give
     up my whole life to atonement.   I repent, Zeus. I
     bitterly repent.

     [_She runs off the stage.   The FURIES make as if to
     follow her, but the FIRST FURY holds them back_.]

FIRST FURY: Let her be, sisters.   She is not for us.
     But that man is ours, and ours, I think, for many a
     day. His little soul is stubborn. He will suffer
     for two.

     [_Buzzing, the FURIES approach ORESTES_.]

ORESTES: I am alone, alone.

FIRST FURY: No, no, my sweet little murderer, I'm
     staying with you, and you'll see what merry games
     I'll think up to entertain you.

ORESTES: Alone until I die. And after that--?

FIRST FURY: Take heart, sisters, he is weakening. See
     how his eyes dilate.   Soon his nerves will be

throbbing like harp-strings, in exquisite arpeggios
of terror.

SECOND FURY: And hunger will drive him from his
    sanctuary before long.   Before nightfall we shall
    know how his blood tastes.

ORESTES: Poor Electra!

[The TUTOR enters.]

THE TUTOR: Master!   Young master!   Where are you?
    It's so dark one can't see a thing.   I'm bringing
    you some food.   The townspeople have surrounded the
    temple; there's no hope of escape by daylight.   We
    shall have to try our chance when night comes.
    Meanwhile, eat this food to keep your strength up.
    [The FURIES bar his way.]   Hey!   Who are these?
    More of those primitive myths!   Ah, how I regret
    that pleasant land of Attica, where reason's always
    right.

ORESTES: Do not try to approach me, or they will tear
    you in pieces.

THE TUTOR: Gently now, my lovelies.   See what I've
    brought you, some nice meat and fruit. Here you
    are! Let's hope it will calm you down.

ORESTES: So the people of Argos have gathered outside
    the temple, have they?

THE TUTOR: Indeed they have, and I can't say which are
    the fiercer, the thirstier for your blood: these
    charming young creatures here, or your worthy
    subjects.

ORESTES: Good.   [A short silence.] Open that door.

THE TUTOR: Have you lost your wits? They're waiting
    behind it, and they're armed.

ORESTES: Do as I told you.

THE TUTOR: For once permit me, sir, to disobey your
    orders. I tell you, they will stone you. It's
    madness.

ORESTES: Old man, I am your master, and I order you to
    unbar that door.

    [THE TUTOR opens one leaf of the double doors a few
    inches.]

THE TUTOR: Oh dear! Oh dear!

ORESTES: Open both leaves.

    [THE TUTOR half opens both leaves of the door and
    takes cover behind one of them.   The CROWD surges
    forward, thrusting the doors wide open; then stops,
    bewildered, on the threshold.   The stage is flooded
    with bright light.   Shouts rise from the CROWD:
    "Away with him!" "Kill him!" "Stone him!" "Tear him
    in pieces!"]

ORESTES [who has not heard them]: The sun!

THE CROWD: Murderer! Butcher! Blasphemer! We'll tear
    you limb from limb.   We'll pour molten lead into
    your veins.

A WOMAN: I'll pluck out your eyes.

A MAN: I'll eat your gizzard!

ORESTES [drawing himself up to his full height]: So
    here you are, my true and loyal subjects? I am
    Orestes, your King, son of Agamemnon, and this is my
    coronation   day.   [Exclamations   of   amazement,
    mutterings among the CROWD.] Ah, you are lowering
    your tone? [Complete silence.]   I know; you fear
    me. Fifteen years ago to the day, another murderer
    showed himself to you, his arms red to the elbows,

336

gloved in blood. But him you did not fear; you read
in his eyes that he was of your kind, he had not the
courage of his crimes.   A crime that its doer
disowns becomes ownerless--no man's crime; that's
how you see it, isn't it?   More like an accident
than a crime?

So you welcomed the criminal as your King, and that
crime without an owner started prowling round the city,
whimpering like a dog that has lost its master. You see
me, men of Argos, you understand that my crime is wholly
mine; I claim it as my own, for all to know; it is my
glory, my life's work, and you can neither punish me nor
pity me. That is why I fill you with fear.

And yet, my people, I love you, and it was for your
sake that I killed. For your sake. I had come to claim
my kingdom. and you would have none of me because I was
not of your kind. Now I am of your kind, my subjects;
there is a bond of blood between us, and I have earned
my kingship over you.

As for your sins and your remorse, your night-fears,
and the crime Aegistheus committed--all are mine, I take
them all upon me. Fear your dead no longer; they are my
dead. And, see, your faithful flies have left you and
come to me. But have no fear, people of Argos. I shall
not sit on my victim's throne or take the scepter in my
blood-stained hands. A god offered it to me, and I said
no. I wish to be a king without a kingdom, without
subjects.

Farewell, my people. Try to reshape your lives. All
here is new, all must begin anew. And for me, too, a
new life is beginning. A strange life....

Listen now to this tale.   One summer there was a
plague of rats in Scyros.   It was like a foul disease;
they soiled and nibbled everything, and the people of
the city were at their wits' end.   But one day a
flute-player came to the city. He took his stand in the
market-place. Like this. [Orestes rises to his feet.]
He began playing on his flute and all the rats came out
and crowded round him. Then he started off, taking long
strides--like this. [He comes down from the pedestal.]

And he called to the people of Scyros: "Make way!"
[_The CROWD makes way for him_.]   And all the rats raised
their heads and hesitated--as the flies are doing.
Look! Look at the flies!   Then all of a sudden they
followed in his train.   And the flute-player, with his
rats, vanished forever. Thus.

[_He strides out into the light_. _Shrieking, the FURIES
fling themselves after him_.]

CURTAIN

30

EDWARD OSBORNE WILSON

Edward Osborne Wilson (1929-   ) is the founder of sociobiology: the extension of population biology and evolutionary theory to the social structure of all organisms, including human beings. In _Sociobiology: The New Synthesis_ (1975) Wilson, a biologist and entomologist, who had previously authored the highly acclaimed and definitive study <u>The Insect Societies</u> (1971), attempted to synthesize what seemed to be an irreconcilable gap between the social sciences and the biological world. He suggested that if man evolved by Darwinian natural selection, genetic chance and environmental necessity, then the social order can be explained by the application of these same principles to all aspects of human existence. In 1978, in his Pulitzer award winning book - <u>On Human Nature</u>, Wilson examined "the reciprocal impact that a truly evolutionary explanation of human behavior must have on the social sciences and humanities." He characterized the book as a "speculative essay about the profound consequences that will follow as social theory at long last meets that part of the natural sciences most relevant to it." His definition of human nature as "the full set of innate behavioral predispositions that characterize the human species" clearly reveals that he is convinced that biology is the "key to human nature." To the extent that this view of human nature is true, Wilson maintains that mankind faces three great spiritual dilemmas: 1. Man has no place to go since any goal external to his biological nature has been shattered by the findings of the natural sciences; 2. Traditional value structures are no longer viable to the extent that they ignore the "hard-won empirical knowledge of our biological nature"; 3. As human knowledge concerning the genetic foundation of social behavior increases, man faces the possibility that through molecular engineering he can alter his nature. In the face of these three dilemmas, Wilson concludes that social scientists cannot ignore the field of biology if there is to be hope for man.

Born in Birmingham, Alabama, Wilson began his career as an entomologist with the Alabama State Department of

Conservation even while he was still pursuing his B.S.
and M.S. degrees from the University of Alabama. After
completing his studies there and doing further study at
the University   of   Tennessee,   he entered Harvard
University where he earned his doctorate in biology. On
completing a three year term in 1956 as a junior fellow
of Harvard's Society of Fellows, he joined the Harvard
faculty as an assistant professor of biology and by 1964
rose to the rank of professor of zoology. Currently, he
is the Frank B. Baird Professor of Science at Harvard
and curator of entomology at the university's Museum of
Comparative Zoology.

   In the ensuing selection taken from the first and last
chapters of <u>On Human Nature</u>, Wilson identifies the three
dilemmas that face mankind but clearly indicates that
there is hope for mankind if it extends the knowledge it
acquires from biology and related sciences to the social
sciences and the humanities.

ON HUMAN NATURE:

Biology the key to human nature.

Chapter 1. Dilemma

These are the central questions that the great philosopher David Hume said are of unspeakable importance: How does the mind work, and beyond that why does it work in such a way and not another, and from these two considerations together, what is man's ultimate nature?

We keep returning to the subject with a sense of hesitancy and even dread. For if the brain is a machine of ten billion nerve cells and the mind can somehow be explained as the summed activity of a finite number of chemical and electrical reactions, boundaries limit the human prospect--we are biological and our souls cannot fly free. If humankind evolved by Darwinian natural selection, genetic chance and environmental necessity, not God, made the species. Deity can still be sought in the origin of the ultimate units of matter, in quarks and electron shells (Hans Kung was right to ask atheists why there is something instead of nothing) but not in the origin of species. However much we embellish that stark conclusion with metaphor and imagery, it remains the philosophical legacy of the last century of scientific research.

No way appears around this admittedly unappealing proposition. It is the essential first hypothesis for any serious consideration of the human condition. Without it the humanities and social sciences are the limited descriptors of surface phenomena, like astronomy without physics, biology without chemistry, and mathematics without algebra. With it, human nature can be laid open as an object of fully empirical research, biology can be put to the service of liberal education, and our self-conception can be enormously and truthfully enriched.

But to the extent that the new naturalism is true, its pursuit seems certain to generate two great spiritual

dilemmas.... The first is that no species, ours
included, possesses a purpose beyond the imperatives
created by its genetic history. Species may have vast
potential for material and mental progress but they lack
any immanent purpose or guidance from agents beyond
their immediate environment or even an evolutionary goal
toward which their molecular architecture automatically
steers them. I believe that the human mind is
constructed in a way that locks it inside this
fundamental constraint and forces it to make choices
with a purely biological instrument. If the brain
evolved by natural selection, even the capacities to
select particular esthetic judgments and religious
beliefs must have arisen by the same mechanistic
process. They are either direct adaptations to past
environments in which the ancestral human populations
evolved or at most constructions thrown up secondarily
by deeper, less visible activities that were once
adaptive in this stricter. biological sense.

The essence of the argument, then, is that the brain
exists because it promotes the survival and
multiplication of the genes that direct its assembly.
The human mind is a device for survival and
reproduction, and reason is just one of its various
techniques....

The first dilemma, in a word, is that we have no
particular place to go. The species lacks any goal
external to its own biological nature. It could be that
in the next hundred years humankind will thread the
needles of technology and politics, solve the energy and
materials crises, avert nuclear war. and control
reproduction. The world can at least hope for a stable
eco-system and a well-nourished population. But what
then? Educated people everywhere like to believe that
beyond material needs lie fulfillment and the
realization of individual potential. But what is
fulfillment. and to what ends may potential be realized?
Traditional religious beliefs have been eroded, not so
much by humiliating disproofs of their mythologies as by
the growing awareness that beliefs are really enabling
mechanisms for survival. Religions, like other human
institutions, evolve so as to enhance the persistence
and influence of their practitioners. Marxism and other
secular religions offer little more than promises of
material welfare and a legislated escape from the
consequences of human nature. They, too, are energized
by the goal of collective self-aggrandizement....
342

At this point let me state in briefest terms the basis of the second dilemma, while I defer its supporting argument to the next chapter: innate censors and motivators exist in the brain that deeply and unconsciously affect our ethical premises; from these roots, morality evolved as instinct. If that perception is correct, science may soon be in a position to investigate the very origin and meaning of human values, from which all ethical pronouncements and much of political practice flow.

Philosophers themselves, most of whom lack an evolutionary perspective, have not devoted much time to the problem. They examine the precepts of ethical systems with reference to their consequences and not their origins....

Success will generate the second dilemma. which can be stated as follows: Which of the censors and motivators should be obeyed and which ones might better be curtailed or sublimated? These guides are the very core of our humanity. They and not the belief in spiritual apartness distinguish us from electronic computers. At some time in the future we will have to decide how human we wish to remain--in this ultimate, biological sense--because we must consciously choose among the alternative emotional guides we have inherited. To chart our destiny means that we must shift from automatic control based on our biological properties to precise steering based on biological knowledge.

Because the guides of human nature must be examined with a complicated arrangement of mirrors, they are a deceptive subject, always the philosopher's deadfall. The only way forward is to study human nature as part of the natural sciences, in an attempt to integrate the natural sciences with the social sciences and humanities. I can conceive of no ideological or formalistic shortcut. Neurobiology cannot be learned at the feet of a guru. The consequences of genetic history cannot be chosen by legislatures. Above all, for our own physical well-being if nothing else, ethical philosophy must not be left in the hands of the merely wise. Although human progress can be achieved by intuition and force of will. only hard-won empirical knowledge of our biological nature will allow us to make optimum choices among the competing criteria of progress....

Reduction is the traditional instrument of scientific analysis, but it is feared and resented. If human behavior can be reduced and determined to any considerable degree by the laws of biology, then mankind might appear to be less than unique and to that extent dehumanized. Few social scientists and scholars in the humanities are prepared to enter such a conspiracy, let alone surrender any of their territory. But this perception, which equates the method of reduction with the philosophy of diminution, is entirely in error. The laws of a subject are necessary to the discipline above it, they challenge and force a mentally more efficient restructuring, but they are not sufficient for the purposes of the discipline. Biology is the key to human nature, and social scientists cannot afford to ignore its rapidly tightening principles. But the social sciences are potentially far richer in content. Eventually they will absorb the relevant ideas of biology and go on to beggar them. The proper study of man is, for reasons that now transcend anthropocentrism, man.

...

Chapter 9. Hope

The first dilemma has been created by the seemingly fatal deterioration of the myths of traditional religion and its secular equivalents, principal among which are ideologies based on a Marxian interpretation of history. The price of these failures has been a loss of moral consensus, a greater sense of helplessness about the human condition and a shrinking of concern back toward the self and the immediate future. The intellectual solution of the first dilemma can be achieved by a deeper and more courageous examination of human nature that combines the findings of biology with those of the social sciences. The mind will be more precisely explained as an epiphenomenon of the neuronal machinery of the brain. That machinery is in turn the product of genetic evolution by natural selection acting on human populations for hundreds of thousands of years in their ancient environments. By a judicious extension of the methods and ideas of neurobiology, ethology, and sociobiology a proper foundation can be laid for the social sciences, and the discontinuity still separating the natural sciences on the one side and the social sciences and humanities on the other might be erased.

If this solution to the first dilemma proves even partially correct, it will lead directly to the second dilemma: the conscious choices that must be made among our innate mental propensities. The elements of human nature are the learning rules, emotional reinforcers, and hormonal feedback loops that guide the development of social behavior into certain channels as opposed to others. Human nature is not just the array of outcomes attained in existing societies. It is also the potential array that might be achieved through conscious design by future societies. By looking over the realized social systems of hundreds of animal species and deriving the principles by which these systems have evolved, we can be certain that all human choices represent only a tiny subset of those theoretically possible. Human nature is, moreover, a hodge-podge of special genetic adaptations to an environment largely vanished, the world of the Ice-Age hunter-gatherer. Modern life, as rich and rapidly changing as it appears to those caught in it, is nevertheless only a mosaic of cultural hypertrophies of the archaic behavioral adaptations. And at the center of the second dilemma is found a circularity: we are forced to choose among the elements of human nature by reference to value systems which these same elements created in an evolutionary age now long vanished.

Fortunately, this circularity of the human predicament is not so tight that it cannot be broken through an exercise of will. The principal task of human biology is to identify and to measure the constraints that influence the decisions of ethical philosophers and everyone else, and to infer their significance through neuro-physiological and phylogenetic reconstructions of the mind. This enterprise is a necessary complement to the continued study of cultural evolution. It will alter the foundation of the social sciences but in no way diminish their richness and importance. In the process it will fashion a biology of ethics, which will make possible the selection of a more deeply understood and enduring code of moral values....

The search for values will then go beyond the utilitarian calculus of genetic fitness. Although natural selection has been the prime mover, it works through a cascade of decisions based on secondary values that have historically served as the enabling mechanisms for survival and reproductive success. These values are

defined to a large extent by our most intense emotions:
enthusiasm and a sharpening of the senses from
exploration; exaltation from discovery; triumph in
battle and competitive sports; the restful satisfaction
from an altruistic act well and truly placed; the
stirring of ethnic and national pride; the strength from
family ties; and the secure biophilic pleasure from the
nearness of animals and growing plants.

There is a neurophysiology of such responses to be
deciphered, and their evolutionary history awaits
reconstruction. A kind of principle of the conservation
of energy operates among them, such that the emphasis of
any one over others still retains the potential summed
power of all.... Although the means to measure these
energies are lacking, I suspect psychologists would
agree that they can be rechanneled substantially without
losing strength, that the mind fights to retain a
certain level of order and emotional reward. Recent
evidence suggests that dreams are produced when giant
fibers in the brainstem fire upward through the brain
during sleep, stirring the cerebral cortex to activity.
In the absence of ordinary sensory information from the
outside, the cortex responds by calling up images from
the memory banks and fabricating plausible stories. In
an analogous manner the mind will always create
morality, religion, and mythology and empower them with
emotional force. When blind ideologies and religious
beliefs are stripped away, others are quickly
manufactured as replacements. If the cerebral cortex is
rigidly trained in the techniques of critical analysis
and packed with tested information, it will reorder all
that into some form of morality, religion, and
mythology. If the mind is instructed that its
pararational activity cannot be combined with the
rational- it will divide itself into two compartments so
that both activities can continue to flourish side by
side.

This mythopoeic drive can be harnessed to learning and
the rational search for human progress if we finally
concede that scientific materialism is itself a
mythology defined in the noble sense. So let me give
again the reasons why I consider the scientific ethos
superior to religion: its repeated triumphs in
explaining and controlling the physical world; its
self-correcting nature open to all competent to devise
and conduct the tests; its readiness to examine all

subjects sacred and profane; and now the possibility of explaining traditional religion by the mechanistic models of evolutionary biology.   The last achievement will be crucial.   If religion, including the dogmatic secular ideologies, can be systematically analyzed and explained as a product of the brain's evolution, its power as an external source of morality will be gone forever and the solution of the second dilemma will have become a practical necessity.

The core of scientific materialism is the evolutionary epic. Let me repeat its minimum claims: that the laws of the physical sciences are consistent with those of the biological and social sciences and can be linked in chains of causal explanation; that life and mind have a physical basis; that the world as we know it has evolved from earlier worlds obedient to the same laws; and that the visible universe today is everywhere subject to these materialist explanations.   The epic can be indefinitely strengthened up and down the line, but its most sweeping assertions cannot be proved with finality.

What I am suggesting, in the end, is that the evolutionary epic is probably the best myth we will ever have. It can be adjusted until it comes as close to truth as the human mind is constructed to judge the truth.   And if that is the case, the mythopoeic requirements of the mind must somehow be met by scientific materialism so as to reinvest our superb energies.   There are ways of managing such a shift honestly and without dogma.   One is to cultivate more intensely the relationship between the sciences and humanities....

Yet, astonishingly, the high culture of Western civilization exists largely apart from the natural sciences.   In the United States intellectuals are virtually defined as those who work in the prevailing mode of the social sciences and humanities.   Their reflections are devoid of the idioms of chemistry and biology, as though humankind were still in some sense a numinous spectator of physical reality.   In the pages of The New York Review of Books, Commentary, The New Republic, Daedalus, National Review, Saturday Review, and other literary journals articles dominate that read as if most of basic science had halted during the nineteenth century.   Their content consists largely of historical anecdotes, diachronic collating of outdated, verbalized theories of human behavior, and judgments of current events according to personal ideology--all enlivened by the pleasant but frustrating techniques of effervescence. Modern science is still regarded as a problem-solving activity and a set of technical marvels, the importance of which is to be valuated in an ethos extraneous to science. It is true that many "humanistic" scientists step outside scientific materialism to participate in the culture, sometimes as expert witnesses and sometimes as aspiring authors, but they almost never close the gap between the two worlds of discourse. With rare exceptions they are the tame scientists, the token emissaries of what must be viewed by their hosts as a barbaric culture still ungraced by a written language. They are degraded by the label they accept too readily: popularizers. Very few of the great writers, the ones who can trouble and move the deeper reaches of the mind, ever address real science on its own terms. Do they know the nature of the challenge?

The desired shift in attention could come more easily now that the human mind is subject to the network of causal explanation. Every epic needs a hero: the mind will do. Even astronomers, accustomed to thinking about ten billion galaxies and distances just short of infinity, must agree that the human brain is the most complex device that we know and the crossroads of investigation by every major natural science. The social scientists and humanistic scholars, not omitting theologians, will eventually have to concede that scientific naturalism is destined to alter the foundations of their systematic inquiry by redefining the mental process itself.

I began this book with an exposition of the often dialectic nature of scientific advance. The discipline abuts the antidiscipline; the antidiscipline succeeds in reordering the phenomena of the discipline by reduction to its more fundamental laws; but the new synthesis created in the discipline profoundly alters the antidiscipline as the interaction widens. I suggested that biology, and especially neurobiology and sociobiology, will serve as the antidiscipline of the social sciences. I will now go further and suggest that the scientific materialism embodied in biology will, through a reexamination of the mind and the foundations

of social behavior, serve as a kind of antidiscipline to
the humanities. No Comtian revolution will take place,
no sudden creation of a primitively scientific culture.
The translation will be gradual. In order to address
the central issues of the humanities, including ideology
and religious belief, science itself must become more
sophisticated and in part specially crafted to deal with
the peculiar features of human biology.

I hope that as this syncretism proceeds, a true sense
of wonder will reinvade the broader culture. We need to
speak more explicitly of the things we do not know. The
epic of which natural scientists write in technical
fragments still has immense gaps and absorbing
mysteries, not the least of which is the physical basis
of the mind. Like blank spaces on the map of a partly
explored world, their near borders can be fixed but
their inner magnitude only roughly guessed. Scientists
and humanistic scholars can do far better than they have
at articulating the great goals toward which literate
people move as on a voyage of discovery. Unknown and
surprising things await. They are as accessible as in
those days of primitive wonder when the early European
explorers went forth and came upon new worlds and the
first microscopists watched bacteria swim across drops
of water. As knowledge grows science must increasingly
become the stimulus to imagination....

This view will be rejected even more firmly by those
whose emotional needs are satisfied by traditional
organized religion. God and the church, they will
claim, cannot be extinguished ex parte by a rival
mythology based on science. They will be right. God
remains a viable hypothesis as the prime mover, however
undefinable and untestable that conception may be. The
rituals of religion, especially the rites of passage and
the sanctification of nationhood, are deeply entrenched
and incorporate some of the most magnificent elements of
existing cultures. They will certainly continue to be
practiced long after their etiology has been disclosed.
The anguish of death alone will be enough to keep them
alive. It would be arrogant to suggest that a belief in
a personal- moral God will disappear, just as it would
be reckless to predict the forms that ritual will take
as scientific materialism appropriates the mythopoeic
energies to its own ends.

I also do not envision scientific generalization as a substitute for art or as anything more than a nourishing symbiont of art. The artist, including the creative writer, communicates his most personal experience and vision in a direct manner chosen to commit his audience emotionally to that perception. Science can hope to explain artists, and artistic genius, and even art, and it will increasingly use art to investigate human behavior, but it is not designed to transmit experience on a personal level or to reconstitute the full richness of the experience from the laws and principles which are its first concern by definition.

Above all, I am not suggesting that scientific naturalism be used as an alternative form of organized formal religion.... I am suggesting a modification of scientific humanism through the recognition that the mental processes of religious belief--consecration of personal and group identity, attention to charismatic leaders, mythopoeism, and others--represent programmed predispositions whose self-sufficient components were incorporated into the neural apparatus of the brain by thousands of generations of genetic evolution....

As our knowledge of human nature grows, and we start to elect a system of values on a more objective basis, and our minds at last align with our hearts, the set of trajectories will narrow still more. We already know, to take two extreme and opposite examples, that the worlds of William Graham Sumner, the absolute Social Darwinist, and Mikhail Bakunin, the anarchist, are biologically impossible. As the social sciences mature into predictive disciplines, the permissible trajectories will not only diminish in number but our descendants will be able to sight farther along them.

Then mankind will face the third and perhaps final spiritual dilemma. Human genetics is now growing quickly along with all other branches of science. In time, much knowledge concerning the genetic foundation of social behavior will accumulate, and techniques may become available for altering gene complexes by molecular engineering and rapid selection through cloning. At the very least, slow evolutionary change will be feasible through conventional eugenics. The human species can change its own nature. What will it choose? Will it remain the same, teetering on a jerrybuilt foundation of partly obsolete Ice-Age adaptations? Or will it press on toward still higher intelligence and creativity, accompanied by a greater--or lesser--capacity for emotional response? New patterns of sociality could be installed in bits and pieces. It might be possible to imitate genetically the more nearly perfect nuclear family of the white-handed gibbon or the harmonious sisterhoods of the honeybees. But we are talking here about the very essence of humanity. Perhaps there is something already present in our nature that will prevent us from ever making such changes. In any case, and fortunately, this third dilemma belongs to later generations....

GLOSSARY

Agnosticism: The view that certain kinds of
                   fundamental claims cannot be known to be
                   true or false. For example, the agnostic
                   maintains that we cannot know whether God
                   exists.

A posteriori: A characterization of knowledge or
               reasoning that follows from experience.
               Opposed to a priori.

A priori: A characterization of knowledge or
               reasoning that is independent of
               experience (i.e., sense experience) or
               reasoning based on such knowledge;
               non-empirical knowledge. Opposed to a
               posteriori.

Atheism: Disbelief in or denial of the existence
               of God.

Behaviorism: A school of psychology that restricts
               study to the objective observation of
               behavior rather than to the study of
               states of consciousness (ideas, images,
               percepts, etc.). The view that man is so
               constituted that every aspect of his
               experience and behavior is the inevitable
               consequence of causes lying outside
               himself. View of B. F. Skinner.

Conditioning: A psychological term which describes a
              type of learning process in which an
              organism, such as man, comes to associate
              one thing with another.

Contemplation: According to Aristotle, contemplation
               (the life of thought and philosophy) is
               the happiest life.

Cosmology: A branch of philosophy which studies the
               origin, nature. and development of the
               universe (cosmos) as an orderly system;
               philosophy of nature; the study of mobile
               being.

Deism: The belief that God is the creator of the
               universe and the lawgiver of the universe

but God is not providential. God is rather impersonal and indifferent about the world and humanity. Therefore, there can be no relation (prayer or revelation) between God and human beings. View was popular in the science-minded 18th century.

Determinism: The belief that every event in the universe is dependent upon other antecedent events, which are its causes. Therefore, every event is predictable on the basis of its antecedent conditions.

Dualism: In general, the distinction between mind and body as separate substances. View of Plato and Rene Descartes.

Empiricism: The theory of knowledge that claims that all knowledge, except certain logical truths and principles of mathematics, come from (sense) experience. David Hume was a British empiricist, along with John Locke and George Berkeley.

Enlightenment: A 17th and 18th century cultural and philosophical movement in Europe which is characterized by a new confidence in human reason and individual autonomy. Major figures of the movement include Rene Descartes, John Locke, David Hume, Immanuel Kant, Diderot, and Jean-Jacques Rousseau.

Epistemology: A branch of philosophy that studies the nature, sources, limits, and validity or justification of human knowledge.

Ethics: A branch of philosophy that seeks to determine the nature of the good of man.

Existentialism: A 20th century philosophical movement that emphasizes the theme of human freedom and responsibility. According to Sartre, an atheistic existentialist, there is no human nature ready-made for there is no God to conceive it.

Forms, Ideas, (Platonic): The really real objects of thought; pure essences that are non-physical, unchanging, and universal. They exist whether perceived by human beings or not and are the causes of what occurs in the material world.

Free Will: Freedom of choice; the doctrine that human beings have the capacity to make voluntary decisions; moderate indeterminism; man has the power of self-determination. Opposed to determinism.

Humanism: Any view in which interest in human welfare is central. There are a broad range of humanistic philosophies treated in this volume from Biblical humanism which sees man as made in the image and likeness of God to existential humanism which sees man as creator of his own meaning and essence.

Idealism: The metaphysical view that asserts that reality is ideas, thought, mind, or selves rather than material forces or entities. Opposed to materialism.

Indeterminism: The theory that at least some events in the universe are not determined or caused by antecedent events. These indeterminate events are unpredictable.

Interactionism: Dualistic theory proposed by Rene Descartes which asserts a reciprocal causal influence between mind and body.

Materialism: The metaphysical view that asserts that everything in the universe. including living reality and mind, can be reduced to, and explained in terms of, matter and motion. Opposed to idealism.

Mechanism: The view that everything, including living organisms, can be entirely explained in terms of mechanical laws. Mechanism rejects the theory that things exist for a purpose or end.

Metaphysics: A branch of philosophy that studies the nature of reality and its causes. The study of being as being. For Aristotle, it is divine science or first philosophy.

Mysticism: The belief that one can grasp certain fundamental religious truths (for example, the existence of God) by way of direct experience but by way of an experience other than ordinary understanding.

Natural Law: According to Thomas Aquinas, a dictate of reason which primarily expresses in universal form the fundamental inclinations of human nature. It is formulated by reason in a judgment that is naturally made with little or no discursive process of reasoning. The primary precept of natural law is usually expressed simply as "Do good and avoid evil." Natural law theory originated in ancient Greek philosophy.

Natural Theology: Any theology constructed by human beings out of the framework of their own experience and reasoning.

Naturalism: The metaphysical view that nature is all that exists. The supernatural does not exist. In ethics, it is the view that moral values are to be found in nature and so have an objective status.

Nihilism: The doctrine or belief that nothing exists or nothing can be known, or nothing is valuable.

Ontology: The study of the nature of being. Sometimes equated with metaphysics but narrower in scope.

Operant conditioning: A type of learning in which the response is instrumental in obtaining positive reinforcement or in escaping (or avoiding) negative reinforcement.

Positivism: The belief that knowledge is limited to observable or positive facts and their interrelations. Thus, the sciences provide the only reliable knowledge. Metaphysical speculations about the ultimate nature of things are viewed by the positivist as meaningless.

<u>Pragmatism</u>:   The view that claims that the criterion of what is true or good is to be found in the practical consequences of ideas in how they work to solve problems and achieve human goals.

<u>Rationalism</u>:   The theory of knowledge which exhibits confidence in reason, and intuition in particular, to know reality independently of experience. Rene Descartes, Benedict Spinoza, and Gottfried Leibniz were leading 17th century rationalists.

<u>Relativism</u>:   The view that maintains that there is no objective or absolute truth. Ethical relativism holds that rightness and goodness vary from age to age, group to group, and person to person.

<u>Revealed theology</u>: Any theology (science of God) based upon the communication to human beings of the divine will.

<u>Revelation</u>:   The communication to man of the Divine Will.

<u>Self-determinism</u>: The view that attempts to reconcile the claims of determinism and indeterminism. It maintains that our actions are indeed determined but not solely by external forces or conditions but also by motives and intentions. These influence our choices but do not necessitate them.

<u>Social engineering</u>: The management of human beings with respect to their place and function in society; applied social science.

<u>Sociobiology</u>:   The study of society in terms of the methods and concepts of biological science.

<u>Solipsism</u>:   The view that only I (the solipsist) exist. Other persons have no independent existence of their own but exist solely as creations of my own consciousness.

<u>Stoicism</u>:   An ethical system originating in ancient Greece and Rome. The belief that virtue

is the only good and is found through knowledge. According to this theory, man is a fragment torn from the divine.

<u>Theism:</u>   The belief that God exists transcendnet to the world as Creator. According to this view, God is both the source and the ultimate end of existence.

<u>Virtue:</u>   In the philosophy of Aristotle, the excellence of a thing which enables it to perform its function well; in man, the activity of reason and or rationally ordered habits. For the Stoics, virtue became associated with manliness and strength of character. For Machiavelli, the word means shrewd prudence.

<u>Will to power:</u> According to Nietzsche, the idea that every act is ultimately aimed at superiority, sometimes over other people, and always according to one's own standards.

Ionesco, xvii
Irenaeus, xliv. 292

James, 245, 259, 268, 281
Janet. xlv. 295. 296
Judaeus, Philo, xliv. 292
Jung, xv, xliv, xlv, xlvi. lv. 289. 290

Kierkegaard, xvii, xxxiv

La Mettrie. xiv, xxxv, xxxvi, xxxviii. xli. l. liv.
95, 195
Law xxii. xxvi. xxvii. xxviii, xxxi, xxxv, xxxvi.
xxxviii. xlix, 3. 4, 6, 8, 9. 13. 25. 26. 89, 97. 121,
136, 137, 139, 145. 200. 206. 265. 272, 318. 328. 329.
331. 334, 356
Leibniz, 187, 196. 324, 357
Locke. xxxv. 173. 187, 264. 354
Lorenz, xvii
Lucretius, 127, 130, 133. 134. 136. 137
Luther, xxxi, xxxii. liii. liv, 139

Machiavelli, xiii, xxx, liii. liv. 117, 118, 358
Malebranche. 196
Manilius. 127, 128
Marxism. 1, 322. 342
*Materialism. xlviii, li. 291. 346, 347, 348, 349, 355
 Matter. xxiii. xxv. xxxv, xxxvi, xl, xlviii. 16. 22,
36, 48, 52, 57. 58, 59, 66. 87. 106. 112. 113, 125,
129, 146. 147. 152, 159, 162, 163, 171, 177. 179. 180.
187. 189. 193. 200, 204, 238. 250. 264, 269, 284, 293,
295, 299, 302. 309. 326. 341. 355
 Mead. xv, xl, xli. xlvi. xlix, liii, liv, 245, 246
*Mechanism. liii. 197, 203, 248, 280. 355
*Metaphysics. xix, xx, xxv, 33. 173. 279. 355. 356
 Montaigne, xiii, xxxi, xxxiii, xxxviii, liii, 125
 Morris. xiii. 245. 259
*Mysticism, 356

*Naturalism, xxxv, xli, xlviii, li. 203. 341. 348. 350.
 356
 Nietzsche. xv. xvii. xxxix, xlvii, liii, liv. 229,
 230. 321. 322. 358,
*Nihilism. li. 230, 256

*Ontology, 356

 Pascal. xxxiii. xxxiv. liii, 165
 Paul, St., xiii. xiv, xv, xvi, xxi, xxii, xxvii.